Outcasts and Heretics

OTHER BOOKS BY DON SHARPES

Sacred Bull, Holy Cow, A Cultural Study of Civilization's Most Important Animal

Lords of the Scrolls, Literary Traditions in the Bible and Gospels

Advanced Educational Foundations, The History, Philosophy and Culture of Schools

Advanced Psychology for Teachers

International Teacher Education Perspectives (Editor)

Curriculum Traditions and Practices

Education and the U.S. Government

Improving School Staffs

Strategies for Differentiated Staffing (with Fenwick English)

Outcasts and Heretics

Profiles in Independent Thought and Courage

DONALD SHARPES

LEXINGTON BOOKS

A division of
ROWMAN & LITTLEFIELD PUBLISHERS, INC.
Lanham • Boulder • New York • Toronto • Plymouth, UK

LEXINGTON BOOKS

A division of Rowman & Littlefield Publishers, Inc.
A wholly owned subsidary of The Rowman & Littlefield Publishing Group, Inc.
4501 Forbes Boulevard, Suite 200
Lanham, MD 20706

Estover Road
Plymouth PL6 7PY
United Kingdom

British Library Cataloguing in Publication Information Available

Library of Congress Cataloging-in-Publication Data

Sharpes, Donald K.
 Outcasts and heretics : profiles in independent thought and courage / Donald Sharpes.
     p. cm.
 Includes bibliographical references and index.
 ISBN-13: 978-0-7391-2317-1 (cloth : alk. paper)
 ISBN-10: 0-7391-2317-3 (cloth : alk. paper)
 ISBN-13: 978-0-7391-2318-8 (pbk. : alk. paper)
 ISBN-10: 0-7391-2318-1 (pbk. : alk. paper)
 1. Philosophy and religion. 2. Theologians. 3. Philosophers. I. Title.
 BL51.S4985 2007
 200.92'2—dc22
 [B]
                                                                    2007029227

Printed in the United States of America

♾™ The paper used in this publication meets the minimum requirements of American
National Standard for Information Sciences—Permanence of Paper for Printed Library
Materials, ANSI/NISO Z39.48–1992.

CONTENTS

PART I
MODERN OUTCASTS

PART II
THE LEGACY OF RELIGIOUS HERESY
AND DISSENT

TABLES

ABBREVIATIONS

AHR	*American Historical Review*
A	*Archaeology*
AM	*Atlantic Monthly*
BA	*Biblical Archaeologist*
BAR	*Biblical Archaeology Review*
CAH	*Cambridge Ancient History*
CHCL	*Cambridge History of Classical Literature*
CP	*Classical Philology*
HR	*History of Religions*
JBL	*Journal of Biblical Literature*
JES	*Journal of Ecumenical Studies*
JECS	*Journal of Early Christian Studies*
JEH	*Journal of Ecclesiastical History*
JHI	*Journal of the History of Ideas*
JHS	*Journal of Hellenic Studies*
JMS	*Journal of Medieval History*
JRS	*Journal of Roman Studies*
L	*Linnean*
NG	*National Geographic*
NYT	*New York Times*
NYTBR	*New York Times Book Review*
NYTM	*New York Times Magazine*
N	*Nature*
NG	*Nature Genetics*
OHBW	*Oxford History of the Biblical World*
SA	*Scientific American*
S	*Smithsonian*

ACKNOWLEDGEMENTS

To the following individuals, a partial list of my indebtedness to them and to so many others who have inspired my research and corrected my omissions and errors: Dr. Retha Warnicke, Professor of History at Arizona State University, author of a biography of Mary Queen of Scots, for her review and correction of some factual errors. Dr. Sam Zeveloff, Professor and Chair, Zoology Department, Weber State University, for his review of Darwin and evolution. Professors Lotte Schou of the Danish School of Education at Aarhus University in Denmark and Peter Widell of Aarhus University for material about Kaj Munk and comments and reviews. Dr. Jud Taylor, President Emeritus of the State University of New York at Cortland, for information about Roger Williams. Dr. Gary Greif, Professor Emeritus of the University of Wisconsin Green Bay, for editing and review. Dr Richard Jacobs, Dean of the Emeritus College of Arizona State University, and members of its Writers Group for support and comments. Steve Pappas, Director in the U.S. Department of Education in Washington DC, for his reviews and astute criticisms. Julia Nishibata of Doshisha University in Kyoto, Japan for insightful comments and thoughtful and careful editing. Chuck Summers who graciously loaned me his volumes of Voltaire from his private collection.

Finally I am indebted to the library of Arizona State University for access to its extensive holdings, archives and online data and retrieval services and the libraries of Oxford University for access to rare books and editions. Special thanks to MacDuff Stewart, Patrick Dillon, Paula Smith-Vanderslice, and Catherine Forrest-Getzie and the staff at Lexington Books for belief in the merit and success of this inquiry.

INTRODUCTION

At any rate you have an ingrained propensity to taking your own course. And
that, in a well-ordered community, is almost as inadmissible. The individual
must subordinate himself to a society, or, more precisely, to the authorities
whose business it is to watch over the welfare of society.

Henrik Ibsen, *An Enemy of the People*

In one of the most famous images of the twentieth century, a slender man carrying shopping bags in each hand stood in front of a column of three Chinese
tanks on the boulevard leading to Tiananmen Square in Beijing and brought
them to a complete stop. The lead tank swiveled three times to try and move
around the lone dissenter and each time he jumped sideways to stand directly in
front of the tank. The lead tank turned off its engine. The man climbed onto the
top of the tank and appeared to speak to the tank commander who stood in the
open trapdoor and waved him away. After a hurried exchange, the man jumped
down, the tank revved its engine, puffs of diesel fumes rose, and the tank
lurched forward. But the man blocked the route again. Seconds later, three men
appeared from off the street and hustled the bold young man away.

The incident occurred on June 5, 1989, the day after thousands had been
shot by Chinese troops clearing Tiananmen Square of demonstrators. This one
courageous act by a daring dissident framed the peaceful Chinese protest that
summer that was so brutally crushed with lethal military force. This unknown
man helped spawn the revolution that brought down the repressive Soviet Union
and the Berlin Wall in the fall of 1989. He is only one contemporary symbol of
profiles in courage, a man who said nothing but who spoke for all peoples, a
dissident about whom nothing is known but whose image of valor galvanized
the globe.

I feature such inspirational leaders in this book. Their ethic of personal responsibility to the truth triumphed over ambition and even personal safety. I will
reach into the archives of our past to resurrect and memorialize them. These are
my chosen Medal of Honor recipients. Many had charisma but that is not a
qualification for candidacy. I will let them crawl under your skin and stay there
for when your time comes to stand valiantly and perhaps alone against the perennial perils of authoritarianism.

Admittedly, heroism and moral courage are nebulous concepts. Some will
not be able to define it well, but say they know it when they see it. Many agree
on the principal icons in world or American history, those who have influenced

the course of events or the lives of others in significant ways, in the arts, science, philosophy, politics, or war. But I will not be writing about those who achieved success, but rather those who sacrificed status in order to make a statement about principle. I am not trying to identify individuals who have necessarily had influence on history, but a few obscure and historically neglected, who have stood for the most important ingredient in their lives with brio and passion. Their courage has often changed the course of history. Their deaths or ostracism solidified their fate and placed them where the rosters of moral courage reside.

Heroism and moral courage is like that, often full of anonymity, faceless, like the photograph of the soldiers raising the flag at Iwo Jima who represent all soldiers. Some real heroes just hold their souls in, not wanting to release their identity, letting their privacy guard their heroic deeds. War heroes and ordinary soldiers have the toughest time after they return home from war, and many can never adjust to the normalcy of life. Some heroes are slightly flawed, some disturbed, some just renegades, but who nevertheless do extraordinary acts. Or they are patriotic individuals like Pat Tillman who gave up a football career in the National Football League to fight and die in Afghanistan. Comparing heroic people to those in fiction is unfair because a Hercules, Superman, Spider Man, or movie action hero has a touch of the divine, the supernatural or unreal, or just the improbable.

Heretics, heathens, dissenters, and iconoclasts are also the common terms from an ancient religious context used to debase individuals who depart from conventional behavior or beliefs. All such terms are considered derogatory put-downs, identifying unsophisticated persons, country bumpkins, destroyers of conventions, social pests to be evicted from the community.

Heathens originally were those who lived on the heath, or rural folk. Pagan meant a country dweller. Barbarians were uncouth, rude, and uncivilized. But literally, in Latin, they had *barba.* . . they were men with beards, and were therefore by implication barbarians, foreigners and strangers. Iconoclasts were destroyers of icon who smashed Byzantine holy images because believers were not supposed to worship graven images. But an iconoclast is also one who challenges established beliefs and institutions, one brave enough to force society to confront pernicious or misguided ways.

The forms of personal independence can be manifold, like saying something forbidden, writing the unacceptable to the government, not taking part in the accepted social ritual, not placing the ablution with the votive offering at the altar of Zeus, or failing to conform an obligatory religious rule, such as not eating pork as a Jew or drinking liquor as a Muslim. Through whatever medium the heretic or dissenter chooses, he or she forfeits social standing and invites the cruelest sanctions and ostracism. Extraordinary personalities lived ordinary lives making a living, perhaps making tents or sails, baking bread, or mortaring homes, weaving garments like Gandhi, as well as having a beer with the guys in the tavern, attending a play, walking in gardens, or enjoying dinner with a spouse or friends.

Contemporary heroes and heroines are often whistle-blowers, those men and women of moral courage who confront their bosses over wrongdoing and unethical behavior in the boardrooms of American government, military, and businesses. The following are some modern examples.

Whistle-Blowers

Joe Darby was from a military family in Cumberland, Maryland, a city in the western spur reaching into Appalachia. Joe was serving in Iraq when a sadistic friend in his unit gave him a CD of about 200 photos to download and copy. Included among the scenes of Iraqi and barracks life were photos of horrible scenes of degradation and torture from Abu Ghraib prison. Joe was disbelieving and distraught. He decided to turn in anonymously a copy of the photos on a CD to the Criminal Investigation Division. Within hours, agents found out who Joe was and questioned him.

After implicating his friends Joe knew his life was in danger and he slept with a cocked 45-caliber pistol under his pillow. After the exposure, all those involved in the prison photos kept their jobs. Joe was viewed as a rat, and even the townsfolk in his hometown of Cumberland considered him a traitor. He was politely told that he could never return to his hometown, as Donald Rumsfeld, then Secretary of Defense had revealed his name before Congress. Everyone he knew turned against him. Angry people who had known his parents and grandparents issued threats. He and his wife traveled with a phalanx of security guards. The Kennedy family gave him the Profiles in Courage award. He cannot say now where he works or lives.

Joe Darby was a prisoner of conscience who held to a higher standard, a man who had a true sense of moral righteousness and who wanted to return the dignity that had been stolen from his army unit by the folly of a few who broke the law. Six of the seven soldiers, but no officers, who terrorized the Iraqi prisoners went to prison.

Mike German, a decorated FBI agent, discovered that other FBI officers had mishandled wiretapping methods. He voiced his concerns to his superiors. Not only were his accusations ignored, but he was compelled to resign, his reputation tarnished and his career terminated. The Office of Special Counsel is an independent federal agency that tracks whistle-blower cases. An average of 537 cases involving national security were reported annually after the 9/11 attacks. Working against government national security whistle-blowers is the exemption enjoyed by security agencies from the 1989 *Whistle-Blower Protection Act*. This law guarantees investigations brought by the whistle-blower but does not guarantee retaliation by law or agency reprisals. Agencies are justifiably concerned that classified information could leak through the media or during a court trial about intelligence-gathering activities.

Other officials who had their agencies retaliate against them for pointing out serious flaws or illegal activities include **Bogdan Dzakovic**, a team leader for the Federal Aviation Administration who consistently pointed out flaws in airport security prior to the 9/11 terrorist attacks. **Sibel Edmonds** of the Federal Bureau of Investigation discovered shoddy translations after 9/11 by incompetent translators and informed her superiors. She was fired in March 2002. **Russell Tice**, a former official with the National Security Agency, testified before Congress on illegal programs. For this truthfulness, he had his clearances revoked and found himself transferred to a furniture warehouse job.

Bobby Maxwell spent twenty-two years as one of the Department of Interior's best auditors of royalties oil companies owed the government, amounting to a percentage of about $60 billion oil companies generate in revenue on federal land each year. Maxwell had filed a lawsuit against a large oil company, Kerr-McGee, using the *False Claims Act* in which an individual can seek damages for unpaid royalties to the government. For his aggressive vigilance, and his legal creativity in using an old law in a new way in pursuing the public's cause, the Interior Department fired him. Technically, officials simply eliminated his position. The department was under investigation by Congress to explain its slipshod and dysfunctional practices in auditing taxed energy monies owed the government.

Like all the figures in this book, government whistle-blowers who come forward with tales of illegal activities or corruption are harassed, are investigated themselves, are subject to character assassination, have reputations ruined, and are often fired. They are lucky if they are only transferred to a less satisfying position. Such individuals who have placed themselves at risk stand out because they believe, for example, that tobacco companies lie about the effects of their products, or that certain drugs cause harmful secondary medical effects, or that there is waste in selected government spending programs, or that there is lying and corruption among elected officials. While exposing themselves to loss of income, reputation, and excessive lawyer legal fees, whistle-blowers earn a place in hearts for their courage.

Independent Thinkers

It is easy to label outlandish views as extremist. It is more difficult to determine whether or not an idea is just contrary to popular opinion, maybe offensive, possibly libelous but not illegal.

Salman Rushdie was born in Mumbai (Bombay) in 1947 and renounced Islam. As a result of publishing his novel *Satanic Verses*, former Iranian leader Ayatollah Ruhollah Khomeini, on February 14, 1989, issued an Islamic death *fatwa* against him, allowing any Islamic believer to kill him without punishment. The outrageous threat of death from a state governed by Islamic clerics against a novelist writing fiction repulsed the modern world and compelled the British and American governments to collude in hiding him. What might appear to be the quiet and uncomplicated life of a writer whose time is spent alone at a desk or in a library was, in this instance, turned into a man hidden from actual executioners because of a work of fiction. Ideas, even ones in fiction, can get you killed. Rushdie is the modern equivalent of a medieval heretic to Islam.

The aftermath of the death threats against Rushdie were extraordinarily violent. Bookstores selling his book were firebombed in Berkeley. In Bombay, his home city, twelve people died in a police shooting and riot outside the British Embassy. Others died in Egypt. Public burnings of his book were held throughout the world. His Japanese translator was stabbed and beaten in Tokyo. His Norwegian publisher was shot and severely injured in an attack outside of his Oslo home. The bounty on Rushdie's head was raised from $3 million to $6 million and endorsed by the Iranian government.

Anna Politkovskaya, forty-eight, the mother of two grown children, and a veteran journalist for *Novaya Gazeta*, one of the few independent newspapers in Moscow, was assassinated in the elevator of her apartment building on October 7, 2006. She had previously received numerous death threats. Her killer shot her four times, three in the chest and once in the head, with a Makarov pistol with a silencer. It was a political assassination and not a random killing or robbery. Anna had been reporting on the war in Chechnya and was a persistent critic of official corruption and state terrorism by Russian officials. At least thirteen journalists were murdered in Russia from 2000 to 2006. After Iraq and Algeria, Russia is the third deadliest country for murdered writers and critics.

Social barriers and limitations, like those that shaped the former Soviet Union and Eastern Europe from 1945 to 1989, also emboldened a few courageous independent thinkers like the Russian **Alexander Solzhenitsyn**, awarded the Nobel Prize for Literature in 1970. Solzhenitsyn chronicled the horror of the Soviet prison camps in *The Gulag Archipelago* (1973), and was the most formidable literary opponent of government policies under Stalin and later Soviet rulers.

Equally courageous, though not in fear for his life, in America was **Arthur Miller**, author of *Death of a Salesman* (1949) and *The Crucible* (1953), who was summoned before the House Un-American Activities Committee in 1956 and questioned about his alliances. Richard Nixon was a congressional member of this committee and one of its most aggressive questioners. At the time a climate of fear permeated all intellectuals, writers, and movie industry personnel for potential association with communists. Miller refused to name individuals he associated with, was cited for contempt of Congress and fined $500, but widely praised for his stand against suppression of free speech and freedom of association. A court later overturned the conviction.

There are thousands of unknowns who performed heroic acts during the ravages of China's Mao Tze-Tung from 1949 to his death in 1976; the horrors of the genocides in Cambodia in the 1970s; the genocide of Tutsis by Hutus in

Rwanda in the 1990s; and genocide by the Sudanese military and its mercenaries in the Darfur region of Sudan in the beginning of the twenty-first century. Gun-toting mercenaries hired by venal, industrial exploiters, land-grabbers, and illegal loggers in the Amazon rain forest kill Brazilian conservationists, small ranchers, and environmental activists like the American-born nun **Dorothy Stang**. She was a sister of the Sisters of Notre Dame de Namur and lived in the frontier town of Anapu near the Trans-Amazon highway. She had dedicated her life to family farmers who pursued their agricultural subsistence in harmony with nature. On the morning of February 12, 2005, two gunmen confronted the seventy-three year old nun on a jungle path and Rayfran das Neves Sales then shot and killed her.

There have been countless other exiles, poets, and pilgrims whose destinies were tied to opposing political factions or who in jest or in print personally offended a chief magistrate or public official. The Red Guards during the time of China's so-called Cultural Revolution from 1966 to 1976 either murdered or forced **Lao She**, an internationally respected novelist, to commit suicide in 1976.

History may be punctuated by the rule of a few enlightened despots and the gravitas of reasonable philosophers, but it is littered with boorish and philistine aristocrats and dictators whose only contributions to civilization are that they filled up some geography and usurped the benefits of others during their limited existences. Whole societies have been subordinated to totalitarian regimes that insisted on thinking only according to the code of the ruling dictator or the aristocratic or clerical class. One doesn't have to read far in the history of any century to find examples of the suppression of independent voices.

The twentieth century is littered with the corpses and dictates of dead dictators, their perverse rules and brutal crushing of any opposition or dissent: Hitler in Nazi Germany, Stalin in Russia, Mao Tze Tung in China, Idi Amin in Uganda, Saddam Hussein in Iraq, Kim Jong Il in North Korea. Perhaps the most insidious was the regime in Cambodia in the 1970s and 1980s of Pol Pot whose nihilistic campaign to impose the most extreme version of Marxist rule eliminated all individual rights, all forms of creativity, originality, and inventiveness and even the idea of individual consciousness. Pol Pot killed over 20 percent of Cambodia's population within three years for its failure to comply with his inflexible suppression of individuality.

The twenty-first century has more than seventy countries, roughly half the nations of the world, still ruled by dictators who cannot be removed from power legally, who exercise arbitrary control over their citizens and routinely suppress freedom of thought, speech, religion, the press, and the right to a fair trial.

Plutarch (c. 46–120) interpreted the past through such biographies as I am undertaking here. His *Lives of Famous Greeks and Romans* was written to illustrate characters strong in moral virtue. Plutarch cared less about how Julius Caesar, for example, shaped history than how his morals exemplified his era. Plutarch was troubled by the decadence of Romans and, as a Greek, wanted to provide literary examples to restore faith in humanity when faith in the divine was eroding. Likewise, Diogenes Laertius in the third century of the Christian era wrote ten books on the lives of famous philosophers, beginning with Thales and ending with Epicurus, an important contribution to biography and the history of philosophy.

I seek to combine biography with moral not physical courage. So again I draw from literature for examples. Henrik Ibsen's (1828–1906) play *An Enemy of the People*, first performed in Norway in 1883, shows the courage of one man fighting against the tyranny of the majority, authoritarianism, political chicanery, and cowardice. The play has a contemporary resonance. Ibsen himself, in a photo taken in his study in Oslo in 1898 looks the part of a lone maverick with his bushy sideburns and full beard as he scowls for the photographer. But Ibsen portrays the local paper and local politicians conniving to silence Dr. Thomas Stockmann, the local physician, who discovers that the local baths, a source of tourist revenue for the community, have contaminated waters. The play evolves to show how everyone collaborates to keep Dr. Stockmann from informing the public through writing in the paper or speaking in a public forum. Stockmann's last line in the play summarizes Ibsen's intent: "The strongest man in the world is he who stands most alone."

Radical, courageous individuals, celebrated in fiction or real life, with a passion for speaking their minds about the truth are generally unwelcome. After having voiced their contrary opinions, or exposure of graft, greed, or corruption, these persons are usually maliciously persecuted for their outspokenness. The virtue of courage is at least as heroic as the idea proposed. The ambitions, quirks of personality, degrees of creative genius, or intentions of such thinkers break the personnel mold and formulate new lines of inquiry. What dissidents have in common is that their ideas initially caused moral outrage. Only subsequent generations gave them acceptance.

There are daily examples of heroism and altruism by people of all ages who are not dissidents or motivated by a cause. When Enterprise High School in Enterprise, Alabama was struck by a tornado destroying the school and killing eight students on March 2, 2007, Andrew J. Jackson, a sixteen year-old weightlifter, hoisted a falling concrete beam long enough for another student to escape before the beam fell and crushed him.

One collective example of courage are America's founders, the 57 signers of the *Declaration of Independence* in 1776, who pledged "our lives, our fortunes and our sacred honor" to declare independence from Britain. The high rhetoric of the opening paragraphs, later used by Lincoln to unite the country at war, are the most memorable. But the heart of the document is the list of offenses the king had brought upon the colonies, "a history of repeated injuries and usurpations … the establishment of an absolute tyranny over these States."

Since many were lawyers, they understood the effect signing this document would create and the danger it implied for them if captured.

The list of kingly actions that the signers enumerated as tyrannous included the refusal of governors to pass needed legislation, the forfeitures of a people seeking representation, the dissolution of representative legislative houses, the obstruction of the administration of justice by refusing to establish judiciary powers ("made judges dependent on his will alone"), the keeping of standing armies without the consent of state legislatures, the quartering of armed troops among the people, and imposing of taxes without the peoples' consent. If caught, all signers knew they would be tried and killed for treason. Less well-known men like George Wythe, William Whipple and Matthew Thornton pledged their lives to the cause.

In *Deuteronomy* we find the admonition: "If there arise among you a prophet, or a dreamer of dreams … saying 'Let us go after other gods' … that prophet or dreamer of dreams shall be put to death." This biblical injunction lends divine authority to kill those of alternative beliefs. Similar passages against infidels are in the Koran. "When you meet the unbelievers in the battle-field, strike off their heads (Sura 47:4). "And fight in the way of God with those who fight with you ... And slay them whenever you come upon them, and expel them from where they expelled you" (Sura 2:190). "When the sacred months are over slay the idolaters wherever you find them" (Sura 9:5). Some monotheistic religions have God's blessings for killing those not of a similar persuasion.

At the height of classical Rome, the state religion, the worship of Jupiter was closely allied with the emperor and both heresy and blasphemy were classed as treason. A Roman judge would convene an *inquisitio*, an inquiry, into the case, and this same procedure was adopted by ecclesiastical authorities in the Middle Ages. Thus, even the Inquisition, which we commonly associate with the Catholic Church's persecution of deviant beliefs, dates from the Romans who had commissions that sought to extirpate unorthodox religious dissent. But the origin of heresy and an inquiry into those suspected of holding of unacceptable beliefs is much older. Ancient Greek laws made failure to worship the gods a capital crime, and this law was used to order the death of Socrates.

But Greek playwrights also created personal heroes. Prometheus was Aeschylus's tragic heroic figure who defiantly stole fire from Zeus and gave it to humans. He was a rebel who defied the ultimate authority to save the whole human race. In retaliation, Zeus had him chained to a rock in the Caucasus Mountains where each day an eagle ate part of his liver that was regenerated each day so the pain was endless. Challenging God has its penalties, but Aeschylus turned Prometheus into a symbol of heroic fortitude of the clashes between humans and deities.

I begin this study by examining modern dissenters in the first two chapters, contemporaries who have lived, and in a few cases still do still live among us, and whose intrepid fearlessness we can admire if not emulate. In the third chapter I describe American dissenters like Roger Williams and Cochise whose lives were symbolic of valor and dissent. Since one of America's perennial controversies is between science and religion, in chapter 4 I examine Darwin who proposed ideas that overturned the beliefs about the biblical origin of biological life. Since many seeking spiritual relief have turned to nature and natural phenomena, I describe witches and other so-called pagan beliefs in chapter 5 to round out Part 1.

I examine the legacy of such individuals in part 2 at the dawn of history and the written tradition to suggest examples from the Greeks who challenged gods and authorities. In succeeding chapters I explore the tumultuous first three Christian centuries and the beginnings of religious heretics in Christianity to form the backdrop to further religious, scientific, and philosophical controversies in western civilization.

Heroes and heroines do not live in a vacuum but have a biological as well as a historical legacy and I have attempted to humanize their lives. In a lifetime, one is fortunate to be able to encounter people two or three generations before and after one's own. Reading biographies of historical figures expands one's concept of the human experience.

There is no pattern to these studies of human character, except that I believe that there are celebrated and unsung heroes and heroines in every age. I omit military heroes and soldiers as the invitation is too strong to have to select only a few when so many are available. Military heroes are under orders and do not act independently, though they often make heroic choices in the face of imminent death. I do believe that there are far too many we will never know about because their stories have never been told and their courage obscured or neglected. Like the persons buried in all the tombs of the Unknown Soldiers, I dedicate this book to the contributions of unknown heroes and heroines. Some saints and numerous atheists are included because courage knows no religion. It is the act of moral courage, not the conversion to any particular religion, which is the defining criterion. The choices profiled are personal but illustrate the theme of moral courage and the varieties of human conditions, without age or frontiers that inspire it.

PART I

MODERN OUTCASTS

CHAPTER ONE
GREAT SOULS OF THE MODERN AGE

Outcasts, heretics, heathens, infidels, and dissenters have boldly challenged petty tyrants, injurious laws, religious bigotry, or traditional or popular wisdom to reveal their intellectual and moral independence and sense of justice. Outsiders but not outlaws—deviants or criminals are excluded—are remembered as subversive, antagonistic, and even hostile to convention, the kind of person you might defame or slander but could invite to dinner even if he or she does not antagonize the caterers or unduly provoke other guests. Courageous men and women do not shy away from prohibited expressions, colonial repression, dictatorial rules, or bad laws.

This book is a journey through a series of biographical profiles throughout the past two and a half centuries. It is about those who challenged the status quo, who stood bold and often alone in the teeth of opposition from common and sometimes uncomprehending minds, and emerged as torchbearers of liberation, captains of their souls and exemplars for us all. Their lives remind us that courage and virtues of principled character are good for their own sake and glorify the human experience. It is common practice among many profiled in this book that individuals are tried, imprisoned, tortured, and often sentenced to death for laws that do not allow criticism of government. I have selected four great souls of the modern age from different continents to begin this excursion into moral courage: Gandhi, Dr. Martin Luther King, Jr., Steven Biko and Ayaan Hirsi Ali.

Mohandas Gandhi (1869–1942)

Gandhi was a giant of moral courage and spiritual habits who spent his life fighting against discrimination, sectarian violence and preached the virtues of nonviolence and saintly behaviors he practiced. If spiritual value is the basis for all action, as Gandhi claimed, then he is a model for how people dedicated to a saintly life can live. During his life he spent the equivalent of six and a half years in prison for his opposition to discrimination and tyranny. His life was his lasting message. He was assassinated for his beliefs on January 28, 1948 by a Hindu fundamentalist, Nathuram Vinayak Godese, thrity-five, editor of a Poona weekly.

13

Gandhi was a dualist believing in the spirit and the body. Like all devout Hindus and Buddhists he felt he needed to curb the senses to attain spiritual enlightenment and purity. And like other mystics, he sought to lose himself in a larger divine presence. "I have but shadowed forth my intense longing to lose myself in the Eternal and become merely a lump of clay in the Potter's divine hands, so that my service may become more certain, because uninterrupted by the baser self in me."[1] These lines could have been penned by any Christian, Buddhist, or Muslim mystic, as they represent a quest for the active consciousness to be absorbed into a transcendental or divine consciousness, or at least to leap beyond limited human consciousness.

Yet since the spiritual life was his chief ambition, not even formal education was relevant to his cause. "I have never been able to make a fetish of literary training. My experience has proved to my satisfaction that literary training by itself adds not an inch to one's moral height and that character-building is independent of literary training."[2] He had not been particularly studious in school. As a law student in England from 1888 to 1891 he had socialized with a group of radicals, vegetarians, and theosophical followers and imbibed theosophy's distaste for formal learning.[3] He spent three years in England but learned little of Western economics, politics, art, science, or letters. His scholarly contribution was a few articles in a vegetarian publication. But while in prison in South Africa and later in India he was able to read more of those authors who inspired him like Ralph Waldo Emerson, Henry Thoreau and his inspirational friends Leo Tolstoy, John Ruskin, and Thomas Carlyle, and even Karl Marx and Friedrich Engels. His reputation was not based on his learning but his zeal for a virtuous life. He only read those writers he preferred, never those who might challenge his existing beliefs. His principal reading and prayer guide was the *Bhagavad Gita*, the Hindu holy book.

He was impressed with the Montessori method for elementary-aged school children. He favored any educational program that was vocational, preferring physical labor to academic study. He advocated for his rural Indian villagers the skills of handicrafts, carpentry, horticulture, the care of animals, and spinning. He chose spinning literally as his home-spun cause, and vowed to spin daily when he returned to India from South Africa. He believed that self-sufficiency was essential and that manual labor gave individuals a sense of freedom from commercial exploitation. He considered big business to be detrimental to Indian life and abhorred the growing influence of capitalism, which is why communists thought they had identified a kindred spirit. In a provocative speech in 1916 at the Muir College of Economics in Allahabad the budding economists in the audience heard that he had never read Adam Smith. He said he preferred reading scriptures to economics and that industrialized progress was a smokescreen because all big business was immoral.

He became an advocate of chastity. He forswore sex with his wife in his middle years. "Sex urge is a fine and noble thing," he wrote. "There is nothing to be ashamed of it. But it is meant only for the act of creation. Any other use of it is a sin against God and humanity." [4] How a couple following this advice, and hoping to conceive and unable to know when an "act of creation" was occurring or not is not disclosed. But Gandhi is not concerned with the science or logistics of sexual intercourse, but in expounding his view of reproductive human actions. He encouraged abstinence even among his married followers at his Ashram in Gujarat. His political innocence was in believing that the subcontinent would follow him in his calls for sexual abstinence.

His sexual perspective was likely influenced by a youthful trauma. He was married when he was thirteen in an arrangement made by the parents, as was customary in India. But when he and his bride both were sixteen, and she was pregnant, he left his father's sick room to awaken his wife and enjoy her. His father suddenly died during his brief absence from his father's sick bed. A few months later, his child died. The guilt over following his sexual appetite and not his duty to his father rankled him for the rest of his life and clearly contributed to his attitudes toward sex in later life.

He not only opposed sexual relations but eating meat, smoking, and drinking alcoholic beverages. His health was always frail and not advanced by his strict dietary regimen and sparse eating habits. He was often ill for months at a time and refused most medical advice. He fasted, not for his own devotion, but to stiffen the resolve of his followers not to engage in violence. His three daily meals in India were always the same and consisted of three slices of bread, two oranges, either raisins or a bunch of grapes, and sixteen ounces of goat's milk.

Gandhi's Life of Protest

At nineteen he left his family, wife, and new son for legal study in England as an unpromising student. He had scored poorly in the Bombay university exams. At the time, no one would have guessed that this shy, poor speaker, and unskilled and uninformed young man would one day rescue India from imperialism and become one of the world's most admired and saintly figures.

From 1893 to 1914 as a practicing attorney he rallied the minority Indians in South Africa against the racist policies and statutes of the Afrikaner regime in the Transvaal. Here he personally experienced the debilitating effects of racism. He mobilized the mostly Muslim Indian community that eventually thwarted the government against punitive laws. The South Africans had imposed a tax on Indians, had tried not to recognize their legal marriages, had imposed immigration and residence controls, and enforced an indentured labor system. With each new discriminatory legislative act aimed at curbing the activities of minority workers and residents, Gandhi parleyed, provoked the government with a series of labor strikes, and used his growing international influence to get the laws overturned or revoked. He founded an ashram community that was able to sustain the lost wages of strike workers with food, and established an organization that published his messages in magazines like *Young India* and *Harijan*, named after the untouchables he sought to integrate into Indian society and to get Indians to change the insidious caste system.

He returned to India after twenty-one years of leadership against white apartheid practices to an India that desperately needed his particular kind of leadership. While he was in South Africa, other serious reformers had attempted unsuccessfully to transform British sovereignty in India into home rule. While these political reformers had been debating and demonstrating, Gandhi was returning as an outright hero, someone who had actually been successful in restraining colonial authorities on behalf of Indians. His arrival would signal a new beginning for Indian politics, a national uprising that put an end to British imperialism in India.

His reformist baptism for the soul of India began in Bihar province bordering southeast Nepal in 1917. Peasants working in the indigo plantations had been systematically exploited by English owners. They were employed like feudal serfs for marginal wages and forced to turn over a large part of their crops to the owners. Gandhi was asked to come to intervene. He organized lawyers, the local peasants, was brought to trial, and convinced the courts to release him. He got regional officials to pass judgment on the owners and order retributive damages for discriminatory financial charges they had imposed on the workers. The British would soon learn that they could not order him, or any Indian, about in his own country. This signal political victory would mark the beginning of his active nonviolent movement. But his own views on non-violence vacillated:

> I advocate training in arms for those who believe in the method of violence. I would rather have India resort to arms in order to defend her honor than that she should in a cowardly manner become or remain a helpless witness to her own dishonor. But I believe that non-violence is infinitely superior to violence, forgiveness more manly than punishment. [5]

As Gandhi's religious influence deepened, his political activities increased, all directed against the British. The period between World War I and World War II were transitional for countries like Turkey that under Kemal Ataturk overthrew the caliphate, or the military movement of Sinn Fein in Ireland that sought to undermine British suzerainty. These movements of throwing off the yoke of authoritarian governments gave encouragement to Indian reformists like Gandhi. But when the passions of unruly, disorganized, and inflammable mobs often rioted in India's cities, Gandhi's response was to undertake a fast. His religious example was exemplary but he was unable to control the humiliation, excited passions for justice, and the need to exclude the foreign domination his countrymen felt.

One of his trials began on March 18, 1922. He had written three offensive articles in *Young India* the previous year. The official charge was bringing contempt or disaffection to her majesty's government established by law in British India. Gandhi was persistent in noting that the British should not have been in

India at all. Gandhi would spend the next two decades of his life pointing out the folly of imperial British claims of ownership in India and for setting its own form of laws upon native citizens.

Gandhi was accused of Machiavellian practices and of being an enigmatic schemer in his politics among his followers and in negotiations with the British. But in reality he was candid and simplistic in his themes that occur repeatedly in his writings. He believed in truth, that God is truth and truth is God, in non-violence, in the spinning wheel for people to learn economic self-sufficiency, in the adverse effects of capitalism, and in Hindu-Muslim unity.

Gandhi was a Hindu preacher, a man who seemed single-handedly to have liberated India from British colonial rule. By 1946 and the end of World War II the British were as anxious to leave India as the Indians were desirous of their departure. His written statements in the bulletins and publications he operated are hortatory and plain, often simple aphorisms that, like comments by Socrates, exhorted his readers to seek justice and virtue, to dispense with selfishness, and find meaning in life's simplicities. His wise sayings were read avidly by India's devotees. His moral authority was unquestioned by his adoring followers. He would earn the title of Mahatma, the Great Soul.

He was not a scholar as his reading in history, science, and the humanities was limited until later in his life when prison time afforded him the luxury of reading. Throughout most of his life his bedside books were the Veda and Hindu holy texts. His wisdom originated from his deep faith, from prayer and meditation. Even his legal training does not reveal him as a logical or especially coherent thinker. He was too focused on the primary goals of his mission: to release India from British occupation, and to eliminate religious and racial hatred and prejudice between Hindus, Muslims and Christians. He was friendly with members of all religious sects. His ascetic life led thousands to adopt his austere lifestyle. But rising sectarian violence between Muslims and Hindus in the days following independence and the splitting off of Pakistan and eventually Bangladesh as separate countries carved out of India, dampened Gandhi's dream of interracial and inter-religious unity. He found the idea of a separate country like Pakistan's founded on religion repugnant. His incessant pleas for multi-ethnic unity, of intransigent attitudes and sectarian beliefs, fell on deaf ears.

> Mutual toleration is a necessity for all time and for all races. We cannot live in peace if the Hindu will not tolerate the Muhammedan form of worship of God or if the Muhammedan will be impatient of Hindu idolatry and cow worship. It is not necessary for toleration that I must approve of what I tolerate. . . . all the quarrels between Hindus and the Muhammedans have arisen from each wanting to force the other to his view. [6]

He was cremated in the Indian tradition and his ashes scattered in the Ganges River. In New Delhi on a ghat, or broad flight of stairs leading down to the Ganges, is a monument to this man's memory and accomplishments, and I once paused in a moment of reflection and silence before it.

Dr. Martin Luther King Jr. (1929–1968)

The problem of race and color prejudice remains America's greatest moral dilemma. [7]

It's difficult to imagine the depth of hatred southern Whites had for Blacks throughout American history and right through the first half of the 20th century. This unfeigned repugnance was exemplified in state segregation laws that applied to housing, jobs, dining facilities, public squares, toilets, even to separate public drinking fountains. The Klu Klux Klan enjoyed the freedom to wear white sheets over their heads, harass blacks en masse and parade in streets undeterred by police or any official retaliation. But when demonstrating blacks congregated in public arenas, police were noticeably absent to prevent white violence on blacks, but then arrested them for parading without a permit. Black churches were routinely burned or bombed during King's demonstrations. Laws in southern states encoded segregation into statutes and prohibited most forms of social contact between White and Black communities.

The unanimous *Brown v. Board of Education* decision was handed down in May, 1954. The desegregation order galvanized at Central High School in Little Rock, Arkansas, when President Dwight Eisenhower federalized the state militia to maintain order from demonstrating whites shouting obscenities and threatening violence to the newly entering black students. The *Brown* decision and all subsequent U.S. Supreme Court decisions about busing to achieve school desegregation highlighted the national social agenda of the late 1950s and 1960s.

The 1960s were a time of explosive change for America. King became the acknowledged national leader for civil rights for African Americans when America was traumatized by the Vietnam War. President John F. Kennedy was assassinated on November 23, 1963. Robert Kennedy, his brother, a former attorney general and senator from New York, was assassinated in Los Angeles in 1968 while campaigning for the Democratic presidential nomination. Malcolm X was assassinated in 1965 and Martin Luther King in 1968. Riots and demonstrations followed each of these tragic incidents in American life. I was a witness to one of the most intense riots in 1968 after King's assassination when I saw jeeps with mounted machine guns patrolling the streets of downtown Washington DC during martial law in the nation's capitol.

This was an era of social turmoil in which King, who spearheaded much of the agitation for the civil rights movement, lived and died. [8] The visceral hatred of most southern whites for blacks, embedded in its mentality and segregated laws, was soon to be exposed by his methods. How can a man whose first two names are those of a formidable revolutionary not be revolutionary in spirit himself?

King graduated from a segregated high school in Atlanta, Georgia, at the age of fifteen, and in 1948 from Morehouse College where his father and grandfather had received their collegiate education. He then attended Crozer Theological Seminary in Chester, Pennsylvania. and received his bachelor of divinity degree in 1951. After receiving a scholarship stipend from Crozier, he enrolled at Boston University where he received his doctoral degree in 1955. It was while he was a student in Boston that he was introduced to Coretta Scott, a southern girl, graduate of Antioch College, then studying music at the New England Conservatory of Music. They soon married and would have four children. [9]

King followed in his father's footsteps and became a Baptist minister. He accepted pastoral duties at Dexter Avenue Baptist Church in Montgomery Alabama in 1954 and the following year led an event that sparked the beginnings of the civil rights movement in the United States. During that time King was arrested, threatened, and his home bombed. In his lifetime he was assaulted four times and arrested nearly twenty times.

The Tactic of Nonviolence

The Southern Christian Leadership Conference, which took its ideals from Christianity and its nonviolent practices from Gandhi, was organized in 1957 and King became its leader. This black leadership organization was to be the inspiration for the civil rights movement throughout the 1960s. On a visit to India in 1959, King was convinced that Mohandas Gandhi, who had won India's independence from Britain with his philosophy of virtue, had been morally right to advocate nonviolent means to achieve political ends. The international recognition King received convinced him that the tactics in the Montgomery bus boycott in 1955 were the most effective to achieve civil rights recognition for blacks. He returned to the United States to use non-violent methods against entrenched southern racism. "We must not allow our creative protest to degenerate into physical violence," he said in his "I have a dream" speech in 1963.

King's tactics of non-violence and direct confrontation were not always welcomed, even among the black organizations. The National Association for the Advancement of Colored People (NAACP), for example, was more cautious in its approach and relied on judicial advancements to achieve its ends. The NAACP was instrumental in lobbying successful in the courts on behalf of the *Brown* decision and did not want to jeopardize its legal gains with a backlash of public opinion.

Meantime, college students had organized the Student Non-Violent Coordinating Committee (SNCC) to rally support for sit-ins in diners, restaurants, hospitals, cinemas, parks, and public places where segregation was still legal. In these sit-ins at segregated lunch counters, in boycotts of segregated public transportation, in support of strikes for workers, and in protest marches and public demonstrations, and in hundreds of speeches, King's support and active involvement drew public attention to the inequities in American society and inequalities in segregated state laws and the administration of justice for civil rights.

BLACK ORGANIZATIONS THAT ADVANCED CIVIL RIGHTS IN THE 1960s

National Association for the Advancement of Colored People
(NAACP)
Southern Christian Leadership Council (SCLC)
Student Non-Violent Coordinating Committee (SNCC)
Congress of Racial Equality (CORE)
Urban League
Freedom Riders
Alabama Christian Movement for Human Rights
Western Christian Leadership Conference (Harry Belafonte)
Council for United Civil Rights Leadership (CUCRL)

In 1963 the combined freedom organizations targeted Birmingham, Alabama, for a peaceful sit-in and marches. The police arrested hundreds. When Judge W. A. Jenkins issued an injunction prohibiting demonstrations, King knew that the campaign to expose the South's racist laws would be fruitful and that he would be arrested. King also knew that law is the bedrock of a democratic society and that to use the law as a means to curtail or thwart civil liberties or freedom of movement and the right to assemble peacefully as guaranteed by the First Amendment was unconscionable and unconstitutional. Though his bail bond was insidiously raised too high for him to pay, he elected to go to jail. He wrote, in *Letter From a Birmingham Jail*, that

> Oppressed people cannot remain oppressed forever. The urge for freedom will eventually come. This is what happened to the American Negro. Something within has reminded him of his birthright of freedom; something without has reminded him that he can gain it. [10]

Demonstrations: Civil Rights and the War in Vietnam

On May 20, 1963, the U.S. Supreme Court legalized sit-in demonstrations and this nullified Alabama's segregation laws. A large number of demonstrators who had been imprisoned were thus freed. After the Birmingham demonstrations, and rioting caused by young black males unconcerned about Black church affiliations or the diplomacy of compromise, the vacillating President Kennedy finally relented in favor of the black persistent quest for justice. Kennedy had secretly favored King's cause but wavered because the South was so important to electoral success, and Kennedy had beaten Richard Nixon in an extremely close election in 1960, winning by only about 200,000 popular votes.

The marches in Selma, Alabama in 1965—there were 30,000 in the last march on March 21—were to prove decisive in revealing the depth of southern police brutality and the injustice of the state's legal system. White protestors who voluntarily came to lend support, were labeled outside agitators or provocateurs by southerners and treated disdainfully, and in a few cases murdered, like the Boston Unitarian minister James Reeb who was clubbed to death by white toughs in March, 1965. The Detroit mother of five and housewife, Viola Liuzzo, a transportation volunteer, was fatally shot through the head while driving a Black man in her car from Montgomery to Selma. President Lyndon Johnson spoke eloquently on March 15, 1965, and announced that he was sending a voting rights bill to Congress, and made a passionate and sincere plea for the acceptance of civil rights for all. It had been a decade since Rosa Parks refused to relinquish her bus seat.

But the 1960s were also a time when America was at war in Vietnam. The war's mounting casualties witnessed nightly on TV polarized the population, many of whom wanted a defeat of communism and others who saw the brutality and senselessness of violence against a people caught in a Vietnamese civil war. The defeat of communism wherever it existed, according to American foreign policy, was a Pavlovian response to the cold war with the Soviet Union and the nuclear standoff. The convergence of the antiwar and civil rights movements traumatized the collective conscience of the nation and resulted in demonstrations, riots, and even a few student deaths on American college campuses.

The rising level of anguish about the war in Vietnam fragmented the unity of the large black organizations in supportive unity with King. Often, criticism of the war took precedence in marches, speeches, and demonstrations over the conditions of Blacks. The unfortunate commingling of the two movements tended to diffuse the impetus of both. Young blacks in particular, like Malcolm X, were expressing more violent reactions. Stokely Carmichael of SNCC, for example, had coined the slogan "black power," which King found unacceptable, even though it energized those who wanted freedom immediately. King was being shunted aside by others seeking the helm of the movement, and shut out by the Johnson administration irked over his criticism of the war. By 1967 King, rising to his responsibilities as a minister and capitalizing on the peace movement, was speaking almost exclusively against the war rather than about the conditions of Blacks.

But, as if a foreign war and a major social upheaval were not enough to provoke trauma, the cold war with the USSR was apparent with its threat of nuclear annihilation. In the United States the hunt for spies and potential communist sympathizers was a national paranoia. On top on the list of J. Edgar Hoover's "subversives" FBI list was King, who was secretly followed and taped. The FBI assumed that since King was causing widespread social anxiety that he might just be an agent of a foreign power or a communist sympathizer, an idea as far-fetched as a sketch from a Joseph Conrad novel. [11]

J. Edgar Hoover, the head of the FBI at the time erected his own cult image around the agency that he managed like a personal fiefdom. Hoover convinced the public, and cowed presidents and Congress, that he and his agency personified the ideals of equal justice when in fact he managed the FBI to serve his personal policies. Hoover used electronic surveillance to pry into the private lives of members of Congress and King himself. Hoover had tapes of King's infidelities while King was traveling. Hoover and his agents knew that King was not a communist, but feared some communist sympathizers would influence him, or worse, hijack his movement. [12]

King's crowning speech, an eloquent statement using biblical phraseology and images, was delivered in Washington DC on a sweltering summer day at the Lincoln Memorial before 250,000 people on August 28, 1963. His speech electrified a national TV audience and drew attention to the civil rights differences in American society and continuing segregation. Here is a part of what he said that day.

> I still have a dream. It is a dream deeply rooted in the American dream that one day this nation will rise up and live out the true meaning of its creed, we hold these truths to be self-evident, that all men are created equal. [13]

It was a phrase he had echoed many times in his speeches and sermons. King's oratory and active campaigning injected a fresh vitality into the civil rights movement, prompted congressional legislation in civil and voting rights, changed the way Americans thought about themselves and fellow citizens, and above all exposed the rawness and intransigence inherent in southern white attitudes and segregated laws.

The success of the demonstrations and mass marches were to be realized through another national tragedy—the assassination on November 22, 1963, of President John F. Kennedy in Dallas. The elevation of Vice President Lyndon Johnson to the presidency accelerated the passage of civil rights legislation. President Johnson convinced Congress to pass the *The Civil Rights Act* (1964), prohibiting discrimination in public accommodations, and *The Voting Rights Act* (1965) prohibiting discrimination in state voting privileges and eligibility, ending centuries of legal oppression and discrimination. King brought essential financing, limited organizational skills, international and national attention, and democratization to the liberation movement.

In 1964 King was awarded the Nobel Peace Prize for his efforts to promote civil rights in America, the youngest at thirty-five ever to receive that prize.

King was assassinated on the evening of April 4, 1968 as he stood on the balcony of the Lorraine Motel in Memphis, Tennessee, while in the city to mediate a garbage workers' strike. He was just thirty-nine years old. His assassin was James Earl Ray, a high school dropout and a small time criminal who had escaped from a Missouri prison in 1967. Ray was apprehended at Heathrow Airport in London the following June, and was tried, convicted, and sentenced to ninety-nine years in prison where he died of liver failure in 1998.

King's crusade restated the moral dilemma in America that the Swedish sociologist Gunnar Myrdal had written in a classic 1941 study of race relations, *An American Dilemma*. Despite his Christian message and style, King incurred the wrath of white supremacists and the ire of closet racists. But he also invoked the consciences of those who saw the value of the full extension of civil liberties for all Americans. His international recognition and Nobel Peace Prize announced to the world his humane authenticity and pricked the ethically hesitant throughout the nation and the world of his moral integrity. He was a charismatic man of his times, a martyr to the cause of human freedom. Streets are named after him in many major cities in America, a token legacy to the magnitude of his accomplishments.

Let's turn now to an equally courageous leader in defense of human rights in an equally segregated country in the same era.

Bantu Steven Biko (1946–1977)

Prior to 1988 when Nelson Mandela assumed the presidency of a new unity government, the Republic of South Africa had been an apartheid government that legally separated black, whites and "coloreds" since 1948. Apartheid South Africa was no different than the southern United States from colonial rule until the passage of congressional civil rights legislation in 1964.

The prime minister then was P. W. Botha, known as the "Old Crocodile," who died in 2006 at ninety. Botha had carried on the ignominious legacy of racist government policies from 1978 to 1989, an implacable defender of apartheid policies and practices. He achieved national notoriety as secretary of defense. As prime minister he gave the police unprecedented powers to repress dissent, and encouraged black tribal and language groups, especially the Zulus and Xhosas, to fight among themselves. He used the communist threat as a way of stamping out opponents and accused black groups of having been infiltrated by communist insurgents. He was reelected in 1987 but had a stroke in 1989 and resigned. In May 1990 F. W. De Klerk, the new Prime Minister, met with Nelson Mandela who had been released from prison after twenty-seven years to discuss the nature of the transitional government in a country that included five million Whites and twenty-eight million blacks. Apartheid started to unravel.

Nelson Mandela spent over two decades imprisoned on Robben Island for his antagonism and defiance of South Africa's racist and segregationist laws, over three times as long as Gandhi spent in prison. Mandela emerged as president when white government domination ceased. Mandela and Fredrik Wilhelm De Klerk were both awarded the Nobel Peace Prize in 1993 for their joint efforts in making possible a peaceful transfer of power and avoiding a civil war. This successful transition helped eradicate segregationist laws. Even without Mandela and the power struggle among blacks, the more odious forms of apartheid had been disintegrating for years, much of it brought on by international attention and economic boycotts. By 1990 trade unions for blacks had been legalized, segregationist laws had been scrapped, and the laws banning mixed marriages rescinded. *The Separate Amenities Act* ended apartheid in restrooms, beaches and other common areas and the *Group Areas Act* that segregated housing was modified. No one was more pleased than I was to witness the peaceful governmental transition. By 1998 when I visited the country again, the government was a majority black government that faced other problems of unemployment, an influx of immigrants from other parts of Africa, and rising crime rates.[14]

The segregationist laws and police brutality that sustained the country were hallmarks of a racist government in South Africa until the late 1980s. There were forty-five known deaths that occurred during police detention from the 1960s onward, all under mysterious and suspect circumstances. Steven Biko's premature death in prison under torture was among them. [15]

Here is a brief background on the European settlement of South Africa as a prelude to Steven Biko's fight for justice.

A majority of scientists have concluded that humans evolved originally in Africa. The discovery in the 1920s of the so-called Tang baby, the skull of a child from over a million years ago found near Cape Town, confirmed that the region once housed hominids. So when the Dutch arrived in southern Africa in 1652 and established a base for their trading vessels that reached to the Dutch East Indies, now Indonesia, Europeans had returned in a sense to ancient ancestral homelands. The British followed the Dutch in 1814 in concessions wrung from the end of the Napoleonic wars and took control of the southern tip of the continent. The Dutch took flight into the interior around what is today Pretoria and Johannesburg in a district known as the Transvaal and the Orange Free State. This Dutch group became known as Afrikaners with their own language, a mixture of Dutch and German.

The discovery of gold at the turn of the twentieth century brought adventurers, prospectors, and miners from all English-speaking countries. Suddenly, the newcomers outnumbered the Afrikaners. These new settlers demanded the vote and other civil liberties and were backed in their claims by the British government. The result was the Boer War in which a young journalist, Winston Churchill, was captured and daringly escaped from confinement to tell the story and later lead the struggle for Britain in World War II.

At the Boer War's end in 1910, the British gave all of South Africa to the united nation of Afrikaners. These two colonial powers had carved up the southern part of the continent, as they and other colonial powers did for all of Africa, without the consultation of any of the native peoples, a recipe for racial unrest. The Nationalist Party that assumed power in 1948 was racist and bigoted and instituted a variety of segregationist policies and statutory restrictions on civil liberties that remained in force until 1989, incurring the universal enmity of the global community. The government's policy was to establish groups of so-called homelands, regions set apart as little countries where inhabitants would have citizenship so that they could be eventually denied citizenship in South Africa.

White South African government officials claimed that Africans in South Africa were better off economically than citizens elsewhere in Africa, and the argument had some legitimacy. But it was an irrelevant comparison because the Africans in South Africa were worse off than the whites in South Africa, and this civil rights disenfranchisement was the direct result of white supremacy.

But a menacing air lurked just beneath the surface of the seemingly placid but controlled society. Enter Steven Biko.

A medical student at Natal University Steven Biko founded the South African Student Organization, a movement to establish a new style of self-reliance for blacks as they struggled for civil freedoms in an apartheid environment. It became known as the black consciousness movement. It broke away from interracial group identification and white liberal groups and individuals like the novelists Alan Paton and Nadine Gordimer. It was to inaugurate a new era in the liberation of all black Africans in South Africa from racial slavery.

White liberals born in South Africa were sympathetic to the African cause and in opposition to the apartheid government and its racist policies. Black political organizations like the African National Congress were banned. Biko's black consciousness movement was not in opposition to white liberal cooperation. Biko wanted to psychologically disassociate the political struggle from it in order to emphasize Black self-reliance. He believed that blacks would never find their self-assurance if they let whites lead the struggle for them, however much each group believed in the injustices perpetrated. Purposefully focusing on raising black consciousness and self-confident attitudes was the right thing to do, Biko believed, in a South African society that denigrated blacks as a part of public policy.

Biko became close friends with Donald Woods, the editor of the *Daily Dispatch* in East London, a newspaper committed to daily editorial condemnation of apartheid. Woods would write the story of his association with Biko and find himself banned for his outspoken opinions against apartheid policies. After Biko's death, Woods was confined to house arrest, unable to write, publish, or even speak about his views. The movie *Cry Freedom* was made from Woods's story of Biko.

In 1976 nine young blacks were placed on trial before the Supreme Court as a danger to public safety because the government believed that mobilizing public opinion against white rule would cause racial confrontation. Of course the black consciousness movement was precisely an organization that was opposed to white racist domination. The prosecution accused the defendants of violent antiwhite feelings in order to foment revolution. The defense argued that there was already widespread resentment among blacks and that they therefore had the right to seek a redress of their grievances.

Biko was summoned by the defense to give evidence of the righteousness of the cause on behalf of the defendants. I have read the transcript of this trial and Biko appears as not only an articulate spokesman for his movement but as an extremely capable oratorical foil for the desperate attempts by the South African government to curtail peaceful opposition to apartheid policies. His testimony is an eloquent witness for civil liberties and an example of modesty and grace under pressure and a brilliant intellect under courtroom questioning.

On August 18, 1977 Steve Biko and a friend Peter Jones were stopped at a roadblock in the Eastern Cape Province, then taken to Port Elizabeth for interrogation. Within three weeks Biko was dead, officially because of a hunger strike. In fact, as an inquest would later reveal, he died of wounds received while in detention. He was only thirty years old.

In the end the government was not blamed or rebuked for Biko's murder. Newspapers that dared print anything favorable to him or his cause were banned. The prime minister and chief of security were known to be culpable but were not accountable to anyone, and blacks in general were universally accused of stirring up revolutionary sentiments. It was not a becalmed atmosphere for civil dialogue. The apartheid government chugged along as if nothing unusual had happened.

Steve Biko was a man of extraordinary talents and courage who challenged an apartheid government with peaceful intentions as Gandhi had done in South Africa and India and Martin Luther King, Jr. in America. He encouraged his native South Africans to find a self-reliant voice of their own. Freedom would come for black South Africans more than a decade after his death when by then even white Afrikaners realized that their racist policies were detrimental to their lives in a majority black nation. The threat of all-out civil war prompted De Klerk and Nelson Mandela to conclude a treaty resulting in a peaceful transition of power. Steve Biko was a young hero and martyr for that ultimate cause.

Ayaan Hirsi Ali (1969–)

I do not believe in God, angels and the hereafter. [16]

Ayaan Hirsi Ali, former Dutch parliamentarian and Muslim, was born in Somalia in 1969, and faced political exile because of her father's agitation against communism in Somalia in the late 1960s. She was raised in Kenya and Saudi Arabia, immigrated to The Netherlands in 1992, and was elected to the Dutch Parliament in 2003. She rejected her Muslim belief after the bombings of the Twin Towers in New York City in 2001. The punishment for renouncing her faith in the Moslem world is death.

She fled an arranged marriage while in Europe in 1992 and made her way to Holland. Hirsi Ali is a heretic and infidel to Muslims, a feminine role model for women who seek political office, and an advocate for public service, the rights of women, democratic values, and a vociferous critic of Islam. [17] She speaks Somali, Arabic, Amharic (Ethiopia's main language), Swahili and English.

She worked initially as a cleaner and then a translator at a refugee center in Rotterdam. She became a political science student at the University of Leiden, graduated, and eventually accepted a position at a think tank. She became better known after 9/11 as the media clamored for interviews from immigrant analysts. Dutch political parties asked her to join their ranks and encouraged her to run for a seat in Parliament. Each time she spoke on TV or wrote opinion pieces in the newspapers about how Muslims had inhibited the prerogatives of women, Muslim officials threatened her and her employer.

In 2002 the populist politician Pim Fortuyn, who claimed that Islam was a "backward religion," was murdered. In 2004 the movie director Theo Van Gogh was shot and stabbed while biking on his morning commute to work. Van Gogh had made a film called *Submission*, shown on Dutch TV, critical of Muslim beliefs and revealed its violence against women. Ali had written the script. The killer, twenty-six year old Mohammed Bouyeri, born in Holland of Moroccan immigrants, had taped a five-page note on Theo's body addressed to her. He was charged with Theo's death, tried, and sentenced to life in prison. Thereafter, the Dutch government provided her with fulltime bodyguards.[18] Suddenly, political violence precipitated by Muslim extremists had penetrated Dutch society, one of the most openly democratic societies in the world. Multiracial and multireligious tolerance was shattered all over Europe. After mosque and church bombings in Holland, she was coaxed into agreeing to leave the country until it was safe to return.

There were approximately 16.5 million people in Holland in 2006 of which 1.7 million were non-Western immigrants or their children. Of this population group, about one million are Moslem and as a group they constitute a third of the population of Amsterdam, Rotterdam and The Hague.

The debate over individual rights, collective rights mingled uneasily in Dutch society until the beginning of the 21st century. Muslim extremists began to take advantage of Holland's tolerance for unorthodox individual beliefs and the beliefs of the Muslim religious minority that sought to undermine the national code of freedom of speech. The rights of women clashed with the lenient national policy and culture towards immigrants. The religious issues became social and legal. There were multiple social issues that applied only to Muslims:

- Some men were taking multiple wives.
- Many Muslim women underwent genital mutilation.
- Clinics specializing in repairing broken hymens were covered by National Health insurance.
- Employers would not hire women wearing head scarves.
- There were killings of honor for violating female virginity.

The Dutch were discovering that their cozy approach to consensus-building, and by forming alliances between disparate groups in Dutch society did not dovetail with Muslim beliefs.

Ali's fear, and that of other Dutch intellectuals, was that the country would be torn between two groups of the far right—the Islamic and non-Islamic extremists. Since 2004 the Dutch Parliament building became an armed fortress when it was formerly entered like an art museum. That same year she published *The Cage of Virgins*, a book that immediately received a torrent of abuse from Muslims, calling it "blasphemous and offensive." She gave up getting married and having children of her own, living then in locked rooms and traveling in bulletproof cars surrounded by bodyguards. Such a dissenter only promotes virtues of courage, intelligence, principled stands, and compassionate advocacy for the rights of women and children.

She commented on an offensive Danish cartoon row at a press conference in Berlin in 2006, speaking out to defend freedom of speech against Islamic intolerance. She stressed that Muslims in the West are individuals who are not under the collective hysteria and the compulsion of violence as Muslims are in the Middle East. European writers, filmmakers, illustrators, and journalists, she said, are afraid of describing, analyzing, or criticizing intolerant sides of Islam. Muslims in Denmark who felt their religion had been violated should have appealed to the courts. Instead, Danish imams, one of whom I interviewed in Copenhagen in the summer of 2006 who is now deceased, went to Lebanon and Egypt and appealed the case to other Moslem clerics and officials.

Regrettably, Ali had provided inaccurate information when she applied for political asylum in 1992 and the Dutch government notified her that her application was therefore invalid and asked for a response.[19] She had discussed the truth of her immigration status with Dutch officials prior to service in Parliament and in interviews. Her neighbors won a lawsuit saying her presence among them constituted a risk to them. She resigned from Parliament in May 2006 and came to the United States accepting a position at the American Enterprise Institute in Washington D.C. When the Dutch government refused to continue to pay for her bodyguards in the United States, she returned to Holland.

She spoke out against the integration of Muslims at all into Western secular society, particularly liberal European countries like Holland and Denmark. The United States made the mistake of supporting the Taliban against the old Soviet Union only to see the Taliban strike back at the United States and destroy its sense of equanimity and tolerance toward Islam. True Muslims think Jews rule the world, that democracy is sinful, and that God's laws are the only laws that need to be obeyed.[20] She emphasizes that only by having Muslims renounce their faith will democracies be safe from Islamic fundamentalist beliefs. It's hard to imagine how governments can begin to change people's religions, even if they believed that that remedy would solve the problem. In fact, democracies tolerate the view that religion is a private affair and not a state matter.

Radical Islam that seeks to kill infidels and blasphemers can find passages in the Koran that ease consciences and give its members divine validation, just as Maoism and Stalinism can be attributed to *Das Kapital*. But to explain the horrors of the Chinese famines and the atrocities of the Cultural Revolution and the Russian gulags by invoking the writings of Karl Marx is to miss the point. Messianic violence can attach itself to any creed or no creed. A disturbed radical who has a murderous cause can find a sacred text to justify his actions, as did

Yigal Amir, the Jewish radical who assassinated Yitzhak Rabin, Eric Rudolph, the Christian antiabortionist bomber or Mohammed Bouyeri, the Muslim extremist who killed Theo Van Gogh.

How to find an acceptable accommodation with moderate Muslims who do seek to integrate into Western societies is a central task of the twenty-first century.

CHAPTER TWO
TWENTIETH-CENTURY
DISSENTERS

Whatever the country, freedom of thought and expression are universal human rights. These freedoms, which modern people long for as much as bread and water, should never be limited by using nationalist sentiment, moral sensitivities, or—worst of all—business or military interests. [1]

Contemporary dissidents have dedicated their lives to alerting the world to the suppression of human rights for women or children, against torture, or for freedom of the judiciary, the press, speech, assembly, and religion. [2] Many are journalists, academics, novelists, or free-spirited individuals, outspoken critics whose valiant actions outshine their expertise or artistry. Sometimes they are in the wrong place at the wrong time or believe in the wrong religion. Fearless men and women have spontaneously emerged to refute regimes that restrict or prohibit human rights, using their voices and pens to proclaim what those with less courage are unable or unwilling to do.

The profiles of dissidents I have chosen for this chapter are representative of the geographic range of continents and countries that have denied human rights. Many individuals like the activist scholar Aung San Suu Kyi from Burma (Myanmar), or the deposed judge and lawyer Shirin Ebadi from Iran have been awarded the Nobel Peace Prize in partial recognition of their bravery and accomplishments. My aim in these short sketches is three-fold: to alert informed citizens everywhere to the ongoing abuse of human rights, to inform the consciousnesses of each individual to the potential for abuse in one's own country, and to aid hesitant individuals to foster their own courage in the face of repression.

The twentieth century was one of the bloodiest in human history. World War I, known as the Great War and the War to End All Wars, from 1914 to 1918, listed about 10 million military dead and another 10 million soldiers missing and presumed dead. World War II, from 1939 to 1945, resulted in over 60 million killed in Europe alone, and countless millions of others in Asia in the war with Japan. Among these dead are innumerable heroes and heroines we will never know, like those immolated by the Germans in World War II death camps.

But one heroine we do know was Helene Deschamps Adams who died in Manhattan in 2006. She was born in China in 1921 and her father was a general in the French colonial army serving in Africa. Helene hated the occupation by the Germans that began in 1940 in her native France. As a young woman, code name Anick, she fought for the French resistance movement. Her stunning good looks and causal manner captivated German troops who allowed her to approach on her bike and flirt with them so she could spy on them.

Her escapades are the stuff of spy novels. She was captured by an alternative resistance movement with fake German documents and nearly executed. A close friend was killed by a sniper in a car she was driving. She hid in a closet filled with apples while drunken German soldiers tormented her protectors. As the secretary for the French collaborator ministry, she stole papers of French citizens the Germans had ordered to be executed. She was partially deaf the rest of her life from a bomb blast that blew up in a building she had just vacated, knowing the bomb was in the building. She was recruited by the Office of Strategic Services, the predecessor of the CIA, and came to the United States in 1946 and married an army lieutenant.

She was not killed for her activities but came close enough to death many times and is therefore a symbol of heroism, someone who forsakes family, friends, and any kind of normal lifestyle to fight an enemy. Others during the Nazi occupation of Europe were not so lucky escaping detection and death.

Dietrich Bonhoeffer (1906–1945)

Dietrich Bonhoeffer's principled views, based on his strong Christian faith, made him one of the few German crusaders against the Nazi regime during Hitler's genocidal Third Reich.

Dietrich was born sixth in a family of eight children (he had a twin sister Sabrina) and the youngest boy. His father Karl was a famous neurologist and director of a clinic for mental disorders, a senior psychiatrist and a professor at the University of Berlin. His mother, Paula, was a prominent socialite. His family lived in the Grunwald district, an upscale, wealthy community in Berlin.

By 1924 Dietrich then only eighteen began his theological studies at the University of Berlin, and by the age of twenty-one earned his doctorate in theology with highest honors. His doctoral thesis had been built around the idea of a social community within a church context. But at the time there was widespread unemployment and hard economic times in Germany, conditions that appealed to emerging nationalists like ex-corporal Adolph Hitler.

Bonhoeffer sailed to America to become a fellow at Union Theological Seminary where Reinhold Niebuhr was a scholar and Bonhoeffer studied under him. He attended Abyssinian Baptist Church services in Harlem and came under the influence of revival music, song, and dance. Such powerful emotional responses captivated him and he included them in his later worship services. He also taught Sunday school in Harlem and met the Frenchman Jean Lessere, a pacifist who convinced him that it was necessary to live, not just preach about, the virtues of the Sermon on the Mount.

By 1931 Bonhoeffer was back in Germany, ordained as a Lutheran minister, and found the Christian churches obedient to political authority and not to the clergy's hierarchy. When Hitler became chancellor in 1933 the racist ideas of the Nazi party became public policy. When he was only twenty-six, Bonhoeffer criticized Hitler's policies in a national radio broadcast. His broadcast was quickly cut short and he never had an opportunity to speak publicly again.

Many clerics and church leaders wanted a strong leader to solidify the German people and restore national pride. But on April 1, 1933, the Nazis began a national boycott of Jewish businesses. Anti-Semitism had always been embedded but usually dormant in the German psyche. Bonhoeffer wrote *The Church and Jewish Questions* (1933) addressed to the Lutheran churches in Germany asking them to stand with the Jews in their persecution. This paper became a defining moment. Most churches refused to condemn the Nazis. Bonhoeffer, though still young, and unlike few others, saw through the false structure, the power symbols, the hoopla and pageantry of the Nazis to their underlying false ideology. Church members who mumbled dissent were arrested.

So Bonhoeffer quietly accepted a parish assignment in London to escape Nazi interference. A small London contingent of about a hundred church leaders formed a group called the Confessing Church that proposed a breakaway from Nazi propaganda. Then, in 1935, Bonhoeffer received an offer to return to Germany to direct a seminary for aspiring clerics of the Confessing Church at Finkenwalde in northern Germany. While in residence he wrote *The Cost of Discipleship* (1937), a book about his beliefs that focused on prayer, study, and mutual service to humanity, noting that sometimes it is necessary to die for one's faith, an irony that would become his fate. In September, 1937, the Gestapo closed the seminary. In 1938 the Nazis organized *Kristalnacht*, an outright attack on synagogues and Jewish houses of worship. By September 1939 Germany invaded Poland, and France surrendered to invading Germans in May 1940.

Bonhoeffer was soon involved in the resistance movement against the regime. Friends arranged for him to accept a teaching fellowship in America, again at Union Theological Seminary. As soon as he arrived in America he realized, like the phrase from Isaiah, "He who believes does not flee," that he had made a mistake and almost immediately caught the next boat back to the continent. He had papers allowing him to travel on behalf of the churches to other countries but in effect became a double agent for the resistance movement and a part of the conspiracy to assassinate Hitler. While traveling he recruited other clerics for the plot.

He was in Sweden in 1942 and attempted to use a helpful Swedish cleric who was also a member of Parliament to send a message to the British government to help in the conspiracy against the Hitler. The British, uncertain of the legitimacy of the message, and believing that this might be an attempt to undermine real conspiracy attempts, remained silent. Bonhoeffer was crestfallen. Between trips abroad, he stayed at Ettal, a Benedictine monastery outside Munich, where he worked on his book, *Ethics*, his defining work that was eventually published in 1949.

After the unsuccessful assassination that injured but did not kill Hitler in July 1944, all organizers of the plot were arrested including Bonhoeffer, his brother Klaus, and brother-in-law. On April 9, 1945, Bonhoeffer was led from the Flossenburg concentration camp to the gallows and hanged together with other conspirators, including Admiral Wilhelm Canaris, head of Military Intelligence, General Hans Oster (who recruited Bonhoeffer), and Hans von Dohnanyi, married to Bonhoeffer's sister, Christine. Hitler himself committed suicide on April 30, 1945. The war ended less than a month later.

Bonhoeffer is a symbol of those who daringly attempted to put an end to a dictatorship that drove Germany into a senseless war, and one who risked his life to pursue what he believed was a Christian duty. Is it Christian to try to kill so that others can live? The answer depends on belief, but does not detract from the courage of one who has made that choice.

Kaj Munk (1898–1944)

For a small country with a population of under 6 million, Denmark has a rich cultural and intellectual heritage for which Danes are exceedingly proud and of which Kaj Munk is a neglected contributor. The astronomical observations of Tycho Brahe (1546–1601) led to the improved planetary calculations and eventually to Kepler's and Newton's theories. The brilliant theoretical contributions of Niels Bohr (1885–1962) have been inestimable to atomic physics. The fairy tales of Hans Christian Andersen (1805–75) are still the stuff of children's literature. The essays of Søren Kierkegaard (1813–55) mark the beginning of existential philosophy. Carl Nielsen's (1865–1931) symphonies are world famous. In this mix of international celebrities are a few heroes and heroines during World War II. Kaj Munk was a Danish Lutheran cleric and playwright known for his literary talents and outspoken opposition against German oppression. His execution at the hands of the Nazi Gestapo during World War II made him a hero and elevated his national status. His original birth name was Petersen but he took the name of the family that raised him after the death of his parents. Munk was educated at the Cathedral School at Nykøbing Falster and at the University of Copenhagen, where he took a degree in theology in 1924 and was ordained a Lutheran minister. He married his housekeeper and they had four children and also adopted one child. Photographs in literary biographies show him in family portraits playing with his children, hunting with friends, walking in his garden, and working on his writings.

German Invasion of Denmark

The German invasion of Denmark changed Munk's life. Germans invaded on April 9, 1940, as a means of preparing for an invasion of Norway. The Danish government capitulated within a couple of hours not having the army, resources. or will to resist forcefully. Germans had no pressing strategic interest in the country except for its agricultural products and was initially pleased to allow the government to function and the king, Christian X, to remain as titular head of state. The German goal was to tout Denmark internationally as a model protectorate, an example of beneficent German rule, and to permit fellow Aryans to manage their affairs without coercion. In the beginning, Germans were successful in this strategy. Danes worked assiduously not to offer resistance and to cooperate together in a unified government despite party political differences, though many were repulsed by Nazi ideology. But by late 1942 Danes became more hostile. A Resistance movement was formed by nine men in the Oskar Davidsen restaurant and active resistance began. Thereafter, sabotages occurred frequently. A small plaque on the wall of the restaurant that marks the space where the first resistance meeting was held.

Underground Press and Writings

As the Germans imposed prohibitions on a free press, an underground press began soon after the occupation. These presses operated within normal businesses including a nail factory and dentist offices, and consisted of daily, weekly, and monthly broadsheets. *De Frie Danske,* for example, had a total circulation of 350,000 to 400,000. *Morgenbladet,* the newspaper daily with a circulation of 8,000–10,000, was mailed to subscribers with fictitious return addresses. It published an article on Munk in its January 5, 1945, edition. Examples of these printing presses and broadsheets are visible in the World War II Resistance Museum (Frihedsmuseet) in Copenhagen. Niels Ebbesen was a national hero in Denmark who died in 1340. Following his standard of using strong men as the protagonists in his plays, Munk wrote *Niels Ebbesen* during the Nazi occupation to show how strong individuals could stand up to oppression. A copy of this play, published in 1942, is in the Resistance museum. Munk was considered a valiant patriot at the time of his execution. But after the war in 1945 critics deliberately altered his writings. Politicians and government officials regarded him as highlighting their collaboration with the Germans. They wanted to appear to have been on the side of the resistance movement, when in fact they had not been. Munk was made the victim of a smear campaign beginning in the late 1940s, to weaken his character. His speeches and poems were distorted to portray him as a Nazi sympathizer. The 2003 biography of Munk by Per Stig Moller, a philosopher and historian from the University of

Copenhagen who served as Denmark's foreign minister, investigated the primary sources and found the distortions that had been republished as late as 1984. Munk wrote thirteen historical plays many of which were performed at the Royal Theatre in Copenhagen. His play *The Word* (1925) was made into a film in 1954. His dramas portray strong characters, like King David, Herod, Napoleon, and Cromwell, willing to stand up and fight for their ideals and principles, a characteristic of his own personality and strong Christian beliefs. The focus on strong leaders and individuals in his plays initially led Munk to feel admiration toward Hitler, perhaps because he was politically naive. But his sympathy soon turned to antagonism in 1936 and the rest of his life he fought against Mussolini's and Hitler's fascism and especially against the German occupation of Denmark until his death in 1944. On January 4, 1944, Munk was taken from his home by the Gestapo and shot in the head on the road to Silkeborg a few kilometres west of Aarhus in Jutland. Over 4,000 Danes attended his funeral as a sign of solidarity.

World War II German Army Deserters

But heroes and heroines did not just come from Danes or Europeans under Nazi occupation. Many conscientious Germans, some in military uniform, became active resisters and deserted because of the regime's malfeasance. The oath quoted below had to be sworn by all soldiers and Germans in the war effort. Those who refused bore the full brunt of Gestapo violence. No one was allowed to hide behind a conscientious objection.

> I swear to the Lord this holy oath, that I will show unconditional obedience to Adolf Hitler Fuhrer of the German Reich and people and commander in chief of the armed forces. I swear that I, as a brave soldier, at any time am ready to sacrifice my life for this oath. [3]

Deserting from an army is a serious crime, but most countries also have an escape clause for conscientious objectors. The German army during World War II had no such legal outlet. The triumphant Allied forces accepted the legality of the brazenly corrupt Nazi war tribunals and let judges be excused from subsequent prosecution for their disregard of legal standards. It was only after the war that the Geneva Conventions were approved as criteria for actions in international conflicts. Article 3, for example, prohibits "outrages upon personal dignity, in particular, humiliating and degrading treatment." The conventions have been followed for more than a half-century by almost 190 countries, including the United States. *The War Crimes Act of 1996* passed by the U.S. Congress makes it a felony to violate the Geneva Conventions.

By contrast, German army deserters who found themselves in East Germany after the war and under Soviet control were treated as heroes.

Over 30,000 conscientious deserters, regarded as traitors in their homeland, escaped from Nazi brutality during World War II, and over 20,000 paid with their lives before firing squads, by beheadings and hangings. In Germany long after the conclusion of the war in 1945, these deserters were vilified and their reputations smeared by charges of treachery. The stories of so many of these German soldiers who refused to fight for the Third Reich during the Hitler regime, men like Ludwig Baumann, Kurt Oldenburg, Peter Schilling, Helmut Kober, and Anton Reschny, have been imperfectly known and seldom acknowledged.

Shortly after he came to power, Hitler instituted a war tribunal system that elevated unemployed lawyers to the status of judges. The legislation for this legal system was passed on May 12, 1933. War trials do not accord the same principles embodied in commonly accepted procedures of justice, such as presumption of innocence, legal representation, due process hearings, or rights of appeal. The Nazi regime's legal system became subordinate to the military. Here are a few of the courageous individuals who for personal and religious reasons, refused to serve in the army or swear allegiance to an unworthy tyrannical leader.

Hermann Stohr, born in 1898, served in World War I as a volunteer. But in 1939 he refused the call to enter the German army. When he also refused to swear an oath to Hitler, he was sentenced to death and beheaded in 1940.

Max Josef Metzger, born in 1887, was ordained a Catholic priest in 1911 and served as army chaplain in World War I. Because he issued a peace proclamation he was sentenced to death in 1943 and beheaded in 1944.

Martin Gauger, born in 1905, was an assessor for prosecutors. He also refused to swear an oath to Hitler and was dismissed. In 1940 he refused to serve in the armed forces and was executed by gas.

Franz Jagerstatter, born in 1907, was the only person in his farming village to vote "no" to the German occupation. He did become a soldier in the German army and came home in 1941. He was redrafted but this time refused. He was arrested and declared that his Catholic beliefs did not allow him to enter the army. He was sentenced to death by a war court and beheaded in 1943.

Josef Ruf, born in 1905, entered a Franciscan monastery as a youth. Because of his Christian beliefs, he also refused to swear an oath to Hitler and was beheaded in 1940.

Gustav Stange was drafted in 1942. He refused the oath to Hitler because he was a member of Jehovah's Witnesses. He was sentenced to death in 1942 and executed the same day.

Ludwig Baumann was born in Hamburg December 13, 1921, the son of a tobacco wholesaler. His mother died tragically in a traffic accident when he was fifteen. By 1938 German law under the Nazis required all youth under 16 years of age to join the Hitler youth movement. Even the future pope Benedict XV, the young Joseph Ratzinger, was compelled to become a member. Then, at age nineteen, Ludwig was forced to join the navy in 1940. He and his friend Kurt Oldenburg deserted from a navy base in the French city of Bordeaux on June 3, 1942. He saw the German war effort as genocide and, although young, he knew that he didn't want to kill people who had no quarrel with him. He was arrested two days later in an unoccupied section of France. On June 30 he and Oldenburg were sentenced to death after a court hearing of forty minutes. While in prison he was tortured but never revealed the names of his French collaborators.

Ludwig's father had heard of his son's death sentence and appealed for clemency to an officer friend who happened to be a friend of Admiral Reder who had already pardoned Baumann and Oldenburg on April 29, 1943. Ludwig's sentence was commuted to twelve years in prison to be served at the end of the war. Until then, he was detained in the concentration camp of Esterwegen but not told of the commutation of his sentence for eight months and feared execution daily. He was later transferred to Fort Zinna in Torgau where he witnessed the executions of other deserters.

As soon as he was well enough recovering from diphtheria, which had rendered him incapable of walking, Ludwig was sent to the eastern front. He was wounded but survived and was treated in a hospital in Brno, the Czech Republic, where he remained, fortunately for him, until the end of the war. Ludwig was awarded the Sieverhauser Peace Prize in 1984 and the Aachener Peace Prize in 1995.

So was the crime of desertion during war a cry for peace and reason and against senseless war, or a crime against the state? Whatever the conclusion, there is no denying the courage of German army deserters in the face of certain death for resisting what they believed was state tyranny and the genocide of millions for a false ideology of Aryan racial supremacy.

Edith Stein (1891–1942)

Edith Stein (1891–1942) was at various times in her life a practicing Jew, an atheist, a Catholic, a nun, and a wide-ranging philosophical scholar, who met her death as a victim of Nazi oppression and Jewish genocide. After her death she became a symbol of Catholic solidarity with murdered Jews.

Born in 1891, she was the youngest of eleven children of an Orthodox Jewish family in Breslau, today's Wroclaw, Poland. As a child she was precocious and temperamental with erratic childhood behaviors according to those who knew her. But she flourished in school with a fierce determination to succeed and was always the head of her class. According to her own account she was an atheist from the age of thirteen until she received her doctorate at the age of twenty-two. [4]

She entered the university of Breslau in 1911 and became a student of psychology, a discipline then in its infancy in theory and experimentation, and quickly became disillusioned with its content and methods. But she read the phenomenologist Edmund Husserl's *Logical Investigations* (1901) that marked a theoretical break with Neo-Kantian idealism and got her intellectually hooked. She would remain a confirmed follower of phenomenology the rest of her life. Husserl, who trained through his doctorate as a mathematician but dedicated his life to philosophy, was also born into a Jewish family but converted to Christianity in 1887 and became a Lutheran.

I note a little about Husserl's philosophy here because it became the basis for Edith Stein's spiritual quest and conversion. She used the ideas of phenomenology and combined them with Christian ideas of spirituality and faith to find her religious vocation as a nun.

The Philosophy of Phenomenology

Phenomenology was Husserl's philosophical interpretation that offered a variation on the ancient philosophical subdivision of ontology, the study of being and how we are conscious of our existence and other existences. Husserl proposed that phenomena, the perception of reality, was the proper course for philosophical inquiry into being, and a new way of looking at essences, or what existences represented. essences and existence, act and potency, substance and accidents, were Aristotelian philosophical classifications for investigating reality. But first, Husserl said, we have to distinguish our consciousness itself from objects it experiences and "bracket" those, a procedure he called *epoche*, a Greek term in which one suspends belief in knowledge of the existence of the real world. His work concentrates of consciousness and how we perceive reality as phenomena. Stein turned these philosophical ideas in later life into foundational spiritual understandings of how humans relate to God and each other.

In 1913 Edith journeyed to Gottingen to study phenomenology with Husserl. She remained there as a student for the next three years, completing her doctoral dissertation, *The Problem of Empathy* (1916). World War I exploded in 1914. She abhorred the war and volunteered at a Red Cross military hospital and witnessed the suffering and despair of wounded soldiers firsthand. These experiences formed the basis for her work on empathy and probably helped in her religious conversion. She was awarded the medal of valor for this work.

Her major work, *Finite and Eternal Being*, which uses perception as the foundation for philosophy, elaborates on this thesis of empathy toward others and God. When Husserl was offered a professorship at the University of Freiburg, he offered Edith the chance to join him as a graduate assistant. She enthusiastically joined him and began editing his papers. This proved to be a tedious chore as Husserl was philosophically incoherent and disorganized in his ideas and writing habits. But this period in Stein's life was transitional, less focused on philosophy and more on the role of religious experiences, even though she had abandoned her Jewish faith, but not attendance at the synagogue when at home with her mother and family.

Conversion

She met Max Scheler, a Jewish convert from Munich, who proposed "prophetic philosophy," a combination study of philosophical investigation with transcendental experiences. Scheler taught that it is religion that ultimately makes us human. She also began to read the New Testament to find out more about Christianity. But in 1921 she read with excitement in an all-night reading session the autobiography of Theresa of Avila, the seventieth century mystical nun, and she was transformed. This one book would lead to her conversion to Catholicism and baptism into the Catholic Church January 1, 1922.

She left Freiburg to take a lay position teaching German in a teacher training college in Speyer operated by Dominican nuns. This teaching post allowed her time to write several articles, including a translation of the doctrine of truth by Thomas Aquinas. In 1927 she undertook a series of lectures to women's organizations like those for teachers, college graduates, and professional women, and she was widely and enthusiastically received. She became the brain trust and spokesperson for Catholic women's movements during the 1920s with her effective oratory.

Finally, after trying for years to enter academia but was politely but consistently rebuffed because she was Jewish and a woman, she was offered a collegiate position in 1932 at the Educational Institute in Munster. The following year, 1933, the party of National Socialism under Adolph Hitler came to power and the lives of Edith Stein and about 60 million others would be changed forever. The Nazis slowly but inexorably began the extermination of Jews in Germany and all the occupied countries of Europe.

In 1933 she entered the Carmelite convent in Cologne, the religious order Theresa of Avila founded. Perhaps she found in the life of a contemplative an element of what she found in philosophy: knowledge of the inner life tinged with the mystical. She identified with Theresa of Avila, and later the mystic John of the Cross, more profoundly than she had with Husserl or any other philosopher or writer she had encountered. She was thoroughly knowledgeable with Thomas Aquinas and Immanuel Kant, and knew Martin Heidegger personally, who had moved from Catholicism to a rejection of all theologies. Stein had read and was dissatisfied with Soren Kierkegaard's description of his personal Christianity of suffering. Her renouncing of the world and assuming the cloth of the convent was a personal transformation that leapt beyond the corridors of academia. Faith for her was a kind of knowledge. In making such active choices in her personal life she exemplified and anticipated twentieth century existentialism.

On the night of November 8, 1938, German SS troops and other state thugs burned synagogues and drove Jews from their homes and businesses in a tragic event since known as *kristallnacht*, the night of broken glass. Edith was psychologically crushed but knew that there was no reasoning with this Nazi mentality or its anti-Semitism. The night of December 31, 1938 she fled to a Carmelite convent in Holland where she assumed she would be safe. When the Germans occupied Holland she applied for a Swiss visa that was slow or delayed in coming. She was arrested in her convent on August 2, 1942, as were all who had Catholic/Jewish affiliations, transported back to Germany, and executed August 9, 1942.

She enjoyed a vigorous intellect and a strong emotional vitality. Her whole life was a search for truth, knowledge and spiritual enlightenment. She had a strong interest in research that she thought could establish a philosophical basis for the social sciences. Though she was herself brilliant, her work is sketchy and undervalued because it is so remote. Entering the scholarly world of being, essences, and perceptions, combined with orthodox religious ideas of transcendence, beatific visions and prayer, renders any inquiry suspect and its conclusions extremely cautious. She was beatified by Pope John Paul II on May 1, 1987.

Aung San Suu Kyi (1945–)

Burma, also known as Myanmar, has been under military rule for most of its history since independence from Britain in 1948. It has been in a civil war since 1948, and has one of the world's most durable military dictatorships with one of the world's largest armies. Its constitution has been suspended since 1988. It has no internationally recognized legal system of justice as the courts are under the control of the military dictatorship. The last legislative elections were held in 1990 but the election results never revealed. Burma is a country rich in resources and ethnic diversity but poor in liberties, with an ineffective economy and an inadequate infrastructure. It is the second-largest producer of illicit drugs. Largely because of the confinement of Aung San Suu Kyi, the United States imposed economic sanctions still in effect as of this writing. Aung San Suu Kyi is a dissident spokeswoman whose detention in Rangoon, Myanmar, and whose Nobel Peace Prize award in 1991, catapulted her into the international limelight as a standard bearer for courage in the teeth of military authoritarianism.

She was born June 19, 1945 the daughter of a Burmese general assassinated in 1947, the year before Burmese independence from the British. In 1960 her mother was appointed Burma's ambassador to India. She attended St. Hugh's

College at Oxford and received a BA in 1967. She journeyed to New York for graduate study but postponed her study to work at the United Nations when U Thant from Burma was secretary general. While at Oxford she met Michael Aris, a student of Tibetan civilization whom she married in 1972. They relocated to Bhutan for two years where Michael tutored the royal family and headed the Translation Department while she worked in the Ministry of Foreign Affairs.

Michael and Aung returned to Oxford where he assumed an appointment in Tibetan and Himalayan studies. By this time the couple had two sons, Alexander and Kim. From 1985–86 she was a Visiting Scholar at Kyoto University as a researcher, and Michael was at Simla University in India. Each had one of their sons living with them.

She returned to Burma in 1988 when her mother suffered a stroke, just in time to witness the resignation of General Ne Win, the military dictator who had ruled since 1962. Massive protests followed his death and the military killed thousands of demonstrators. In these turbulent first days of the revolution, She wrote to the forming government trying to compromise and seeking the formation of a legitimate legislature. She spoke in public to thousands for the holding of parliamentary elections. Suddenly the repressive government banned political assemblies of more than four people, and individuals were arrested and sentenced without trial. She was prohibited for standing for election, and in 1989 was placed under house arrest.

She began a hunger strike and her husband Michael came to Rangoon and asked to be incarcerated with her. As international attention was drawn to this drama, officials granted her more freedom and improved detention conditions. The government announced that she could leave the country, but she refused knowing she would never be allowed to return. Michael did leave the country to return to England and his work and to care for their two sons.

Her book, *Freedom from Fear and Other Writings* (1995), was reissued and widely read throughout the world. Her children accepted the Nobel Peace prize on her behalf in Oslo in 1991. Representatives from all countries in the English–speaking world called for her release. She continued to call her home country Burma. In 1995 she was released from house arrest, but her movements were greatly restricted and then she was detained again. She was forbidden to speak to large gatherings though her popularity among her people remained high.

In 1999 her husband Michael Aris died in London of prostate cancer, not having seen her since 1995.[5] Her motorcade was attacked in 2003 in an assassination attempt. The Myanmar government extended her house arrest in May 2006, after she had been detained more than a decade already despite intense international pressure seeking her release.

Authors and Outsiders

The eighteenth century produced a notorious case of the suppression of freedom of the press, a cornerstone example that led to press for individual rights and freedoms in the First Amendment to the U.S. Constitution.

John Peter Zenger (1697–1746) was an American journalist trained as a printer who had emigrated from Germany as a boy of thirteen in 1710. He published The *New York Weekly Journal* in New York, a paper backed by several prominent professionals and merchants, to oppose the policies of arbitrary rule by the odious British governor William Cosby. His first edition (Monday, November 5, 1733) was on the freedom of the press. Zenger was arrested on charges of libel and false and seditious writing and imprisoned for failure to reveal the names of the authors who had been published anonymously. He languished for nine months in jail, then on the top floor of the Federal Hall still standing today at Wall and Nassau streets in New York. He was defended by a young lawyer, Alexander Hamilton, who conceivably wrote one or more of the articles offensive to Cosby's administration. Hamilton brilliantly argued that in Zenger's defense that his case went beyond the innocence or guilt of Zenger but to the cause of freedom. Hamilton admitted to Zenger's printing the statements but said that they were not false statements but true, and that therefore a man could not be charged for telling the truth or for exposing tyrannical government. The jury deliberated only ten minutes and returned a verdict of not guilty. The rights of self-government, of juries to reach judgments without interference, of subjects to be free of foreign rule, and of freedom of the press were established in America with the trial of John Zenger.

Freedom of the press, however, has not yet been enshrined in much of the world. Beginning in 2000 Iran systematically began a campaign to silence dissident writers, and this included the closure of newspapers and websites. From this purging, dissident intellectuals and writers are now dead from this purging, in prison, in voluntary exile, or have ceased being critical of government actions.

Akbar Ganji is a modern man of principle, obdurate and courageous, willing to lay down his life for his principles, who has consistently criticized the Islamic Republic of Iran and spent the last few years in Tehran's Evin prison, confined since April 2000 for his criticism of the government. He was charged with "spreading propaganda against the Islamic regime." While in prison, he was beaten, sent to solitary confinement, and refused medical attention. He is rumored to have been denied regular meals and required medicines. He suffered from acute asthma and other respiratory disorders. Ganji's wife was ordered by the Tehran court not to give interviews nor to report on her husband's condition.

His cause has been taken up by Amnesty International, Human Rights Watch, Reporters Without Borders, International PEN, and International Freedom of Expression Exchange, among numerous other independent international organizations. Even Iranian newspapers are afraid to report details of his incarceration.

Akbar Ganji was imprisoned for exercising his right to freedom of expression as guaranteed by Article 19 of the International Covenant on Civil and Political Rights, to which Iran is a signatory. Little information is available for a man who symbolizes the loss of freedom of the press and his personal freedom. But knowing that such freedoms are perilous and still occurring in the modern world makes the struggle for freedom all the more intense and compelling.

In Turkey similar persecutions were happening against those who wrote or spoke out against historical crimes or present usurpations. **Elif Shafak**, a Turkish citizen born in France and a professor of Near Eastern Studies at the University of Arizona, was put on trial for publishing a novel that ultranationalists found offensive. Ultranationalists were a numerically weak but politically powerful group that sought to derail Turkey's attempt to enter the European Union and to retain the country's oriental and Muslim character by stifling free speech. Article 301 of the Turkish penal code prohibits, among other things, anything that insults "Turkishness," an ambiguous legal term if there ever was one, and a definition that might even have legal scholars scratching their heads. Conviction brings three years in jail. Elif Shafak was brought to trial under the legal article for remarks in her novel *The Bastard of Istanbul* (2005). She successfully argued in her first trial that the comments were made by fictional characters who could not be prosecuted. A judge agreed and dismissed charges. But a second attempt at prosecution found her on trial again in late 2006.[6] She was again acquitted.

These disturbing trends of limiting free speech and freedom of the press, the bedrock of Western values, do not occur only in the Middle East or Muslim world. Europe is currently the chosen venue for the struggle between expression of free speech and no criticism of the Muslim religion. **Robert Redecker**, fifty-two, the author of several books on philosophy and teacher of high school philosophy in a school near Toulouse in southern France, wrote a scathing article in the paper *Le Figaro* in September 2006 denouncing Muhammad and calling the Koran a book of violence. Immediately thereafter, he began to receive death threats on online websites and via telephone and emails. The French Interior Ministry described the threats as dangerous and assigned the police to place him under surveillance. He and his wife and children are in hiding as of this writing. The irony is that the West is under the ideological surveillance of Islam.

> If the 21st century wishes to free itself from the cycle of violence, acts of terror and war, and avoid repetition of the experience of the 20th century—that most disaster-ridden century of humankind, there is no other way except by understanding and putting into practice every human right for all mankind, irrespective of race, gender, faith, nationality or social status.
>   —Shirin Ebadi, from the Nobel Address

Shirin Ebadi (1947–) is an Iranian human rights activist, a former dismissed judge in Iran in 1979. She won the Nobel Peace Prize in 2003, the first Muslim woman to win this distinguished award. She lives in Tehran and defends freedom of the press, gender equality, and dissidents against the government, taking on politically sensitive legal cases. [7]

She attended the Faculty of Law at the University of Tehran in 1965 and, after obtaining her law degree and an apprenticeship, she was appointed a judge in 1969, the first woman in the history of Iran to serve in such an esteemed position. She was awarded a doctorate in law from the University of Tehran in 1971.

Following the Revolution of 1979 she was summarily dismissed by the Islamic government and given clerical jobs. She requested, and was granted, early retirement. But because of the Muslim intolerance for lawyers who might bring suits against the regime, the Bar Association was closed and she was unable to obtain a law license to practice until 1992. In the interim she wrote several books including *Criminal Laws* (1972), *The Rights of the Child* 1987), *The Rights of Women* (2002) and similar books on rights and Iranian laws.

She still takes on challenging legal cases, such as that of a student killed for protesting repressive practices by the judiciary and intelligence forces. This case exposed the role of vigilante groups associated with highly placed government officials in the intelligence ministry, the chief of which later resigned. For exposing them, she was detained and arrested in 2000 and subsequently released but banned from practicing law in her own country. She is the president and co-Founder of the Human Rights Defense Council, and the Association for Support of Children's Rights. She has been awarded ten honorary doctorates from universities in North America, Europe, and Australia. [8]

In July 2003, an Iranian-Canadian photo-journalist, **Zahra Kazemi**, was arrested outside Evin prison for taking unlawful photos, imprisoned, tortured, denied medical attention, and died in prison. The Canadian government was prohibited from having representatives attend the trial of the security agent, Mohammad Reza Aghdam Ahmadi, accused of her death, and within days the court barred all foreign observers. Canada recalled its ambassador from Tehran. Two Iranian newspapers were closed and the court prosecutor warned Iranian journalists to censor their own stories.

Ebadi was barred from representing the family of Zahra Kazemi at the trial of the security agent charged with her death. This case created international attention. Ahmadi, the accused agent, was acquitted, but the case was reopened in 2005 when the court determined that other factors might have been involved in Kazemi's death. Ebadi regularly receives threatening letters and emails. [9]

Dr. Wafa Sultan (1958–), forty-seven, a Syrian-born Muslim mother of three, was largely unknown as a psychiatrist living near Los Angeles until February 21, 2006, when she gave an interview on Al Jazeera TV based in the Persian Gulf emirate of Qatar and became an overnight sensation in the Muslim world for her outspoken beliefs against Islam. Here is what she said in that interview as noted by the Middle East Media Research Institute:

> The clash we are witnessing around the world is not a clash of religions, or a clash of civilizations. It is a clash between two opposites, between two eras. It is a clash between a mentality that belongs to the Middle Ages and another mentality that belongs to the 21st century. It is a clash between civilization and backwardness, between the civilized and the primitive, between barbarity and rationality. It is a clash between freedom and oppression, between democracy and dictatorship. It is a clash between human rights, on the one hand, and the violation of these rights, on other hand. It is a clash between those who treat women like beasts, and those who treat them like human beings. [10]

During the televised interview she criticized Muslim clerics, so-called warriors and leaders whom she believed distorted the teaching of Islam and the prophet. She questioned why young men in the prime of their lives were killing themselves by suicide to settle a misguided religious score.

Afterwards, Muslim clerics universally condemned her, clerics in Syria denounced her as an infidel, and she received numerous death threats, though a few moderate reformers praised her for speaking out. Even the American Jewish Congress invited her to speak in Israel.

Her own life changed dramatically in 1979 as a medical student at the University of Aleppo in northern Syria when a radical Muslim group was attempting to undermine the government of Hafez al-Assad. Militants burst into the classroom and gunned down her professor, chanting "God is Great," shooting hundreds of bullets into him as she and the class watched horrified. From that moment on she began to question all her beliefs and every single teaching in the Koran. She now proclaims herself "a secular human being" and no longer practices the faith of Islam. [11]

Abdul Rahman, forty-one, attempted to gain custody of his two daughters in Kabul, Afghanistan, in 2006, an action his family opposed. The family told authorities he had converted to Christianity sixteen years previously. At the time of his conversion he had worked for a Christian aid group in Pakistan helping refugees. He was jailed in March 2006, but not formally charged for rejecting Islam, and could have been sentenced to death under Shariah law on which Afghanistan's constitution is based. One part of the constitution upholds the rule of Shariah, the Islamic religious law, while another grants religious freedom to its citizens. But the Afghan constitution did not adequately protect religious freedoms, according to the U.S. Commission on International Religious Freedom, a bipartisan government groups that works closely with the U.S. Department of State. In his own defense Rahman declared: "I am not an infidel. I am a Christian. I believe in Jesus." Islam reveres Jesus as a prophet. [12]

The Afghan government tried to find an acceptable medium to calm the international outcry and at the same time mollify its constitutional constituents even while Islamic clerics called for his death during Friday prayers. The judge said he would not be swayed and would resist any interference. The Council on American-Islamic Relations, a group based in Washington D.C., called for his release. President George W. Bush and Secretary of State Condoleezza Rice both phoned Afghanistan's President Hamid Karzai to intercede. Karzai said he would not intervene in order to protect the separation of executive and judicial powers. Pope Benedict XVI sent a letter to President Karzai requesting pardon for Abdul Rahman.

The prosecutor noted that Rahman was "a microbe who should be killed." Calmer heads suggested that he be released for mental incompetence. But of that tactic, Abdul Raoulf, a cleric at Herati mosque in Kabul, in an interview to the Associated Press, said of Rahman: "He is not mad. The government is playing games. The people will not be fooled. This is humiliating for Islam. Cut off his head."

Within weeks of his confinement, charges against Abdul Rahman were unexpectedly dropped for lack of evidence. The attorney general of Afghanistan notified the Justice Ministry to release him. Apparently, one month had elapsed, the time limit for retaining a person without charging him. On that technicality Abdul Rahman was a free man. He was granted asylum by Italy and Italian secret service agents whisked him to Rome almost immediately. Remaining in Afghanistan were the built-in tensions that were always there: The struggle between Islamic politics and Western, secular values like freedom of religion.

This brief sampler of heroes and heroines from twentieth century society is illustrative of the fight individuals must endure to proclaim their independence and support humanity's causes. As we shall see, free speech battles throughout history have been between individuals struggling against authoritarianism in its many guises, masquerading as the imposition of religious dogma and clerical domination or as just dictatorship. The courage of just these few biographical choices emboldens all of us in the vigilance and fight to maintain the rights, privileges, and freedoms of all the world's people.

CHAPTER THREE
AMERICAN OUTSIDERS

The reason for our journey is our religion. You see, we are not the Pope's people nor the King's really, but God's people. We are Saints of the Holy Discipline . . . and if we go to this New World, free from old King James and all the fancy church rituals that are not to our way, we can worship as we want. You see, we believe that the church is in our heart and not in a building. So 'tis our hearts that lead us.

From the diary of Remember Patience Whipple, 1620

Western history is filled with the animosities between religious factions, mostly feuds between Catholics and Protestants but also Sunni and Shiite Muslims, sprinkled with anti-Semitism, and laden with prejudice, discrimination, hatred, arsons, and bombings of churches, synagogues, and mosques, and selective assassinations. Religious intolerance is rarer in Asia where, for example, a Japanese can be married in a Shinto wedding, live life as a Christian, and be buried in a Buddhist ceremony. The traditional culture of Japan recognizes both its animistic Shinto past and adopted Buddhism. On the other hand, sectarian strife between Muslims and Hindus in India shows the depth of Asian religious divisiveness.

Constitutional creators in America in the 1770s knew the ferocity and madness of the religious wars in Europe after the Protestant Reformation and the rebellions of kings like Henry VIII against the papacy, and the subsequent bloodletting brought on by nationally preferred religions and denominational practices. In North America, Congregationalists had established a theocracy in Massachusetts. The Dutch had introduced a moderate form of Protestantism in New Amsterdam. Catholics had settled Maryland, and Anglicans controlled Virginia with laws against Methodists. A national identity would require the kind of tolerance Rhode Island had purposefully established under Roger Williams. The wisest course dictated a clear distinction between secular politics and personal religious liberties. It would not be easy to convince each generation that, righteous as God's laws were in prescribing behavior, that the laws of the people would have to maintain the delicate balance between order in civil society and contenting religious beliefs. Government neutrality seemed the best vehicle. The First Amendment in clear and precise language spelled out the prevailing precedent and at once became the most admired code in history and the most litigated.

Roger Williams (c. 1603–1683)

John Clarke, a leader of the Baptist church in Newport, Rhode Island, received a request in 1651 from a blind Baptist in Lynn, Massachusetts to hold a worship service in his home because he was unable to travel. A 1644 law prohibited Baptist churches from even existing within the borders of the Bay Colony. Notwithstanding that prohibition, John and three other Baptist members journeyed to Lynn and held ceremonies in the home of the man who had invited them. On July 20, 1651, as Clarke was preaching, two constables interrupted the services and arrested three "strangers." After spending more than a week in jail, they were eventually summoned before the court, tried, and sentenced. There were no accusers, witnesses, and no jury. Clarke was not allowed to be heard by the court that fined the men.

The following month, friends raised funds to pay the imposed fines of two of the men, but Obadiah Holmes refused to pay his fine and would not allow others to raise the money for him. On September 5 in Boston he was tied to a post in the marketplace, stripped, and received thirty lashes with a three-pronged whip.[1]

At the time no one was more outraged than Roger Williams residing in Providence Plantations. This was just the kind of religious injustice and lack of respect for the freedom of conscience he had fought against all his life.

> Being by God's ordinance, according to our just title, Defender of the Faith and Supreme Governor of the Church . . . We have . . . thought fit to make this declaration following . . . that if any public reader in either of our universities . . . or any person respectively . . . shall affix any new sense to any Article . . . other than is already established in Convocation with our royal assent; he, or they the offenders . . . we shall see that there shall be due execution upon them.
> English Royal Proclamation, November 1628

Roger Williams was a dissenter from the original Dissenters, a broadminded visionary who trumped his Puritan colleagues and fellow ministers by escaping the intolerant Massachusetts encampment and founded a religiously tolerant state. Even today signs of his religious tolerance are visible in the town center of Bristol, Rhode Island (see table following). The proximity and diversity of so many active houses of worship today in Bristol, Rhode Island, is a testimonial to Williams's prescient sense of religious tolerance and the endurance of his foresight. By contrast, the Mormon Temple in the heart of Salt Lake City, established by Mormons who were themselves fleeing persecution in Missouri in the nineteenth century, is only a few blocks from a Catholic cathedral.

But no other house of worship exists for several miles within the city and fewer still in neighboring towns.

Much of America consists of such cities dominated by a single religious and sometimes ethnic presence. Cities like Bristol, Rhode Island, mark a departure from the traditional homogeneous American settlement where a variety of religious and ethnic persuasions came to mingle with people of other faiths in colonial times prior to the First Amendment to create what America symbolizes today.

Moreover, Williams befriended Narragansett Indians and had a profound respect for their laws and customs. He also founded the city of Providence, an urban sanctuary for seekers of religious tolerance, or what he would call in a declaration of the founding of the city of "Liberty of Conscience." He believed that the Indians were the rightful owners of the land and that a king's title to settlers was illegitimate. The Puritans were therefore trespassers.

THE DIVERSITY OF CHURCHES WITHIN SIX BLOCKS IN DOWNTOWN BRISTOL, RHODE ISLAND

Cheora Agundas Achin, United Brothers Synagogue
First Baptist Church (1814)
Our Lady of Mount Carmel Convent
St. Mary's Catholic Church
St. Michael's Church in Bristol (1718)
First Congregational Church (1680)
St. Elizabeth Portuguese Catholic

No one is sure exactly when Roger Williams was born, where he died, where he is buried, or even what he looked like. He did have more enemies than friends because of his principled theological and legal positions. The statute of him in the plaza of Roger Williams University in Bristol, Rhode Island has the likeness of Ted Williams, formerly of the Boston Red Sox, famous as the best hitter in baseball history.

Williams was born about 1603 around the time of the death of Elizabeth I, who in her forty-five-year reign had sought a delicate balance in civil and religious affairs. James I of Scotland ascended the throne the same year, a year that ended the rule of the Tudors and inaugurated the Stuarts.[2] Williams entered Pembroke College at Cambridge studying to become a minister in the new Protestantism of England, the Anglican Church. Some attempted to persuade him to join in an even more reform-minded group that sought to eradicate all ritualistic signs of the Roman Catholic Church, to have books of prayer in English, to abolish bishops, and allow ministers to marry. However, the regal and civil authorities in England, not wishing to entertain any new religious experiments, strictly ruled against any further reform. The consequences were imprisonment and in some cases execution for straying from the new Anglican version of Christianity. Labeled Dissenters, these puritan reformers left England by the thousands to seek a new life elsewhere and most settled in liberal Holland, and a few migrated to America.

Williams graduated from Cambridge in 1629, became an ordained minister, married Mary Barnard, the daughter of a clergyman, and fled England to join the dissident reformists settled in Massachusetts. He was immediately offered a ministry at a congregation in Boston but declined because he felt that the church had not yet completely divorced itself from the Church of England. Many believed the Anglican Church still held too many remnants of Catholicism. Salem needed a minister but Williams declined the appointment. After a brief sojourn in Plymouth, whose inhabitants were totally separated from the Church of England, the Salem church accepted him in 1633.

This independent streak, so early manifested in his career, and so refreshing in the New World, would never in his lifetime yield to orthodoxy in thought or belief. Within just a couple of years of his arriving, he was engaged in controversies about the veiling of women in church, the legality of the land grant given by Charles I to the Bay Colony, throwing the foundation of the government into questionable legitimacy. He was called into court and asked to answer charges of loyalty to the crown, but they were dropped.[3]

Williams then questioned whether or not magistrates as civil officers had a right to enforce religious duties. Remember, this is a young man in his early thirties challenging the established customs of his elders, men like Governor John Winthrop, John Cotton, also a Cambridge graduate, and Thomas Hooker, who later established Connecticut. Who was this upstart who lacked prudence if not adherence to stubborn and disquieting principles?

His Salem church had requested an additional plot of land to accommodate expansion. The Boston clerical congregation declined because it was offended by his preaching and contentious ideas. Williams wrote to the elders in Boston and claimed they were lacking in charity by punishing the whole Salem congregation for a peevish attitude toward him. In July and October, 1635 he was summoned before the court to answer for erroneous and dangerous opinions. The views hardened as neither Williams nor the court compromised on their positions. Some in his own congregation believed that he had offended too many clerical and civil authorities too often. Charged with defaming and defying the clergy, he was asked to depart the jurisdiction within six weeks.[4] Rather than be exiled on a boat back to England, he fled into the wilderness and arrived at the headwaters of Narragansett Bay, purchased land from the Indians and settled in, eventually sending for his family. By 1640 over forty families had joined him.

He earned the trust and learned the language of the Narragansett Indians. In 1643 he published in London *A Key to the Language of America*, the first study in cultural anthropology of American native peoples and a handy guide to their language. He had tentatively ventured back to England that year to secure a wider audience for his writings.[5] This book was a sensation in its day satisfying a hunger among the British for an understanding of the natives of the Bay Colony and their environs. This particular study was not only a demonstration of his studious scholarship, but his bonding fellowship with Indian men, sympathy for native customs, and strong feelings of amity for their way of life. He never tried to convert them to Christianity, arguing that one should only enter a church voluntarily.

He was called upon by the Bay Colony to act as diplomatic mediator between the colonists and the natives, a duty he accepted regularly. He was unable to negotiate a truce between the Bay Colony and the Pequots, a tribe that had killed a colonist, and the resulting slaughter eliminated the tribe. The colony never repaid him any courtesy for these services. It was only in 1676 that Massachusetts lifted his forty-one year banishment. This and this was only temporary and conditioned upon his not venting any further dissenting opinions. Williams was then in his seventies.

Williams remains a beacon of religious tolerance, a dissenter among the Dissenters, and one of the first American men of courage, an exemplar for all times.

Thomas Paine (1737-1809)

Those who expect to reap the blessings of freedom must, like men, undergo the fatigues of supporting it. [6]

Thomas Paine, born in Thetford, England, exercised all his courage as a British expatriate in America during the days of revolution against England, and in 1776 wrote one of the most moving documents in American political literature, *Common Sense.* One would not suspect that a young Englishman who had held nine different jobs, including sailor and schoolteacher, by the time he was in his mid thrities, been married twice, been dismissed from two government positions as a customs' officer, and had failed every business he entered and then became bankrupt, would eventually compose a pamphlet so popular that it altered the course of American history. He was tried in absentia in England for slandering the aristocracy, nearly died in a French prison for his activities on behalf of the French Revolution, neglected by his American compatriots, and died in obscurity and poverty in America, shunned by Americans for his attack on Christianity in his book *The Age of Reason* (1793–94).

His first wife, Mary Lambert, died when he was only twenty-two years old, and he separated permanently from his second wife, Elizabeth Ollive. He was pretty much washed up in his late thirties, but picked himself up and decided to immigrate to America. He did not expect to be one of those destined to captivate an American and British audience with rapturous prose and revolutionary rhetoric in the popular pamphlets of the day. Paine was indeed a radical thinker and his motive in writing his numerous political tracts in his productive life was to rescue mankind from tyranny and false principles of government so people could be free.

Paine arrived in Philadelphia on November 30, 1774, with a letter of introduction from Ben Franklin whom he had met in London. He soon met Robert Aitken, publisher of the *Pennsylvania Magazine*, who made Paine managing editor, and the circulation doubled within a year. Paine became a journalist that year when he was thrity-seven and knew no other occupation the rest of his life. He was to broadcast the plight and sentiments of the working class, and not the professional, clerical, and landowner elite of the colonies. But, most significantly, he abandoned any fervor he may have entertained for England and instantly became a staunch advocate for American independence.

In 1775 he published an article with Thomas Prior, an officer in the Continental Army, in the *Pennsylvania Journal* and signed it "A Lover of Order." The Pennsylvania Assembly had instructed its delegates to the Constitutional Convention "to dissent from, and utterly reject, any propositions, should such be made, that may cause, or lead to, a Separation from Our Mother Country, or a change of the form of this Government."[7] Paine pointed out that the Assembly exceeded its powers because the delegates to the Convention were not delegates of the Pennsylvania Assembly but of the people, a remarkably keen insight. By using the same logic, Paine noted his own preference for a potential independent separation from England and for a national and not a provincial action from each colony.

MEMORABLE 1776 PUBLICATIONS

The Wealth of Nations (Adam Smith)
The Decline and Fall of the Roman Empire (Edward Gibbon)
Common Sense (Thomas Paine)
Virginia Declaration of Rights (George Mason)
The Declaration of Independence (Thomas Jefferson)
The American Crisis (Thomas Paine)

In 1775 many colonists still held for allegiance to the British crown and alliances with England and wavered about independence or armed struggle. When Paine set foot in Philadelphia, disputes with England were viewed as a kind of lawsuit, to be settled with gentlemanly reserve and decorum. The attitude of Britain was to treat the American colonies as a conquered country. This was a rash and subsequently ruinous policy. The onset of hostilities fractured this comforting alliance and reset the mood of Americans toward a political divorce.

Common Sense appeared on January 10, 1776, in an edition of 1,000 copies and immediately sold out. The pamphlet eventually went through fifty-six printings and sold roughly 120,000 copies in three months, and 150,000 by the end of the year. By the end of 1776 Paine had enlisted in the Continental Army and served with the rank of brigade-major under General Nathanael Greene, who introduced him to George Washington under whom he served until 1779.

Paine promoted the idea of a Constitutional Convention in February 1776 that would frame a charter, "answering to what is called the Magna Charta of England," that would secure "freedom and property to all men, and above all things, the free exercise of religion according to the dictates of conscience."[8] The convention of delegates met in Philadelphia for three months beginning in May 1776 and proclaimed independence on July 4. His pamphlet *Common Sense* rallied Americans and delegates to the Constitutional Convention to declare for independence from England using biblical arguments, like the *Book of Samuel*, against monarchy and hereditary rule. Paine wrote in *Common Sense*:

> The sun never shined on a cause of greater worth. 'Tis not the affair of a city, a country, a province, or a kingdom, but of a continent—of at least one eighth part of the habitable globe. 'Tis not the concern of a day, a year, or an age; posterity are virtually involved in the contest, and will be more or less affected, even to the end of time, by the proceedings now. [9]

He argued for a representative form of government. The only king he wanted was the law: "The law is King." He saw early and presciently that the colonies needed to form a political union if they were to survive and not succumb to a dictator's sword. With the publication of *Common Sense*, Paine tapped into a dormant energy from all classes of American society, a people who had already forged a vision of an independent set of colonies and an embryonic idea of national identity. Paine called on men to fight for their freedom, not just think about it. He appealed to the new American sense of practicality and action. Nearly everyone literate in America had read his pamphlet.

The American Revolution was the first mass political movement in history that did not result in a palace coup or the death or assassination of a king. It included all classes of individuals from southern plantation landowners and slaveholders, to merchants, professionals, and artisans. Its written expression was an Enlightenment ideology based on reason and not on traditional religion. We shall examine more of these ideas in the chapter on Enlightenment dissenters. Hence, Paine was one of the creators, along with Thomas Jefferson, Franklin and James Madison, of a secular language that formed the origins of democratic government absent religious principles unlike, for example, the founding of the Massachusetts Bay Colony. The most important business of government, Paine thought, was to protect the diversity of religions, an interesting proposition for many who claimed he was an atheist, for "securing freedom and . . . above all things, the free exercise of religion, according to the dictates of conscience ..." [10] To protect all religions was indeed a novel idea for government.

Common Sense is the most significant document favoring independence that *The Federalist Papers* is arguing for a federal Constitution. *Common Sense* is not just a rhetorical and journalistic paper but a tightly woven argument against reconciliation with England and for Independence. It reveals a keen sense of the political context of the era and the dramatic decision facing the colonies and citizens. It expresses what no one in America had articulated previously, and does so with journalistic flair, carefully selected historical analogies and sound logic. *Common Sense* drew scores of rebuttal pamphlets from English Loyalists. But unquestionably Paine initiated and spurred on the debate which culminated in the July 4, 1776, Declaration.

Common Sense was just the first volley of journalism from Paine. He wrote throughout the course of the war with Britain. The first essay in the series of articles titled *The American Crisis* was published on December 19, 1776, as the Continental Army under Gen. George Washington finished its first skirmishes with British forces and Hessian mercenaries. Paine described the military situation in this essay that opened with these ringing words:

> These are the times that try men's souls. The summer soldier and the sunshine patriot will in this crisis shrink from the service of his country; but he that stands it now, deserves the love and thanks of man and woman. Tyranny, like hell, is not easily conquered; yet we have this consolation with us, that the harder the conflict, the more glorious the triumph. What we obtain too cheap, we esteem too lightly: —Tis dearness only that gives every thing its value.[11]

The American Crisis was an ongoing analysis of the Revolutionary War and an avidly read set of essays. Many were republished in England. Paine's clever turn of phrases and coining of memorable lines was unique in American history. No one previously had written so passionately, plausibly, and argumentatively about the political future of America. "Those who expect to reap the blessings of Freedom," he wrote on September 12, 1777, "must, like men, undergo the fatigue of supporting it." He was emotional and adamant about cowards and those who wavered in their commitment to the cause of independence. This was reportage with an edge at a time that defined America as a republic. And it issued from the pen of a recent British immigrant.

His views on war itself were also memorable. "Mankind are pretty well convinced that it can never be worth their while to go to war for profit sake. If they are made war upon, their country invaded, or their existence at stake, it is their duty to defend and preserve themselves, but in every other light and from every other cause is war inglorious and detestable."[12] It is a statement applicable to contemporary foreign policy. But nations go to war for something called national honor, and this motivation seems to know no excesses.

The irony of his life and argument on behalf of the independent colonies in *The American Crisis* is that as a British citizen who immigrated to America and who repudiated his native country, he then called Americans who did not support independence traitors. Were not all Americans who supported independence traitors to England? In our own day, are all Kurds who support independence from Iraq traitors to Iraq? The controversy over who is a patriot and who is a traitor is perennial, and nobody expressed that dilemma more powerfully than

Paine. The answer of who is a patriot and who a traitor, who a conformer and who a maverick, also defines who is an outsider.

I am a Farmer of Thoughts, and as all the crops I raise I give away. [13]

His essays were a welcome tonic for independence, for union among the states, and for restrictions on the expansion of western lands. He successfully disputed Virginia's claim in a pamphlet called *Public Good* that its patent granted by James I in 1609 extended to the Pacific Ocean. He also wrote on taxation, credit, monetary policies, trade and commerce, and for the natural and civil rights of all citizens. His lasting contribution to political thought, *The American Crisis*, is neglected reading in American literature and history.

Paine entered Pennsylvania in 1774 penniless and unknown, and sailed back to Europe at age fifty in the spring of 1787, an international celebrity. He returned to England to discover that his father had died of smallpox the previous year. His mother died in 1790 at the age of ninety-four. He returned to Paris where his friend Thomas Jefferson was then ambassador. The Marquis de Lafayette presented him with a key to the destroyed Bastille prison that Paine dutifully sent with an accompanying letter to George Washington. The key hangs on the wall next to the staircase at Mount Vernon, Washington's home on the Potomac River.

Paine published *Rights of Man* in London in 1791, a book that condemned his friend Edmund Burke's defense of aristocracy and made Paine an enemy of British interests and the king. Paine wrote his two-part book as a rebuttal to Burke's *Reflections on the Revolution in France* that appeared in 1790. Burke extolled the English political system of monarchy and repudiated the political developments in France. Paine, of course, felt exactly the opposite.

Paine was tried for libel in absentia in 1792 before Lord Kenyon and a specially commissioned jury in Guildhall on December 13, 1792. Prosecutors contended that Paine was "wicked, malicious, and of seditious disposition." Interestingly, no legal violation was cited, only that Paine's book caused the government to be maligned. Paine's defense lawyer gave a stirring argument in defense of freedom of speech, but the jury returned a verdict of guilty. Paine's book was condemned and his life put in jeopardy. Clearly, England was not yet ripe, as France was, for abandoning its monarchy or the concept of hereditary succession. And because of the popularity of his ideas the government sought to discredit him.

His English friends informed him of his peril and helped escort him one night to Dover, embarking just minutes before the arrival of the order to arrest him. He never again set foot in England. But *The Rights of Man* stirred the political pot in England as vigorously as had *Common Sense* in America. The pamphlet breathed new life into reform movements, and inaugurated scores of labor and grassroots organizations that allowed workers to enter into social and political discussions on their status and economic conditions. He was revered for putting into prose what many already felt but could not articulate. As a member of the English working class himself he was able to express the grievances and resentments of the labor majority, and promote a daring program of social legislation and tax reduction that inspired the poor.

His reputation and stand for the common man gave him unwarranted credentials to enter France and become a part of that revolution. It was to be short-lived.

King Louis XVI was persuaded by the French Constituent Assembly, which was unable to govern the country or agree on any resolution to the turmoil, to sign a declaration of the Rights of Man in August 1789. (See chapter 13) This declaration recognized the equality of rights for all, but retained the rights of property and became a death knell for the aristocracy and the divine right of kings.[14] French mobs marched on Versailles in October 1789. The French revolution soon turned on itself and mutilated its ideals along with its citizens during the Reign of Terror. France's futile foreign wars with neighboring countries, which saw France as weakened in its politics as in its currency, ensued. The rise of a dictator to lead France away from its murderous excesses and misadventures in governance was inevitable. The arrest and guillotine of King Louis XVI and the queen, Marie Antoinette followed in 1793. Europe was thereafter in thrall to the conquering French military until Napoleon's defeat at the hands of Wellington on the plains of Waterloo in 1815.

Paine arrived in the middle of this revolutionary fervor and humanitarian nightmare.

Once in Paris Paine supervised his book's translation, hoping to inspire the revolutionary spirit in France. He did not recognize France's political weaknesses and that France's revolution would not be like America's. He was affectionately received in Paris and made an honorary citizen, one of only nineteen together with Washington, Jefferson and Madison, and was elected as a member of the National Convention in 1792. He had hoped that the French would emulate the American resolve and transform society peacefully, but was dismayed by the terror the revolution unleashed in 1792, its vengeance, malignancy, lack of proper judicial proceedings, and guillotines, including the regal executions. His honorary French citizenship did not prevent his enemies from mischief. He was imprisoned for nearly a year from suspicions of political machinations, and suspected as an English spy. Paine became as disillusioned with the political folly and insanities of the French Revolution as the French did. His idealism crushed, he scurried back to America in 1802.

Paine's major political study was *The Rights of Man*. He distinguished between natural rights, where an individual acts intellectually freely and for his own comfort in happiness, and civil rights, or those who pertain to one's membership in society. Paine did not adequately address the question of property rights, a sticking point central to both the American and French revolutions. The French declaration included property among natural rights. French church property was confiscated by the state. Philosophical speculators like Paine writing to establish a foundation for emerging democratic principles did not always satisfy the conditions or requirements of practical economics, nor did politicians and leaders follow the sound advice of the most esteemed Enlightenment authors.

Paine subsequently wrote *The Age of Reason* while in Paris, a book that condemned religious superstitions and organized religions for associating with the corruptions of the aristocracy. He completed it while living with James Monroe and his family in Paris while Monroe, later to become the fifth President of the United States, was ambassador to France. It's unnecessary to go into the details of this hastily written two-volume work except to note that his views on scripture were as skeptical as was this age in Europe and France's anticlerical, antireligious government. Not until 1801 when Napoleon, in a concordat with Pope Pius VII, reinstated Catholicism as the preferred religion did France return to a religious fold. By then Paine was packing his bags for a return to America.

The Age of Reason was a bold enterprise, a work that alone would symbolize his moral courage in challenging superstitious beliefs in both the Old and New Testaments and, in an era prior to the historical criticism of the nineteenth century and accuracy in scholarship, for proclaiming his opinions so openly.

Like Thomas Jefferson, George Washington, Ben Franklin, and other prominent figures of this age, Paine was a Deist, one who believed that there was a Divine Being, but not one who transcribed works of literature to humanity outlining his plan for them, but a benevolent Creator whose chief gift to mankind is reason. Paine was especially hard on the beliefs and practices of Christianity that would not endear him to his admirers. He was thus unprepared for the storm of criticism that greeted him because of this one work when he returned to America in 1802. This potent book dogged him the rest of his days as former allies deserted him.

His last major book was the short but persuasive *Agrarian Justice* in 1797 in which he wrote in the opening lines: "To preserve the benefits of what is called civilized life, and to remedy, at the same time, the evils it has produced, ought to be considered as one of the first objects of reformed legislation."[15] His proposal in *Agrarian Justice*, a pamphlet of twenty-four pages, is a naïve solution to poverty. But it illustrates his sense of social justice, not charity, for all people, and he especially notes that the lame, the blind, and the elderly poor need special assistance. Whenever intellectuals, academics or politicians are in doubt about a topic to write or speak about they can always promise to eradicate poverty.

Paine's proposals did not get as much mileage as Marx's theory of communism but the sentiments were similar. Paine in many ways anticipates Marx who viewed capitalism and the holding of personal property as evil and who saw the exploitation of workers as the greatest threat against humanity. Both Paine and Marx argue for a sharing of the wealth of the world, though Paine used biblical analogies to support his argument.

Paine proposed that the earth in its uncultivated state is "the common property of the human race," and is therefore a joint proprietor with all the produces of the soil, both vegetable and animal. He noted that there was no landed property in the beginning of human history. The produce of cultivated land belongs to the cultivator. He believed that every person has a natural right to a portion of the fruits of the earth. He proposed to give everyone who has been despoiled of such rights a monetary entitlement so they can live their lives respectfully and not in poverty. He did not believe anyone has a right to a monopoly of natural inheritance.

Paine was a sincere advocate for the rights of ordinary citizens. Since he was born poor, and worked as an ordinary day laborer, he identified with the American sense of justice, fairness, and freedom. He was uncompromising in his principles, and he made no attempt to seek a fortune or to benefit by running for political office either locally or nationally. He refused all royalties from *Common Sense*, the book that made him famous. Although not killed by assassins or authorities—he was adroit enough to escape jail and possible death in England and France—his opinions and beliefs made him prominent enemies and ostracized him from polite society.

He not only refused payment for many of his major writings, believing them to be for the common good, and also any government position, ostensibly because he did not want to embarrass his government officials by appearing to be writing to gain favor. I happen to believe, however, that because he was not of a propertied class that even his friends at one time, like Washington, Jefferson, and Gouverneur Morris saw him for all his rhetorical writing skills and service in the military, as unqualified in property, money, or education to represent the interests of the United States either at home or abroad. This is an unflattering conclusion but there is enough historical evidence to warrant it.[16]

Though not an elected delegate of the Continental Congress for independence or the U.S. Constitution, he was certainly one of the most prominent spokespersons for both independence and constitutional liberties and equality for all. As a widely popular journalist, he was one of America's first intellectuals. His style appeared reckless but robust, always biting and incisive, and portrayed an honesty that was memorable. A reader roused to action felt inclined to reach for the sword and do battle with the adversary, or give money to the cause of those who would.

He died in New York City June 8, 1809, at age seventy-two. Only six grievers, and no representative of any government, attended his funeral services. Two of the six were Blacks who sympathized with his written arguments to abolish slavery. He was buried on a farm in New Rochelle given to him by the State of New York on behalf of his patriotic service in the fight for American independence. His life and legacy were revived a generation or two after his death as the labor movement gathered influence and American workers recognized the value of his working-class radicalism and his enduring faith in human nature.

For our next hero we journey to America's western states, the nineteenth century, and the Native American culture.

Cochise (c. 1815–1874)

I noted in the introduction that I would not include soldiers in these profiles but I have made two exceptions: Cochise and Red Cloud, soldiers only in the literal sense. They were chiefs fighting for the survival of their peoples, unwilling to be driven from their land by invaders and occupiers. Native Americans were all considered outsiders as European Americans moved into their territory and found excuses for exploiting them and the land. Cochise and Red Cloud are two prime examples of how native peoples courageously defended their people and lands to death or exile. They might not be the best exemplars of how to defend against oppression through guerrilla warfare, but they are representatives of a people who stood up for their rights.

The Apache rangeland in the nineteenth century extended roughly from today's Phoenix, Arizona, east to Socorro, New Mexico, south to Chihuahua in Mexico and east again to Hermosillo in Mexico, an area roughly the size of Arizona or New Mexico, a region of arid deserts and daunting mountains. This untamed and unsettled desert belonged to the Spanish until the latter part of the nineteenth century, home to countless bands of Apaches, and visited only by a few, intrepid explorers. The main settlement was Santa Fe, founded by the Spanish in 1607. A few other settlements had been established as early as 1654. The territory then became a part of Mexico after its independence from Spain in 1821. In 1846 the U.S. Cavalry invaded during the Mexican-American War.[17]

Cochise was the chief of the Chiricahua Apaches whose homeland was southeastern Arizona. Cochise was taller than most men in his tribe and had more leadership stature based on his courageous exploits against Spanish, Mexican, and American invaders. Geronimo, another Chiricahua Apache of the next generation, is more widely known because of movies and legends.[18] Cochise and his affiliated Apache tribes were relatively peaceful until Mexicans killed his father, and the Americans hanged his brother and murdered his father-in-law. For decades there were revenge killings on both sides accompanied by raids to secure food and provisions.

The Apaches were not a settled agricultural people like their adobe cousins in the north or natives in southern Mexico who grew corn, beans and squash. Apaches were nomadic, supplementing hunting by gathering berries, nuts, and fruit as the seasons provided. From about the 1780s to the 1820s, the principal adversary of the Apaches had been the Spanish who had more than two dozen presidio forts and settlements in the southwest. The Spanish policy was to pacify the natives, who generally stole horses and cattle to keep them from raiding. To avoid these raids, the Spanish offered staples of food, weapons for hunting, and liquor. This pattern of providing provisions was later adopted by the Mexicans and Americans. Accepting rations from the Spanish or Mexicans kept the relative peace, reduced travel for Apaches to find food and establish encampments, and reduced raids on presidios and settlements. Throughout this extended period

Apaches learned about Spanish and Mexican customs, and many even learned to speak Spanish.[19]

When Mexicans won independence from Spain in 1821, the conditions for the Apache intensified. The war had drained the coffers and the men to staff the northern regions so Apaches did not receive the accustomed allotments of food and equipment. By the mid-1820s Apaches were raiding settlements again to survive. Cochise honed his skills as a young warrior during the 1830s. For a few decades the Indians raided settlements throughout northern Mexico, southern Arizona, and New Mexico to obtain supplies, and the Mexicans, depending on the strength of their finances to raise men and their own equipment, periodically tried to contain or subdue them from overrunning presidio settlements.

A civilian trader named James Kirker organized countless war parties against the Apaches in northern Mexico in the 1840s. When he and his group of mercenaries, recruited from farmers and settlers, killed over 130 Apaches in 1846 in the settlement then known as Galeana in Chihuahua, Mexico, hostilities commenced again and became revenge killings, and not just raids. In May 1846 the U.S. Congress declared war on Mexico, which then had to divert its limited resources to fighting the American invaders at the lower end of the Rio Grande River south of Corpus Christi, Texas, and around Matamoros.

As the Mexicans fought the Americans in 1846, northwestern Mexico became a raiding playground for Apaches. Typically in this tenuous relationship, there would be an Apache raid, then a peace offer when the Mexican town would supply provisions, then an incident in which someone or a scouting group or members of a supply-wagon team would be killed, then a revenge raid in Apache territory. This pattern of raids by Apaches for sheep, cattle, and horses in which Mexican men, women, and children were killed, and the inevitable Mexican military team that followed Apaches into their strongholds to avenge the killings, lasted throughout this period. Typically, Mexicans accepted peace, the Apaches entered the town, everyone got drunk, someone got killed, and the slaughtering cycle repeated itself.

Eventually, the Apaches reached out to the Americans, a relationship feared by the Mexicans because it meant that their two enemies would be aligned, with Americans providing the Apaches with arms and ammunition. The Apaches could not entertain the prospect of having enemies on both sides of the border. The American presence was strengthened by mining activities, the presence of Fort Buchanan about forty-five miles southeast of Tucson, and the Butterfield Overland Mail Company that crossed through Apache territory. By 1860 the Butterfield stagecoach system stretched 2,800 miles from St. Louis to San Francisco with over 200 stage stations approximately twenty miles apart manned by a total of over 2,000 employees. Because Mexican forts in Sonora had been fortified to avoid Apache incursions, Cochise and his warriors knew that raids south would be more difficult and costly in life.[20]

But the peace pacts Cochise made with the Mexicans and Americans were always fragile. Revenge was the motive and killings and pillage the main activity. By 1862, in the middle of the Civil War, parts of the southwest like Santa Fe and Tucson fell into the hands of Confederate troops. The Congress of the Confederate States had passed a law declaring for extermination of all hostile Indians, giving Confederate troops legal authority to massacre. Brig. Gen. James Carleton, with 2,350 troops commanding the California Column came in 1862 to drive out the Confederates from the southwest and reestablish federal control and revitalize commerce in the region.

American policy toward the Indians pursued opposing directives. One policy, manifested by the welfare handouts of blankets and provisions at reservations and Indian Bureau offices after the Civil War, encouraged compassion, a doctrine promoted by church groups who sought to convert Indians. Settlers in the Southwest, however, with the backing of the military, pursued a policy of extermination. Cochise was able to seek refuge occasionally in places like Fort Apache and receive provisions and offers of peace between raids and the killing of stagecoach employees, farmers, and mine workers. In time, the military's countless incursions in his territory hunting him and killing small parties of his people, convinced Cochise that he needed to make peace to survive and keep his band from total annihilation.

It would have been impossible to be a chief and a pacifist, although eventually Cochise surrendered in the face of superior forces, convincing his tribal members that they would have to live on reservations or be exterminated. Cochise himself was certainly responsible for the deaths of many innocent victims. But he is no different than a George Washington commanding the Minutemen militia of the Revolutionary War as each presided over the defense of the homeland. The ghosts of those he killed may cry foul for this reasoning, but many of them would have tried to kill him too if they could have.

Cochise eluded capture for decades from both Mexicans and Americans until he witnessed the slow decimation of his tribe and sued for peace shortly before his death in 1874. Except for regional historians he is a largely unknown and neglected figure in American history. But his courage and resourcefulness in the teeth of survival in a harsh landscape and extinction by soldiers of his tribe and people is a testament to heroism in any culture.

Red Cloud (1822–1909)

I was born a Lakota and I shall die a Lakota. Before the white man came to our country, the Lakotas were a free people. They made their own laws and governed themselves as it seemed good to them. The priests and ministers tell us that we loved wickedly when we lived before the white man came among us. Whose fault was this? We lived right as we were taught it was right. Shall we be punished for this? I am not sure that what these people tell me is true. [21]

Many Indians in the Great Plains, like the Sioux, Cheyenne, Arapahoe, Pawnee, and Comanche, were frequently warring among themselves as they followed the buffalo through one another's territory in the mid-nineteenth century. They made peace as often as they made war with each other, and then joined in councils and common festivities. But by 1860 it was clear that they had a common enemy in the U.S. army and the encroachment of settlers. Smaller tribes, more prone to extinction in intertribal warfare, thought it expedient to make peace with the newcomers who would end the Indian infighting. Red Cloud, a Lakota Sioux, refused to submit to U.S. rights for passage through his territory and to settlement demands.

The white man didn't help his cause by giving shiny trinkets, plying the Indians with liquor, or lying over agreements and intentions. Before the ashes of council fires cooled, the axes of the whites were cutting down pine trees to build forts and settlements. Indians preferred to keep their homes and traditional hunting grounds without intrusion. This is a part of Red Cloud's story.

There are at least a dozen famous Indian chiefs that could have been profiled who were as illustrious and brave, men like Crazy Horse, Black Elk, Chief Joseph, Chief Seattle, Lone Wolf, Ten Bears and Sitting Bull. But I believe that Red Cloud was both a warrior and a statesman, one who concluded agreements during the difficult last decades of the nineteenth century and, in most instances, made the U.S. government adhere to them. He was full of integrity in his private life, and exemplified outstanding service on behalf of his people through diplomacy—he made several trips to New York and Washington D.C.—and militarily through victories over other tribal enemies and the U.S. army. Let Red Cloud represent, like Cochise, the principled stand all native peoples made in defense of their survival and homeland.

Because there were no written records and only uncertain verbal accounts from those who knew them late in life, little is known of the early lives of Native Americans. The early years of Red Cloud are sketchy. He was born about 1822 somewhere along the forks of the Platte River in Nebraska. He learned horsemanship at an early age and actively took part in the buffalo hunts.

When he was twenty-eight years old, Bear Bull, an Oglala chief, enraged and probably drunk at the time, killed Red Cloud's father and brother over the failure of the Sioux tribes to submit to an agreement requested by the army to pass through Sioux territory. Red Cloud faced Bear Bull and his son silently and then shot them both, an action his tribe endorsed.

Raised as a warrior from his birthplace in western Nebraska, Red Cloud became the proud chief of the Lakota Sioux and emerged as the most successful native military strategist against the U.S. cavalry. His campaigns resulted in the Fort Laramie Treaty in 1868. The U. S. government agreed to pull back from forts and travel excursions along the Bozeman Trail that led to the gold fields in Montana. The treaty did not last long as Custer's raids and the Black Hills operations in 1874 quickly brought about the destruction of all Plains Indians' independence.

The settler trails that led through his land to Montana and on to Oregon brought more people through to the West Coast, and the military might that sustained them made the old way of life of the Plains Indian doomed. Although personally brave in battle, like his killing of Capt. William Fetterman and eighty soldiers at Camp Phil Kearney in 1866, Red Cloud was eventually outnumbered and outgunned by the U.S. army and forced to relinquish control over his territory. He was restricted to the Pine Ridge Reservation in 1880, a heroic figure who presided over a transitional period in U.S. history as hordes of settlers fled west for the acquisition of land, gold, and adventure. They cared less for the privileges of the native peoples than their own aggrandizing pursuits.

Red Cloud was a dissident because he would not agree to the possession of Sioux lands by either the military or the migrating settlers who saw the Sioux as savages. He believed in a Great Spirit and his own spirit as he noted in his last speech to his people:

> Taku Shanskan is familiar with my spirit and when I die I will go with him. Then I shall be satisfied. Wi is my father. The Wakan Tanka of the white man has overcome him. But I shall remain true to him . . . Shadows are long and dark before me. I shall soon lie down to rise no more. While my spirit is with my body the smoke of my breath shall be toward to the Sun for he knows all things and knows that I am still true to him. [22]

When the Ghost Dance became popular in the 1880s among the Sioux, he urged his people not to participate. Like the Romans feeling the religious turbulence among Christians in the early days of Christianity, Red Cloud knew that the military would think the spirit movement a sign of insurrection and would crush it. His sensible advice went unheeded and was a partial cause for the massacre at Wounded Knee in 1890, an abhorrent event that ended all American Indian rebelliousness.[23]

His ruddy, stern, weathered features made him the delight of all photographers of renown in the nineteenth century. There are 128 known photographs of him from his prime in 1872 on his first visit to Washington D.C., until a 1905 photo when he was eighty-three at Pine Ridge Reservation.

CHAPTER FOUR
SKEPTICAL SCIENTISTS AS DISSIDENTS

Religion and science are two separate realms of human experience, like different colors filtered through the same prism. When Europe was dominated by religious authoritarianism for over a thousand years, heretics and dissenters were routinely and often savagely silenced. Today, religious authoritarianism still exists and dissidents and infidels are likewise persecuted. Science does not define morality, nor does religion explain nature. Science, indifferent to human needs and sufferings, as earthquakes, hurricanes, and floods attest, helps us understand nature better. Besides intolerance, dogmatism, and some preaching and plenty of posturing, the real adversary in this perennial debate is neither religion nor science but broad misunderstandings of both of these twin pillars of human thought and their differing contributions to humanity.

In this chapter I examine individuals less and examine more of a new battle over an old war of ideas between faith and reason, religious belief and evidence, myth and science. I figure Charles Darwin as a model for this debate.

What Americans Believe

Religion is based partially on faith in unobservable phenomena, or in scriptural and spiritual values. Some beliefs of each religion may be based on superstition, some on rituals like singing, and much may be speculative and subject to interpretation. But whatever is believed is usually based on teachings or writings transcribed or dictated by God or a by prophet who claims God has spoken to him or her. In the 1990s conservative church participation witnessed the largest growth rate of all religions in America at nearly 20 percent, while more liberal churches like the Presbyterian and United Church of Christ lost membership. With 65 million adherents, the Catholic Church is the nation's largest of the 149 religious groups in the Unites States, at about a quarter of the population. Pentecostalism, at over 60 million, like Charismatic advocates whose faith centers on emotional responses, is the fastest growing branch of Christianity. Evangelicals generally believe that the Bible is literally true.

Astrology is in some ways like a religious persuasion because it seeks to predict the future controlled by the stars. Astrological forecasts are ambiguous enough to approximate certain behaviors and occurrences. The test of astrology is the degree to which adherents believe that the motion of the planets and stars dictates their fortunes or behaviors. Palm readers and fortune-tellers may be dismissed as charlatans, but too many still believe there is value in knowing an astrological sign as indicative of a personality and the future.

Science, on the other hand, is about what can be observed and measured. If it is not observable or cannot be measured it cannot be science. If scientific investigators use the right instruments they can uncover the secrets of matter and how it interacts with other material substances. Science has theories or hypotheses about how material substances combine and disconnect. Accumulated evidence about a theory tends to confirm its credibility, even though the answer may not be the ultimate truth. For example, the existence of atoms did not automatically lead to the discovery of subatomic particles. Einstein predicted in his general theory of relativity that a curved space-time dimension to the universe is distorted by matter and energy, a twist to the once popularly held linear theory of how light and gravity function. Steven Hawking has shown that the big bang theory of how the universe began is the most probable, and that therefore time had a beginning. Hawking also promulgated the theory of black holes, first proposed by John Wheeler in 1969, in which matter becomes so dense and heavy no light can escape. Time ceases to be in a black hole because there is no motion.

Neither science nor philosophy admits orthodoxy. Only faith and religion presume to know absolute truth. Science is skeptical of all opinions unless tested with rigorous methods and validated repeatedly, but rightly disdains transcendental theories without methods for validating them. The Federal Drug Administration, for example, does not allow pharmaceuticals to be released to the general public unless relevant organic tests have been performed for primary and secondary effects. The general public would resist efforts to curtail this standard scientific process that deters oversight on public health. In the final analysis, if we don't accept evolution, we may as well abandon or discard all we know about the life sciences.

Polls on Creation

So what do Americans believe?

In a November, 2004 CBS News/*New York Times* poll, Americans were posed three statements and asked to indicate which best described their beliefs:

- We evolved from less advanced life over millions of years, and God was not involved.
- We evolved from less advanced forms of life and God guided this process.

- God created us just the way we are.

Only 5 percent were unsure how to answer, but 55 percent indicated that God created us in our present form, while 27 percent said God guided the evolutionary process and only 13 percent believed that God was not involved in evolution.

A Pew Forum on Religion and Public Life found similar poll results in 2005. Two-thirds of Americans surveyed said that creationism should be taught alongside evolution in public schools. The survey found that 42 percent of respondents believed that "living things have existed in their present form since the beginning of time." By contrast, only 42 percent thought humans had evolved over time, and only 26 percent of that group thought humans evolved through natural selection. The other 18 percent thought humans evolved, but were "guided by a supreme being."[1]

On the other hand, only 13 percent of American adults know what a molecule is. This is the lamentable condition of U.S. science understanding. While knowledge in all sciences expands exponentially, scientific illiteracy remains high.

More than half of all Americans believe that the universe is more than 6,000 years old. They are wrong, not about their faith in a creator, but in the age of matter. The biblical myth in *Genesis*, and the belief that the Bible was literally transmitted by an omniscient deity, can trump reason, science, and all accumulated and corroborated evidence. The millions of galaxies, the infinity of space, the microscopic life forms that constitute all biology offer a realistic if awe-inspiring and incomprehensible view of reality. But the biblical reality of creation is a world of imagination, myth, and borrowed stories from the first civilizations. Biblical creation is an improbable story that offers no realistic account of reality at all, but does parse well with existing stories of creation from the Sumerian *Epic of Gilgamesh* and the Akkadian *Enuma Elish*, both composed hundreds of years before biblical compositions.

Yet despite the intellectual advances of the past 2,000 years, biblical literalists persist in asserting that the biblical creation story is the only valid one. Some zealots have hijacked science classrooms with creationist dogma, or fought to place commandments in courtrooms. With the exception of mathematics, all the discoveries of seminal ideas in science—like energy, quantum mechanics, the cosmology and complexity of the universe, the atomic structure, DNA, and evolution—contravene the biblical story of the spontaneous creation of matter and human life. The discoveries in all the sciences both inform and challenge our most elemental principles and beliefs about who we are and what constitutes the world we live in.

Let me highlight the one brilliant and intrepid scientist, a religious outcast, who makes the hair of biblical creation literalists stand on end: Charles Darwin. Let him represent all skeptical scientists in all centuries.

Charles Darwin (1809–1882)

Darwin was one of the most observant, careful, and thoughtful scientists in history, and one of the most maligned. I include him here as the first among modern scientists because, although Darwin was not burned at the stake or killed as he might have been in the Middle Ages, he was assaulted by establishment religious forces, not for attacking the sanctuary of creationism, but by supplying evidence and a theory for his observations of nature. Science and religion have been at odds ever since religions began, and Darwin was the regrettable target of fundamentalist religious enmity in the nineteenth century and still is today. I use him as an exemplar to discuss one of the most central issues of the twenty-first century, the theory of natural selection that, despite the accumulative and convincing body of scientific evidence, fails to convince a sizeable segment of the American population of its validity. Skeptical scientists advocating evolution are inevitably pitted against a scientifically uninformed but voluble public majority.

What Darwin achieved is astounding. He gave the biological sciences the theory of natural selection around which investigations into life processes occur by dispelling the unhelpful classification of the permanence of species and the separateness of creation. He synthesized his own observations on animal and vegetative life with a profound theory, natural selection, and a validated hypothesis of how natural life evolves. He assembled a huge body of formidable evidence from his own observations of natural phenomena and collections of botanical and animal forms to bolster his theory. And he did all this with a rare gift for self-deprecation, modesty, and kindness even to his adversaries.

His writings read as if the author were a courteous man gently trying to urge the reader into understanding, and not like a pompous professor lecturing. This is evident even when one reads *The Origin of the Species*, as the style is disarming and convincing, the opposite of a fanatical advocate. It's almost as if Darwin sided with a skeptical reader to ease him or her through doubts. Although primarily known for *The Origin of the Species* (1859) and *The Descent of Man* (1871), he published widely (see chart on p.73) in thirteen other books and scores of papers in the natural sciences.

> Everything about which I thought or read was made to bear directly on what I had seen or was likely to see; and this habit of mind was continued during the five years of the voyage. I feel sure that it was this training which has enabled me to do whatever I have done in science.[2]

Charles Robert Darwin was born February 12, 1809, the same day as Abraham Lincoln. His father was a successful physician. His mother died when he was only eight. He came from a distinguished pedigree, born the fifth of six children and was raised by doting sisters. His grandfather, Erasmus Darwin (1731–1802), was a notable English physician, scholar, and poet. Darwin wrote a biography of his famous grandfather in 1879. Erasmus was also the grandfather of Francis Galton, Darwin's cousin, who conducted the first studies of gifted people and gave impetus to the first tests on intelligence.

Charles studied medicine at Edinburgh University and later for the ministry at Christ's College, Cambridge but lost interest in both professions before receiving a degree, though he graduated from Cambridge in 1831. He could not pass on an opportunity to journey on a botanical voyage on a ship called The *Beagle*. From 1831 to 1836 he circumnavigated the globe and collected specimens that changed his views of how biological development evolves. He collected fossils in South America, and continued to experiment with animals and plants all his life. As a man who retired in semi-luxury, Darwin was able to pursue his scientific interests without needing employment, though he suffered from poor health much of his adult life.

Darwin and his wife, Emma Wedgewood, his cousin whom he married in 1839, were to have ten children, seven of whom survived childhood. William, the eldest, became a banker. George was an astronomer and mathematician who became professor of astronomy at Cambridge. Francis followed his father as a naturalist and botanist, and edited his correspondence and his father's autobiography. Leonard was a career soldier in the Royal Engineers. Horace was a graduate of Cambridge and worked as an engineer and builder of scientific instruments. He was also mayor of Cambridge.

Classifying Species

What puzzled Darwin during his *Beagle* travels was the number of species that seemed so similar and yet were so suitably and subtly adapted to their environments. How had they have evolved over time, he asked himself, and how had individual variations adapted to survival needs? The key to population growth, he reasoned, must be because each species somehow self-regulates its survival and population growth. That insight was to become the theory of natural selection, or the proposition that individual organisms that survive are those that reproduce most successfully in their environments and pass on modified traits to succeeding generations. Weaker members of the species die out and are replaced by the stronger, more resilient survivors. And this process, like all those in the universe, is random.

The systematic modern classification of species began with the publication of *Systema Naturae* in 1735 by the Swedish botanist Carl von Linne, hereafter known as Linneaus, his Latinized name. Linnaeus introduced an organic pyramid of types descending from phylum, class, order, family, genus, and species. Humans are classified under this system as *Homo*, the genus, and *Sapiens*, the species. This system recognizes descriptive similarities, like downward pointing noses or opposable thumbs, rather than organic relationships. DNA is a more precise identification of how living beings are intricately interrelated. For creationists, species are unchanging. For scientists, all organic life is constantly changing. It was by theoretically challenging the classification of species, based on his solid observations and comparisons, that Darwin challenged how we even classify living organisms, including humans.

Darwin's *Notebooks*, composed from 1837–1844, contains a drawing of a branching tree, just like a genealogical tree, the first evolutionary tree diagram. As he was later to describe in *The Origin of the Species* (1859), many more individuals of each species will be born than can possibly survive. Thus, there is a recurring struggle for existence even among individuals. Any organism varies ever so slightly to advance itself under the complex and sometimes varying conditions of life and will have a better chance of surviving, and thus be naturally selected, as will its descendants. From genetic inheritance, any organism will tend to propagate its modified features. All life forms are modified descendants of earlier life forms.

Darwin's Research

Darwin was a meticulous researcher and spent his life thinking over copious notes from careful observations of flora and fauna taken during his travels and from available written sources. His first summary resulted in *The Origin of the Species* (full title: *On the Origin of the Species By Means of Natural Selection, or the Preservation of Favoured Races in the Struggle for Life*) that appeared in 1859. A. R. Wallace, then collecting biological samples in Southeast Asia, (he returned to England with 125,000 specimens) had come to a similar conclusion independently about evolved life, a debt that Darwin acknowledged when both had abstracts of their works read at the Linnean Society in 1858.

Although *The Origin of the Species* and *The Descent of Man* were Darwin's most notable books, his other experiments in natural science are also significant. His book on insectivorous plants, for example, sold better than *The Origin of the Species*. The venue and laboratory for nearly all his experiments was his home and garden. He worked for eight years on a study of barnacles.

Darwin's home, Down House in Kent, England, is located about sixteen miles from London. The house was originally built in 1650 as a farmhouse until extensions were made in 1778. Darwin made additional improvements in this home he lived in for forty years. It is regularly maintained and remains almost exactly as it was when Darwin lived there. A five-year restoration was completed in 2003. The study contains his chair, writing desk, and many artifacts collected during his travels on the *Beagle*. The grounds are extensive and I took the opportunity to walk around the property on the footpath known as the Sand-walk that Darwin took daily in the afternoons. The bluebells still bloom as they did in his day. The apple orchard, the gardens, the greenhouse, and flowerbeds remind us of his love of nature and his study of it. I marveled at the mounds planted by his son Horace, created for his study of earthworms, the subject of his last book published in 1881, the year before his death.

DARWIN'S BOOKS

1839	*Journal of Researches* (his first book on volcanic islands)
1842	*On the Structure and Distribution of Coral Reefs*
1846	*Geological Observations on South America*
1854	*Cirripedia* (Barnacles) in two volumes
1859	*On The Origin of the Species*
1862	*Fertilisation of Orchids* (second edition 1880)
1868	*Variation of Animals and Plants Under Domestication*
1871	*The Descent of Man*
1872	*The Expression of the Emotions in Men and Animals*
1875	*Climbing Plants*
1875	*Insectivorous Plants*
1876	*The Effects of Cross– and Self–Fertilisation*
1879	*Life of Erasmus Darwin*
1880	*Power of Movement in Plants*
1881	*The Formation of Vegetable Mould Through the Action of Worms*

The orchids are still flowering in the greenhouse. Darwin was fascinated to observe how some bees and insects were attracted to orchids. When this interest became evident to the public he received orchid cuttings from all over the country for his experiments and published a book on orchids in 1862. Six of Darwin's experiments can still seen around the garden, most significantly the weed garden that was used to confirm his theory of natural selection. Climbing plants, like ivies and Virginia creepers, and flowers are also in the greenhouse. Darwin wrote four books on plants.

Thomas Huxley was the most vocal advocate for Darwin's theory of natural selection and held debates and made speeches throughout the United Kingdom on Darwin's behalf, as Darwin was often in ill-health, and traveling little and then only to spas for health reasons. Herbert Spencer's book, *Principles of Biology* (1866) contained the phrase "survival of the fittest," thereby describing a key aspect of natural selection. Darwin received an honorary doctorate of law from Cambridge University in 1877 for which he was exceedingly proud.

He died in his bed at Down House on April 19, 1882, and is buried in Westminster Abbey next to his friend, the astronomer John Herschel and about twenty feet from Sir Isaac Newton.

His legacy is permanent and lasting. The bibliographic references for all the books and publications in the Darwin Correspondence Project fill nearly 200 pages and all are available online. His theory has been numerously validated in all the experimental sciences and continues to provide the theoretical incentive for investigations in all the academic categories and scientific disciplines. Darwin ranks with Copernicus, Galileo, Kepler, Newton, Freud and Einstein among those who have capsized our certainties and intellectual comfort zones. I say comfort zones purposefully because he stripped away the notions that there is a guarantee of progress and that each organism, whether a bacterium, wildebeest, or human, has a special purpose. No one has influenced our knowledge of organic life more than he, one of the most original thinkers and finest writers in the history of science.

Natural Selection Over Time

Some day, if the earth isn't destroyed in a cataclysmic collision with another astral body, or if humans don't destroy themselves and the planet through wanton exploitation or reckless endangerment, humans will be regarded by future archaeologists as merely an intermediate form to an emergent organic creature existing then that we can't imagine now. Time is the awesome perspective that natural selection brings to minute modifications in organisms.

When we look at the beauty and fragility of the fossilized bones of a trilobite, a marine creature that lived 600 million years ago during the Cambrian period, we can begin to fathom time as an enduring factor in the evolution of biological life forms. Trilobites flourished long before the dinosaurs and existed on earth for more than 350 million years.[3] By comparison, hominoid fossils are only between 6 and 7 million years old. It is that chronological immensity that generates mental limitations to understanding the scale of life on earth and yet which defines its slow progression. Darwin was one of the first to acknowledge this duration on the evolution of natural phenomena as he argued in one of his first books, *On the Structure and Distribution of Coral Reefs* (1842). The formation of coral reefs is an example of the long formation of geological strata.

> The effects produced on the land by the later elevatory movements, namely, successively rising cliffs, lines of erosion, and beds of littoral shells and pebbles, all requiring time for their production, prove that these movements have been very slow . . . that the movements must either have been effected by small steps, separated from each other by long intervals of time, during which the reef-constructing polypifers were able to bring up their solid frameworks to the surface.[4]

As the boundaries of organic life have receded into greater stretches as found in archaeological sources and DNA studies, more millions of years and greater precision in their calculation, we can see the value of Darwin's early conclusion about the relevance of geological and biological selection and evolutionary processes. Darwin made the same kind of conclusion about humans in *The Descent of Man*:

> We are far from knowing how long ago it was when man first diverged from the Catarhine stock; it may have occurred at an epoch as remote as the Eocene period. (54.8 to 33.7 million years ago) . . . We know that some may have retained the same form during an enormous lapse of time.[5]

By the beginning of the third millennium, it was clear to all scientists from DNA studies that chimpanzees, bonobos, and humans were all distant cousins.

A QUICK PRIMER ON EVOLUTION

What is evolution? An idea that all organic development has occurred over long periods of time.

Is evolution just a theory? Evolution is theoretical, like gravity or the atomic structure, an assumption supported by a series of validated observations from the natural world.

How does evolution occur? Most likely through natural selection whereby many species die out and others survive.

What is the evidence against evolution? All evidence supports evolution, and no other scientific theory is a viable alternative.   (Mayr 2001)

Genetics and Molecular Biology

The greatest contribution of genetics and molecular biology to science, especially the decoding of the DNA sequence, has been the similarity of human biology with other organisms. The tools of molecular biology and comparative genomics can distinguish specific changes in the DNA of 17,000 species of butterfly and why some insects have only six legs instead of twelve. The Human Genome Project confirmed that, despite the seeming complexity of human biology, humans have about 25,000 genes, about the same number as many fish and mammals, and about twice as many as fruit flies. George Church, one of the earliest proponents of Project, predicted that within a decade individuals would have their personal genome or DNA sequence encoded on a disc for doctors to reference for diseases and sicknesses. Some recent research has confirmed some phenomenal findings.

For example, former Harvard professor of anthropology William W. Howells demonstrated through the measurement of cranial cavities that all humans are of one homogeneous species.[6] Cann and Wilson showed through global analyses of mitochondrial DNA, which only passes through females, that all humans came from the ovaries of one woman in Africa about 150,000 years ago.[7] Radiation analyses of African skulls dated to 36,000 years ago, plus or minus 3,000 years, are nearly identical to skulls found in Europe about the same time, indicating that there was a migration from Africa to Europe approximately 40,000 years ago or longer.

In 2006 Sarah Tishkoff and her associates reported a recent instance of human evolutionary processes from a genetic study of peoples in East Africa. Genetic changes in humans occurring as recently as 3,000 years ago have developed an ability to digest milk. Normally, the lactase tolerance for milk is switched off after weaning. But among cattle-raising and pastoral peoples in Africa, and later in northern Europe, people with a persistent lactase resistant gene flourished. Nearly all Dutch and Swedes are lactase tolerant. This genetic mutation allowed the owners to leave many more times descendants than those who didn't have this gene.[8]

The conclusions from genetics and molecular biology point firmly toward evolutionary changes. But let's jump right to the central controversy Darwin initiated—the origin of human life and see what science has discovered.

Evidence About Human Origins

New exhibitions of our ancestral relatives showing the progress of human evolution now include the results of DNA and molecular biology in addition to the discoveries from paleontology. These dual forms of forensic science are indeed like the strands of a double helix. Advances in technology, like MRIs, carbon testing, radiation detection, etc., have rendered the remains from paleontology more precise about where we come from and how long ago. DNA gives more conclusive results about lineage and organic affinities. The overall conclusion is that evolution is still at work and its development has been inexorably slow but organically traceable.

Let's do a quick review of some of the earlier results to follow the history.

The twentieth century world was shocked in 1924 by the discovery in South Africa of a child's hominid skull, or a humanlike species that walked upright. The discoverer, Professor Raymond Dart, called it *Australopithicus Africanus*, or southern African. It came to be known as the Tang Baby and was only about six-years-old when it died over 1 million years ago. Nothing that old previously had ever been found that approximated a hominid species. Paleontologists assumed that earlier forms of human-like beings had died out as a species. Scores of additional hominid primates have since been found.

In the 1930s Louis and Mary Leakey began looking for clues to human ancestry in the Olduvai Gorge in northern Tanzania. In 1959 they made one of their most remarkable discoveries, that of a teenage male, not a true human, but a hominid. The Leakeys discovered a complete male skull in 1959 they christened *zinj*, the first *australopithecus* found outside of South Africa, and reliably dated it at 1.8 million years old.

Richard Leakey, Louis and Mary's son, searched for human fossil remains in Kenya for decades. He found about 15,000 biological fossils remains, including over 300 early hominid remains. About seventy pieces are of *Homo erectus*, a development of hominid species that lived approximately 1.5 million years ago.

The female fossil known as Lucy, discovered in 1974 by my colleague Donald Johanson, became famous as a member of the new hominid classification of *Australopithecus afarensis* dating from 3.2 million years ago.

The latest hominid discovery is of another child fossil known as the Dikika baby, a girl of about three when she died, dating from 3.3 million years ago, found in the same Afar region of Ethiopia.

Neanderthals lived in western Asia and Europe 250,000 years ago. By 28,000 years ago the fossil record vanishes and presumably Neanderthals disappeared.[9] The consensus among scientists is that Neanderthals (named after the valley in Germany where the first fossil was found in 1856) is an extinct hominid species distantly related to modern humans. Speculation about whether or not Neanderthals and *Homo sapiens* interbred has not been altogether discounted.

Tests on the mitochondrial DNA of twenty-four Neanderthals and forty early modern humans by Drs. David Serre and Svante Paabo of the Max Planck Institute of Evolutionary Anthropology in Leipzig showed no signs of genetic contributions. The conclusion is that they are two distinct species.[10] By 20,000 years ago a new, more resilient strain of hominids began to be found everywhere on the earth: the Cro-Magnon branch of *Homo Sapiens*. Specialists assume that this hominid species originated in Africa from a single female about 200,000 years ago, and that this woman is the common ancestor of all living humans.

One of the most complete humanoid skeletons is *Homo Ergaster*, a six-foot tall specimen known as Turkana Boy, a species that lived from 1.4 to 1.9 million years ago. The most amazing conclusion is that human DNA is a 98.8 percent match with chimpanzee DNA, and about a 96 percent match with other primates. By 2005 even chimpanzees would have had cause to rejoice as a species since they, together with humans, chickens and mosquitoes and a few other inauspicious creatures have had their genomes completely sequenced.

Great accuracy had been achieved in dating procedures to decipher more precise ages. Volcanic ash, for example, in which human fossil evidence is often found, yields potassium and argon gas which decay at a fixed rate and which therefore can be precisely dated. But DNA evidence tells the tale of human origins more compellingly. By the mid-1980s scientists extracted DNA from a 40,000 year-old baby mammoth and found that it only differs by 1 percent from modern elephants. This implies a common ancestor from around 5 million years ago.

A new process known as Preimplantation Genetic Diagnosis (PGD) allows prospective parents to test their embryos for the possibility of children developing genetic diseases like cancer, cystic fibrosis, or sickle cell anemia, or other cripplers like Huntington's disease. The mother's eggs are collected after hormonal stimulation, and then each egg is fertilized by the prospective father's sperm. The fertilized eggs grow in a Petri dish and at the 8-cell stage of division, a cell known as a blastomere is removed to see whether or not its embryo contains any defective genes from either parent. If there are any defective genes they are discarded and donated for research, and the good genes implanted back in the prospective mother or frozen for future use.[11]

SIGNIFICANT DATES IN HUMAN HISTORY

- Human skeletons have been found in the Republic of Georgia dating from 2 million years ago.
- 38,000 years ago western Europeans were mass producing beads making holes with sharp edged stones; 32,000 years ago a man carved an ancient horse from mammoth ivory, found at Vogelherd, Germany.
- More than 30,000 years ago artists were painting animal figures on the walls of caves in southern France.
- 28,000 years ago a 60-year-old man was buried in an elaborate burial ceremony, interred with rich grave goods and bracelets, necklaces, and pendants. Found in Sungir, Russia, he was cloaked with a tunic on which hundreds of mammoth ivory beads had been sewn— the oldest and most exotic human burial yet uncovered.
- 26,000 years ago Cro-Magnon man, in what is today's Czech Republic, was baking clay statuettes in kiln.

This genetic testing is especially helpful if parents already have a child with an inherited disorder and want to prevent further children from its ill effects, or if one or both parents know that they, or other members of their families, carry a genetic disorder that they might pass on to their children. The process is expensive and raises the questions about whether anyone should be meddling with the natural order in human propagation.

The ethical debates spawn more questions than answers: When does human life begin? For that matter, when is something, like a virus or a cell, alive? The human body consists of some 100 trillion cells, each alive in a sense. So is the human body only an aggregate of many living cells and not a single living organism? Will every human organ be able to be reproduced for replacement as one or another organ becomes diseased or damaged? The reality of implementing that science, despite the controversy, is technologically years away. And the ethical controversy is that human embryos are not always destroyed in the process of obtaining stem cells. On one side of the argument are advocates for the sick, and on the other side advocates for the unborn.

Moreover, we're not even sure of what matter is yet.

The present state of atomic, nuclear, and high-energy physics is using particle accelerators to detect smaller and smaller bits of matter with no evidence that there might not be even smaller particles to be detected. When I was studying chemistry and physics in high school, I was fascinated by the atomic theory. Since then, scientists have discovered that protons in the nucleus of the atom are composed of two "up" quarks, each with a positive two-thirds electrical charge and one "down" quark with a negative one-third charge. A neutron consists of two down quarks with a negative one-third charge, and one up quark with a positive two-thirds charge.

The issues of the Future a wise God
Veils in the dark impenetrable Night,
And smiles if mortals stretch
Care beyond bounds to mortal minds assigned. [12]

The progress of our understanding of the natural world has advanced but runs head first into the myths embedded in religions.

Intelligent Design

Clashes of cultural values are integral to the continuing experiment in democracy, and conflicts between religion and science are a perennial subtext to that unique American experience. However, because U.S. Supreme Court rulings now prohibit creationist accounts of the origin of life in schools, arguments favoring divine intervention, known as Intelligent Design, have emerged as an alternative voice against the teaching of evolution in science classes. Intelligent design suggests that some organisms, such as human eyes, are far too complex to have developed chaotically or randomly and that, therefore, evolution alone cannot explain biological phenomena. [13] The public controversy with creationism has created a sideshow to science. Science showed that humans are related to animals by slightly modified degrees and not by kind, or by a special category known as species.

Intelligent Design advocates are fond of using a complex part of the anatomy to suggest an intelligent designer. The eye is a frequent example. But the evolution of an eye can be traced in mollusks. The limpet, for example, has a layer of transparent membranes that senses light with photosensitive cells but cannot form an image. Beyrich's slit shell has a deeper eyecup and gives more direction about a light source but again has no image. A chambered nautilus has a gap at the top of an eye chamber that focuses light on a rudimentary dim image. A murex has an enclosed eye pocket with fluid that acts like a primitive lens and focuses light on a retina. An octopus has more advanced vision, a complex eye with a protective cornea, colored iris, and a focusing lens. [14] In other words, eyes have evolved from simple to complex over long periods of time with changes in eye-building genes.

Yet I discovered to my dismay when I had both an appendix and a gall bladder removed that these were useless organs. I politely asked whether there were others I should know about. Perhaps ancient ancestors had need of them for unknown reasons. Why a designer would insert useless organs only for the purpose of having others remove them surgically when they became troublesome is worrying as it implies an imperfect design.

Yet the concept of intelligent design is ancient and appears in both pagan and Christian literature. The idea appears in *On the Nature of the Gods* written by Cicero about 50 BCE:

The first point then, said Lucilius, does not seem to require any argument to prove it. For, when we look up at the heavens and contemplate the celestial bodies, what can be so plain and obvious as the existence of a supreme divine intelligence by whom all these things are ruled?[15]

Likewise, Boethius, the Christian author of *The Consolation of Philosophy* who was Roman Consul under the Emperor Theodoric, noted in about 520 CE:

I could never believe that events of such regularity are due to the haphazard of chance. In fact, I know that God the Creator watches over His creation. The day will never come that sees me abandon the truth of this belief.[16]

If the evidence for evolution, with all its compelling data, were to be laid out alongside intelligent design, with only weak argument and logic in its favor, the contrast would be unmistakable. Even the logic is flawed. I see a pheasant and shoot it. I kill it designedly. An innocent golfer stands under a tree and is struck by lightning. Does anyone believe that God designedly killed this man? Where is free will in the equation? If neither the death of a mosquito nor a man is designed, then there is no reason why their origins should be designed either.

And although Intelligent Design advocates see design in individual organisms they do not argue about the similarities between species. There are hundreds of genes that occur in both humans and bacteria. Why would an Intelligent Designer design common genes in both humans and bacteria and parasites that make it harder to treat infections? Drugs that can kill the bacterium can also kill the human, an important evolutionary prescription to know if you want to remain healthy . . . or just alive.

Great indeed, we confess, is the mystery of our religion. (Tim. 3:16)

The simplistic argument that evolution is *just a theory,* as if that offhanded comment made its findings mere hunches, is meant to deride the discoveries and promote the inerrancy of scripture. A theory in science may appear to be speculative, but actually is not just a guess, but a model that best describes the preponderance of evidence. What Intelligent Design advocates fail to recognize is that the idea of intelligence, and the existence of one or more deities, are themselves just theories. Creationism and Intelligent Design are not theories, as we understand statements for testing truths, but political and religious promotions. Yet almost half of all Americans, as we saw, believe that the earth and humans were created nearly simultaneously.

Despite unambiguous U.S. Supreme Court rulings, many school districts repeatedly and insidiously attempt to undermine students' full entry into the modern world by promoting a biblical interpretation of the universe, which in turn frustrates science teachers.[17] Moreover, some school boards confuse the concept of evolution, even the facts of human development, with natural selection, or a theory of the origin of organic life and humans. Such combined unambiguous religious persuasions, flawed political activities, weak judicial knowledge, and fiscal irresponsibility in challenging established legal principles damages the image of education as a source of learning and free inquiry and makes schools appear as mere extensions of churches.

When kindergarten students in one class found a mouse for their animal exhibit they were unsure whether it was male or female. Their teacher decided they should vote on their choice. This was good for teaching democratic thinking, but bad science. Democracy and science are not competing theories. Neither are creationism or Intelligent Design and natural selection.

Such misapplied political correctness is dangerous not only to American culture but also to education. No one can blame parents for wanting to protect their children from negative influences of popular culture and themes that are offensive to their religious beliefs. Even though the religious right consistently has lost court battles, it effectively has bankrupted many textbook publishers and maligned the professionalism of science and science teachers. Projecting only a biblical version of biological life is an affront to practicing scientists and an indignity to all informed citizens.

A geological argument against intelligent design can be found in subterranean caves, such as Kartchner's cave in southeastern Arizona, which was discovered only in 1974 and not opened as a state park until 1988. The limestone deposits in this cave were formed about 330 million years ago when sand was deposited from ancient seas. When the movement of tectonic plates and volcanic activity caused the earth to buckle and mountains to form about 200 million years ago, these deposits tilted. As water trickled through crevices in the earth, some deposits eroded and escaped through fissures in the rocks. About 1 million years ago, as a large cavity displaced crusted matter, water began to seep from the cave ceiling. The slowly dripping water seeping through innumerable cracks left deposits of carbonic acid forming calcified stalactites hanging from the ceiling and stalagmites forming on the floor. For a stalactite to form one inch takes about 750 years.[18]

There is no fundamental difference between man and the higher mammals in their mental faculties.[19]

If Darwin had not proposed the theory of natural selection, his co-discoverer Alfred Wallace, who spent more than twelve years in the field, more than twice as long as Darwin did, would have alerted the public to its relevance. So Darwin today absorbs the brunt of the criticism, and he has indeed been its greatest exponent and descriptor. But the theory itself would have still been validated over time regardless of its first expositor. Darwin and scientists maligned like him deserve inclusion in this study for courage in fostering the publication of their research and not retreating from conclusions or implications drawn from observations of the natural world.

CHAPTER FIVE
WITCHES AND OTHER PAGANS

O well done! I commend your pains;
And every one shall share i' the gains;
And now about the cauldron sing,
Live elves and fairies in a ring,
Enchanting all that you put in.
(Hecate in Shakespeare's *Macbeth*, Act IV, Scene 1)

Except for the Black Forest in Germany, large woodlands prevailed throughout Europe until the twentieth century. It is convenient to juxtapose pagans with the primitiveness of forest life, an irresistible comparison between the light of the city and dim light under a canopy of forest leaves. Dark, uninhabited, mysterious, and secretive, forests were the perfect locales for pagans, demons and mythical denizens not found in cities, creatures not only like elves, fairies, and pixies, but also goblins, Gorgons, and exorcised devils. Forests were saturated with evil spirits and shadowy satyrs where groves of trees hid temples of witchcraft, dens for warlocks, and sacrifices to Satan. The only sensible Christian thing to do was to cut down the trees and deny these creatures sanctuary and in their place erect cities and cathedrals of worship.[1] Cities emerged as the tabernacles of Christianity, and forests were denied their natural habitats for hunters and gatherers, where Hansel and Gretel get tricked into being cooked and Dorothy can never find the yellow brick road.

The forest will not support agriculture because rainfall is uncertain and sunlight reaching the floor precarious. It is a vast, dark place receptive to contemplation, which is why monasteries were built there, but hostile to ritual celebrations, except for covens. Only scavengers, predators, and non-Christians live in forests, creatures that live perpetually on the dark side, more animal than human, in a permanent state of arrested development. The mythical tales of Romulus and Remus, suckled by wolves before founding Rome, is a symbolic story of the emergence of cities from forest life. The shaggy wild man Endiku, from *The Epic of Gilgamesh*, also represents in fable the noncivilized in the hinterlands. Endiku is raised by wild animals that reject him after he has had intercourse with a human. Gilgamesh has to literally wrestle him in order to be tamed into the urban culture.

83

The great civilization of Angkor Wat built over a millennium ago, then lost for a half a millennium, extracted itself laboriously from dense undergrowth in the Cambodian jungle. Cities with pyramids of the Maya in the Yucatan Peninsula in eastern Mexico are exceptions to city life, an illustration of how an agrarian society flourished in a fetid and torrid jungle environment, urbanity in stone in the midst of tropical green, the prime incubators of diseases. Whatever the level of civilization attained, always a tenuous description, regardless of the devotions of believers, or however monumental the houses, edifices, temples and sanctuaries, the swamps, jungle, and forest inevitably reclaim their domains and swallow humanity's finest refinements. Forests do not long sustain burgeoning populations.

The urban/rural classifications, along with the Christian/pagan distinctions, are another example of mankind's ambition to create a hierarchy of social classes with the designers of such schemes invariably at the top of the anthropological pyramid. Eventually the barbarians, those outside the gates, would be subdued and joined the ranks of urbanites until a rising social consciousness in the twentieth century, the "greenies," made it fashionable to be connected to the environment.

Pagan Rites: The Quest for Spirituality

Pagan devotees, those observers of religious rituals who belong to occult associations existing at the margins of religions and the fringes of society, constitute only a fraction of seekers of a creative force or heightened consciousness. Witches, sorcerers, shamans, druids who worship the old Celtic gods, Satanists, Goths, and Heathens like the Forn Sidr group in Denmark who worship the old Norse gods, are a few of these groups. Christianity has portrayed them as possessed of the devil when mostly they are only intent on finding a form of spirituality outside of organized religion. Buddhists, Hindus, and most native peoples also seek spirituality. We have been acculturated through literature to believe that all witches are sorcerers, and are prejudiced against, for example, the Egyptian magicians in *Exodus* 7:11 "Pharaoh in turn summoned wise men and sorcerers, and they also, the magicians of Egypt, did likewise by their magic arts." Shakespeare's witches in *Macbeth* are a similar example. "Double, double toil and trouble; Fire burn, and cauldron bubble" (Act IV, Scene 1).

Rarely does a single shamanistic figure demonstrate his faith by dying for it. Nevertheless, witches and pagans are generally regarded unfavorably because they are outside the religious mainstream. Members of pagan practices and covens have largely come from former membership in established religions. For the purposes of this study they are dissenters broadly speaking and included here as a group, together with a few figures, because they are repeatedly referred to as heathens.

Pagan rituals include initiation rites, greeting behaviors, cleansing ceremonies, a sacred meal, chants and songs often conducted in a circle, an officiating priest, priestess, or shaman, and a code of ethics. Their ceremonies appear no different than those of a formal religion. The primary difference is that there is no standard creed or dogma, no prohibitions on food or drink (though often on drugs), and in some cases no god or deity to be worshipped.[2] Moreover, witches, conjurers, and sorcerers, who are presumed to have un-natural or magical powers, and assumed to predict the future, are viewed differently from priests, rabbis, medicine men and women, and chaplains whose occupations are consoling and healing, and who serve as official agents or intermediaries between earth and heaven.

Contemporary covens imitate the most ancient religious ceremonies. The stone circles of Stonehenge and Ashdown in England containing 800 megaliths are universally assumed to be Paleolithic centers of religious ceremonies that likely included dances, sacrifices, and festive and funeral processions. The inner sacred space becomes symbolically the center of the world, like the ancient site of Eleusis in Greece, where members enter into communication with the divine within the earth and from the sky.

Greek Origins

Pagan rites are of greater antiquity than monotheism, and therefore closer to the authentic origins of religious emotions and practices. Myths of heroic figures celebrated in literature often represent the quest for transcendence and immortality. The frenzied activities of followers of the cult of Dionysius, for example, had very ancient roots. Initiates into the mysteries of the Eleusinian rites—sworn to secrecy so no one knows what practices they conducted—were cultic rituals that sought communion with the Demeter and Persephone, the goddesses of agriculture.

The Greek myth of Hephaestus symbolizes the divine use of magic and the wizardry of the gods. Hephaestus was reputedly born crippled without male insemination by Hera, Zeus' wife. His ugliness and deformity caused Hera to throw him onto the island of Lemnos where he was rescued by two Nereids, Thetis and Eurynome, who hid him in a deep cave. For nine years he learned the crafts of the artisan and the smithy. In Homer's *Iliad* he makes the shield of Achilles. He builds a golden throne for Hera and makes nets, cords, and chains that bind goddesses like Aphrodite and hold men captive. The master of bondage, so to speak, the power of restraining, is the magician's power.[3]

But if Hephaestus is an illustration of the deity with physical limitations but extraordinary powers, Hermes (Mercury to the Romans) is the god who most represents a mythical magician. He is the son of Zeus and a nymph, Maia. He possesses a magical rod, the caduceus, the symbol of pharmacists, and a hat that makes him invisible. He steals the cattle of his brother Apollo, so he is a thief, but also the protector of herds and flocks, the patron of those on journeys, and can travel anywhere in the blink of an eye. He can guide the dead to Hades but is himself no lord of the underworld as that role belongs to Pluto. In short, Greek myth saw him as a mediator between the deities and men, a perfect agent for a magician, witch, or shaman. Hence, the mythology of semi-divine intervention, not always for human good, precedes both Judaism and Christianity and continues to reside in contemporary consciousness.

Today, common controversies are court challenges to compel the Pentagon to allow a Wiccan pentacle to mark the grave of a veteran. The Department of Veterans Affairs permits thirty-eight symbols on government-issued grave markers. The Wiccan pentacle had not been among them. Patrick Stewart of Fernley, Nevada, who was awarded the Bronze Star and Purple Heart, died in Afghanistan when his helicopter was shot down. His wife fought the government to honor the memories of Wicca veterans killed in battle with the Wiccan symbol on their grave markers. The Department of Veterans Affairs agreed to add the Wiccan pentacle to its list of approved religious symbols on April 20, 2007.

Neo-paganism and witchcraft practices are a continuation of a heritage of ancient religious practices that predate both Judaism and Christianity. They are not devil-worship rituals represented by sadistic-looking semi-human figures with cloven feet and tails, or figures like the Wicked Witch of the West in *The Wizard of Oz* (1939), or the three witches in *MacBeth,* associated with fertile medieval imaginations. Wiccans do not worship Satan or practice black witchcraft.

The following example comes from medieval Ireland during a period in civilization when superstition appeared to be the principal source and inspiration for human motivation.

Alice Kyteler, Medieval Irish Witch

Lady Alice Kyteler was born in Kilkenny, Ireland, of Anglo-Norman parentage. Her family came to Ireland from Normandy in 1169. Her father died in 1298, and as a young woman of eighteen she inherited all his family property and business. She married William Outlawe, the brother of the chancellor of Ireland, and bore him a son. But within a few years husbands William, Adam, and Richard all died under mysterious circumstances, some said because Dame Alice was engaged in demonology. Then about 1320 she married her fourth husband, Sir John Le Pour, while she was still seeing Robin Artisson, her lover and, some claimed, a demon.[4]

When Sir John took painfully ill he went to see the local Bishop where he presented a case that his wife was a witch and devil-worshipper. Dame Alice had already been suspect because of the mysterious deaths of all her former husbands, so she was under serious ecclesiastical investigation. The Bishop of Ossory, Richard de Ledrede, excommunicated her. Here were the charges against her:

- Denying the faith of Christ and the Church; not worshipping the body

of Christ and not hearing the mass or receiving the sacrament.
- Propitiating the demon, Robin Artisson, by sacrificing animals and scattering pieces of them at crossroads.
- Seeking advice from demons.
- Using the church for nocturnal meetings in which candles were burnt.
- Making powders and ointments of ingredients like the flesh of non-baptized children, worms, herbs, and the intestines of cocks all boiled in the skull of a beheaded robber.

In parts of Ireland today these activities might be considered common, but in the fourteenth century they could ruin your reputation and get you torched.

But because of Alice's wealth and status the bishop was arrested and placed in Kilkenny castle prison. The bishop retaliated by placing the diocese under an interdict, meaning that no religious ceremonies of any kind could be performed. The lord justice entered the fray and ordered the bishop to lift the interdict. The bishop officially requested that Dame Alice be charged with sorcery under civil law. At this point the lady thought it prudent to visit her relatives in England, including King Edward II. Her maid was not so fortunate, and after confessing to the standard medieval menu of demonic atrocities, she was burned at the stake on November 3, 1324.

After a thorough search of her quarters after Alice's escape, some incriminating evidence emerged: a "pipe of ointment." Even then men were unaware of what a dildo was.

Kyteler's Inn in Kilkenny, established in 1324, still accepts patrons.

The circumstances of this bizarre figure and incident, which today might be grist for a TV documentary, crime scene investigation, or police blotter episode, are not so odd as is the conclusion—that this eccentric woman, who may indeed have been wholly or partially responsible for the deaths of her husbands, was possessed of evil demons and conducted sorcery, at the time a civil offense. This thinking prevailed right through to colonial America.

By 1484 the practice of witchcraft was so widespread that Pope Innocent VIII issued a papal bull forbidding the faithful to consult witches as it was then popularly believed that their presumed powers were actually real, but under the influence of the devil, who was after all a spiritual being. However, witchcraft became more popular simply because the pope had stated his belief in it. Nevertheless, in 1485 forty-one women were burned in Como alone, and scores more condemned by secular authorities in Brescia to a similar fate. Then, in 1510, another 140 were burned at Brescia for witchcraft and more than 300 in 1514, again at Como.[5] Clearly, something wicked was in the air . . . or water.

Witches Among the Puritans

When my granddaughters Carlie and Stephanie went trick-or-treating during Halloween, they had no idea of the origin of dressing up as a witch in order to frighten adults into giving them whatever they asked. Witches could be scary because they could make you become possessed of evil spirits, or the devil himself, and place a curse on your household. Superstition historically has had a stranglehold on peoples' beliefs. But when superstition was combined with authoritarian ecclesiastical and civil rule, as it was in medieval Europe and the Massachusetts Bay Colony, the result may have been dishonor for suspect individuals, and historical infamy for institutions like the Inquisition and Salem witch trial magistrates.

> You must understand, sir, a person is either with this court or he must be counted against it, there is no road between. This is a sharp tie now, a precise time—we live no longer in the dusky afternoon when evil mixed itself with good and befuddled the world."
>   Judge Danforth in Arthur Miller's *The Crucible,* 1953

The dissenters to the Anglican religion fled from England to Holland in 1607 and then journeyed on the *Mayflower* to New England in 1620 with the intent of establishing a model religious commonwealth in the New World. The *Mayflower* was built as a cargo ship and was supposed to land in Virginia and not New England. Poor navigational skills were the least of its problems. There were 102 passengers on board, but only forty Puritans. The other passengers just wanted to go to the New World to make a better living. Will Butten, a young orphan boy serving as a servant for one of the families, died during the voyage as did one sailor. A baby boy was born to the Hopkins during the sailing, and Peregrine White was born right after the landing. Dorothy Bradford, William Bradford's wife, slipped on deck ice after the landing at Plymouth, fell overboard and was drowned. Six additional people died in December, 1620. Myles Standish's wife Rose died in January 1621 and another seventeen people in February. By March nearly half of the colony had died. They had all come to the wrong part of the New World at the wrong time of year with inadequate knowledge, skills, and provisions.

A second wave of about 1,000 immigrants arrived in 1630, and another 20,000 between 1630 and 1650. These believers established a theocracy in colonial New England, where church and state codes were combined into one legal system. By the time of the arrival of the Puritans, hundreds of witch trials were occurring throughout Europe and there were thousands of victims, 75 percent of them women.

Once admitting to the presence of evil in the world, it is a relatively easy to anthropomorphize it, demonize its presence, then to ascribe to it powers to enter humans and change behavior. The Catholic Church has rituals for exorcising the devil from individuals thought to be possessed. Witches are also thought to be a substitute for the devil operating through vulnerable women and impish intermediaries. Sometimes girls just want to have some fun at the expense of somber adults by playing tricks and manufacturing amusing stories. But in an age of superstitious adults, this could imply they were possessed by the devil, no fun at all. You have to know your audience.

The Puritans, who had lived in England since 1564, followed the strict teaching of John Calvin, the Swiss Protestant reformer. They exercised strict codes in dress and liturgical practices, and deemphasized all outward symbols of religious authority and ritual. They deplored, for example, the *Book of Common Prayer*, and relied exclusively on the Bible. They emphasized the authority of scripture and the community of the baptized. The characteristics of Puritanism included a hatred of popery, a dedication to preaching, obedience to church rules, and a loathing of depravity and licentiousness. Today's definition of a religious fundamentalist might be too liberal for a Puritan, but both would be united in opposition to reason, science, and the follies and dangers of secular learning.

Puritans used the legal authority of legislatures and forced all students to conform to Puritan beliefs. Since Puritans believed that the child was born in sin, children needed strict discipline to control their appetites and impulses. Man is evil, Satan or Lucifer is present, and everyone must be vigilant about preventing satanic influences.

But it wasn't always clear in the interrogations, ordered to determine whether or not a woman should be held for trial, or whether those questioned were witches or just the victims of witchcraft. Muttering might be perceived as a placing curse. Was a dead horse, a limp ox, a sick cat, or fits among the maids a curse that had been inflicted on a household? Indeed, several dogs were also massacred together with victims of alleged witchcraft as these wretched animals too were thought to have been possessed. Welts on the body might signify that the devil inhabited one's body. Afflicted girls, often exhibiting seizures (or faking them), who might bring testimony against a widow neighbor for alleged abuses, seem to have been standard courtroom theatrics used as evidence of the presence of evil in the accused. No one suggested the evil might be in the law or the minds of judges or authorities.

It is therefore not surprising that witchcraft imported into America was also a statutory offense punishable with death in England from 1563 to 1736.[6] Two especially zealous men, Matthew Hopkins and John Stearne, instituted a vicious campaign of witch hunting in England. They toured Essex on horseback and found evil demons and witches everywhere. From 1645 to 1647, during a time of turmoil when Oliver Cromwell's Parliamentarians were conducting a civil war with the royalists of Charles I, Hopkins and Stearne caught, interrogated, and brought before magistrates at least 250 suspected witches, of which more than a hundred were hanged. Hopkins and Stearne were popular with the clergy and villagers, even though their legal methods were suspect.[7] In 1676, eighteen people accused of witchcraft were burned at the stake in Essex. The last known hanging for witchcraft in England was in 1716, and the last execution in 1722 in Scotland. Laws against witchcraft were repealed only in 1736.

From 1638 to 1691 more than 120 people, 88 women and 32 men, were suspected of witchcraft in all New England. About thirty-eight of these cases were discovered to be slander suits, and of the eighty-three actual trials only eleven to seventeen resulted in convictions. Three guilty verdicts were reversed. [8] Some sense of justice and commonsense had prevailed. But the following year, from March to October of 1692, hundreds of suspected witches were imprisoned in Salem village (now Danvers) Massachusetts, ranging in age from four to seventy-one, as witchcraft fever ran high. Nineteen were hanged, many were tortured, and all were asked to name accomplices in alliances with the devil.

These actions in colonial America against presumed witchcraft, like the machinations of the Inquisition in fifteenth century Spain and the religious upheaval and wars in Europe in the sixteenth century, demonstrate the abuse of combining civil and ecclesiastical power. The Puritan ethic of hard work, self-discipline, self-reliance, moral rectitude and spiritual values has informed the collective American consciousness. Nevertheless, the ruthlessness of religious persecution in America's early history reminds us of the need for perpetual vigilance against the abuses of religious zealotry.

Zealous magistrates in seventeenth century England, combined with conniving people who harbored grudges against neighbors and plentiful doses of superstition, were the combustible ingredients for waging a war against Satan. Surprisingly, accused women often confessed to the most outrageous behaviors, like copulating with the devil and keeping creatures that were his familiars as pets.

The Latin word *incubus* means nightmare and its mythology arose in medieval times to symbolize a male demon having intercourse with women at night. The woman will usually experience coitus as a dream and not typically awaken. Should a child result of this questionable union, it might be deformed or possess magical or even evil capabilities and tendencies like a wizard. This medieval superstition still dominated Puritan thought and hence the presence of a deformed child, absent the modern knowledge of the multiple causes for such biological anomalies, fuelled the concern that somehow a demonic presence had literally inserted itself into a Puritan stronghold.

Vulnerable women were essentially coerced into fabricating horrendous tales to please their accusers so they could find some solace for intimacy and kindness in an indifferent world. The mania for witchcraft hunts were fueled by innuendo, gossip, superstition, bad blood, bad faith, and bad laws. Ironically, few men were found to be warlocks.

Mary Dyer (1611–1660)

In 1959 the Massachusetts General Court ordered a bronze statue erected in Mary Dyer's memory on the grounds of the State House in Boston. Who was this extraordinary woman to have a statue in her likeness erected in one of Boston's most esteemed locations?

Mary Dyer was born in England in 1611 and hanged on Boston Commons in 1660, a victim of religious ignorance, intolerance, and bigotry. Authorities viewed her Quaker belief, which she triumphantly proclaimed on the scaffold, as an affront to their presumed sanctity and a threat to the religious purity of the colony. She was convicted only of being a Quaker, not a witch. But in Puritan Massachusetts in the mid-seventeenth century, there was no legal difference among the magistrates between possession by the devil and sectarian beliefs.

There was a relatively high intellectual ferment in colonial New England in the seventeenth century, but it was primarily theological, not tempered by enthusiasm for scientific inquiry or literary and aesthetic pursuits occasioned by the Renaissance. The Puritans were not the only adventurers escaping from the turbulence of religious conflicts in Europe, as the Spanish settled in St. Augustine in 1565, the French in Quebec in 1605, the Dutch in New Amsterdam in 1624, and the Swedes in Delaware in 1638. But the Puritans made the largest contribution to American letters of any seventeenth century colonists, though the output was essentially devotional. The peculiar combination of a dogmatic, intolerant, and authoritarian religion with an educated leadership created an unusual community that regarded learning as sacred as belief and moral behavior. However, it also regarded sectarian belief as heretical and worthy of death, an unenlightened view.

In the church at St. Martin's in the Fields in London in 1633 Mary married William Dyer, a milliner and a Puritan. The young couple immigrated to Massachusetts in 1634 and was admitted into the Puritan church in December 1635.[9] By 1637 Mary had given birth to a stillborn daughter (she would eventually have six children), whose deformity was speculated to be the devil's work. Once it became known that Mary had given birth to a deformed child she had it secretly buried. According to existing midwife instructions, the Boston authorities had the body exhumed. This resulted in the exile of William and Mary from the colony by Governor John Winthrop.

Moreover, Mary had become captivated by the personality and teachings of her friend and midwife, Anne Hutchinson, who would be excommunicated for her beliefs in personal conscience and individual revelation.[10] On the face of it, such pacifism seems to be a minor theological difference. But in the seventeenth century, Quakers believed in the power of personal and direct revelation as the key to salvation, and did not believe in the trinity, the divinity of Christ, or the scriptures. Such individuals lived in peril in colonial New England.

Banished together with Anne Hutchinson, Mary left Massachusetts in 1638 for Rhode Island where her husband was one of the founders of Portsmouth and Newport and later attorney general. The Dyers established a farm in today's Newport. But when news arrived that Charles I had been beheaded in 1649 and Oliver Cromwell installed as protector, Mary felt compelled to return to England alone. She left William and her six children in 1650 and remained in England until 1657. William came to London in 1652 to negotiate a new charter for Rhode Island but left on the return voyage without Mary who stayed on for another three years. While in England she fell under the spell of George Fox, the founder of the Quakers, and seemed to have found in him her religious calling. When she landed in Boston in 1657 she was immediately arrested for being a Quaker. Husband William had to hasten from Newport to Boston to demand her release, a request that was granted because of his official position in the Rhode Island colony, with the promise that she never return. Her independent spirit could not resist the challenge to her new religious courage.

Unknown to William, Mary slipped out of Newport in 1659 to go to Boston to visit fellow Quaker Christopher Holder and inmates William Robinson and Marmaduke Stevenson. She was arrested again. William wrote a long letter pointing out that no law existed allowing for her imprisonment. Holder was released and immediately returned to England. Governors Thomas Temple of Nova Scotia and John Winthrop of Connecticut, and son of the late governor of Massachusetts pleaded for her release. Mary's eighteen-year-old son William, with his father's blessing, journeyed to Boston, re-directing the ship he captained, to plead for his mother's release personally.[11] By a vote of 12 to 11, with one absent sick member, the General Court in Boston on October 19, 1658, made the practice of being a Quaker punishable by death. Thus, on October 27, 1659, with this new pernicious law as their precedent, the jailers walked Robinson, Stevenson, and Mary Dyer to the gallows.

While still on the scaffold, and after Stevenson and Robinson had been hanged, using the threat of death as a symbol of intimidating power, the authorities reprieved Mary at the last minute by the primary intervention of her son, William, who carried the signed document for her reprieve with him on a ship to the Azores. Her sentence was commuted with the understanding that she was to leave Boston and never return.

Later, Mary was visiting fellow Quakers on Shelter Island off eastern Long Island. She was instructing African slaves and Indians, at their request, in her Quaker faith, when news came that the Massachusetts authorities were ready to circulate a document about her in England justifying their use of the legal system and courts against her. The document noted that a similar law had been passed in England against Jesuits. Mary was incensed, and in late April 1660 she left Shelter Island for Boston.[12] Husband William, still tending the farm in Newport, and sympathetic to his wife's religious ideal but unconvinced of the necessity of flaunting it, did not find out about her decision to return to Boston for another week. He knew the law was inexcusable but did not believe it necessary that his wife should challenge it with her life. He loved her deeply after twenty-seven years of marriage. Nevertheless, he wrote to the Boston magistrates again pleading to show mercy toward women.

On June 1, 1660, refusing to recant her beliefs, at age forty-nine she was hanged on Boston Commons.

Days later, on June 4, 1660, London was celebrating the return of royalty after eleven years of parliamentary rule and the accession of Charles II as king of England. When news of Mary Dyer's hanging reached the continent there was general outrage. On September 9, Charles II forbade the killing of Quakers and told Massachusetts to send all dissidents to England for trial if need be. Emissaries with this royal writ arrived in Boston in November 1661 just in time to cancel the planned hanging of Winlock Christison the following day. All Quakers were immediately released from prison. The death penalty law was not fully repealed until 1681. The Royal Charter for Massachusetts was withdrawn in 1686 and settlers lost titles to the land. A British governor assumed control of the colony and he established Anglican rule in Boston. Thus, the Puritans lost both civil and ecclesiastical control of the colony, a crucial distinction that they had not accepted from the beginning of the colony's establishment.

The Salem Trials

The case of Mary Easty during the Salem Witch trials in 1692 is similarly instructive for the lack of proper legal procedures and the high level of toxic superstition of the townsfolk and the magistrates.

Mary Easty was baptized in Norfolk County England on August 24, 1634 and hanged in Massachusetts during the witch trials of 1692. Easty was fifty-eight-years-old. She and her husband had seven children and lived upon a large farm. Her interrogation followed the pattern of accusations by girls who said they had fits, and were speechless at times, this latter characteristic the more difficult to believe. The magistrate apparently never thought to question these girls separately, nor to offer counsel for the defendant nor allow them to have witnesses. The magistrates, in other words, assumed guilt and not innocence on the part of the accused.

After her initial interrogation Mary Easty was sent to prison but was unexpectedly discharged shortly afterward. She and her family mistakenly thought she would now be safe from further accusations. But after the same girls claimed to have been perturbed again because of Mary's so-called machinations, a second warrant was issued two days later for her arrest. She was awakened at midnight by the town Marshall and taken back to prison where she was placed in chains. She was tried and condemned to death on September 9 and executed on September 22, despite her own eloquent plea to the court for reconsideration.

Easty's surviving family was compensated twenty pounds from the state government in 1711 for her wrongful execution.

Viewed impassively, the court, magistrates, and Massachusetts officials were simply eliminating potential threats to community harmony and promoting social cohesion. In the process, however, they conferred the worst historical blotch on colonial America, corrupted the very virtues they preached, and vitiated all known legal procedures. Their dictatorial use of the courts condemning vulnerable women based on the word of conniving adolescent girls even stung England which had long since given up the use of star chamber courts. The crown eventually restored Anglican rule in New England.

We easily use the term "medieval" to describe such barbaric illegalities in the name of religion as those in colonial New England in the 1690s, thinking that such abhorrent practices are anachronistic. Then we recall that even today tribal and clan beliefs exist in the Middle East, where men can murder their wives, daughters, and sisters with impunity for violating the family's so-called honor and that cases against the perpetrators are rarely prosecuted. In Malaysia in 1976, newspapers routinely reported on factories where young women worked suddenly emptying when so-called *bomohs*, local devil spirits (also a Malay witchdoctor), entered their workplace. One woman would sense the presence of a bomoh spirit and scream full throttle. Then all the women would run screaming from the factory and supervisors would have to close work for the day because the women would not return until the devils they thought present had exited the building.

A few conscientious men like Increase Mather, father of Cotton Mather, argued that although witches needed to be exterminated, every precaution should be taken to make convictions based on hard evidence. After all, the supposedly evil deeds were actually performed by devils who could not be prosecuted, so that convicting an intermediary human had to be beyond a reasonable doubt. How could any court prosecute a woman harboring evil intent whose body, and by implication her mind too, was assumed by an intangible spirit? Confession, usually provided by torture, became the evidence of choice for conviction.[13]

Besides the Rhode Island Charter, it would take more than another century before legal statutes embodied religious toleration. The next crucial document came from Virginia, written by George Mason.

> That no man shall be compelled to frequent or support any religious worship, place or ministry whatsoever, nor shall be enforced, restrained, molested or burthened in his mind or goods, nor shall otherwise suffer on account of his religious opinions or beliefs; but that all men shall be free to possess, and by argument to maintain, their opinions in matters of religion, and that the same shall in nowise diminish, enlarge, or affect their civil capabilities.
> Virginia Statute for Religious Freedom, 1786

But not until the First Amendment to the U.S. Constitution would Americans, especially women, feel reasonably safe from fundamentalist religious threats.

Modern Wiccas

Neither witchcraft nor paganism has died in America, and witches still practice their merry craft. The rites of spring festival was held in southwestern Massachusetts in 2005, and about 500 assorted wiccas, druids, faeries, and Norse and Celtic practitioners danced around a Maypole to celebrate the link between the earth and sky. Paganism is an umbrella term like animism that partially describes some of those who worship nature and the outdoors and who celebrate ancient mystery rites. It includes a variety of activities that fall under the general category of earth-based spirituality. Thus, liberally defined, paganism is one of the fastest growing religious movements with more than fifty sites in the United States.[14]

I have studied scores of profiles of individuals of all ages, sexual orientations and occupations who are, or seek to be, engaged in pagan rites and activities. They all have given themselves new names, such as "Willow Raven," or "Saturn's Child," that reflect their natural proclivities, or animistic or astrological inclinations. The profiles they use to describe themselves are revealing because they are self-descriptive. Most want to learn more about themselves and the intuitive processes. Many have recently moved into a new community and seem to be escaping a distraught past. Discounting those who are simply lonely and seek to move in a broader social circle not a part of formal religion, I sense insecurities coupled with longings to join people of like-minded natural and mystical and transcendent interests. All appear to have an independent personality streak.

There is no one defining characteristic of a wicca nor any single one ritual that encapsulates witches' belief, unless it would be an earth-based spirituality. In fact, modern pagans go by a variety of names and covens as broad as there are Protestant denominations, such as Druids, faeries, Dianics, Asatru and ceremonial magicians. The pole, symbolized by the May Pole dance, may be the closest to identifying their beliefs as the pole represents an axial relation to the center of the earth. One current website (at: http://www.witchvox.com) listed over fifty festivals in the United States in 2005.

Other naturalistic religious forms hold similar views of the sacredness of nature. Shintoism, for example, is a lingering Japanese belief that views the natural world as sacred. Animism, a word originating from the Latin *animus* for breath or spirit, is a religion that reveres the sacredness of all objects, even inanimate ones. Scholars think animism is the oldest form of religious belief, dating to the Paleolithic era about 40,000 years ago. Animism is a belief that still permeates much of Africa. In these natural contexts, polytheism, monotheism, and idolatry—designations used by subsequent religions to disparage and demonize beliefs without a written revelation—have no real meaning to animists.

The Maenads and Greek Mystery Rites

Similar festivals existed in the ancient world. The maenads, or *bacchae* after Bacchus, were women votaries and priestesses of Dionysius or Bacchus, the god of the vine, celebrated in Euripedes' play *The Bacchae*.

> But should the Theban state
> In rage attempt with hostile arms to drive
> My Bacchae from their confines, I will head
> My Maenads, and lead them to the fight.[15]

Maenads accompanied Dionysius on his journeys and officiated and danced at his orgiastic festivals. Their ecstatic frenzies are celebrated as the touchstone of heightened experiences. At least one feminist English coven imitates parts of the maenad rituals.

The story of Euripedes' *Bacchae* goes like this. The skeptical King Pentheus thinks the new youth in town has arrived to steal all the young women;

therefore, he has him arrested. In fact the attractive youth is the god Bacchus who has concealed his divinity, and the maidens are his women votaries. Miraculously, the women who had been confined in chains are freed and escape back to the woods. Bacchus tells Pentheus that he may not know the mysteries of the rites chosen by Zeus because "the orgies of the god abhor the impious." He promises to show him the mystery rites and clothes him in the dress of the occasion. He then commands his women maenads to exact their vengeance on him. They discover him and tear him apart as they would any hunted animal. The moral of the story is that the gods are not be mocked or denied, and that the mystery rites they attend or sponsor, like the bacchanal, shall never be known to the uninitiated.

The mysteries of Bacchus are secret rites held at night, generally in the mountain forests or woods. Women dressed in white vestments (or naked wearing only strings of beads) are dancing, perhaps to the accompaniment of flute music or drums, if the rite happens to be far removed from people. Hymns are chanted or songs sung. Divinity is present but infrequently observed. Wine or some narcotic is drunk, or sex or some ecstatic behavior is enjoyed to induce rapture or a light madness. This communal power gives the devotees uncommon strength.

The ceremonies and circumstances of ancient Greek mystery rites are similar with contemporary covens. It is more likely that current witches, as described by Margot Adler in *Drawing Down the Moon* (1979, 2006), resemble the Greek maenads, as described by Euripedes in *The Bacchae*. The modern idea of witches as demonic visionaries possessed of evil spirits is tainted by a Christian perception when the ceremonies are really derivative of much older rituals. The main difference is that modern covens view the deity present as female.

A recurring experience for a pagan newcomer is putting aside the rational explanations of what pagan culture means and simply digesting it. Some find the teachings and ritual silly and frivolous, while others find that there is a consoling sensation, that a force overcomes them when they find themselves in nature, or with witches at a ritual, and that they want to tap into that vibrant energy.

The journey of finding oneself in nature, through nature, or with nature is as old as humankind. Many who join covens have experienced an intuitive and responsive dimension to the attraction of joining a naturalistic religion. It is an uplifting feeling, perhaps of cosmic transcendence that characterizes the personal experience of animistic religions, accentuated by a bonding of social cohesion if one belongs to a coven. Regardless of how pagans categorize themselves or perform their rituals, they are almost universally regarded as heathens, if not sons and daughters of the devil.

The mythology we live by, enlivened with the belief in unknown powers we anthropomorphize as divinities, is overlaid with the realities of existence. We enter the world through the mysteries of conception (gods and goddesses), are born in a womb (the cave), and warmed with heat (fire), nourished by milk (mother archetypes) and the life of plants and animals (sacrifice). We struggle to find meaning and attribute problems to our fate or the intervention of deities.

Formal Western religions summarize in dogmas how God has revealed the plan for existence and formulas for deliverance. Informal religions like Shintoism have no divine plan and instead seek enlightenment like Buddhists and linkage with the powers in nature.

All religions, whether laden with systematic divine plans or with energies directed at experiencing transcendence, have imperfect conclusions about the mission of human life. Proposing the existence of spiritual beings excelling humanity in powers and truths, or in the energy of nature like Brahma, or through the expansion or emancipation of consciousness like the Buddha, lends a sense of significance to the ordinariness of human existence.[16] At the same time, many religions like witchcraft, introduce beliefs that are intellectually suspect, even ludicrous, with overtly personal experiences that are beyond validation. Nevertheless, the collective bonding of communities seeking any kind of spiritual union and fulfillment is a perennial human quest to better the present condition and to quiet perturbed anxieties about the future. Often, defending one's belief is something to die for.

PART II

THE LEGACY OF RELIGIOUS HERESY
AND DISSENT

CHAPTER SIX
PRE-CHRISTIAN DISSENTERS

Or as the heresies that men do leave
Are hated most of those they did deceive,
So thou, my surfeit and my heresy,
Of all be hated, but the most of me!
    Shakespeare, *A Midsummer Night's Dream*, Act 2, Scene 2

To understand how heretics emerged and dissented from orthodox religious faith, we have to return to the mists of prehistory to examine religious origins. My purpose in this chapter is to tell the story of ancient dissenters like ancient Greek philosophers who predate monotheistic religions and who challenged popular beliefs about deities. Their courage in challenging religious beliefs is as valuable as the heroism of contemporary dissidents. I add a couple of Chinese sages to illustrate the differences in religious thinking between Asia and the West. Then I explore Cicero, that illustrious Roman and perspicacious lawyer, orator and scholar whose treatise on the gods prepares us for the theological controversies and multiple heresies and heretics Christianity generated. Once Christianity became the established religion of the West, the idea of heresy became ingrained in culture and law.

Paleolithic Beliefs

The period roughly 40,000 years ago is known as the Paleolithic and represents a period when Neanderthal and early Cro-Magnon peoples lived in Europe. This was a time when early hunters who had a culinary affinity for cave bears began the peculiar burial practices of placing bear skulls and bone marrow in cave niches. One particular ancient bear skull was found in a tunnel cave high in the Austrian Alps. Here Neolithic man butchered, ate, and buried bear skulls in a ritualistic ceremony that some scholars speculate constitutes a primitive example of religion.[1] These ancient hunters apparently thought fit to keep the head and selected body parts apart from other eating practices.

Whether ancient humans pierced a tooth to wear as a pendant, drank beverages from the skulls of enemies or ancestors, placed bones, skulls, and carved amulets in crevices as so-called votive offerings, or believed that a carved stone figure of a woman with a distended belly was a goddess does not lead one to conclude that ancient peoples worshipped a divinity, or even that they believed in an afterlife. Not every cave with painted wall art was a sanctuary in our sense of a place for religious sacrifice. Rather, what these fossil remains could suggest is that Paleolithic people feared their ancestral dead returning to life to taunt them.

All such interpretations of ancient art, whether a drawn stick figure on a wall is a shaman or the scattering of human bones represents cannibalism or that a bird drawing on a pole symbolizes a tutelary spirit, must be approached with caution. Belief in spirits is old and its origins covered with millennia of dirt and rocks, but to thrust modern religious beliefs into that distant past is popular but pure speculation.[2]

A 2004 report in *The Proceedings of the National Academy of Sciences*, noting that carbon 14 dating was used in a five-year investigation from Oaxaca, Mexico, revealed changes in religious ritual that accompanied human social evolution. Before 4,000 BCE, a dance ritual existed from which no one was excluded. But with the establishment of permanent villages and a more sedentary lifestyle accompanied by the cultivation of maize, certain rituals were scheduled by solar or astral events and restricted to initiates who enjoyed a privileged social status. Whether this indicates that religion evolved with the development of society is problematic. But the correlation of astral and formalized rituals with known religious practices like the establishment of clerical hierarchies and the erection of temples in the Middle East and Mexico seems to indicate that religion, however understood, certainly matured with advanced societal development and cohesion in developing communities.

I note this caveat because the temptation to read the modern context back into prehistory is strong but unwarranted. We prefer not to categorize pre-historical peoples as heathen since in a religious sense they had not gotten the message yet from written revelation. So the temptation is compelling to somehow want to make them believe in a god who had not yet been revealed. Yet in another sense this insults the intelligence of these people about whom we can only surmise beliefs.

It is difficult to imagine a cultural context in which organized and doctrinal religion did not exist, which is why it is essential to mentally transport ourselves back into an era when mythic literature and poetic expression were the principal classifications of knowledge. There were no separate categories of learning and most of the subjects we consider elementary to our schooling existence did not exist. The varieties of religious impulses take many forms and we can understand much about religious diversity and the impulse for transcendence and new age visions from an examination of the Greek mystery rites.

Greek Mystery Religions

You were.
You are.
You will always be,
Supremely sacred Zeus.[3]

I include ancient Greek heretical thinkers because they raised the first questions about the gods and the relationship of humans to all deities, thereby defining what impiety and heresy would be and who heretics were. A formal heretic is a dissenter from established church doctrine. But its popular use as a non-conformist is widely accepted. It is in that nonconformist sense that I discuss in this section, and in the lives of a few early Greeks who gained notoriety through literary satire and philosophical dissent. Diagoras of Melos, for example, was branded a notorious atheist, and the Athenians sentenced him to death in 415 BCE for mocking the Eleusinian mysteries and discouraging people from getting initiated. You couldn't get more heretical 2,500 years ago.

Religion for the Greeks between the sixth and third centuries BCE was integral to Athenian civic life. Temples existed on most islands and on prominent hilltops. Mystery rites associated with designated deities like Orpheus drew devotees and initiates. Prayers, hymns and animal sacrifices occurred before and after major events like battles, treaties, celebrations, and even seasonal dramas. There was universal belief in multiple gods but no doctrine, sermons, or personal testimonials.[4]

Divination, oracles, and soothsayers were widely accepted because everyone wanted to know the future, to discover if the gods were favorable to their lives or petitions. Yet outright atheists like the Athenian aristocrat Critias, author of prose, poetry, biography, and city constitutions, and who was possibly implicated in the condemnation of Socrates, prospered with impunity. Dissent from traditional belief was not courageous for men like him because his aristocratic status gave him privileges denied commoners.

Philosophy originally arose independently from religion, and philosophers began openly to speculate about the gods, as they did everything else. By the third century BCE, the intellectual quest had largely incorporated religion into its speculative domain. When Christianity emerged as a new religious movement, having assimilated all of Greek philosophy and ancient religious beliefs not in opposition to its creeds, this process was reversed and forced the methods and substance of philosophy into conformity with its beliefs. Heretics then replaced dissenters.

The earliest dissenters, the so-called Pre-Socratic philosophers, were the first we know who examined the nature of the world, and the connection between divinity and humanity in the universe. Xenophanes may have been the first to declare that God could not exist in any human form. As philosophy matured into a staple intellectual pursuit, and one of the richest gifts investing the Eastern mind, it formulated the questions that would define free speech, wide-ranging discussions of humane ideas, ethics, and the early exploration of scientific inquiry.

We have only fragments of their works. They dissented as much from each other as from any ideas they had. We know more about them from subsequent commentators than from their own documents. The written fragments we do possess have been retained like post-it notes for inspiration by unknown owners, and they yield little about a consistent program of thought. But because they are fragmentary does not mean they are trifling. The remnants reveal insights into the nature of reality, into the nature of humans and divinities at the dawn of the age of speculation.

One man's ideas stimulated another's, someone challenged and disagreed with the proposals of a predecessor, another made radical interpretations, and soon a genius like Plato arrived to synthesize all existing knowledge and elevate the quest itself into a divine pursuit thereafter imitated by millennia of scholars. The themes of a god distant from his creation, the immortality and preexistence of the soul, the power of contemplation to make the soul divine-like are all Platonic in origin. The fact that we think of them as Christian themes shows how comprehensively Plato has been assimilated into Christian thought.

With tape recordings, videotapes, CDs, and instant messaging we have access to what people say and think and can know more or less simultaneously whether it is agreeable, controversial or explosive. Without modern devices we can only speculate from fragmentary writings what ancient writers actually believed and the degree of dissention their ideas generated. Momentarily return to this epoch millennia ago when literature itself was a modern invention.

Sources of the Literary Tradition

Had it not been for the discovery of the ancient Assyrian king Ashurbanipal's (669–633 BCE) library of 22,000 tablets preserving studies in astronomy, medicine, literature, and science on baked clay tablets we might never have known of the ancient world's intellectual treasures prior to biblical composition. Copying and editing literary works began at least six centuries prior to Ashurbanipal's library, so that 1,200 BCE is a reasonable estimate of the expansion of literature.[5]

No culture exists in isolation but each adds another layer on the artistic foundation by building on existing knowledge. Humans proliferate; the earth is oppressed; the gods are angry; mankind needs to be eliminated; the gods repent and allow one man to regain their trust. These themes resound in the *Epic of Gilgamesh*, in the Akkadian epic, the *Atrahasis* (c. 1,800 BCE), in the Greek story of Prometheus, and in *Genesis*. Greeks borrowed literary themes from the Babylonians and Akkadians, and biblical scribes borrowed from Greeks, Babylonians and Assyrians. It was only when religious orthodoxy reigned, among the Greeks prior to and during the lifetime of Socrates, among Jews after

Philo, or among Christians after Constantine adopted Christianity as the state religion, that those dissenting from the accepted religious persuasion became the subjects of opprobrium, exile, and in some cases death.

Pre-Socratic philosophers were impelled by dissatisfaction with mythical explanations of the universe and the origin of life, or by overpowering intellectual curiosity, or both. They speculated on how the natural world began and how and why it continues to exist. The creative spirit necessary to embark on speculative ventures about the composition of matter, the nature of stellar existences has marked the progress of civilizations of which we are the heirs. The fact that one or more particular view has become entrenched in our consciousness as specifically religious and not just theoretical is regrettable because canonical designations of truths have stultified further creativity and encouraged religious interpretations of reality.

Beliefs about gods during these early Greek centuries are not based on revelatory truths but on minds projecting the presence of omniscience, claiming that someone out there must be a know-it-all. The divinity of the gods arose, not just because of inherited mythical literary traditions from the Babylonians, but because of epistemological quests for knowledge. The argument became that if men could know so much there must be someone who knows not only what men know, but how and why everything fits together.

The Athenian legislative assembly between the sixth and third centuries BCE sometimes passed laws prohibiting "wrong-doing" against the gods because Athens had numerous deities. One of the first decrees was promoted in 432 BCE. The law allowed for prosecution of offenders who did not acknowledge the gods or anyone who taught that the heavens were not their habitations. This included most philosophers, an unpaid occupation that suddenly became more dangerous than infantrymen in war. Euripedes was accused but was acquitted. Anaxagoras, who wrote that the heavens were like rocks, fled into exile. Socrates fell ultimate victim. Athens about this time was on a war footing and would eventually engage Sparta for military supremacy the following year after this decree. It's possible that the legislature felt that any anti-patriot movement would dampen war enthusiasm and overturn divine favors, an argument that resonates in today's public policy debates.

As old as the study of philosophy is, it has fallen into disfavor among modern intellectual pursuits. Those who exercise one or more of its attributes, such as clarity, logic, and persuasion, generally are journalists or academics, occasionally lawyers, rarely politicians. But when philosophy was in its infancy in ancient Greece it was the principal pursuit of the mind, for conversation in drinking establishments, for study and contemplation, and not for just idle talk or as preparation for a job or occupation. It was pursued for its own sake, as art once was, as the monogram of Universal Pictures with the roaring lion, *Ars Gratia Artis*, "art for the sake of art," still reminds moviegoers. "Philosophy for the sake of philosophy" would not win any advertising slogans nor prizes for a catchy jingle selling commercial products. Consequently, to return to an epoch when philosophy was king, so to speak, we have to imagine that the discussions and writings about what the universe is, how it works, and how humans fit into nature—questions that still tickle our curiosity—were at an embryonic stage but universally pursued. And even then, antiestablishment types, which could include most philosophers, might find that they were unwelcome to authorities.

Anaxagoras (c. 500–428 BCE)

Anaxagoras, like all the earliest Pre-Socratic philosophers, was skeptical of the proclaimed deities and sought to provide a scientific explanation of the universe. Unlike Anaximander, who escaped official opprobrium, Anaxagoras was charged with impiety by his political opponents. Whether this meant that officials thought he was an atheist or merely a nonconformist to the civil order is unclear. At the time in Athens, impiety was considered a denial of the recognized state gods. The Romans adopted this code and applied it to Christians. Whatever his belief, Anaxagoras offended ordinary Athenians and their sacred rituals and claimed that neither the sun nor the moon were gods. He was acquitted through a friend's influence but sensibly thought it prudent to leave Athens and immigrate to Lampsacus (in today's Turkey) where he died at the age of seventy-two.

Absent an understanding of microscopic life, neither Anaxagoras nor any of these early philosophers could understand how visible elements could change from one substance to another, though everyone could observe that fire changed everything. He proposed that everything was composed of *seeds*, a term close enough to atoms or subatomic particles. His mechanical description of celestial bodies was not rivaled until Newton.

He proposed the concept of *nous*, or mind. He writes in *Fragments*: "Mind controls all things, both the greater and the smaller, that have life. Mind controlled also the whole rotation, so that it began to rotate in the beginning." This is a different version from Plato's chaos or the Genesis version of the beginning of existence.[6] By introducing mind and matter with such ingenuity, he proposed dualism before Descartes. "In everything there is a portion of everything except Mind, and there are some things in which there is Mind as well."[7]

Mind means that philosophy is a way for humans to approach the immortality of the gods. Mortals were similar to and yet somehow different from the gods the Greeks accepted, and certainly unlike the remote, transcendental god of monotheists. It was the Greek quest to find what seemed to be attainable, of ways to be like the gods, or at least find a solution to immortality. By the time of Plato and Aristotle, this mental leap of trying to reach immortality through poetic expression to approximate godlike attributes had extended to intellectualizing about the universe. This was playing mind games. A person who did not use thought processes was not alive. Philosophy replaced the old Greek religion.[8] Not until Christianity, and later Islam, when faith replaced thought, would heretics be formally condemned.

Mind might seem like a perfectly normal philosophical proposition since everyone thinks they have one. Discoveries in the neurosciences are slowly eroding that ancient concept, as the brain appears to perform all the functions associated with mind. But the interplay becomes problematic if one introduces a Divine Mind. If a Divine Mind knows the human mind, and all its thoughts and motives, then the extent to which the Divine Mind is a part of the human mind complicates philosophy and theology. If the Divine Mind knows all and pervades all, then it is everywhere at once—and this is pantheism—and the human mind is a participant in God's thought. On the other hand, if individual human minds participate somehow in a universal Human Mind, one must explain, but cautiously so as not to incur the wrath of officials, how this differs from a Divine Mind.[9]

Anaxagoras' original idea of mind would come to dominate the relationship of God to humanity and Christian theology for centuries. When the *Logos* was introduced by the evangelist John as a term for Christ (a term the Greeks would not have used for a deity, using instead a divine *Nous*), Christianity fell into the same ontological trap the Greeks created. By conceptually differentiating the mind and body and not emphasizing the unity of a person, and then accepting the idea of a soul from the Egyptians, theological commentators never could fully explain how mind was different from soul. Nor could they explain why mind, thought to be immaterial, had to die when the body did. No one explained whether or not, or how, the individual mind rejoined the body in the resurrection of the body as Paul proclaimed. Nevertheless, in the process of minds thinking about mind and soul after the establishment of Christianity, many heretics would be spawned, and a lively number of dissenters who decided that the silence of discretion was preferable to the boldness of disagreement against prevailing orthodoxies.

Protagoras (c. 490–420 BCE)

Young man, if you associate with me, on the very first day you will return home a better man than you came, and better on the second day than on the first, and better every day than you were on the day before.

Protagoras in Plato's *Protagoras*

Protagoras was an itinerant scholar who taught rhetoric and was a forerunner of the sophists who believed that anyone could be trained to use argumentation to persuade anyone of anything. Many users of rhetoric were unscrupulous, intellectually dishonest, and irreverent, many like people you may know or have encountered, especially those who want to sell you something. Rhetoric acquired a bad reputation in Athens because its cleverness promoted skepticism, adulterating the whole budding discipline, when its original purpose was simply to sway crowds or win lawsuits.

Protagoras claimed that man was the measure of all things, a radical idea because it implied that human knowledge and judgments are relative to the person and not emergent from a deity. "Then my perception is true to me, being inseparable from my own being; and . . . to myself I am to judge of what is and what is not to me."[10] If everything is relative, there is no basis to conclude that one appearance is truer than another. For the next few hundred years, Democritus, Plato, and Aristotle responded to this intellectual challenge and engaged the Western world in epistemology, philosophy's quest to discover the nature of knowledge as their Greek predecessors had coped with the nature of matter.

THE EVOLUTION OF RELIGIOUS IDEAS

ORIGIN	SOURCE	RESULT
Sumer	Awe & Wonder	Deities, Temples
Egypt	Burial practices	Immortality
Babylon/Canaan	Literature	Ritual & Sacrifice
Greece	Heroes	Semi-Divine persons
India/China	Consciousness	Meditation
Palestine	Literature	Sin, Loss of God
Greece	Gnosticism	Transcendental
Asia Minor	Philosophy	Doctrines of Belief
Roman Empire	Authority	Institutions of Religion
Arabia	Inspiration	Personal Revelation
Europe	Rebellion & Belief	Personal Interpretations of Christianity & Bible
America	Personal Revelations	New Religions (e.g., Mormonism)

Protagoras claimed that no one could know if the gods existed or not. "Concerning the gods, I have no means of knowing whether they exist or not or of what sort they may be. Many things prevent knowledge including the obscurity of the subject and the brevity of human life." Ancient sources claim that these positions led to his having been tried for impiety in Athens and his books burned.

The final word in this dialogue is a plea for virtue, not knowledge. Plato uses Socrates as an intellectual discussant to discover just how ignorant men are, and that the enjoyment of dialogue is honey enough to the mental palate. If there is a message here it is that there is no room for dogmatism in discovering truths, an admirable attribute lacking in later theological commentators. The key tribute is that the Athenian philosophic world moved from an investigation of the heavenly spheres to knowledge, and then to virtue and ethics. With Plato and Aristotle the West was introduced to human behavior and what constitutes the right kind of behavior. Ethics is born and its birth is secular, separate from conformity to divine commandments.

Empedocles (c. 492–432 BCE)

Empedocles was unusual because not only did he philosophize about the properties of the universe by proposing that the four elements of earth, air, fire and water permeated everything, but he was venerated in antiquity as a kind of shaman, mystic, proponent of democracy and holy man to whom miracles were attributed. The following quotation from a work attributed to Empedocles called *The Purifications* speaks to his self-proclaimed extraordinary powers.

> Friends . . . I give you greetings. An immortal god, mortal no more, I go about honored by all, as is fitting, crowned with ribbons and fresh garlands; and by all whom I come upon as I enter their prospering towns, by men and women I am revered. They follow me in their thousands, asking where lies the road to profit, some desiring prophecies, while others ask to hear the word of healing for every kind of illness.[11]

If not swooning from wine, Empedocles here is declaring that he is an immortal god. Was he fantasizing, or was he the product of the enticements of the Pythagorean mysteries or the mysticism of someone in a meditative trance? What people actually thought of him is unrecorded, but this passage is an example of a man who was not just contemplating the composition of the universe but revered for superhuman accomplishments.

He thought of himself as a healer, a philosopher, a prophetic mystic, and a god, and no one appeared to take offense at these declarations. Nonetheless, they are exactly the kind of characteristics that would be attributed to the contemporaries Apollonius of Tyana and Jesus nearly 500 years later. Thereafter anyone who claimed such qualifications for himself would assuredly be classified as a blasphemer. Nor were distinctions accepted between those convinced of the veracity of their claims and those merely deluded or mentally unstable.

We can regard these centuries as the beginning of the merger of philosophy and religion. Prior to the Pre-Socratic philosophers, the myths of Hesiod and Homer prevailed in the popular culture of the day and reinvigorated the deistic myths of the Babylonians. But beginning in the seventh century BCE we see intimations of the questioning of mythic beliefs. Xenophanes criticized divine anthropomorphism and would say God could not exist in a human form. Anaximander would say the gods are like humans in some ways. Most philosophers would conclude that it was impossible to know the certainty of divinity but that no one should minimize ritual practices and the cult of divination. It was an age in which it was possible to be a heretic without knowing it. Socrates didn't know.

Socrates (469–399 BCE)

I tell you that to let no day pass without discussing goodness and all other subjects about which you hear me talking and examining both myself and others is really the very best thing that a man can do, and that life without this sort of examination is not worth living.   Socrates, in Plato's *Apology*.

Socrates not only defined his age with high intelligence and personal courage, but influenced all succeeding philosophers. He represents that rare person, a teacher willing to die for his ethical principles, the epitome of a dissenter. He was interested in having people define themselves through a quest for moral knowledge. Like Confucius and Buddha, he is the ancient world's highest example of moral integrity and intellectual honesty, a teacher, and is rightly credited with founding morality and ethics in the Western experience.

Socrates follows in the philosophical tradition of free intellectual inquiry by challenging superstitious beliefs and social conventions, using logic to confound myth. He neglected his personal life to favor a role as a seeker of the truth and teacher of wisdom, less interested in scientific facts or cosmological wonders than in values and beliefs. But he was also practical, believing that philosophy was useful only for wisdom and right conduct, not just for idle speculation. He formulated the dialogue or dialectic, a questioning process for people to follow as they sought moral character. The Socratic method is essentially a technique whereby discussants pursue the implications of a statement, its truth or its falsity, until they discover some new truth. His incessant questioning and criticism of faulty thinking did not always win him admirers or converts to his cause. His death gave philosophy its first martyr. His martyrdom status would become widely accepted when Christian martyrs found his example illustrious and imitated his composure and assurance in meeting their chosen deaths for faith.

Socrates went daily to the agora, the marketplace, just below the Parthenon built during his lifetime on the hill in Athens, to teach and converse. He never considered himself a "public" person, that is a politician, but he was eventually persuaded to serve as chair of the executive committee of the world's first democratic legislature. Once, when the populace wished to put to death generals who had acted cowardly in war, Socrates resisted and refused to put the matter to a vote, thus earning many enemies.

Socrates' main question—can there be a natural ethic without a supernatural belief—challenged the conventional belief about the Greek gods. The religiously orthodox considered him dangerous. He was brought to trial before Athenian magistrates on charges of corrupting the youth of Athens with his ideas and of religious heresies against the gods. He was found guilty and allowed to commit suicide.

With Plato, Socrates' recorder, we have a well-rounded theology of the gods, and the rituals of necessary piety humans must show deities. By the third century BCE in Athens it was commonly understood that men were the possessions, if not the playthings of the gods, and that after death humans would receive divine judgment for their actions in life. Plato's dialogues of *Phaedo, Timaeus, Theaetetus,* and the *Laws,* which contain a section on how religion should be treated in an ideal state, would become incorporated into Christian dogma. After that, mere speculative dissenters would be heretics and all hell, literally in the minds of persecutors, would be available for their fate.

The Greek religious and philosophical experience is the meat and potatoes of the Western experience. But the Eastern experience is no less rich in virtue and in spiritual and mental experiments to find enlightenment.

Chinese Ideologies

The message of the Tao is renunciation in order to achieve wisdom, a call that is part philosophy, ethics, and search for enlightenment. It was first conceived and developed by Chuang-Tzu who lived c. 370–300 BCE. The Delphic-like oracular sayings collected by Lao-Tzu known as the *Tao-te Ching* would become more popular and definitely pithier. Life is subject to the eternal transformation of the Tao, in which there is no better or worse, no good or evil. Things should be allowed to follow their own course, and men should not value one situation over another. A truly virtuous man is free from the bondage of circumstance, personal attachments, tradition, and the need to reform his world. Chuang-tzu declined an offer to be prime minister because he did not want the entanglements of a court career.[12]

Although not as well known in the West as his immediate predecessors Confucius and Mencius, Hsun-Tzu (c.305–235 BCE) was one of the most seminal minds China ever produced. Like many compatriots in the Greek-speaking world in the third century BCE, Hsun-Tzu based his ideas on nature and reason, on human affairs and not on divine predilections, on the nature of mankind and not on spirits and seasons as the sources for human actions.

Unlike Mencius who thought that human nature came from heaven and is therefore good, Hsun Tzu believed humans were born evil with desires that left unchecked would result in misery and conflict: "order and disorder do not come from Heaven." Humans are evil and good character only acquired through education and training, an idea parallel to the belief about all humans born with original sin. By the time of the Sung dynasty (960–1279 CE) his writings were declared heterodox, just like a heretic, and he remained thereafter outside the mainstream of Chinese philosophy. He was eclipsed altogether when Buddhism dominated Chinese thought.[13]

His thoughts on behavior are pragmatic. If born with a fondness for profit a person will indulge in greed and it will lead him or her into personal strife. Courtesy and humility will disappear. If born with feelings of envy and hate, and a person indulges these, these negative characteristics will lead him or her into excess behavior, and all sense of loyalty and good faith will disappear. On the other hand, if one is born with sensual desires, a fondness for beautiful sights and sounds, one will indulge these and they will lead that person into wantonness. In these statements Hsun-Tzu anticipates the contributions of genetic propensities in influencing behavior. He seems also to anticipate the pessimism of Thomas Hobbes but his wide experience gives his views a sense of realism.

He invented the essay form about 2,000 years before Montaigne and wrote on a variety of topics: music, the emotions and desires, the operations of government, the dynamics of heaven (nature, fate, karma), military affairs, rituals (for example, the rites concerning burial and mourning practices), and rules for princes and kings like Niccolo Machiavelli's *The Prince*. But his most consistent theme is that of the qualities for a gentleman, whom today we would identify with the sage or scholar, men of "benevolence, righteousness and proper standards." His analogies are clever and insightful and his logic impeccable. There is a touch of stoicism in his essays, betraying his strong feelings for parsimonious living as worthy of a sage. Like the Essenes, the Stoics and Jesus, he favored simple living standards and poverty the better to free the mind for contemplation.

The transformation of behavior will occur when man is guided by the instructions of a teacher and guided by ritual principles. Only then will he be able to observe the dictates of courtesy and humility, obey the forms and rules of society, and achieve order.

Hsun-Tzu sought the abolition of hereditary titles and rulers and heralded the need for meritorious men in governance. The resumption of official examinations in 1646 during the Ming Dynasty, revived only recently, demonstrate the need for merit in positions of influence. He supported ritual and religious practices but not superstitious activities like divination or rain dances, as he believed they were frequently used for selfish and ambitious purposes.

Extol the classics, he said, yet repudiate the authors who have authored them. Give the honorable their due and belittle the petty, tedious, and inferior men who lack understanding. Extol virtues and denigrate evil deeds. Praise wide rulers and condemn the actions of ignoble tyrants.

Zoroaster had claimed that the supernatural forces of light and darkness competed for mankind's soul.[14] Mencius argued that men were born good, and Hsun-Tzu that they were born evil. *Genesis* argued that humans had once been born good but had lost semi-divine goodness forever through disobedience and needed to be cleansed by baptism of a universally inherited sin. Christianity claimed the need for a savior, Jesus, and for the soul to be resurrected.

These early doctrines placed a value of either good or evil on humans before any individual human (except Adam and Eve in the Western literary tradition) had an opportunity to declare a choice in the matter. Let's assume that these philosophies do not express reality and that humans are born without either a positive or negative condition and that neutrality of values is the real disposition. The result is that without values that are universal, and certainly not absolute, then there are no heretics, and the history of persecution and suffering would forever have been mitigated through enlightened tolerance for diversity of thought and creativity.

We can argue that change occurs because of social, economic, and political conditions but that human nature remains always and everywhere the same. But for the sake of argument let's assume the reverse, that human variability is unpredictable, that a Marcus Aurelius does not equate to a Nero or Caligula, nor a Baptist preacher to a serial killer, and that anatomically everyone is born with a similar pancreas, but that each has behavioral dispositions that do not even allow the person acting to know the motives. In effect, human nature is a myth and bipedal similarities are overwhelmed and obscured with bizarre and arcane individual human behaviors too differentiated to form a common category.

If we can hold that playful idea in mind, then we can understand better Cicero who wrote on the nature of the gods, a topical issue in his era. Standing an idea on its head, so to speak, however whimsical, challenges our ingrained ideas in the culture that can strangle creativity.

Cicero (106–43 BCE): *On the Nature of the Gods*

There are many aspects of philosophy that have not as yet received the attention they deserve, and one of the most difficult and puzzling of all subjects of philosophic inquiry . . . is the nature of the gods.

What is more impetuous and more inconsistent with that dignity and steadfastness that should characterize a philosopher than to entertain unsound opinions or to defend with dogmatic assurances a hypothesis that has been inadequately examined and understood. [15]

Cicero (Marcus Tullius Cicero) wrote extensively on religion and his insights based on his essays *De Natura Deorum* (*On the Nature of the Gods*) and *De Divinatione* (*On Divination*) reveal much about Roman religion in the century prior to Jesus. Cicero believed that if humanity lost its reverence toward the gods that good faith, brotherhood, and justice would be lost as well.

Had Christians been less dogmatic, had they followed Greek and Roman examples, their debates would have resulted in multiple Christian philosophies and not, as it did, in one theological orthodoxy with multiple heresies. This would have resulted in innumerably fewer exiles, purges, burnings, calumnies, defilements, and deaths. Cicero's dialogue about philosophies describing the gods as satirical and engaged in polemical invective was a literary device all Christian commentators would in time emulate.

Cicero opens this essay, as Plato does in the *Symposium*, by setting the venue for the discussion in the home of a friend who has gathered together various philosophers who are to spend the evening debating the merits of the various schools of philosophy. Cicero has one of the proponents of the Epicurean school that satirized the teachings of most ancient writers. He lays out the absurdities and weaknesses of proposed theories about deities from the hypothesis, that, for example, they embody the ether, or all or each of the planets, or personify nature itself.

The speaker, a student and teacher of Epicurus, then states that the gods exist because men have a concept of them formed in the mind. The existence of gods is thus inferred from intuitive preconception. Then Cotta, the Stoic exponent, says that everyone believes in the gods but nobody can say where they come from, where they live, how they are constituted, and how they live. But like all ancient religions, most Roman gods and goddess, in addition to Diana on earth, Luna in the heavens, and Hecate in Hades, were linked intimately to agriculture, food production, and farm management.[16]

Balbus, another Stoic proponent in this dialogue, spends his discussion extolling the stars and planets and notes how systematic have been ancient writers in making deities of various stellar orbs. Who can gaze upon the firmament, one might ask, and see the precise movements of the heavenly bodies and the whole sidereal panorama and then deny that reason dwells in them? The argument of transposing the gift of human reason to inanimate objects was a common philosophical technique. If ancient writers could have known about heavenly bodies what we know today, that they are inhospitable lumps of gas and unforgiving geology like the planets or flaming bodies of fire like the stars, their enthusiasm would have been diminished for granting the gift of reason to them.

As a lawyer, Cicero aptly uses his oratorical skills and logic to set up straw-men arguments from known writers about the gods and then picks apart the reasoning. In particular he laments the logic of finding proof of the existence of the gods inferred from intelligence in the heavens. This is similar to the proposals today of intelligent design enthusiasts who claim that perceiving the order and beauty in the universe is evidence of a higher intelligence and a creator god.

Cicero bemoans the fact that the gods should have withheld the power of reason in mankind since it is so often tragically perverted. Reason destroys so many men and gives blessings to so few that its existence is more a cause for general regret than of congratulations. "Can we believe, then, that this vast crop of sin was planted by the immortal gods? For if they bestowed reason upon mortals they also bestowed malice."[17] He claims that his purpose has not been to destroy belief but to describe the confusing conception of the gods in explaining beliefs.[18] Cicero was in fact a supporter of religion but an opponent of superstition. Neither Cicero nor any of the knowledgeable and illustrious philosophers of significance describes the beliefs of the Hebrews.

INVOKED ROMAN DEITIES (116–27 BCE)
(Varro, *De Rerum Rusticarum*, Book 3)

DEITY	PURPOSE
Father Jupiter	Agricultural Fertility
Mother Earth	Agricultural Fertility
Sun and Moon	Sowing & Reaping Seasons
Ceres	Grains
Bacchus	Wine
Flora	Fruitbearing
Minerva	Olives
Venus	Gardens
Lympha	Fountains (water)
Bonus Eventus	Good Fortune (Order & Good Luck)

Cicero states that there are four ways he believes the idea of the gods are implanted in the minds of men. The first is the foreknowledge of future events. The second is the advantages we derive from our environment. The third is the terror we experience that demonstrates the power and displeasure of the gods. The fourth is the harmony, motion, and revolution of celestial beings. This last is the most convincing. Today he might easily be considered a believer in Intelligent Design. The irony is that Cicero saw the intelligence in the universe as evidence of the plurality of gods, not in a single god.

> Both among us and among other nations the worship of the gods and respect for religion grows stronger and deeper.
> Cicero, *On the Nature of the Gods*, Book 2, 5.

Cicero approved of Julius Caesar's assassination though he did not take part in it. When Octavian, who would become Caesar Augustus, occupied Rome after Caesar's assassination, allowed Marc Anthony, who hated Cicero, to place Cicero's name on a proscribed list and Cicero was executed in 43 BCE.

The Religion of the Romans

Even the words we use today for the gospels, "good news," or literally "God's spelling" in English, or *euanggelion*, "good news" in Greek, and its messages, are adopted from the cultural usage of the first century. By the time of Augustus, beginning with the celebrations of 17 BCE, Roman writers like Horace were beginning to mark the beginning of a new age. In Halicarnassus the local calendar was changed so the year could begin with the emperor's birthday: "the beginning of the good news (*euanggelion*) of safety and welfare for mankind."[19] The rituals associated with Roman religion practices were integral to the state's administration of society. Roman religion and secular activities were not separate. Performing the sacred rituals, what emperors saw as compliance with good civil order, and what Christians saw as idolatry, would complicate Christian life in later centuries and inaugurate an era of martyrdoms.

Thus, in spite of the dispensations of Moses to the Hebrews and prior to the revelations of Christianity, the common belief was that there were divine existences (singular or plural), but not the deities of the Homeric myths. Thoughtful men considered apparitions as fairy tales, divinations as useless, and philosophical arguments, at least those not totally irrational, to be invalid and disagreeable. If God did create human reason, he should have withheld the gift since so much misfortune results from its use.

The Roman religion and its practices dominated civic life for hundreds of years. The vast array of temples, many erected to virtues believed to be divine, the rites of purification, the prayers and ablutions, the auguries, all these and other practices were a testimonial to the codification of what became known among Christians as paganism. The Romans saw their religious practices and exercising of virtues as unifying the people toward purposeful common goals and civic ideals. The pantheon of the gods was both a blessing and a curse. Like Greeks, Romans inherited a multiplicity of gods from older civilizations and christened them with new names, Jupiter for Zeus, Mercury for Hermes, Neptune for Poseidon, Venus for Aphrodite, among others.

Skeptics like Cicero questioned the nature of belief and sought to embrace a virtuous life unburdened of so many deities and their divine attributes. A Christian convert named Arnobius, whose fourth century life parallels that of the emperor Diocletian wrote a treatise in defense of Christianity known as *Against the Nations* in which he mocks the polytheism and idolatry most Greeks and Romans practiced.[20]

Abundant examples of Roman household deities have been excavated in Pompei. Examples include the popular *lares*, similar to the *teraphim* that Rachel stole when fleeing with Jacob. The *lares* were the household Roman deities that protected the home and were often found as small statuettes with knee-length tunics in niches near the kitchen. The *genius*, a kind of guiding spirit of a family, its procreative force of family ancestors, was usually symbolized in illustrations as a man pouring a libation. The *penates* are the least understood and scholars often consider them the equivalent of the *lares*, but seem to be a more abstract form representing the deity, but they too are also linked to the family's sustenance.[21] Moreover, cultic and mystery practices of Bacchus (Dionysius) were held in Roman villas.

Xenophobic Romans distinguished between *religio* and *superstitio,* contrasting their national beliefs from fringe Eastern beliefs with prophetic visions and occultism, like the alluring festivals of Cybele and Isis celebrated with colorful garments, masks, and musical instruments imported into Roman households by slaves from Asian provinces. Romans were pious but austere in their devotions. Devotees of Asiatic and Egyptian deities injected festive practices into the more serious Roman devotions. Soon, Rome became a city where all religious beliefs and practices mingled with myriad commodities and peoples. Christianity fell within this purview for the first 300 years prior to the codification of its dogma and acceptance as the state religion. By the fifth century CE the perception of what religion was became reversed, and Christianity was established as the Roman religion and all previous beliefs became superstitions.

According to Plutarch in *Moralia* the atheist thinks there are no gods, and the superstitious person wishes there were none. The superstitious person believes in the gods and would become an atheist if he were not afraid of death and its consequences. The intermediate state is where true religion lies.[22]

The last renowned defender of Roman paganism symbolizing the virtues of the empire was Quintus Aurelius Symmachus (c. 345–410), who came from a distinguished line of Roman public servants. He is an outstanding representative of the old school of Roman life and eloquent spokesperson for its values against Christian emperors who were unfavorably disposed to the old state religions. He rose quickly through the senatorial ranks to become proconsul of Africa and *Pontifex Maximus*. He had enormous wealth that complemented his high moral character. But the emperor Gratian banished him from Rome in 382 because he protested the removal of the Statue of the Altar of Victory from the Senate.

He argued that he was defending the institutions of Roman ancestors and the rights and destiny of the country and demanded the restoration of religious affairs that had for so long been advantageous to the state. He implored the emperor that the altar preserved public concord that appealed to everyone's good faith, and kept a symbolic place where men can take an oath at a sacred site and not give perjury. He argued for the continuation of the sanctity of the role of the Vestal Virgins who through no fault of their own were being deprived of an esteemed role in public observance. His eloquence and good faith, his obvious honesty and intensity of sentiment, are evident in this rare document. But it was the last gasp of a dying pagan world. Ambrose, the bishop of Milan, rebutted Symmachus' request in two known letters to Emperor Valentinian, the younger brother of Gratian and who prevailed as chief spokesman for Christianity in the fourth century.[23]

Public religion in major cities like Carthage was controlled by selected committees composed of the elite, the *decurions*, who defined the individual religious identity of the city. There was no official Roman religion until Christianity since each city chose its cults and festivities.[24] In effect, the collective civic religion of the major cities self-selected the favored religious celebrations and cults in Rome. This also conforms to the general rule in the provinces where the governor or proconsul had remarkable autonomy. The imperial cult, which linked the empire together, and the municipal cults of Jupiter, Juno and Minerva were Rome's designated religious choices. The senate or the emperor could and did prohibit certain activities like magical or astrological practices, and did levy a tax on Jews beginning in 66 CE.

The persecution of Christians did not have an imperial or Senate law prohibiting their form of worship or rituals. Instead, local officials brought Christians to trial because of refusal to honor recognized local deities and the imperial cult. Christians were private religious worshippers but public dissidents and nonconformists. In a supreme irony then, early Christians were dissenters from Roman ways, as later clerics would be persecutors of those they designated as heretics.

The Edict of Decius in 250 (the text has not survived) was an imperial attempt to win favor throughout the empire in troubled times by establishing a shared religious experience of ritualistic sacrifice to the recognized deities. All who refused, not just Christians but also Manichees and a few cantankerous philosophers who dissented when they couldn't dissemble, were exiled or killed. Emperor Decius overturned the prerogatives of local rulers who allowed wide-ranging religious freedoms by an imperial order using religion as a force for collective unity. His decision had wide implications for imperial rule and for religion by placing in the hands of the emperor the executive right to govern religion, usurping it from the local provinces and the Senate. This centralization of religious control had the unintended effect, through the conversion of Constantine, of ultimately reversing the occasional persecution of Christians and making Christianity the state religion to the exclusion of all others and leading to the persecution of pagans, the former defenders of civic and religious order.

Theodosius (346?–395) did more to favor Christian ecclesiastical order and destroy paganism than all previous emperors. Gratian withdrew official rights, immunities and revenues from the pagan priesthood. Theodosius, the Christian emperor, demolished pagan temples and sacred grounds and prohibited all pagan ceremonies, rites, sacrifices, and assemblies. It was like the Taliban blasting to dust a thousand-year-old statue of Buddha because it stood for a disallowed idolatrous symbol. Sensible Christian bishops accommodated the new but perhaps reluctant converts by incorporating under the rituals of saints and relics many of the old pagan customs. They thus politically defused any questions about the inherent superstitions, mythical origins, and philosophical inconsistencies of triumphant Christianity, the new religious authority in the neighborhood and in the realm. Thereafter, pagan heretics and dissidents would be harder to find, but Christian ones flourish.

CHAPTER SEVEN
HERETICS IN THE FIRST CHRISTIAN CENTURIES

The generation after the death of Jesus witnessed the Roman extinction of a revolt that decimated the population and the Jewish quest for political independence and religious idealism. Jews were hungry for a hero like Judas Maccabeus (died 160 BCE) to rescue them from the malaise and uncertainty that permeated the dispersed population, especially despondent residents living among the actual and spiritual rubble of Jerusalem. Many looked back to a nostalgic time a few decades earlier when a certain Jesus of Nazareth had offered hope through religious reform. They recalled then how excited and expectant some were about the message he preached, a combination of a vision of the future and devotion to God that recalled biblical prophets. Some scribes felt they could recast vignettes of his career to satisfy growing interest in a Jewish leader who could inspire hope in the Torah in the midst of the catastrophe that was Judaism.

Thus, in the first century after the death of Jesus, the destruction of the temple in Jerusalem as the central place of worship, the slaughter of the people, and the scattering of the few living Jews to the far reaches of the Roman Empire, Diaspora believers associated with the early Jesus movement wrote scores of documents. These writings described the life and activities of Jesus and his followers and letters purportedly written by his disciples. A select few of these documents in subsequent decades would be canonically recognized. The remainder would be designated inauthentic and consigned to neglectful oblivion if not actual flames. But the variety of letters, testimonials, semi-biographies, novellas, epiphanies, and hymns are evidence of widespread interest in the movement. The Nazarene movement grew partly through readers of these writings. And as the meaning of Christianity crystallized into dogma, this in turn created the first Christian heretics.

The gospels are not authentic biographies of Jesus. Yet they flourished in a time when biographies were widespread. From the same time period, roughly 70 to 140 CE, Suetonius wrote biographies including the *Lives of Famous Men and Lives of the Caesars,* scholarly and informative biographies of the lives of Julius Caesar, Augustus, Tiberius, Claudius, Nero, Vespasian and Titus, among others. This time span covers the life of Jesus through to the approximate date of the composition of the last recognized canonical Christian documents in c. 90 CE. Suetonius exhibits a special care for facts, quotations from his abundant sources, divides his topics into sections, and he writes with diligent detail. The gospels have none of these characteristics. The only literary traits the gospels and Roman biographies share in common are auguries, mysterious events common in Roman biographies like flying eagles dropping chickens, laurel trees wilting at the death of an emperor, figs blooming in the off-season, and dreams predicting an ominous future. During the period when Christians were composing their first documents, exemplary Greek and Roman historical models—among them, besides Suetonius, were Tacitus, Dio Cassis, and Plutarch—writers that could have served as models for biographical emulation that Christian writers chose not to use and may not have even read.

The common critique of Plutarch in his *Parallel Lives of Famous Greeks and Romans* was that he included as many legends in his biographies as he did documented facts. But he addresses this feature at the beginning of his study of Alexander when he writes about his search for "the signs of the soul in men." In other words he was not proposing exact descriptions but personality profiles. He was forthright about the difficulty of writing the lives of famous men that did not always include written confirmation of details and so instructed his readers about the limitations of writing biography and history. Thus, the literary fashion of the time, indeed of all time, was to make any biography as popularly palatable as possible. Fanciful stories about a man's legend were considered a part of his biography. The gospels are no different and are illustrative of the Greek literary style of the era.

> I think I have confessed my own experience to you from the beginning of the conversation: I am inclined to disbelieve legends. This is the reason: Until now I have not met anyone who has seen such fabulous things, but rather one person claims to have heard it from another, that other believes it, and third one a poet convinces.[1]

The gospel narrators portrayed a passionate man filled with holy conviction compared to epic heroes, exactly the kind of person who could inspire and uplift the spirits of a dejected generation. Gospel scribes were not philosophers, historians, or even biographers, but simple men, like Paul, engaged in the revival of a religious dream. There was no established doctrine, and religious belief grew as its adherents matured.

As the Roman Empire became more centralized and the Nazarene movement spread, especially under emperors Tiberius, Vespasian, Trajan, and Hadrian, the Mediterranean culture became more homogenized. Both Jews and Gentiles evolved in a Hellenic and Romanized cultural mix where ideas and fashions clashed and merged. The dominant feature of the written story of Jesus had been apocalyptic, grounded in the personal reform necessary for Jews to prepare for the coming Last Days, filled with ideas about personal resurrection and eternal life. The mystical movements known as Gnosticism and the Orphic mysteries had long circulated in Hellenic circles and their melding with Jewish eschatology into this cultural mainstream helped form Christianity. In the first few decades this movement remained essentially Jewish with the Bible as the main text. *The Gospel of Mark* is representative of the Jewish side of Jesus and *The Gospel of John* of the Gnostic appeal of emergent Christianity, a new face given to Jesus by a mystical scribe that Jesus himself might not have accepted. Paul essentially Hellenized the Jewish message and created Christian theology.

We might think that a hundred heresies could easily be identified and flushed out. But Christianity as an agreed-upon set of doctrines was not initially evident. Heresy hadn't been categorized in the first couple of hundred years, and no one was sure what the basis of Christianity was supposed to be besides a mixture of Jewish, Persian, Egyptian and Greek beliefs, mystery cults, and concepts of the hereafter. This was exactly the kind of religious diversity that flourished in the Roman Empire, until it became obvious that Roman authorities looked disapprovingly on theological differences that turned into civil disturbances. Christian ecclesiastics decided that peace with Rome was preferable to theological contention. Hence, with the insistence of the clerical community Christian clerics sought unity of dogma that, once established with imperial favor, made heresy and dissent unfashionable and then dangerous.

There was no Christian capitol in the first century. After 70 CE and the destruction of the Hebrew nation small communities of Nazarenes lived in Antioch, Corinth, Ephesus, and Rome and probably met in homes and rented rooms. Members consisted of Jews who believed Jesus was the Messiah, Gnostics who thought he was the divine demiurge, dualists who saw him as "the light of the world" (*John* 8:12-58) conquering the forces of darkness, Christians who thought Jesus was Spirit/God with only the phantasmagoria appearance of a man, apocalyptic believers who perceived him as a Divine Deliverer, and various lost souls who wanted to join the latest new age mystery cult. All would have had to be baptized, no special trial, not like walking on hot coals. A diversity of believers could adopt one or another characteristic of Jesus and claim to be Christian without damaging dogma since none had yet been defined. To become a heretic one must first be clear about what one is opposing and what is standard belief. Before the establishment of an authoritative structure enforcing dogma and validated documents pronouncing what is non-Christian this was not obvious.

We don't find any heretics in the first century because it isn't clear what one is, and if any existed how they differed from all the legitimate but widely differing interpretations of faith. Apart from Hebrew adherence to the Law, ancient religions did not have dogmas but strict regulations for the behavior of the initiates and followers. Catechumens and those not yet initiated into the "mysteries" of a religion had to follow rituals and observe certain actions, some of which included fasting and abstinence from sex or certain foods, traits certainly true of the earliest Greek and Jewish communities.

A brief synopsis of the Roman world with the emerging Christian influence will set the context for how heresy was born.

First Century Rome

Rome becomes significant for Christianity because of the destruction of Jerusalem in 70 CE and the scattering of Jews, but also because, with the adoption of the Pauline theology of preaching and converting gentiles to the Christian movement, there is no established religious urban center, no temple, only loosely regulated rituals, and, most important, no defined set of beliefs. Yet Christians, beginning with Peter and Paul, chose Rome because it was the seat of imperial government.

Claudius had expelled the Jews from Rome in 49 CE because of turbulence over a certain "Chrestus." Whether this was the same as Jesus the Nazarene or another is unknown, since the Greek word *Christus* refers to one who is anointed and is therefore a designation not a family name.[2] Neither Jews nor Christians returned to Rome until after the death of Claudius in 54, or about the time Paul was composing his epistles, the first New Testament documents. There are no laws at this time making Christianity illegal, although the whim of emperors like Nero, who even expelled philosophers from Rome in 66, had the power of judicial decree. But by the time of Trajan (53–117) imperial laws prohibiting associations from forming and meeting were applied to Christian groups. Romans were suspicious of novel groups that might pose an imminent danger to civil order, as the Jews had in 66 in Palestine, with nationalistic tendencies and a rebellion against Roman occupation. Such groups might incubate a new prophet calling for secession or revolt.

This was not a specific injunction Rome devised to torment Christians. Rome had a long history of the suppression of secret conspiracies starting with the Punic Wars against Carthage over two centuries earlier, as Livy describes in his *History of Rome*, and always sought to stop secret cults or religious organizations from spreading among the lower classes. The slave revolt of Spartacus was still vividly recalled. A decree dated to 186 BCE suppressed the Bacchanalian festivals and prohibited anyone from becoming a priest of Bacchus. Rome was conservative, circumspect, and suspicious of the potential danger foreign religions posed to peace in the empire.[3] The irony in this context was that Christians at this time were dissenters. In fact, by the time of Justinian, ancient Roman decrees against forbidden societies were still being enforced under Christian rule in Justinian's *Digest*, published in 533 CE.

Paul, who had traveled throughout the Levant establishing churches, essentially relocated his headquarters in Rome after his arrival in 59. Paul's *Epistle to the Romans* names twenty-eight individuals he sends greetings to, so the community cannot have been that much more extensive in number. Paul in *Epistle to the Romans* brings his gospel message, "the power of God unto salvation to everyone who believes, to Jew first and then to Greek." (*Romans* 1:16). On the face of it this passage is odd for a man who has spent his whole adult life bringing his gospel message to the Greek-speaking world to affirm that the message of Jesus should come first to Jews in the Latin world. Paul's message in Romans is to demonstrate that the Law is important but that a new covenant is now in the ascendant requiring a new faith and observance. Perhaps it is a salve to Peter who is already in Rome. So why didn't Paul, if indeed *Romans* was actually written by him, send Peter greetings? What is omitted in these early documents is at least as significant as what is written.

Ministering to the gentiles directly contradicts Matthew's text which quotes Jesus himself in giving instructions to the first missionaries: "Go nowhere among the Gentiles and enter no town of the Samaritans, but go rather to the lost sheep of Israel" (*Matt.*10:5-6). However, at the time of Paul's ministry the Gospel of Matthew had not yet been written and was only composed between 80-90, long after Paul's death in Rome. Nevertheless, Paul's defense of a mission to the gentiles and a gospel directly forbidding such activity, quoting Jesus himself as authority, places a clear contradiction in the center of Christianity's mission and intended audience. But if we assume that the gospels were intended for different audiences, and not a single group with a collective purpose, the inconsistencies vanish.

The Epistle to the Romans is clearly intended to exhort Christians and discouraged, even reviled Jews in Rome. It argues for accepting the new Jesus covenant that will allow members to proclaim that there is now a former Jew who is a God, an acceptable and non-threatening condition in polytheistic Roman society in the first century. Accepting the new faith would have allowed Jews to keep the Old Covenant and inspired them to maintain some dignity as an ethnic Jew, but with a Christian twist in belief. Devotees were already circumcised. All they needed was to be baptized. Becoming a Christian for a Jew in Rome in the latter half of the first century, assuming Paul's epistle had the intended conversion effect, moreover, did not entail acceptance of any idol, which would have been contrary to Mosaic Law, or the violation of any of the old precepts, or do any violence to Roman beliefs. *Romans* is a masterful, clever proselytizing document for wavering and skeptical Jews and encouragement for minority and isolated Christians.

Marcion in the next half century, later to be classified as one of the first Christian heretics, would divorce himself from this Pauline missionary ploy and reject the Mosaic Law altogether. He would assert that the new covenant of Christianity does not need the Old Testament, its books or prescriptions. Paul's attempt to recruit Jews as Christians would become one of Christianity's first doctrinal stumbling blocks. In the end, orthodox Christianity would agree with Paul and accept reluctantly the Jewish tradition into the code and condemn Marcion.[4]

What is clear is that near the beginning of the second century, or as early as 96, everyone does distinguish between Jews and Christians, as the ranks of the new religion were augmented by converts already in the city or entering it. *The*

Letter to the Hebrews was probably written in Rome about 90-115, but as scholars acknowledge not by Paul. It has a marked Jewish frame of reference grounded in biblical but not gospel scriptures. It draws on *Psalms* primarily to demonstrate how Christ is the key to salvation and how he is the new high priest like Melchizedek. It too is a document intended to convert sympathetic Jews to a Christian interpretation.

An epistle written about 100–120 by Clement of Rome known as *I Clement* is a letter of advice to Christians living in Corinth, who had deposed church elders and replaced them with younger teachers. Clement was the third pope and this letter underscores how toward the close of the first century Rome felt impelled to intervene in local affairs, just like Roman authorities felt obliged to impose their wishes on territorial disputes. But what is unusual in this document is that the author never cites any gospel scriptures, only Old Testament writings and even Greek mythical analogics like the Phoenix bird for the resurrected Christ. The widespread use of biblical writings and the omission of gospel citations demonstrate the reliance on Jewish traditions in early Christian documents. Even if all the canonical gospels had been written by the early second century not everyone would have necessarily been aware of their existence or considered them the only requisite documents of revelation.

By the middle of the second century Rome had a population of about 1.5 million. If any writings existed about Christians at that time they were archived in Rome since it was the governmental hub of the empire and library of everything worth knowing or collecting. Gibbon, citing Livy and Pliny, estimated that there were 50,000 Christians in Rome or approximately five percent of the total population. But even this number is far too generous.[5] Yet there is scant extant documentation about Christianity, other than Paul's epistles.

On the other hand, Roman Christians encountered uninhibited practices of idolatry, temples to innumerable deities, and rituals and performances laced with the polytheism of private and public life. It would have been impossible to live in the city and not observe or participate in activities that honored the recognized deities unless one renounced all ties to business, commerce, entertainment, and public celebrations. The celebration of public holidays always involved sacrifices and so-called pagan festivities. It is difficult to imagine a pious Christian engaged in any public observance or function where official duty required obeisance to the gods and goddess without feeling guilt and estrangement. Yet even as the second century begins everyone of Christian importance seems to be congregating in the streets of Rome as if it were Jerusalem and not the supposedly impious city it was. The persecutions of the emperors Decius and Valerian in the third century would make these very issues central to Rome's coercion of Christians into the *Pax Romana* by forcing Christians to pay official homage to state-approval deities. Many refused and the cult of martyrdom for the faith began.

But not only Christians despised things Roman. Tacitus was pessimistic about imperial Rome and its emperors, although he wrote masterfully about his gloom. Juvenal (55–127) was condemnatory of imperial Rome and just about everyone in it. He satirizes Jews but not Christians, and this omission has its own significance: There weren't enough Christians in his lifetime to denounce and against whom to express indignation.

The bishop of Rome, who was to emerge as the successor of Peter, was domiciled in Rome and serviced members of the flock there. In subsequent centuries, however, the patriarchs of Alexandria and Constantinople held more power because of the growing numbers of Christians in their congregations. But why was Rome chosen to be the first permanent capitol of Christendom, a city where Peter and Paul died, and not, for example, Nazareth where Jesus actually lived, or Antioch the city of the first converts of Paul? The likely answer is that at the time Rome had more Christian followers than any other city and that many converts had originally been Jews from the Diaspora who adopted the new religion to escape the stigma of Judaism after the collapse of Hebrew revolt by the forces of Titus in 70.

Titus (39–81 CE) was the Roman emperor and son of Vespasian who completed the crushing of the Jewish revolt. The Arch of Titus was erected at the top of the Forum's *Via Sacra* in 81, a visible symbol even to this day of Jewish defeat and humiliation. Not only had the conqueror of Jerusalem and the Jews been Roman, Titus had been proclaimed a god at his death.[6] Temples to the divine emperors were everywhere in the major cities of Asia Minor. Jews had once been welcome in Rome but after 70 it must have been difficult to identify oneself as Jew even in Rome and easier to say one was a Christian if only because Jesus had once been a Jew and was now, like the Emperor Titus, proclaimed a deity, a convenient Jewish counterbalance to a Roman deity.

The Nazarene movement in the first decades, according to *Acts of the Apostles*, was centered in Jerusalem. It consisted of Peter and James, Jesus' brother and a few disciples, and they performed Jewish rituals and ceremonies in Jerusalem, and no act that was noticeably Christian.[7] Although it is perilous to accept *Acts* as history, since Luke is building a case like Paul did for carrying the Nazarene message to gentiles, it is clear that in these early decades leading up to the destruction of Jerusalem that Christians were Jews following the precepts of a dead, sanctified rabbi. Paul, not Peter, assumed missionary leadership. Jews expelled from Jerusalem took up residence in Antioch, and it was here that Paul's first converts likely appeared.

The Ebionites, for example, Syrian-based early Christians, practiced circumcision, adopted *The Gospel of Matthew* as the only authentic document, and persevered in the observance of Jewish customs and the Law. They considered Paul a heretic for corrupting the real Christian message. How's that for Christian irony?

CHRONOLOGY OF CHRISTIAN DOCUMENTS

Document	Author	Date (CE)
First Letter to the Thessalonians	Paul	50–51
First Letter to the Corinthians	Paul	53–54
Gospel of Mark	Mark	69–75
Gospel of Matthew	Matthew (?)	80–90
Gospel of Luke/Acts	Luke	90–100
Gospel of John	John (?)	96–?
Letter to the Hebrews	unknown	90–115

(Source: White 2004)

The Shepherd, a first century document, reveals how fluid faith was and how distant it is from today's Christian belief. It is a curious allegory written in Rome as early as 89–99 or as late as 140 by Hermas, reputedly a brother of Pius, the bishop of Rome. It was found in some canonical texts in the *Codex Sinaiticus* lying among copies of the gospels. The text speaks about a Son of God, but someone who is not Jesus. It is a polemical, mystical text, bemoaning the lack of righteousness among believers, like a long sermon filled with more prophetic visions than a theological tract, with the appearance of a ghostly woman named Ronda who plays a part that is both temptress and castigator. Several men of unknown origin (are they angels?) appear and relate stories. The author could be composing a book of revelations, an epistle, a prophetic book in the Bible, or a fictionalized dream. The writing identifies the author as more knowledgeable about Hebrew than Latin prose. It is the work of a pious, almost puritanical early Christian who seeks to get everyone to repent from lust and wantonness. Hermas cannot be classified as a heretic yet because few know what it meant to be a Christian, though many assumed the book was divinely inspired.

Within the Roman Empire, if not within the boundaries of Rome, the Christian movement, according to Gibbon, was relatively insignificant and unlikely to receive official or even scholarly notice. Contemporary historians like Seneca, Pliny the Elder, Tacitus, Plutarch, Galen, Epictetus, and the Emperor Marcus Antoninus wrote nothing about it. Tolerant Romans, more concerned with civil unrest than religious cults, would have exercised caution in moving against Christians. Until Diocletian, individuals who happened to be Christians were punished for various offenses, usually for failing to perform imperial religious rituals relevant to official deities, like failing to burn incense on the altar of Venus or at the temples of the dead emperors, or for forming prohibited organizations. Septimus Severus from Africa was favorably disposed to Christianity. His son Caracalla had a nurse who was a Christian. Marcia, Commodus' favorite concubine, was friendly to Christians, though her status might have impeded her baptism.

Christians had longer periods of tranquility in their practices and beliefs than they had periodic bouts of martyrdom that in most circumstances were confined to Rome. Rome was the seat of imperial government that destroyed Jerusalem, obliterated the Temple, and killed over a million Jews. Yet it was chosen as Christianity's capitol and not Nazareth, Ephesus, Alexandria, or Antioch, more logical choices in the Greek-speaking world. After all, Greek was the language of Paul's epistles and the gospels except for Matthew. It appears Christians were more drawn to the gravesites of Peter and Paul than to the sites or urban vicinities of the activities of him they called Lord and Savior.

The non-canonical *Gospel of Peter* exemplified how many in the Christian communities held Jewish traditions dear. But the second upheaval, the Bar Kochba revolt in 132–35 CE, dissipated all collaboration between the two religions, especially in the minds of Romans. Jewish converts to Christianity thereafter had to choose between their identification with wider Israel and belief in Jesus as the Messiah, or disaffiliating themselves completely from Judaism.[8] The anti-Jewish *Gospel of Peter*, a polemical work considered heretical, was in its day just another composition written to justify a political position in a religious debate.

By the beginning of the second century manuals of instruction like *The Didache* appear that describe the procedures for liturgical worship, for baptism rites, for prayer and fasting, ways of conducting the meal of fellowship (the Eucharist), Sunday services, and even support for the clergy. At this stage in Christianity's development there is more formalization about services and practices than consensus about the substance of belief. *The Didache,* only discovered in 1883 and composed toward the close of the first century, is a short treatise on what are prohibited behaviors, mostly re-enumerating the Ten Commandments and the gospel entreaties of loving one's neighbor, and describing the first documentation about the liturgy of the Mass. A third and final section outlines how to act toward prophets, apostles, and wandering fellow Christians. It suggests that if they plan to stay more than three days they be put to work, a good rule also for visiting relatives. Many rituals are extenuations of pagan rites. Justin Martyr (c.100–165) describes the common practices of Christians in Rome in his apology *Acts of Justin,* a text surprisingly contemporary with present Christian observances.

As the first century closes new documents written by apocalyptic Christian visionaries produced quasi-biographies, pseudo-letters (that is, not written by the claimed authors), and poetic visions many falsely attributed to the first converts to satisfy the communities for church reading material while seeking to define beliefs and behaviors Christians needed to survive in a Roman world. These writings are like the Chimera, the great beast of Greek mythical lore with the head of a lion, the body of a goat, and the tail of a serpent. The anatomical parts were recognizable individually but together they seemed like a fanciful representation of reality. It's possible their intent was merely to entertain and not instruct or sermonize.

The question was, which documents are divinely inspired and which are fictional accounts of visionaries and artists using Christian symbols? The abundance of non-canonical and apocalyptic writings and false attributions of authorship in these early centuries is staggering. Only exacting modern scholarship has revealed the spuriousness of a few, like the letters of Peter, John, Jude, Timothy and Titus.

The fumbling to find some doctrinal clarity was just beginning. Several New Testament documents warn against "false teachings" "false brothers" (*Gal.*, 2:4) "false apostles" (*2 Cor.*, 11:13) and various deceivers and anti-Christs. In the second century the apocryphal, pastoral epistles decry against "false teachings" and "teaching of demons" (*1 Timothy* 4:1-4). The anonymous literary figures who wrote such documents creating the illusion of author authenticity probably just thought they were contributing to the dialogue, or conveniently borrowing the names of the earliest men in the movement to compose catechisms and hortatory messages. What was a member of the new movement to think? Since there was no universal church, no copyright laws, and no defined body of beliefs, what could possibly be considered "false?"

Apollonius of Tyana, Contemporary of Jesus

One religious reformer whose life paralleled that of Jesus was Apollonius of Tyana. Little is known about him or any of these early figures, as their writings were destroyed in the various purges to blot out ideas opposed to established Christian doctrine, or, because their works were later branded heretical. His one biographer, Philostratus (170–c. 224), writing two centuries later is unreliable and implausible, containing quixotic tales more fanciful than factual. Under the pretext of prose elegance the author describes miraculous visions by Apollonius's mother of the birth of a godlike son, and her son's miracle risings from the dead and healing cures. Philostratus, in the biographical spirit of the age, developed a hagiography as fantastic as the gospel narrators did about the life of Jesus. But because he intended to write a biography, unlike gospel narrators whose purpose was to describe a mission, we know more about Apollonius than we do about Jesus.[9]

The similarities of the two lives—wondrous birth, demonstrated youthful intelligence, ascetic lifestyle, wearing only a simple tunic, temple visits, silent retreats, adulation of the crowds, writing nothing, engaging public speaker, pithy parables, miracle cures, disappearance from among a crowd, a Roman trial, after-death apparitions—are too thematically numerous to dismiss as coincidence. Gospel narrators and quasi-biographers were writing a combination of novella and fanciful life story following well-defined literary themes. Christian commentators branded Apollonius a charlatan so he would not be compared to Jesus. Yet his long life in the first century was critical in the development of Gnosticism, mysticism, and apocalyptic beliefs, an historical moment when Paul was composing epistles and the gospels not yet written.

The collective energy of this era was filled with mystery rites, secret societies, and religious cult groups energized by mystical beliefs flowing into the empire from Persia and India. Again, little is known about this flurry of religious activity because documentation was literally nonexistent or guarded secrets. Sworn members of the Knights of Columbus, Masons, or Mormons guard their documents, as secret oaths and rituals are only for members. The most intensely private secret associations were Pythagoreans. Apollonius was indeed a follower and also an initiate into the Eleusinian mysteries. As Philo relates about 25 CE there were myriad examples of young men who abandoned their property or left their homes to seek wisdom and devote themselves to the pursuit of virtue. The Essenes are another example of a sect practicing austerity.

A travelogue of Apollonius would be worthy of merit by itself even without his other writings, for he was as well traveled as anyone in that fascinating century, venturing possibly as far as Nepal, and exceeding the number of places visited by Herodotus. His journeys extended to Arabia, Nineveh, Babylon, the Ganges, the foothills of the Himalayas, Ephesus, Troy, Lesbos, Pergamus, Athens, Cyprus, Crete, Rome, Spain, Sicily, Rhodes, and Alexandria where he has several interviews with Vespasian and, a year after in Tarsus, with Titus then emperor. Thereafter he journeyed to Ethiopia, back to Rome where he was tried and acquitted, then to Asia Minor, and from there he is lost to history but estimated to have lived into his eighties or beyond, the final twenty years in Egypt. By contrast, Jesus, the teacher with a message to deliver and not a student like Apollonius, never left Palestine.

These international excursions brought Apollonius into contact with many of the most learned and mystical men of that fruitful first century, and his teachings must have enlivened the temples, shrines, and sanctuaries he visited. The shrines of Asclepius were healing hospitals and the attendant priests were like psychiatrists resorting to psychic healings rather than surgical relief. These shrines, like that of Aphrodite at Paphos in Cyprus, and temples like that of the Orphic mysteries on Lesbos, were Apollonius's favorite residences and his religious retreats. He lived longer than Jesus, accomplished more in his lifetime than any philosopher or religious reformer, and was more universally esteemed by more people of notoriety.

He absorbed the mystical ideas of Persians in Nineveh, the Magi in Babylon, and Hinduism and Buddhism in India. He resided in temples and spoke to priests. His eastern travels confirm that thoughtful individuals seeking wisdom and enlightenment were traveling to the sources. It is impossible to airily dismiss the influence of Persian or Indian thought on Mediterranean mysticism and subsequently its incorporation into Christian thought.

His virtuous life could have served as a model for gospel portraitures of Jesus. The whole of the Mediterranean world certainly knew him. He may have possessed some psychic abilities. There are multiple external pieces of evidence for his existence and the respect for his life and accomplishments, as the accompanying table shows, that outnumber the amount of external documentation about the life of Jesus apart from the gospels. Ammianus Marcellinus, the last, great Roman historian on whom Edward Gibbon based his *Decline and Fall of the Roman Empire*, wrote that Apollonius was a renowned philosopher. Others, like Eunapius in Constantinople and Volusian, proconsul in Africa in the fifth century accorded him semi-divine status. Despite these encomiums in the first centuries, Apollonius eventually succumbed to the prejudices of Christian theology and the blotting out of his name and records from recognition.

APOLLONIUS OF TYANA

Figure	Event
Justin Martyr (c.100–165)	Speaks of the powers and "consecrated objects" of Apollonius
Emperor Caracalla (188–217)	Honors the memory of Apollonius with a chapel or monument
Flavius Philostratus (c. 175–245)	Composes a biography of Apollonius at the request of Caracalla's mother
Emperor Alexander Severus (d. 235)	Places a statue of Apollonius in his private niche for deities (*lararium*)
Emperor Aurelian (c. 212–275)	Vows a temple to Apollonius after seeing a vision of him while besieging Tyana
Vopiscus, Roman Historian (Third century)	Apollonius a renowned sage, a manifestation of the godhead who resurrects the dead
Soterichus, Nichomachus, Tascius Victorianus	Write biographies of Apollonius that have not survived
Hierocles, Roman Governor c. 305	Criticizes Christianity; miracles of Apollonius more convincing that those of Jesus
Eusebius, Bishop of Caesarea, Church Historian	Rebuffs Hierocles; miracles of Apollonius the work of demons (*Eusebii Pamphili Contra Hieroclem*)

Source: Mead 1966

The Empress Julia Domna, the beautiful and brilliant wife of Emperor Septimus Severus (146–211) and mother of the murderous emperor Caracalla (188–217), commissioned Philostratus to write the life of Apollonius. She was from Syria and therefore familiar with famous men in the region and likely supplied Philostratus with manuscripts from her extensive library. But his biography is embellished with contrived fantasies and legendary beliefs, a common enough literary practice of the time, certainly found in Eusebius's *Ecclesiastical History*. Such fictionalized books erode confidences in historical authenticity.

Pointing fingers at disbelievers and non-conformists will become a Christian sport, and eventually emerge as theological commentary, a perpetual, interpretative discipline with no renewed validating evidence. As the authority of doctrine comes to authoritarian rule under Theodosius enforced through imperial decrees, the idiosyncratic opinions of creative thinkers outside the theological umbrella evaporate. Heresy becomes the equivalent of HIV/AIDS.

Marcion (c. 85–160), The Heretic

Christian heresy starts with an original thinker named Marcion in the century following Jesus and Apollonius. He caused the first theological and doctrinal anxieties by proclaiming which texts he thought authentic and which not. The bishop of Rome excommunicated him.

Marcion was born in Sinope (a port on the Black Sea) the son of a bishop, and became a wealthy ship-owner and merchant. What we know about him is sketchy, and what those opposed to his views wrote about him is contradictory if not purposefully legendary. The reason so many wrote so fervently against him is that even by the fifth century there were Marcion churches all over the Mediterranean world and in Asia Minor.[10]

We know he arrived in Rome about 140 and apparently donated a large sum to the church. At the time Christian churches maintained the rituals of baptism, scriptural readings, a differentiation between initiates (catechumens) and full members, the communion or the Eucharist, marriage (but not among the Marcionites who were celibate), ordination, and the last rites. Many of these communities were merely extensions of Greek or Roman mystery rites and ceremonies and Jewish Passover celebrations.

Marcion sought a pure Christianity, an unadulterated new covenant without Judaic trappings. He proclaimed that the God of the Law and the Prophets, the Creator God of *Genesis*, was not the Father God of Jesus.[11] He dispensed with the Old Testament. As an honest reader of texts he saw the difficulty of reconciling Jewish scriptures with gospel narratives. To justify how God's revelation to the Hebrews could be deemed unworthy, he proposed that a lesser divinity, a demiurge not the father of Jesus, had dictated Old Testament books to scribes. His postulation of twin gods to satisfy this imponderable dilemma, on the face of it, seems no more incongruous than the three divinities orthodoxy decreed in 325 at the Council of Nicaea. Christ is God, not just the Son of God, and whatever messiah the Jews expect, it is not the Christ of the gospels. Marcion could not believe that the Hebrew God, who condoned the slaughter of peoples, was the same God who preached the Sermon on the Mount.

Marcion claimed that the God of the gospel is the true God. He maintained that twin gods rule the universe and made separate revelations. But nobody ever claimed that reason alone should dominate faith or dogma. Within two centuries after Marcion's death the Nicene Creed established belief in three persons in God, a concept that even later councils rejected, as we shall see in a following chapter. A different scholarly view prevails today regarding the confusion found in chosen sacred writings, that biblical books partially imitate literary works from older cultures.[12]

It would have been difficult to convince a philosopher in the imperial age to admit there was only one God. The belief was strong in the Platonic and Persian hierarchy and even progression of divinities. A little known follower of Plato and Pythagoras named Numenius, who was acquainted with Greek, Hebrew, and Christian traditions, argued for three gods, the Father or Pure Intellect, the Creator or Demiurge, and the Creation God of the Universe. It's impossible to speculate how popular this idea was, since only fragments of Numenius' writings remain.[13] Ubiquitous Hellenized myths lent credence to widespread belief in multiple deities. This clearly influenced embryonic Christianity even though it was prohibited among the Hebrews.

Marcion dismissed all the gospels except Luke's. He even purged parts to purify it of Hebraic influences by eliminating Luke's first two chapters and some of the third. He knew the Apostles did not write any gospel. Only subsequent disciples in later generations penned the gospels, and thus he assumed that the titles given the gospels, like *Matthew* and *John*, were not by the authors' hands. He felt compelled, therefore, to treat *Luke* the same way the author of *Luke* had treated *Mark*—by copying some parts and rejecting others. Indeed, Marcion may not have known all four gospels as they might not have been written at the time, and possibly not *Acts*.

His major work (*Antithesis*) has not survived, but from his opponents and disciples we learn it was a document that set out parallel examples of inconsistencies between books in the Septuagint and phrases in the gospels, a literary technique that would be later used by Peter Abelard (1079–1142) in *Sic et Non* (Yes and No). The brilliant medieval theologian Abelard showed various disagreements among theologians and implied that they could not agree on the meanings of scripture among themselves so how could they enlighten the laity. This was an acknowledgement that truth was plural and not singular and challenged the absolute dogma of the church by using reason that appeared to threaten faith.

Marcion's faith was molded by his understanding of selected texts: out with Old Testament, he said, and only keep one Christian gospel, *Luke* (and that severely edited) and ten of Paul's epistles. His understanding of Paul may have been the most profound of his generation, though, unlike Paul, he did not believe in the resurrection of the body. He preached chastity, viewing procreation as the kind of evil Mani would subsequently uphold, a form of dualism between body as evil and spirit as good insinuated in Christian theology and the foundation of monastic living.

One known date of Marcion's career is 144 CE when he was expelled from the church at Rome and when he formed a separate religious organization. His wealth as a ship owner allowed him to journey freely throughout the Roman world to carry his message and to establish churches. Apparently he was a chaste man, austere, and ascetic, intensely pious and practical, ready to die for his beliefs, a perfect candidate for this study. He took his cue for his religious meaning directly from defined texts, which he altered to conform to his beliefs. Today he would be a devout Protestant.

Marcion was the first to determine a canon, a specific set of texts that defined Christianity, a rigorous editing of Paul's epistles and a rejection of some of them as inauthentic. Marcion knew that Paul's epistles were the earliest Christian writings and therefore an unadulterated expression, he thought, of Christ's meaning. He wanted the Old Testament from the latest religious books, the epistles and gospels, even though both sets of combined texts were collections of separate documents. Had he gone further and showed the mythical origins of all these writings he would have anticipated German biblical criticism by 1,800 years and been hailed as an eminent biblical critic instead of a dissident heretic.

It is decades between the probable death of Marcion in 160 and the orthodox writers like Irenaeus and Tertullian who condemned him. Tertullian felt obligated to write five books against him, the most extensive of any of his writings. It would be 165 years after Marcion's death before a Christian creed was formalized. During these time new contexts evolved and merged as the Christian movement struggled with ancient religious beliefs, absorbing philosophical fashions like Gnosticism, church modalities, mystery rites, and mysticism. Early Christianity during Marcion's lifetime existed in a fluid cultural and religious environment. There was no Catholic Church or recognized set of beliefs. There were local patriarchs, bishops, and clerics who exercised authority in their own name, just like Roman governors. It is only after a doctrine has been shaped and validated over more than a century did the writings of orthodoxy's strict adherents survive and those opposed or dissenting disappear. Churches devoted to Marcion's teachings existed everywhere at one time but no favorable writings, including his own, have survived.

One could rightly debate the merits, as Tertullian did ad infinitum, of the attributes of the two opposing gods Marcion proposes.[14] But the convincing argument lies not in metaphysics or theology but comparative literature. Marcion does have the reading right. Even a casual reader can easily note differences in the tone, directives, and actions of the God of *Genesis, Exodus* and the gospels. But what both Marcion and his critics like Tertullian missed is the mythical interpretation of the texts themselves, that the behaviors of the gods in the Bible and gospels are not descriptions of real entities, not divine revelations, but copies of ancient myths from existing literatures.

By 200 Marcion was regarded as the most heretical of those who professed Christianity, or some version of this communion, and this opprobrium is manifest among those who castigated his views. Marcion made the church anxious because he challenged it with the purity of his chaste and ascetic life. He ventured into doctrine where no one had gone before by rejecting Jewish sources to the gospels. He sought to divorce the purity of the Christian movement from its Jewish roots and the second Jewish revolt by Bar Kochba in 132–35 CE may have been the accelerating event. He had no subtle philosophical theory and used no sophisticated logic, metaphysics, or abstract apologetics, but was theologically inventive. He stuck to the texts, or the few he believed were essential like his selection of Paul's epistles, and boldly proclaimed that his bowdlerized version of Luke's gospel was unique and needed to stand alone as dogma without Hebrew prophecy, messianic purpose, or fulfillment, and without any other repetitive and redundant gospels.

Tertullian (c. 160–230) and the Montanists

Tertullian was born in Carthage the son of a Roman centurion. He was highly educated for his time, probably in the law according to Eusebius. According to Jerome he lived to an advanced age although we don't know how or where he died. He converted to Christianity late in his adult life, as would Cyprian and Augustine, and became the most formidable defender of Christianity in its early centuries. It is reported that he converted because of the fortitude of Christians during martyrdom, events he could have witnessed in the amphitheatre in Carthage. Unlike Augustine, he wrote no autobiography so we know nothing about his conversion. Though events of his life are sketchy he left behind volumes of writings that stamp him as one of Christianity's most diligent apologists. He is the ancient equivalent of a witch-hunter and church attack dog.[15] I describe him briefly because he was highly esteemed by the church as its Latin defender against heretics, and then in later life became a heretic himself. According to his critics he was a prolific writer accustomed to excessive moralizing, and his ruthless prose with its stinging sarcasm gave free rein to future writers excoriating heretics.

Carthage was a city of some panache and notoriety settled by the sea-faring Phoenicians, descendants of the ancient Canaanites, as a trading post around the ninth century BCE. Schoolboys pouring over their Virgilian prose would remember that Dido's tragic farewell to Aeneas occurred there and that the First and Second Punic Wars were between Rome and Carthage. Carthage honored its homegrown boy, Apuleius, author of *The Golden Ass*, one of the first novels, and was receptive to the entreaties of the first Christian missionaries sometime in the middle of the second century. It had the distinction as the city of the martyrdom of the first Christians in 180, and finally was home in successive generations to Cyprian of Carthage, Tertullian, and Augustine. Few cities could boast of so illustrious a setting in literature, philosophy, and theology, exceeded only by that other African city to the east, Alexandria.

Montanism: Christian Fortune-Telling

Later in his life, Tertullian joined a charismatic movement known as Montanism that spread throughout the Roman world about 170. It began in Phrygia, today's eastern Turkey. Here's the setting for that heretical movement.

People naturally feel vulnerable when disasters strike, like earthquakes, floods, or epidemics that decimate a city or community. It is at such perilous times that millennium movements tend to emerge, when previously muted voices enunciate pronouncements and prophecies they claim are divinely inspired. In the winter of 165–66 the Roman army destroyed Seleucia on the Tigris River. After the army's departure a plague eradicated the remaining population. In the wake of these calamities came Montanus and two priestesses, Priscilla and Maximilla, uttering entranced oracles they said were coming from the Holy Spirit. Church elders were challenged by this creative and often frenzied impulsivity because individual inspiration as a source of God's voice was popularly preferred above ecclesiastical authority. Ecstatic movements like the members of the cult of Cybele, the ecstatic trances of the maenads, the whirling dervishes or Holy Rollers have arisen and have an appeal to a spiritual awakening that many believers find irresistible.

There were innumerable literary precursors to religious inspiration and fortune-telling. Cassandra, Priam's daughter in *The Iliad*, had fame as a prophetess. No one ever believed her prophecies but they always turned out to be true, including the atrocities she saw in the future committed in Priam's house. The Oracle of Delphi also prophesized the future. The prophet Helenus confided to Aeneas that he should seek out that woman of deep wisdom, the Sibyl of Cumae, who would foretell his future. She had to guide him to the underworld (no ordinary undertaking this, as Ulysses discovered when he was led to meet his mother) so he could learn from his father Anchises. Journeying to the underworld is what Dante, guided by Virgil, would imitate in *The Divine Comedy*. Theseus, Hercules, Orpheus, and Pollux had all been guided to the underworld, so the story was a staple part of literature by the advent of Christendom. The maenads, frenzied mad women, worshippers of Dionysius, crazy with wine, ran through the mountains and grasslands, always fierce with ecstasy. They were not prophetesses, but obviously had more fun.

A man claiming visions and to be a prophet leading women with similar utterances and visions might appear, on the face of it, to be on a fool's errand, or someone who had imbibed too much wine from a Bacchanalian festival. But according to Tertullian the bishop of Rome initially approved Montanist utterances as genuine expressions of the Holy Spirit, but soon changed his mind. Tertullian did not change his mind. After all his defensive writings on behalf of

Christian beliefs, his allegiance to Montanism both symbolized and stigmatized the end of his career.

But in the beginning of his career Tertullian was a master craftsman of Latin prose and used all his rhetorical and lawyerly skills to castigate those he disagreed with, vilifying them with his own peculiar bombast and righteousness. He slandered as a way of enlarging his eloquence and considered it normal to impugn character when disagreeing with an opponent's ideas.

Tertullian Against "Heretics"

One of those receiving his vituperation was Hermogenes, a contemporary, whose works are missing and about whom we know nothing except Tertullian's tract against him. How reliable is the authority of an adversary to reconstruct a doctrine whose distortions are often exaggerated for ridicule? Tertullian calls Hermogenes a "born heretic." The key point of Hermogenes is that he described the central issue of creation, which was biblical but not from gospel texts. Had Hermogenes claimed to be a Jew and not Christian he might not have invited Tertullian's classical prose to be directed against him and certainly not merited the distinction of a heretic.[16]

Hermogenes was a logician who said that God must have created all things 1) out of himself, 2) from nothing, 3) from something. If God created all things out of himself, then we must reject this conclusion because evil, which exists, cannot come from God. He concludes that matter was eternal with God since God could not create something corporeal out of incorporeal substances, and in this he agrees in general with Plato's description of creation in *Timaeus*. Why God could not make such a creative transformation is hard to explain. How evil arises from matter he does not explain. This kind of tortuous discussion was the literary spectator sport of the age, a debate that has nothing at all to do with Christian doctrine. But because Tertullian brands Hermogenes a heretic, and because Tertullian has survived because he defended Christian doctrine, the writings of men like Hermogenes and Marcion have been irreparably lost and we are denied the evidence for their arguments.

Tertullian's combative style, much of it imitative of Juvenal, was forged among Latin rhetorical and Greek literary sources and employed against doctrinal vagabonds like Marcion. Tertullian would have been appalled at those like Origen, Justin and Clement who sought to reconcile Christianity with classical philosophy, even though he was steeped in such learning himself. He rejected such an intellectual plan, disdaining the use of allegory to interpret scripture, and concentrated on rhetorical responses to critics, using the artifices of persuasion, like a good lawyer, to combat attacks against the faith. The result was an ennobling Latin Christian prose for his admirers who could in the future quote him as an eminent authority.[17]

Lesser-known heretics crowded the small stage of early Christianity. One was Noetus who established a school in Rome around the year 200. He taught that God the Father came to earth and it was he that died and rose again, not the Son. This became the Patripassian heresy. Noetus was questioned before a tribunal of presbyters. "Is it heretical," he is said to have asked before the tribunal, "to believe in just one god?" His question was never really answered, just ignored. Noetus was nonetheless branded a heretic, excommunicated, and buried without rites after his death. Eventually in 325, presumably to end such theological quibbling, the church declared that there was only one God, but then named three, and then unconvincingly subordinated the Son and Holy Spirit to the Father as if they were a hierarchy, as indeed they were in Greek mythology. The question of how a deity could have a son equal to the Father would be raised a century later by Arius, an alarming heretic who caused apoplexy among ecclesiastics and for a time had claims to a rival church.

About a decade after Noetus, in 215, an African priest named Sabellius came to Rome. He taught that God was not a divisible substance but that the different parts of God were activities or modes that exhibited different godlike actions, such as creating, giving laws, redeeming, and conveying spirit graces. Like Noetus, Sabellius believed that there can be only one God and that everything else was philosophically untenable. But entrenched dogma, not yet codified, prevailed. He and his followers were excommunicated by Pope Callistus (or Callixtus) in 217.

Early Christian theology was, as I noted, a combination of Hebrew monotheism, Greek polytheism, Persian dualism, Gnosticism, and mystical and apocalyptic visions. It tried to reconcile its multiple Middle Eastern literary inheritances not by defining what it believed, but by excommunicating those with whom it disagreed. Heretics were created in the first centuries from the negligence of Christianity in enunciating from the outset what the substance of its creed was.

Reading these polemics we enter an unforgiving world of Greek metaphysics where intimacies of a Greek tragedy are abandoned for an expanded world of divine multiple meanings conferred on chosen words like Logos, Father, Son, and Spirit. These writers are anxious to transform the discourse into a justification of the nature of Jesus but without the subtlety of Greek humor and empathetic understanding found in Greek plays. Abandoning humor and good sense these budding theologians plunged into disassembling each other's supposed fallacies.

The ancient Greeks introduced boxing in the Olympic Games. But the early Christians like Tertullian with opposing views of the nature of God and Jesus fought as pugilists using the salty language of adversaries as a form of redemption from charges of heresy. These language toughs were hardened by their self-righteous sense of religious correctness and absolute authority as Episcopal leaders. Their writings contain no warmth or wit, little spontaneity, with the possible exception of Origen, and tendentious, repetitive, and excessive verbiage.

The Proliferation of Heresies

When Jesus died his immediate followers were not only bereft but confused as to what to do next. There are ample passages testifying to this dilemma in *Acts*. But within a couple of centuries the teaching model of a Jewish rabbi, him whom the Apostles called "teacher," was dispensed for a more Roman organizational hierarchy based on military distinctions. The Catholic Church did not adopt an Apostolic model of following one leader as did the disciples of John the Baptist and Jesus. Jesus left no norm for church organization, no principle message other than love and mercy, no apostolic succession, and no manual for instructions. He died intestate. The Iman, with degrees of pious acceptance like a revered Ayatollah, is still the preferred Islamic religious structure. Had the Roman episcopate not been adopted, Christianity would likely resemble the Arabic model of differentiated clerical authority as it was in the first two centuries.

Hence it is not surprising that a confusion of voices and a proliferation of scrolls in the first two centuries sought to explain the purpose of the brief life of Jesus and all opinions appeared to be equally valid. Neither the ecclesiastical church nor its growing membership knew which doctrinal opinions were necessary for belief, which just informative, and which detrimental. Converts must have been attracted to communities because of the fashionableness of the religion and because it was unclear exactly what the religious beliefs were and only grouped around the figure of a new divinity. All this would have been perfectly acceptable in the expanded pantheons of Greek and Roman polytheistic belief.

It would have been unusual if differences had not arisen to flavor Christianity. The often conflicting and rival claims of Gnostics, Neo-Pythagoreans, Neo-Platonists, and Orphic mystery followers certainly added color to the culture of the Mediterranean. Many of the several rituals, ideas, and practices of these Greek philosophies actually found a ready home in Christianity. But the variety and ingenuity of beliefs about Jesus and his mission were enough to test the most imaginative of theological inventors.

- Jesus was a different God from the Old Testament (Marcion).
- The message of Jesus had been simplicity and austerity, and the Kingdom of God was already at hand through the Spirit (Montanus).
- Christ's body was a phantom (Docetus).
- Jesus was born a man but achieved divinity through his morals (Paul of Samosata).
- The Father and the Son were the same person (Sabellius).
- The Father and the Son had only one nature (Monophysites).

Who wouldn't be confused?

It was easier to assimilate existing rituals and ceremonies than to define the new dogmas. For example, Theon of Smyrna (c. 70–140), a contemporary of gospel scribes, described five steps in the process of initiation into the Eleusian mysteries. This step-by-step initiation resembles Catholic sacraments. The first is the preliminary purification. Then, second, sacred things are presented, but what these are is unclear. The third step is opening up of the full vision. The fourth part is the investiture, at which time the initiate is authorized to communicate the sacred rites. But the fifth and last step is friendship and interior communion with God, and the enjoyment of that gladness which comes from intimate converse with divine beings. These steps of entry into the faith, belief, or mysteries compare favorably with many Christian sacraments, and because so many converts to Christianity may have been familiar at one time with many of the mystery rites or knowledgeable about them, it would have been easy to adopt and assimilate the process into the Christian mysteries.

Two episodes contributed to the expansion of Christianity in the early centuries: the destruction of Jerusalem in 70 and the influence of Pauline theology. It was not merely the utter eradication of the city that diminished Jewish influence but the psychological debilitation of the Jewish Diaspora that Christian followers rushed to fill that enabled the church to close the membership gap more quickly. Such were the Ebionites, an ascetic group who thought poverty more esteemed than fidelity to one code of belief. Judean Ebionites followed Mosaic Law faithfully and believed Jesus had been a Jewish miracle-worker. It was the Ebionites who thought Paul was the real apostate for injecting Hellenism into the Jewish/Christian modality.

Paul preached in synagogues and his message must have appealed to Jews who saw the destruction of the temple as a sign of God's wrath and the people's infidelity. The fall of Jerusalem gave credibility to the Jews that Jesus just might be the promised redeemer since those in the Diaspora were mercifully spared ruin and annihilation and had an opportunity to convert to the new religion. Additionally, while Paul preached a Hellenic flavor to the new religion, he was from an ultraconservative Jewish background and this enhanced his credibility among synagogue communities. The fact that he was at odds with the Jerusalem contingent of original Apostles seemed less relevant than his contagious enthusiasm for his message. Moreover Paul was uninterested in a church structure. He preached about the spirit, a very Gnostic idea. His letters reveal his interest in the communities he had established where he left locals in charge of services and practices, but set out no plan, other than preaching, for how to enforce a common belief.

Within about fifty years after the death of Peter and Paul *Acts of the Apostles* and the *Gospel of John* were produced which made the message of Paul more important than the message conveyed by the Apostles. *The Gospel of John* clearly identifies Jesus as the Son of God, an accusation Jesus himself would have been embarrassed to hear and likely would have repudiated, or so it appears in *Mark*. But these political documents solidified Pauline theology and rescued the church from its backwater moorings amid a destroyed city and a disenfranchised and broken people. Christians were then able to roam wherever Roman roads and water-corridors led them. Of course all roads led to Rome.

A COMPARISON OF ELEUSIAN MYSTERIES AND CATHOLIC SACRAMENTS

Purification	Baptism
Sacred presentations	Catechism/ instruction
Opening full vision	Confirmation
Investiture	Holy Orders
Communion with the Divine	Eucharist

Meanwhile orthodox Jews did not wait for further events to overwhelm them, and about eighty-five Jewish officials anathematized the Nazarene movement and made it a part of their liturgy thus officially branding all Nazarenes heretics.[18] Christian heresy would soon follow this precedent. In quick succession came six heretics—Basilides, Marcion, Valentinus, Montanus, Nestorius, Arius—each with his own interpretation of who Jesus was, and what the writings about him meant. Indeed some of the most notable propagandists in the history of the church were first members of banned sects: Tertullian was a Montanist as we saw, and Augustine a Manichaean. It was as if the scurrilous abuse and toxic polemics originating between Peter and Paul about the direction the fledgling church should take in Jerusalem in 49 and in a later acrimonious meeting in Antioch were to be propagated endlessly through all the Nazarene communities.

The destruction of so many early documents, whether deliberately or through natural means, denies us access to the multitude of Christian-like ideas, blends of Judaism, mysticism, Persian dualism, and Gnosticism, that incubated in the free intellectual Roman air. Paul's epistles record some of the doctrinal divides amid lingering and unresolved controversies in the communities he addressed. The 1945 discovery of the Nag Hammadi library cache alone contains over four dozen otherwise unknown epistles, letters, visions, novels, and treatises that constitute a proliferation of Christian-related literature in the first centuries. We cannot therefore tell whether heresiarchs were only articulating the views of communities, forming communities based on their own novel theological interpretations, or simply writing literature for eager readers. But intellectual diversity obviously infected the religious polity. The rise and establishment of orthodox doctrine led to the burning and burying of unacceptable writings.

The Donation heresy was popular in this period. Donatus (313–355 CE) denied that the sacraments were efficacious if administered by an unworthy and sinful minister. This movement quickly spread through North Africa and was in full swing during the life of Augustine. A minor theological squabble grew into a large civil revolt within the church and the military were called to expel aberrant members from their churches. But by the middle of the fourth century, Donatists outnumbered orthodox Christians and had their own hierarchy of bishops in the same cities as orthodox bishops. It became clear that differences in theology could lead to sectarianism that would cleave the church as a whole. In fact, the Donatist schism did leave North Africa weakened from its political unrest and theological turmoil. As a result, the area was easily overrun by Vandals and then Muslims. Heresies of the early church were fueled by the political ambitions of localities like Alexandria to secede from the rule of districts like Constantinople, as much a quest for political independence as theological.

ROMAN CUSTOMS ABSORBED INTO CHRISTIAN ORGANIZATION AND LITURGY

Roman Law as the Basis for Canon Law
Roman Government Structure for Administration
Bishops as Roman Prefects
Archbishops as Roman Governors
Synod of Bishops as Provincial Assembly
Priestly Religious Vestments (chasuble, stole, alb)
Equestrian *latum clauum* stripe becomes the Deacon's Shoulder Stole
Use of Incense
Holy Water in Purifications
Burning Candles Before the Altar
Worship of Saints
Architecture of the Basilica
Latin as the Official Language

(Source, Durant 1944, 618-19)

The Protestant Reformation would again expand Christianity's multiple messages. But even today within the Roman Catholic Church there are widening chasms. Liberation theology was a movement that sought to broaden Catholic appeal to Latin America's underclass, to address issues of poverty, the empowerment of the laity in the rituals and ceremonies of faith, and the decentralization of authority. Liberation theology, the equivalent of early Christian interpretations of dogma, traumatized ecclesiastics with the kind of fear that galvanized the early church into strengthening church authority from liberal thinking. Opposed to this liberal view of the church is the organization known as *Opus Dei* (the work of God), an ultraconservative fraternity that emphasizes the enthronement of church hierarchy and preaches strict obedience to church doctrine.

The Apostolic model of succession in the first centuries was set aside so that the church could assume an organization structure from Rome that suited its mission of unifying doctrine and enforcing regulations. The Jewish model was impractical because it assumed that a high priest and king like David would be synonymous, impossible in an imperial Roman world where an emperor was both absolute secular ruler and *Pontifex Maximus*, a religious title later assumed by popes. Borrowing the Roman hierarchical structure seemed practical, and using the biblical symbols of a high priest and sacerdotal kingdom as rationales for clerical domination was eminently acceptable. The bishop, like a Roman prefect, would rule over presbyters and deacons who, in turn, like centurions, would govern the laity, the foot soldiers of the faithful. Bishops ruled dioceses, a Roman military and administrative subdivision. Doctrine was momentarily set aside as the movement slowly became institutionalized.

Cyprian of Carthage (c. 200–258)

One of the chief defenders of church unity was Cyprian, a name once invoked in the Roman Catholic Mass, an educated Carthaginian and admirer of Tertullian who was ordained a priest two years after his conversion and elected bishop of Carthage shortly after his ordination. The early church often embraced mature men who converted to Christianity and then, like Ambrose, Bishop of Milan, the mentor of Augustine, were quickly promoted to responsible clerical positions. Seniority in life, however, did not always translate into organizational or diplomatic experience in administering the affairs of restless and ambitious local clergy, wavering church members or potential heathens.

Cyprian quickly had to cope with troublesome topics and quarrelsome clergy in his diocese. In *de unitate ecclesiae* (On Church Unity) Cyprian wrote that the authority of the local bishop was preeminent. In other words, there was no pope or chief bishop, nor was any bishop more preferential than any other. The "keys of the Kingdom" had indeed been given to Peter but as an individual, he said, not an inherited authority. Cyprian sought unity in the local church membership and the avoidance of theological discord.

The Christian community in Rome about the year 253 consisted of one bishop, 46 presbyters (priests), seven deacons, seven sub-deacons, forty-two acolytes, and fifty-two exorcists, lecturers and porters, all serving a community of about 1,500, a fraction of the total population.[19]

But what happens when local communities depose a bishop? The following story typifies the dilemma early churches faced over organizational unity.

Cyprian would soon discover the complexities of ecclesiastical authority even in local disputes unrelated to doctrine. Two Spanish bishops, Martial and Basiledes, were deposed by their churches in Merida and Leon in 254, probably for cowardice during the persecution under Emperor Decius. African churches, including Carthage, concurred in new Episcopal appointments. But the deposed bishops appealed to Stephen, the Bishop of Rome, for reinstatement and he agreed. Cyprian was outraged. What right did Rome have to overrule a decision by a local church authority? Moreover, a new doctrinal matter intruded: If lapsed bishops were to be reinstated, did they also have to show penitence for their misdeeds and be, in effect, re-baptized? Cyprian believed that by their schismatic actions they placed themselves outside the Holy Spirit and had to become Christians again before they could be reinstated as bishops. As incensed as Cyprian was for this violation to his ecclesiastical and doctrinal opinions, Christian clerics were acting exactly like Roman governors or prefects in appealing to Rome as if to an emperor in civil matters. The bishop of Rome would in time become the de facto emperor of the church, the pope, using the same biblical argument Cyprian had used to support the idea of the authority of the local bishop.[20]

Valerian became emperor in 257 and immediately organized a general persecution of Christians beginning with bishops, who had to pay reverence to the Roman gods. Cyprian refused and was beheaded in 258. Thus his martyrdom installed him as a saint when his real views, had they been known and accepted, may have prohibited him from that status.

By the middle of the second century Rome was beginning to experience the fatigue of running an empire and the strain of holding its imperialism intact against the insurgencies of the Huns, the strains on the economy, and the listlessness of its citizens. The ruminations of Marcus Aurelius, tinged as they were with stoicism, also held a hint of disillusion that would sift through the Latin west and imperil the creative genius during the Augustan Age that gave such a vibrant life to art and literature. Placating the ancient Roman gods, and forcing Christians to do likewise, seemed easier than reinvigorating the polity with doses of pride to relieve a widening sense of resignation and ennui. The invasion of the Christian God arrived two centuries prior to the barbarians and insinuated its divine character into a disintegrating Roman civic and aesthetic vitality.

Meanwhile, decade after decade heretics would plumb the biblical and philosophical inconsistencies in the new religion and compose their persuasions, while established ecclesiastics preached church unity and uniformity. The church would eventually conquer and rule, but heretics raised the right questions and proposed more creative theological solutions. Even the voluble Plutarch, writing in *On the Cessation of Oracles*, was able to muse:

> For it is silly and very childish to suppose that the god, like the ventriloquist spirits, enters into the bodies of the prophets and makes proclamations, employing their mouths and voices in a way of instruments; for in mixing himself up with human means, he does not respect his own majesty, neither does he maintain his dignity, nor the superiority of his being.[21]

Such realistic and healthy skepticism about prophecy among the Greeks at Delphi speaks volumes about what educated authors and pagan priests felt about the superstitious beliefs in the divine. But the myths propagated, and though popular were so inane that only an intellectual, or by implication a philosopher turned theologian, could swallow them.

Attaining the richness of the divine and leading a virtuous life were twin processes in everyone's life according to Greek and Roman philosophers and moralists. According to the typical beliefs of the time, people have been given the faculty of reason to avoid sin and do good deeds, so that when a person died his soul could enter into communion with the godhead. "To be cleansed of the body is the beginning of life for divine and thus blessed souls," says the Phoenician to the Vinedresser in Philostratus's *Heroikos*,[22] and evil people endure a painful purgation. These ideas were very Hellenic, emphatically believed by Plutarch, the most systematic organizer of ancient thought, and the so-called pagan high priest at Delphi from 99 to 120, about the same time as the gospels were composed. Literate Christians were so Hellenized they may not have realized they were totally assimilating the traditional beliefs of the religious, non-Christian world of the first century.

CHAPTER EIGHT
THE AGE OF RELIGIOUS DISSENSION

The Pantheon in Rome built between 118–127 CE is one of the world's most illustrious monuments to plural gods, the only monument to survive from antiquity intact. The Romans were as superstitious as anyone and did not want to neglect a temple to a god they might have forgotten so it was consecrated to all gods. Its height of 142 feet is the same as the diameter of the rotunda. The oculus opening in the center of the dome is twenty-nine feet across and admits natural light and the elements into the awesome interior. Its timelessness represents a rare achievement in architecture as well as to plural divinities. It was converted to a Christian church in 609. It is therefore a respectable symbol and survivor of the age of religious dissension and dissenters.

The ultimate collapse of the Roman Empire culminated with the fall of Rome in 410 by the Visigoths under Alaric, and the conquest of North Africa and Carthage by the Vandals in 439 under Gaiseric. The personal hygiene of the Visigoths and Vandals was the least of the problems of the vanquished Romans, as the impressionable and untutored conquerors capitulated throughout the empire to the Christianity of their captives.

The unification of Christianity offered civil order and the fabric of an ethical code that approximated the old Roman order. Christianity captured the essence of Roman stability and military precision and married it to an organizational unity that had no historical precedent until the armies of Islam swept across the Middle East, South Asia, and North Africa in the eighth century. For a people weary of famine, internecine warfare, the skepticism of misplaced loyalties, the hope of a new belief that would rescue the population from pillage, and bring even an uneasy peace and restore justice, this stability was welcomed even if it meant believing in an eternal damnation for personal misdeeds. That heretics like Nestorius and Pelagius described in this chapter died for the absurdities embedded in grammar and metaphysics carrying theological weight was not the least of the consequences.

Just as the debate about the substance of doctrinal belief was evolving, so too was the authoritative structure of the church and the decision about who constituted ecclesiastical authority. Clearly, bishops were elected in their dioceses, not appointed by a distant authority. But could a council of bishops convened by the emperor create dogma? Everyone seemed to agree that it could.

But a council of bishops acting on its own did not seem to fulfill legitimized authority. The secular and civil authority, the emperor, was in these early centuries the seat and origin of ecclesiastical authority. It was the emperor who anointed the patriarch of the capitol city, Constantinople. This may seem to be a minor point in the discussion, but the implication is that the legitimate Roman authority still took precedence over any so-called church authority and was subject to it. Divine authority was assumed to flow through imperial power, a concept as ancient as the Babylonians, an idea that permeated Europe for hundreds of years as the divine right of kings.

The age during which Christianity matured from the second to fourth centuries was contentious. The enemies of authority were as numerous as there were members of the extended imperial family, which is why the extirpation of imperial sons, mothers, brothers, and assorted cousins were carried out so systematically by the Praetorian Guard. The allegiance of the troops had to be constantly reinvigorated with bribes and booty. Each general had an army of legions ambitious for greater authority, ever eager to quell real or imagined insurrections. The enemies without the walls were far more numerous and, though removed at a distance, better equipped and more ravenous for the city's resources. Goths, Visigoths, Ostrogoths, Persians, Huns, Alemanni, Vandals, and Franks were a few of the tribes that created serious military headaches for Romans. With incursions along the dwindling fringes of the frontiers they perpetually challenged the resolve and finances of the empire.

Add to this combustible mix an assortment of superstitions, degenerate vices among the aristocracy, barbarian ambitions, and the massacre of violent leaders and you can begin to estimate the insecurities of the age. Taxes levied for maintaining the army, together with the excesses of the aristocracy, caused the middle class to collapse. Christianity became so ascendant that by 418 Emperor Theodosius began purging pagans from the ranks of the army. Peace, safety, and security from the fragilities of the economy were principal sources of tension and distress. The collective anxieties of the age were enough to get any citizen to change his religion to obtain divine favors. Actual heretics surely outnumbered the ones we know from history.

Constantine (c. 288–337)

Soldiers declared Constantine emperor in York when his father died there in 306. From that year until 337 he fought a series of civil wars against rival claimants and conspired in the death of a few blood relatives. Adhering to a trend begun in 284 by another soldier emperor, Diocletian, Constantine separated the military from civil administrations, strengthened the economy, and consolidated power that brought stability to the empire. He moved the imperial capitol to Byzantium in 330 to distance himself from further military threats, in essence abandoning Rome to the barbarians. The isolation and confusion in the empire eventually led to the elevation of the church and its hierarchy as the main civilizing and stabilizing power in the East.

In the middle of his soldiering campaigns in Europe, Constantine convened the Council of Arles in 314 to help resolve the Donatist controversy. Donatists were a group of strict Christians from North Africa, as we saw in the previous chapter, who believed that the sacraments were only as valid as the sanctity of the cleric administering them. The Donatist movement began when Christians in Africa had been incensed that certain authorities had turned over sacred books and articles of faith when Christians were persecuted. The Council of Arles condemned them, but they established a rival hierarchy in Africa and remained a potent religious force for another century when the movement disintegrated.

The Nicene Creed

In 325 Constantine held the Council of Nicaea, a town across the water from Constantinople. The intimidated assembly of bishops concluded its hesitant deliberations under duress, undoubtedly not realizing they held the fate of Christianity for all time in their questionable and hurried votes. Constantine was intemperate when it came to Christian controversies. Knowing the emperor's wishes for haste and his lack of forbearance, council delegates declared somewhat hastily in the Nicene Creed what appeared to be a code of acknowledged new religious truths. It incorporated the most fashionable philosophy laden with Greek Gnosticism expressing Hebrew notions of a Messiah with Greek ideas of divinity about a Jewish religious reformer. The Creed couldn't get any more religiously complicated than that.

The result was torturous terminology that baffled later bishops, councils, and proponents of the new message. The Nicene Creed was subsequently declared invalid by some councils, valid again by others, and finally orthodox without equivocation by Christian emperors like Theodosius who equally detested controversy and insubordination in religious affairs. Constantine died happily deprived of the doctrinal vicissitude Christianity would generate despite his efforts to consolidate the council's awkward reasoning.

Not everything religious changed suddenly by this creedal definition. The altar and statue of Victory in the Senate had been kept in place by Constantine. It was removed by his son Constantius, reinstated by Julian, and then removed again by Gratian. The statue was a symbol of fluctuating beliefs and imperial dispositions toward the new religion. The fourth and fifth centuries witnessed a surge of religious expression in the new religion and a scramble among Christian thinkers to discover what the nature of the new divinity was. Paul had kept reminding Christians in his epistles to be true to the faith. But it was unclear what that faith actually was since so many crucial definitions were ambiguous.

Before Christianity was established as the religion of the Roman Empire in 325, the multiplicity of creeds dictated that toleration for the peace of the empire among religious beliefs was necessary. So on April 30, 311, the dying Emperor

Galerius issued an *Edict of Toleration*, in effect a pardon to Christians so they could return to the faith of their Roman ancestors. He then extended a pardon to those Christians who wished to return to their faith, a condition in which he apparently sought the prayers of Christians in his dying moments. Galerius' imperial successor, Maximinus tried unsuccessfully to counteract the degree.

Two years later, the new emperor of the West Constantine, and emperor of the East, Licinius, in 313 issued the *Edict of Milan* granting to Christians, and to members of any other religious sect, full rights to practice their religion as they saw fit. The new imperial degree also removed all legal obstacles to Christian worship and practice and the return of their property, if any had been confiscated. Constantine violated his own edict in 325 when he proclaimed Christianity as the sole religion for the empire, thus invalidating those "others (not Christians) to observe that religion which each preferred." Religious toleration can be viewed as a political tool for emperors and kings who seek the prayers and supplications of certain religious members, or by the highest authorities when it is convenient to establish totalitarian religious dominance. The outcome in all cases is that those excluded become automatically branded as heretics or heathens.

Some saw Christianity as another level of Judaism and a return of the expected Messiah. Others believed in an entirely new revelation by God. But in practice, Christianity became a religion that absorbed all the elements of past religious beliefs. In the quest to seek justification for Christ and the message to be proclaimed, ecclesiastical authorities, in collusion with imperial power, standardized belief in the Nicene Creed and compelled adherence to its tenets. In a heartbeat, everyone not on board the Christian system was classified as a heretic and excommunicated. This now included emperors like Julian.

Emperor Julian (331–363)

History remembers him as "The Apostate." It's true that he personally reverted to the old Roman gods but only because he concluded that Christians did not practice their beliefs well and exhibited none of the charitable qualities their religion taught. He banned Christianity from the empire to allow pagans once again to practice their beliefs.[1] He is the first imperial heretic.

Emperor Julian (Flavius Claudius Julianus) was born in Constantinople in 331, the nephew of Constantine. When Constantine's surviving three sons, Constans, Constantius, and Constantine II, secured the empire after the death of Constantine, Julian's father, oldest brother, and cousins were slain. Julian alone escaped, undoubtedly because he was only five years old. However, he and another older brother were held in castle confinement until 350. Julian was allowed to pursue his education partly in Nicomedia but mostly in Athens where he excelled in Greek literature, rhetoric, and philosophy.

In 355 Julian was summoned to Milan, then the capitol of the western Roman court. There he was protected by the Empress Eusebia from court intrigues.

Constantius, the sole emperor after the other two brothers died violent deaths, raised Julian to the status of Caesar and dispatched him to Gaul to control the provinces. He proved to be a capable and courageous soldier and general. Unlike Caesar's commentaries on his wars, Julian's campaign book of commentaries against the tribes of Gaul is lost.

"The life of this young man was guided by some principle which raised him above the ordinary and accompanied him from his illustrious cradle to his last breath," writes Ammianus Marcellinus.[2] He was compared to emperors Titus, Hadrian, Antoninus Pius, and Marcus Aurelius whom he consciously imitated in character and actions. He divided the night into three parts and slept the first, conducted civil administration business in the second, and personal study in the third. He preferred philosophic studies but did not neglect poetry, rhetoric, languages, or history. Meanwhile, he feigned belief in Christianity so as not to arouse opposition to his authority.[3]

In 356 he recaptured Cologne, repulsed attacks by the Alemanni (after whom Germany is named), and defeated them at Strasbourg with clever military tactics and uncommon courage. He then moved against the Franks on the Meuse River and forced them back across the Rhine. While stationed at Paris, then the provincial capitol, he repopulated devastated lands, strengthened the economy, reduced taxes, and helped restore the prosperity of the region. He is credited with establishing the principle that a man is innocent until proven guilty.[4]

Meanwhile, the emperor of the east, Constantius, fighting a fierce campaign against the Persians ordered Julian to send some of his Gallic legions to the rescue. Julian would have obeyed but his soldiers were reluctant to fight in Persia. So in 359 Julian's army unanimously proclaimed him emperor. In 361 Julian began his march to encounter Constantius's army when suddenly Constantius died of a fever and Julian, now only thirty, rode triumphantly into Constantinople as emperor.

He immediately replaced the courtiers with philosophers, dismissed all the court staff, and instituted administrative reforms. As a secret devotee of paganism, he reinstituted its multiple devotions while tolerating Christian worship. From the time he was a boy he had been inclined towards the pagan gods, a possible response to the fact that Christian emperors had killed most of his family while he was only a toddler. His ardor for paganism grew but fear of exposing his true beliefs kept him from practicing any rituals except in the secrecy of his most trusted confidantes. During campaigns in Gaul he attended Christian holy day ceremonies. As emperor he proclaimed that the temple be re-opened and the worship of pagan gods reestablished.

He summoned Christian bishops whom he knew to be of schismatic minds about their own beliefs, as were their parishioners, and admonished them to accept tolerance of other religions.[5] This was an astute political strategy as he knew that imperial toleration meant that religious groups would become even more divisive and hence unable to become a coherent political threat.

His tolerance extended to the Jews as well. In his zeal to build a monument worthy of his reign, he embarked on restoring the temple at Jerusalem, destroyed almost 300 years earlier by Titus. But clearing the foundations of rubble proved hazardous as fireballs burst out when stones were cleared and some workmen were burned to death. The project was soon abandoned.

Julian's proclamation of religious freedom on February 4, 362, was a sort of reinstatement of Constantine's *Edict of Milan* in 313, a return to a time when everyone could practice religious choice without government interference. He banned the practice of clerics getting free public transport and reserved the right to appoint teachers. He lifted the taxes on Jews and allowed them to renew their sacrifices. Throughout 362 he involved himself in the Senate to settle disputes and paid close attention to military and civil affairs by strengthening the military along the routes where trouble was likely to occur and raised men of proven ability to positions of power.

But the business with the Persians was unfinished and Julian had to turn his attentions eastward to subdue the rebellion. He entered Antioch in the fall of 361 and remained until March 362. During the winter he composed *Against the Galileans*, his critique of Christianity. His austere personality and enthusiasm for philosophy did not endear him to the local population. Antioch was a largely Christian city opposed to the restoration of paganism. But it was also a city of frivolity and luxurious living, recognized as such even by Hadrian three centuries earlier. Julian had restored the pagan temples and their services but the people refused to attend them. Christians had invaded the temple of Apollo at Daphne in the Antioch suburbs and Apollo priests had abandoned it under the threat of violence. As a result, Julian destroyed the Christian church there and restored the cult of Apollo. A bishop of Antioch, Babylas, had been buried in a grove in Daphne, a nearby suburb. When Julian had the church in which he was buried demolished, officials removed the body of Babylas to Antioch and that same night the Christians burned the temple of Apollo Julian had restored.[6]

As a result of the irreverent response to him and his pagan gods, Julian wrote a satire, *Misopogon* (Beard-Hater), scolding the Antioch citizenry for its unseemly habits, its wantonness and lasciviousness, and its ridiculing of pagan symbols. Julian had a beard, but the men of Antioch were clean-shaven. The satire also attempted to explain his own character and how his habits were formed early and were lasting. He recalls how well he was received among the barbarian Celts more than he is now among his own people. It's a biting satire outlining all the injustices Julian received even though he was moderate, reasonable, and cautious in his judgments and actions while in the city. The city fathers relented after his departure and sent a delegation to make peace but Julian was unresponsive at the insult to himself and to the gods he believed in.[7] He left for Persia with his army and was killed by a javelin in the first major battle. He was only thirty-two.

Julian the Scholar

In his short life, he wrote three volumes comprising several treatises, panegyrics, hymns, and tracts, making him the most learned, erudite, and noteworthy authors of the fourth century, and the most prolific writer of all the emperors. Though a courageous military man, carrying several books with him on campaigns, he considered himself first and foremost a student of philosophy. He comfortably quoted Isocrates, Plato, Homer, Xenophon, and Demosthenes, and extolled Diogenes and Zeno whose stoic virtues he admired and practiced.

He wrote of his studies: "Thus when I was initiated by those guides, in the first place by a philosopher who trained me in the preparatory discipline, and next by that most perfect philosopher (Maximus of Ephesus) who revealed to me the entrance to philosophy; and though I achieved but little on account of the engrossing affairs that overwhelmed me from without, still for all that I have had the benefit of right training."[8]

To the end he remained humble about his abilities: "I am fully conscious that by nature there is nothing remarkable about me—there never was from the first nor has there come to be now—but as regards philosophy I have only fallen in love with it."[9] One of his most telling attributes is in a sentence in his satire *Misopogon* where he writes: "In fact, he who grants indulgence to one whose aims are the opposite of his own is, in my opinion, the most considerate of men."[10]

Julian's *Letter to a Priest* is an epistolary fragment, missing its opening and ending, and contains a summary of his belief about the status and conduct of priests.[11] It is addressed to a pagan not a Christian priest, as he wanted religious officials to act in accordance with certain principles and above all to give to the less fortunate. He insists first that the priest conduct himself in accordance with the laws of the state and to exhort men not to transgress the laws of the gods.

He insists on philanthropy, to treat slaves kindly, quotes both Moses and the goddess Athene, and, following his own example, urges the priest to share with others, "because from the little that I had I spent money on those in need and gave them a share."[12] It is also acceptable, not only to give generously to those who are good, but also to share "clothes and food even with the wicked," including those in prison. He believes that when we give we donate to man's humanity and not his morality. He calls every man kinsman not strangers, and thinks everyone should make virtue the basis for all conduct, and that priests be held to high standards and high honor if they follow honorable precepts. He believes that it is everyone's duty to honor the images, temples, and sacred precincts of the altars and the gods. Priests should not read licentious works (and Julian mentions specific authors), speak dishonorably, or take part in shameless acts, and encourages reading of the main philosophers. Priests should not attend the theater, and Julian says he would close them if he could.

This fragmentary document is a lucid description of Julian's belief about the state, the powers and influence of the gods, how the role of priests should be honored, and how priests should conduct themselves. It reveals an emperor who is just, conscientious, educated, well disposed to the poor and unfortunate, and who seeks a well-ordered state that reflects civil pride and a disciplined life, as his own life was. Indeed, this document would fit into any Christian canon with its virtuous themes were it not for his belief in the plurality of gods.

His letters reveal a man of moderation, conscious when injustices have been performed but never intolerant or vengeful toward those who opposed him. As a youthful student in Athens he impressed everyone with his modesty, grace, and charm and of his intense interest in learning and intellectual pursuits. It was during this tenure in the esteemed city that he was initiated into the Eleusinian mysteries. He always favored adherence to laws above all other behaviors. He wrote as often to philosophers about academic concerns in his short career as to government officials. He was dedicated to his administrative chores and shunned the games in the Hippodrome to the dismay of the populace. In his personal life he never remarried after the death of his wife, did not take a mistress, and did not cavort in the company of women. Ammianus says that after the defeat of a Persian city, "He would not touch or even look at any of the lovely young girls who were captured, though Persian women are renowned for their beauty. In this he followed the example of Alexander and Africanus who would not allow themselves to succumb to desire after showing themselves invincible in hardship."[13]

He ate plain food and dispensed with the court cooks. He lived and dressed simply, slept on a hard bed in unheated rooms, and lived an ascetic life like Plato's philosopher king or a soldier's soldier. Had he been a Christian he would have been thought a saintly monk for his virtues. As a judge he was moderate in the dispensation of punishments and fair in claims of equity, careful to secure all the facts about a case before making a decision. He would be the prime exemplar of a Christian prince had he remained a Christian, and not an example for a Machiavellian conduct for a prince. His life could be a valiant illustration of how devotion to principle triumphs over passion, a superabundance of riches and ultimate power. He renounced the religion of his youth because of the conduct of Christians, embraced the religion of his ancestors, and adhered strictly to ethical standards that can be classified as saintly.

In a letter titled as a *Rescript on Christian Teachers*, he writes: "I hold that a proper education results, not in laboriously acquired symmetry of phrases and language, but in a healthy condition of mind, I mean a mind that has understanding and true opinions about things good and evil, honorable and base. Therefore, when a man thinks one thing and teaches his pupils another, in my opinion he fails to educate exactly in proportion as he fails to be an honest man."[14] In a letter from 362 he wrote: "I affirm by the gods that I do not wish Galileans to be either put to death or unjustly beaten, or to suffer any other injury."[15] In another letter in the same year he wrote: "I have behaved to all the Galileans with such kindness and benevolence that none of them has suffered violence anywhere or been dragged into a temple or threatened into anything else of the sort against his own will."[16]

Did Julian stand up heroically to Christian intolerance, or was he merely opportunistic and principled in favor of social conformity? He did tell bishops to be accepting of other religions. Was this for political reasons or religious convictions? Did Julian hate Christians because of what Christian emperors did to his family? As I noted in the Introduction, it's impossible to assess motives. As emperor he obviously felt some obligation to keep the peace, and religious disturbances in the empire were the source of as much civic discord as barbarian intrusions.

But though he maintained the highest ethical virtues and stoical ideals of both the Greeks and the Romans in his personal life and official capacity as ruler of the empire, history written by Christians has been unkind to his memory. In the end, he demonstrated rare courage in the face of lethal danger when he marched in the front line with his troops without breast armor and thus exposed died of a javelin stuck in his liver. His fault is not so much in trying to debunk Christianity as it is in forcing paganism onto an unwilling and intolerant populace. The church at the time was not bold enough to classify an emperor as a heretic. An apostate would do. But the church did condemn patriarchs like Nestorius.

Nestorius (381–451)

Now in my opinion whoever is about to investigate the truth in all seriousness ought not to compose the discourse with preconceived ideas but should bring forward and explain everything opposed to the truth.
Nestorius, *The Bazaar of Heracleides, c. 435*

So begins Nestorius, patriarch of Constantinople, in his book *The Bazaar of Heracleides*. And what a superb opening declaration it is because it expresses a search for truth by stating all issues seemingly opposed to it. This rhetorical method of persuasion would later be favored by scholastics in the Middle Ages, notably Thomas Aquinas who first stated a premise, then listed the arguments against and then for a position, and then wrote a conclusion. Nestorius's arguments revolved around the nature and person of Jesus. Was Jesus the Christ and the Logos also God? Was Jesus the man also Jesus the God? Was Jesus half man and half God? Did he have a human soul in his manhood as well as the person of the divinity? How were these diverse natures joined? Nestorius is heroic in the sense that he maintained his ideological position, later declared a heresy, in the face of bitter condemnation.

Nestorius claimed that Mary was the mother of Christ and not the mother of God since she only gave birth to his humanity not his divinity. He was challenged in this sensible view by the indomitable and antagonistic Cyril of Alexandria. With the blessing of Pope Celestine, Cyril anathematized Nestorius and convinced the Council of Ephesus in 431 to condemn him as a heretic when he was not present to offer his views. Not even Roman citizens were convicted in absentia.

If apologists admitted that Jesus was a separate god they were open to the charge of polytheism. They had to engage in laborious distinctions to attempt to explain that somehow Jesus was, and always had been, a part of the biblically revealed God, and that all descriptions gospel scribes had said about him—God, Son, Word, Christ, Messiah—could somehow be resolved into a divine unity. Somehow, they argued, the scripture had to be explained with Greek philosophy in order to satisfy belief in the undivided unity of the Hebrew God, otherwise faith in monotheism was threatened. If they failed, statues of Jesus would fit just as protectively in another niche in the pantheon of accepted Greek and Roman deities and Christianity would lose its privileged status as a state-sponsored religion. Thus did Greek philosophy and Roman politics triumph over Hebrew prophecy and scripture to fashion Christianity.

Myths about the gods that the Greeks found enlightening and even entertaining were inspiration for understanding the uncertainty of life's problems. Christian apologists took these at face value and transformed such stories into religious orthodoxy in which heretics and nonbelievers were consigned to the most fearsome indignities and even death. There had been innumerable half-men and half-deities in literature beginning with the Sumerian Gilgamesh and Enkidu. But the literate Greeks made the combination of humans and deities into an art form with Perseus, Dionysus, Orpheus, Theseus, Adonis, Hercules, and others, and heroes like Achilles and Ulysses who were able to summon divine help almost at will. By the time of the early Christians the combinations of humans impregnated by the gods and their progeny was a commonly accepted literary feature. Christian apologists turned these myths into metaphysical muddying that formed the basis for Christian dogma.

Hence, resurrecting Nestorius and reexamining his ideas, trial, and condemnation at the Council of Ephesus in 431 is a way of seeking intellectual and religious justice. This exercise is not only fruitful for satisfying what was an early inquisition and to exonerate persecuted individuals like condemned heretics, but also for viewing the context of the fourth century religious debate that resulted in the dogmas defining Christianity.

Theological Contentions

Does a conscientious contender make a trinity of substance out of a trinity of persons, or make a unity of a person combined with a unity of essences? If this seems so much quibbling over ambiguous terms, welcome to the world of the first Christian centuries and the first heresies. Somehow belief must accommodate the unity of substance while acknowledging the differences in the biblical godhead. Father, Son, and Holy Spirit are not separate gods but distinct persons in one god. At the same time, according to this theology, there are no parts to God. In another time, in another place, they could have been debating the essence of Zeus or his control over the laws of nature using the same terminology, but everyone would have been laughing.

Some discussants in this age of questions and dissent argued that if the godhead truly inhabits the body and becomes flesh in being (*ousia*), the vision of Christ's body is illusion and what is witnessed is only the appearance of the body. The metaphor of water and ice (or a burning bush) as one in being but of two differing appearances supposedly satisfies the argument. These are tidy philosophical distinctions but in contemporary understanding chemically incomprehensible.

The claims of divinity for Jesus are found only in the last gospel, the *Gospel of John*, principally in chapters 5 and 14 where Jesus says that he and the Father are one. Some of the unaccepted proposals proposed to resolve the union of God and man were the following:

- That the Incarnation was a fiction and an appearance in order that God might appear to mankind.
- That the divine existence became flesh so that it could become its own existence for the nature of mankind and free it from sin.
- That God was made flesh as a complement to nature instead of soul. That Christ had two natures before the union with God, but that after the union they are no longer two natures but one existence united in substance (ousia)
- That the Incarnation was in animate flesh with a rational and intelligent soul and did not change in substance (ousia) but was one person (prosopon) with both natures.

You might think that it easier to solve quadratic functions without paper and pencil or calculator, or to compute the densities of black holes than to decipher the meaning of the words and the significance in these early theological exercises. However, this was the intellectual coffeehouse discussion of the day, and for a couple of centuries men debated these apparent contradictions at great length. The entire argumentative structure is based on belief in the Incarnation and what it meant for humanity. Without this belief, Christianity, as we understand it, has no doctrinal basis. We can associate Jesus, as Muslims did, with a prophet, or as the Jews did, with a religious reformer. But underlying all these early Christian arguments about the nature and person of Jesus, raised to the status of the Christ and thereafter not called by his real name, elevated myth to unerring belief.

Trying to conceptualize the nature of Jesus as a natural or unnatural union resulted in more disjointed logic. Nestorius tried to explain the union of the natural and the godhead as a combination of natural elements that formed a new union, like water and cold temperature to produce ice. But Nestorius argues that the godhead in the Christ was not imposed externally but freely chosen. The godhead in the Christ would appear to be an imprisoned entity inside a human body. If this is the case, the godhead is limited and not infinite and becomes passive inside humanity, subject to the body's sufferings and not active in divinity. These are contradictory, and ultimately logically unresolvable. As if the impossible were not enough to believe, doctrinaire authorities added another God, the Holy Spirit, into the mix making the divine fire of the Zoroastrians, the dove found in Herodotus, and the grace spoken of by Paul into a separate god.

The union of divinity and humanity in the person of Jesus resulted in a new nature unlike all other natures, and this nature was neither God nor man. "Not one nature but two are we constrained to concede in Christ." The union of these two natures, one divine (*ousia*) and one human (*ousia*), however, are not two natures, says Nestorius, but one *prosopon*.

Defining a Divine Person

Defining *prosopon* has been one of the most illusive ambitions in understanding Nestorius and indeed biblical terminology. The English word "person" is derived from the Latin *personae* and the Greek *prosopa*, translations of the mask over the faces of actors in plays often denoting the "person" of a god or semi-deity like Hercules. The etymological root is *pros*, Greek for "before," and *ops*, "eyes." Hence, the word refers to a mask designating that the hidden actor is portraying a deity, hero, or heroine. Nestorius's use of *prosopon* is equivalent to a metaphor for God playing a role hidden behind the mask of humanity in the person of Jesus. This is ingenious but still a metaphor.[17]

John 6:46 reports that Jesus says that no one has seen the Father. And in *John* 5:37 we find: "And the Father Himself, who sent me, has testified of me. You have neither heard his voice at any time, nor seen his face," where the Greek is not *prosopon* but a Greek word for "himself." The same word *prosopon* occurring in the common (*koine*) Greek of *Mark* 12:14 is translated as "person." Its continued popular use over time led to the meaning of "outward appearance" and eventually came to stand for the colloquial understanding of "person."

An example of *prosopon* also occurs in Paul's *Letter to the Hebrews*. "For Christ is not entered into the holy places made with hands, which are the figures of the true; but into heaven itself, now to appear in the presence [*prosopo*] of God for us."[18] If Christ is appearing before the face, person or "presence" of God the Father, then how can his presence also be the same presence before which he appears? Either there is a face of God that one cannot see and live, or there is another face of God which chosen individuals like Jacob and Moses can see and live. Does then God have many faces, many masks, many persons, more than one *prosopon*? Indeed, the orthodox position (but not commonly accepted even in the fourth century) is that there are three persons (*prospons*) in God.

Prosopon can also be compared to a kind of iconic symbolism embodied in our multiple understandings of the word "image." For example, icons in the Byzantine tradition represent the missing persons in the liturgy, usually Jesus, Mary, and selected saints, not actually present but serving as embodiments of spiritual presence. The schema of the icon, or the appearance of Jesus, is what we observe, but the *prosopon* is the spiritual essence it implies. Add to this mix the nature and role of Satan, sin, and redemption and it is easy to see how the first theologians were supremely challenged in extending the reach of metaphysics and the limitations of logic and language to compose Christian doctrine.

Nestorius compares the union of God and Jesus to a second genesis, a new creation, different from the creation that linked the body and soul in one person. Nestorius preached that Christ was not one person but two, one human and one divine. When Jesus spoke, according to Nestorius, he spoke as one person (*prosopon*) enclosing the union of two natures, one human and one divine, and not, as Cyril proposed, from one *hypostasis*, or from a combination of natures. Even the Delphic Oracle, much less a collection of bishops, would have trouble deciphering these subtle distinctions as central to forming the doctrinal basis for Christianity, and then accepting and explaining them to unlettered laity.

For example, try to get your head around these supposedly clarifying sentences from Nestorius: "For this reason the properties of the two natures befit also one person (*prosopon*) not that of the substance (*ousia*) of God the Word. And the person is not in the substance, for it is not in the substance of God the Word, nor is the person of the union of the natures which have been united in such wise as to make two substances befit the one person of God the Word, for he is not both of them in substance."[19] This explanation comes from a patriarch of the most prestigious episcopate in Christendom that was intended to simplify what people believed. He should have been condemned both by grammarians and language teachers if not theologians.

Analogously, we can think of three parts of a human personality, as Freud proposed, of Superego, Ego. and Id. These three components are not three different persons, as at times one or another appear to be in control of mental operations. Nestorius is proposing something similar with Greek terms that imply real distinctions. Both Freud's and Nestorius's ideas have been superseded by advances in the neurosciences rendering their hypotheses clever and inventive but not descriptive of reality.

Or consider another analogy from the psychological sciences and the idea of appearance. In a Platonic sense, appearances are illusions and are only symbolic of a transcendent reality. Among neuroscientists appearances are only optical images of reality. Brain images are neuronal and only resemble the reality they portray. This playful analogy has the same kind of logical difficulties Nestorius faced in attempting to describe the union between God and man outside of myth without incurring the wrath of other ecclesiastics. The weapons he used, metaphysical terms, were the only recognized methodologies of the time apart from allegory. Myth linked to metaphysics crystallized Christian dogma forever, and woe to those who got caught on the wrong side of the argument or challenged the premises.

Nestorius summarized the debate about the nature of the man Jesus, the Christ, the Son of God, and the Word when, writing about Cyril, the patriarch of

Alexandria, he penned these words. "State clearly the deposit of faith of the fathers and set down the things which are both alike for me and everyone to say, for you have not made clear the meaning which we ought to mean and state."[20] In fact, none of the discussants stated it clearly and all got caught up in circumlocution, meaningless philosophical distinctions, and tortuous explanations of what is essentially in the gospels a mythical presentation of an imitated Greek hero. The doctrines of Nestorius were declared by the Council of Ephesus to be "abominable and profane" and "sick with many strange blasphemies."

Nestorius appears to have had an inkling of his fate when he wrote: "I have not renounced the just course of the orthodox nor shall I renounce it until death; and although they all, even the orthodox, fight with me through ignorance and are unwilling to hear and learn from me, yet the times will come upon them when they will learn from those who are heretics while fighting against them how they have fought against him who fought on their behalf."[21]

Nestorius relied too much on his ecclesiastical position and reason and logic to retain his beliefs, and not enough on precise scriptural quotations or political diplomacy to bolster his position among influential clerics. His reinterpretation of the central mystery altered ever so slightly the meaning of the Nicene Creed and this became his undoing. He did not go to the basilica where the delegates were meeting at the Council of Ephesus for fear of being outvoted, thus not only excluding himself from the proceedings but denying to delegates the opportunity to hear his case. In this he was not very heroic.

Nestorian churches were isolated from the rest of Christendom for over a thousand years, separated by geography and language, existing on the margins of other civilizations, mostly Muslim, where they were a despised minority.[22] According to an inscription on a stele in Xian in China written in Syriac and Chinese erected in 781, Nestorian Christianity was brought to China from Iran in 635 by a man named Alopen who convinced Emperor Tai-Tsung (627–650) to become favorably disposed to the new religion and to allow him to open a monastery.[23] Before the end of the century Nestorians had spread to ten provinces and had established scores of monasteries. As Buddhism gained favor in China, Nestorianism declined while subsequent emperors allowed the religion to maintain its identity and were benevolently tolerant toward it. By 987 churches were in ruins and hardly a Christian could be found in China. The Ming dynasty assumed control of China in 1369 and its insufferable attitude toward all foreigners reduced Nestorians to insignificance, a policy not reversed until Jesuits like Matteo Ricci came calling in the seventeenth century.

Pope Paul united the American Chaldean Church with the Roman Catholic Church in 1982. The one U.S. diocese is composed of twelve parishes: five in Michigan, two in Chicago, four in California, and one in Arizona. The number of American Chaldeans is over 100,000, served by one bishop and eighteen priests. They abandoned their Nestorian cloak and were accepted into communion into the Catholic Latin rite.

I attended a Chaldean Catholic Mass in Phoenix, Arizona, one Sunday to listen to Aramaic and observe whether or not there were substantive changes in the ritual from other Catholic ceremonies. The Mass, with the accompanying rituals and chants, in fact resembled other Catholic masses except for the language. It is closer to the Greek Orthodox or Armenian Mass than the Latin equivalent. Father Paulus was the officiating priest and there were about 300 families in attendance, all members studiously quiet and attentive, no crying babies and no whispers, their voices energetic when it was time to sing. Everyone looked Arab and most could have easily served as soldier extras in a movie about Alexander the Great.

The small, architecturally simple building serving as a church and social hall was packed with chairs in the aisles and many men standing at the rear. Some of the more elderly gentlemen serving as deacons and the men's choir were wearing shoes that appear to have been cobbled before even wingtips were invented. A women's choir was at the right of the altar and both men's and women's voices alternated to the accompaniment of amplified music. The Chaldean Mass was ceremonially long, about an hour and a half, longer than a Roman Catholic Mass but shorter by about a half from a Greek Orthodox Mass that typically runs three hours.

It's difficult to know when ritual is just a substitute for cant, and a sermon a replacement for political bombast. At the conclusion of the Mass, Father Paulos lashed into someone, or something, and sounded exactly like a harsh judge presiding over the sentencing of a serial killer. At the end he said in English, "I'm sorry," whether for his outburst, his ill temper, the substance of his message, or his belief was unclear. Afterward I mingled with the parishioners and introduced myself to a few men who were hospitable and who seemed a little wary of a stranger. This is after all an integrated ethnic and religious community whose roots extend over 2,000 years and whose social engagements come almost exclusively from that tight community.

Nestorius never spoke of the human Jesus as simply a man but did distinguish between his human and divine natures. He refused to attribute to the divine nature the human acts and sufferings of Jesus. Nor could he attribute to Mary the designation of mother of God because this would imply that she, a human, was the mother of both the divine and the human natures of Jesus. However, both Nestorius and Cyril of Alexandria, his opponent in this controversy, neglected the gospel narrators' use of literary artifices to tell the story of Jesus, and instead thought of the gospels as divinely inspired history and not derived from literary mythical and heroic origins. What should have been a controversy between literary critics instead became a theological dispute won by Cyril that settled forever what became Christian dogma.

Pelagius (c. 355–425): Original Sin and Grace

Pelagius probably came from Britain or Scotland, was portly though ascetic, conversant in both Latin and Greek, and lived in Rome a long time as a monk but not a cleric. As with most heretics, most of what we know about him comes from opponents. He was knowledgeable in theology, a contemporary of Augustine, and they met on several occasions in North Africa. His theological writings on the Trinity and scripture, once extolled by contemporaries, are now lost or were deliberately trashed by the overzealous.

Christians consider him a heretic because he denied original sin and grace. But in the fourth century it was unclear how passages in Paul's epistles and the gospels were to be reconciled. Think of original sin like an undetected virus, a crack cocaine addiction or HIV infection that spreads through to the next generation. Despite the endorsements of Paul and Augustine, grace (Latin *gratia* = favor, thanks) was more undefined and ambiguous, considered a special divine privilege given to the unworthy for assistance toward sanctification, like a spiritual merit badge or frequent flyer miles. Pelagius believed that humans could be saved and cleansed of sin through faith alone. Justification by faith alone became one of the central distinctions that separated Catholics from Protestants in the Reformation and that made Luther in effect a follower of Pelagius, if not an exponent.

Here are a few of the questions raised by Pelagius and his erstwhile disciplines and companions.

- If Adam had not sinned, would he have still died?
- Did Adam's sin harm only himself and not all subsequent humans?
- Do humans die because of Adam's sin and death?
- Is the Law of Moses as good a guide to salvation as the Gospels?
- Before the advent of Christ were there men who were without sin?[24]

Augustine, bishop John of Jerusalem, and others inquired into the orthodoxy of Pelagius, and while he sojourned in Palestine they began to question his beliefs. In 417 before a synod convened to hear complaints about him, Pelagius distinguished himself with argumentation and favorable writings and was acquitted of all charges. Subsequently, however, bishops in North Africa, Augustine among them, wrote to Pope Innocent I of the charges leveled against Pelagius and sought his advice. Innocent presumably clarified church views about original sin and grace, but left unresolved the question of who held such views. Innocent died forty-five days later and Pope Zosimus replaced him. But the controversy did no go away.

Pelagius had written a defense of his theology in a work now lost in which he distinguished between the Kingdom of God and eternal life. But it was his contrite humility and obedience to the Pope that allowed pope Zosimus, reversing Innocent's position, to absolve him from heresy in letters sent to bishops in

North Africa from which the indictments originated. Pope Zosimus pronounced the creed of Pelagians to be orthodox, and Pelagius himself to be a man of unblemished faith. But the North African congregations were alarmed and pleaded with Zosimus to reconsider. Zosimus sent the case back to the Africans who hastily assembled a synod of 200 bishops in 418 known as the Council of Carthage. The council then performed the useful service of defining beliefs about original sin and grace and agreed to the following views.

- Death came to Adam because of sin and not naturally.
- Infants must be baptized because of original sin.
- Grace is necessary for the forgiveness of sins and avoids future sins.
- Christ's grace helps illuminate God's commandments and gives strength to execute them.
- Without grace it is impossible to perform good works.
- We are all sinners.

This spelled doom for Pelagius. Zosimus, with a little persuasion from the emperor who sided with Augustine, reversed himself and branded Pelagius a heretic and excommunicated him by sending a papal encyclical to all bishops asking them to sign or at least agree to its contents. Pelagius was never called to appear before the Council of Carthage or to have a session with Pope Zosimus to answer charges against him. He was not given the customary privilege of facing his accusers as would be true in any Roman trial. Pelagius was pronounced orthodox in theology by a synod in Palestine and by two popes, then hastily condemned by a council in Africa prompting one pope to reverse himself (with a little extra-judicial help from an emperor) and brand him a heretic. Since Pelagius was himself then living somewhere in the Middle East he could not be exiled so it is assumed he died there, possibly in Egypt where he had friends.

This is the fate of these early dissenters, often the victims of political ploys more than despicable adherents of controversial policies, to not appear before their accusers and answer charges and then to be condemned without the benefit of a trial.

The controversy over original sin and grace revealed not so much the discomfort of Pelagius, who sought only to be a reasonable part of the theological good guys, but the triumph of Augustine whose views prevailed and became canonical doctrine, even though his ideas like humans not dying for natural causes, or that unbaptized infants who die cannot be saved, are affronts to reason. Theologians had to juggle common sense with reason and mythical concepts from the Bible and Gospels to concoct a theological message that supposedly revealed God's truths.

Pelagius, a gifted intellectual and linguist, had attempted to illuminate ambiguous ideas from Paul's epistles. But his sensible explanations, like denying original sin, were thwarted by ambitious theologians and those who pursued mystical interpretations of concepts like grace and sin. Pelagius argued that sin was not a divine substance that could be quantified but a quality that resided in human actions. Pelagius did not want humans blamed for actions they did not commit, as there was quite enough for which they could be blamed. If sin implies a moral choice made wrongly, then we also have to assume that there was the possibility of a right choice. Original sin does not allow for this to be true because there is no choice, no exercise of free will. Moreover, original sin is punishable by eternal damnation. But if sin is some kind of wall between man and God, then it is possible that original sin is such a barrier between the human and the divine.

Why did Jesus have to die, since he had no sin? This question stretches the idea of "original" in sin. If Christ freely chose death was he also choosing the death imposed on God for Adam, or just assuming the death accorded all natural bodies? Neither Augustine nor Pelagius posed or responded to this perplexing dilemma. It does not speak well of a God described as all-loving and benevolent that from the outset of creation he should condemn all humanity to lingering depravity, an evil blot apparently transmitted physically which must be cleansed with water, and yet be moved enough to answer individual prayers for temporary favors.

If baptism cleanses original sin, why are the children of parents who have been cleansed born into sin? The answer to this question actually defines how sin is interpreted, what original sin is, and its purpose and devolvement into each generation. Pelagius admitted that Adam's sin harmed all humans but by disobedient example. Having relegated science to the trash heap of faith, theologians then added nature as one of the obstructions to belief. Once a synod or pope ordained that he alone spoke the truth of God's revelation, anything as undignified as dialogue was totally unnecessary.

If one concedes that the biblical account of Adam and Eve is borrowed mythology from Sumerian and Babylonian myths, then the whole argument is a wash, only so much redundant bickering about unreal abstractions unconnected to reality. But in fact Pelagius the Brit got it right as the synod at Palestine and Pope Innocent agreed. Had he been allowed to hold his views without condemnation the church would have interpreted scripture more widely and not allowed mere myth to achieve the status of dogma. A century after Pelagius Christian dogma was entwined in the social fabric of Western Europe making overt heretics scarcer than exotic herbal remedies. But dissidents emerged from time to time to enliven and educate a provincial public of its once-glorious past. Boethius was such a figure.

Boethius (c. 475–524)

You cannot impose anything on a free mind, and you cannot move from its state of inner tranquility a mind at peace with itself and firmly founded on reason.

                                                                                Boethius

For nearly a thousand years before the invention of printing, the works of Boethius, author, chronicler, and statesman, who served as prime minister to the Roman Emperor Theodoric (454–526) in Ravenna, were the most famous in the Western world. Today he is forgotten. He is seen variously as the last of the Romans by Gibbon, and, together with Cassiodorus and Benedict, as the founder of the Middle Ages. In fact, he is a bridge between the rust left over from decaying Roman civilization and the intellectual darkness that would characterize the epoch before the Middle Ages. Boethius provided the Middle Ages and Renaissance with a literary and philosophical work of profound genius. His enduring legacy is that he is a dissenter from barbarism, one who took the intellectual high road by preserving the standards of refinement, grace, and even compassion.[25]

He earned his reputation through brilliance and practical intelligence. He lost his life because he did not relinquish his educational or civilized standards to the unpolished and boorish Goths. He used his office to protect the entire Roman Senate from charges of treason, fellow senators from persecution, and farmers from having their property confiscated.[26] Boethius tried to domesticate Theodoric and the victorious Goths ruling the Western empire into imperial Romans. In turn, Theodoric saw mentoring as insubordination and reacted as the arrogant military barbarian he was and not just a petulant student. Theodoric's domed gravesite in Ravenna symbolizes his lifestyle: It resembles a large mound of dung.

Boethius was born of high Roman heritage into a wealthy family (his father was a consul), and he became a consul and prime minister under Theodoric. He was arrested on a trumped-up charge of court conspiracy for which he was likely innocent, jailed, convicted, and executed. While in prison in 533 he wrote *The Consolation of Philosophy*, the most widely read book after the Bible and Augustine right through to the Renaissance. The *Consolation* is part poetry, part prose read for the celebrity status of its author rather than the liquidity of its prose, an expressive blend of Roman stoicism and Christian resignation. Boethius wrote in *The Consolation* that the source of true happiness is the love of God and the pursuit of wisdom. He spoke with the voice of an elegiac poet of philosophy to speak about religion. Although a Christian, he never mentions personal immortality or any of the doctrines of Christianity.

Here is a man who was the equivalent of a prime minister or vice president, and though innocent suddenly finds himself in prison falsely accused by enemies and without an exit strategy. He imaginatively contrives to admit a wise woman, an anthropomorphized figure of philosophy into his prison presence who will dialogue with him about the mysteries of life. Some of it seems artificial, like the use of stylized Latin poetry alternating with the prose, the platitudes about life's fortunes, the classical references. But through it all there is a touch of fatalism and resignation, a kind of musing about what it all means and how fickle and fragile the human condition is.

His story and influence is that of a heroic figure in the face of death who treasures philosophic principles more than his life, a man whose stature had not received such personal acclaim since Socrates. The Vatican cautiously waited 1,350 years and then belatedly beatified him in 1883.

Together with Cassiodorus, another contemporary high court official who chronicled biblical writings, Boethius, in his love for the liberal arts and studies of the Greeks, was the first to propose an academic classification system. He suggested that arithmetic, music, geometry, and astronomy be grouped together. He called this grouping the *quadrivium*, or the four strands. Throughout the Middle Ages these subjects became the courses of study in secondary and higher education and the curriculum for study after the BA to the MA.

Boethius looked backward to the high culture of the Greeks absorbed by the Romans, and yet forward to the Renaissance, that rebirth of classical culture that transformed the dormancy of the Middle Ages into vibrant intellectual stimulation. As Augustine created Plato for theology, Boethius made studying classical philosophy appear to be a primary Christian virtue.[27]

Meanwhile in the Eastern Empire, the epoch of Justinian (483–565) witnessed the triumph of Christianity as the state imperial religion to the exclusion of all others. The Roman Empire in both the east and west were to become bastions of anti-intellectualism, and this corresponded with the rise of Christianity.

Justinian closed Plato's Academy in 529 ending centuries of philosophical discourse and intellectual excitement, thereby condemning "the sick follies of the impieties of Hellenism." The *Codex Justinianus* (l, 5, 18, para. 4) in its first decree excluded all heretics, Jews, and soldiers from any official teaching at Plato's Academy, and moreover reserved all public teaching salaries strictly for Christians.[28] In effect, this decree closed each Neo-Platonic school since few philosophers actually were or aspired to be Christians. Those who said they were philosophers were actually theologians. Orthodoxy had been defined and everyone not orthodox in belief was heretical, and were persecuted or exiled. Official discrimination began and became entrenched in Europe for a thousand years. All intellectual activity declined, art and literature vanished, and piety, transcendental investigations, and soul searching became substitutes for mathematics and independent thinking. The barbarians within the gates, not the invading hordes, triumphed throughout the decaying Roman Empire through forcible intellectual suppression.

Damascius (c. 480–550), a Neo-Platonist and the last of the academy's directors, chose exile to Persia with six other philosophers rather than cease his occupation. Years later he was allowed to return to Alexandria where he composed his few books, notably *The Life of Isidore,* a biography about his predecessor. His principal work, *Difficulties and Solutions of First Principles*, reveals a keen, logical mind that attempts to describe the notion of an absolute principle like God, and then questions how God can be everything and yet have parts. Damascius uses reasoning as old as Parmenides and the philosophical riddle of the one and the many.

I found his reasoning as tight as Aristotle's in *The Metaphysics* and equally sound and consistent. How can the First Principle, God who is everything, asks Damascius, have any secondary principles or parts? He concludes that the Ineffable is Unknowable, not a difficult conclusion to arrive at philosophically, but one that causes anxiety among Christians who believe that there is more than one person in God. By the sixth century the academy had become a staunch defender of intellectual questioning that challenged Christianity and the most prestigious institution that taught students alternatives to Christian doctrine. Given the political circumstances, it had to be closed. The academy was the last gasp of the freedom of intellectual pursuit in the Western mind until the modern era.

Finally, in the Dark Ages, between the defeat of Rome in 410 and the beginning of the Crusades, the Manichean heresy whose adherents believed in two gods, one good and one evil, slowly insinuated itself into Europe, settling in strength in Bulgaria in the seventh century and lasting for about 500 years.[29] Its dualist religious ideas migrated throughout Europe and are sometimes credited with having an influence on medieval English literature like *Piers Plowman*. It certainly spread to southern France where it was known as the Albigensian heresy discussed in the following chapter. The Bogomils, named after an obscure priest, Bogomil, who brought the movement to Bulgaria in the ninth century, believed that Satan was a coequal God who created the material world. Consequently, they renounced all material objects and held even their bodies as sources of evil and practiced extreme forms of asceticism. They rejected all the sacraments and church liturgical functions.

Shortly after Islam overran the Middle East and North Africa, and at the dawn of the Crusades in the eleventh century, patches throughout the nominal Christian world were still incubating drifting currents of Persian dualism, Platonic and Gnostic transcendentalism, Greek mystery rites, Roman Mithraic codes, Jewish apocalyptic beliefs, and Christian theological assumptions. The boiling pot of religious stew challenged both the Orthodox Greek East and the Latin Catholic West. Had a poll been taken of actual beliefs throughout Europe in the arbitrary year of 1000, it is possible that Christianity as understood in contemporary society would not be recognizable, except perhaps among Unitarians and a few Masons.

CHAPTER NINE
HERESY IN MEDIEVAL ISLAM
AND CHRISTIANITY

No one could have imagined that an inhospitable desert would yield more than camels, frankincense, and clouds of blowing sand. But religion knows no special geography. Between 634 and 718 a new religion blew like a sirocco out of torrid Arabia, divided the already disintegrated Roman Empire, shook the remnants of classical civilization to its foundations, and gobbled up great swaths of Christians some of whom actually welcomed release from imperialism and petty theological controversies. Islam transformed disputes about Christian heretics into a holy war against all unbelievers. Muslims brought no cultural refinements and asked only unswerving allegiance to Allah. Enfeebled culturally and economically, residents in Europe and the Middle East, in a bizarre twist of religious irony, reeled from the knowledge that they were engulfed by a militaristic people of faith who saw Christians as infidels and not just as theological opponents.

Toward the end of *The Decline and Fall of the Roman Empire* (1776) Edward Gibbon mused on a startling possibility. If the Muslim invaders had defeated the forces of Charles Martel at Poitiers in 732, western Europe would have been under the influence of Islam as southern Spain was for 500 years. As conquering armies go, so goes the language of the occupiers, as Latin was throughout the Mediterranean with the Romans, Spanish through Latin America, English in North America, and Arabic for all the Middle East and North Africa. But the language of the conquerors may not have been as hard to accept as the faith they brought. It was not Islam that picked a fight with Europe in the Middle Ages. But when Christendom launched the Crusades both Islam and Europe became infidels to each other, a mutual animosity that reached far beyond mere theological dissent. Both religions condoned the worst kind of atrocities in the name of their beliefs.

Neither Islam nor Christianity tolerated religious dissent. Notwithstanding the advance of culture in the relatively peaceful Islamic world compared to the turmoil and conflict in Europe, the Arab world did not sustain independent religious thinking. Islam dominated all affairs as Christianity did in medieval Europe. Both religious worlds had heretics and enough brave souls to offer subtle but controversial positions that challenged the authority and integrity of religious purity and established beliefs. Morally courageous Islamic and Christian men and woman in the Middle Ages would occasionally rise up to challenge the strict religious rules and be quickly suppressed if not tortured. Regal and papal authority sometimes abolished a military religious order, like the Templars, after torturing its members. The arrogant abuse of power created martyrs on behalf of the spirit of independence. That it was deemed necessary to have a military religious order at all demonstrates the futility of the militancy of the Crusades and its twisted religious mission. Once the Crusades were over unofficially in 1291 when the Christian armies lost the Levant, it was difficult to sustain the rationale for any military order regardless of the nobility, status, or sanctity of its members.

Islam and the Infidels

God—
there is no god but He, the
Living, the Everlasting
Slumber seizes him not, neither sleep;
to Him belongs
all that is in the heavens and earth. Koran 2:255

Islam is a monotheistic religion founded in the seventh century by the Prophet Mohammad (570–632). The faith today has more than one billion believers, about 20 percent of the world's population, who comprise a majority of the population in forty-five countries. The Koran is considered the word of Allah. Islam recognizes Adam, Noah, Abraham, Moses, and Jesus as prophets but believes Mohammad is the last and greatest. There are five basic Islamic tenets:

1. *Tawheed*: or "There is no god but god."
2. Prayer: Muslins are required to pray five times daily. (On Fridays, the holy day, prayer is often preceded by a sermon).
3. Alms: Muslims must give annually to the poor a part of income or possessions.
4. Fasting: The holy month of Ramadan is a month-long fast from food, drink, smoking and sex during daylight hours.
5. Pilgrimage: All devout Muslims are encouraged to make a pilgrimage to Mecca once in a lifetime.

The beauty of Islam is its theological simplicity. While Christians, in attempting to define the nature of their belief over three centuries dissipated energies in endless controversies over spiritual and philosophical entities, Islam mobilized armies that swept over the southern Mediterranean and Middle East with incredible rapidity. With military consolidation came leisure, and soon Islamic scholars were probing into the literature, science, and mathematics Christian scholars had abandoned for the aridness of theological speculation.

While Europe slid into cultural decay and aesthetic desuetude, the Muslim world benefited from a prolonged period of intellectual leisure. By the Middle Ages, Islamic scholars and artists, stretching from Delhi in India to Cordoba in Spain, were superior to Europeans in architecture, engineering, navigation, geography, mathematics and astronomy, medicine, horticulture, crafts, metallurgy, calligraphy, literature, music, and philosophy—just about every field of civilized high culture.[1]

The Muslims were not completely cut off, as Europeans were, from the culture ancient Greeks and Romans enjoyed. In fact, they borrowed extensively from Greek geometry, medicine, art, and architecture. The texts of such works were in philosophy, math, medicine, and optics from the cities where European and Arabic culture interacted, in cities like Toledo and Cordoba where trade intersected with ideas as the principal commodities. Jewish scholars borrowed from Islamic scholars, Islamic from Jewish, Christian from both Jewish and Islamic, and all drew their inspiration from a rediscovered Aristotle promoted by the great Islamic scholar Averroes. You can still walk down the short street named Averroes in Cordoba where he once lived.

The first modern centers or seminaries of learning, always associated with religious learning, began in the Islamic world. The comparative leisure of the Muslim world, unlike northern Europe where Viking raiders brought a halt to the promotion of arts and letters, contributed to an intellectual cultivation among Islamic scholars.[2] Islamic universities as centers of learning, whose entire curriculum was theological and based on the Koran, had a 200-year educational head start over the origin of universities in Europe.

For example, in the year 825, about 300 Kerouan people settled along the riverbanks in the city of Fez in Morocco, an ancient city that has not changed much in the intervening centuries. Settlers built a mosque with a roof of bright green tiles which still stands today in the old section of the city. It is reputed to be the world's oldest center of learning still in existence, dating from 857. The library at Fez contains 30,000 volumes, including a ninth century copy of the Koran. A thousand years ago there were several active Muslim learning centers, later to emerge as formal colleges, in Cairo and in Cordoba where religious instruction blended with secular knowledge.

At a period comparable to the height of Arabic culture and refinement in the eighth century, European civilization existed at only a few, lonely, isolated outposts, literally islands clustered around Ireland like Skellig Michael, Iona and Lindisfarne along the English coasts, where monks transcribed and illuminated gospel texts, when they weren't fending off Viking plunderers. So, while Europe was busy fighting off marauders, the Islamic world basked in unprecedented civilized refinement. Islamic culture reached a zenith from the eighth to the fourteenth centuries, promoted in part by high intellectual achievements in Jewish culture within which it was allowed to flourish as it was not in Europe.

There was one exception between these two worlds and that was in theology. The same theological dilemma that Aristotle's secular view presented to Christian and Jewish scholars occurred to Islamic thinkers. Plato had believed in personal immortality, which is why he was popular among Christians and influential with Augustine. But Aristotle presented challenges to established monotheism because of his use of reason and his acute scientific mentality. When Aristotle was re-discovered and translated into Arabic by Moslem scholars in 9th century Syria (from texts provided by the Arians), he became quickly known throughout the Islamic world.

Sharia: Muslim Law

The alternative law among Muslims is *Sharia*, a system of religious laws similar to Deuteronomy that govern behaviors in marriage, divorce, inheritance, and theft. These medieval religious rules and practices are enough to make even the most valiant antagonists queasy.

A woman's testimony in court carries only half the weight of a man's. Alcohol is prohibited and there are severe rules for sexual conduct and behavior. Nobody makes men wear veils, when many actually should. There are wide differences in the Islamic world on enforcement of selected procedures like public floggings, beheadings, hand cuttings and stoning. Strict Islamists want to cut off the hands of thieves and stone adulterers to death (the size of the stones is properly prescribed), as did Jews in the time of Jesus. Fundamentalists usually win acceptance in Saudi Arabia, Iran, Sudan and northern Nigeria, and in all Sharia nations, but not in Turkey, a secular state with a majority Muslim population. Indonesia, with an 88 percent Muslim population, has allowed Sharia courts to rule in Aceh province in northern Sumatra. Jordan has separate courts for Muslims and Christians, but all are subject to Sharia law for inheritances.

In 2004 Afghanistan adopted an enlightened constitution that recognized the plurality of Muslims and the rights of religious minorities and sidestepped the issue of enforcement of strict Islamic laws. Attempting to uphold the traditional religious tenets of Islamic law is akin to national identity. Pakistan, for example, has a federal Islamic court that can invalidate any law it sees as unacceptable to the injunctions of Islam. In practice, the government in many cases simply refuses to accept its rulings. The conclusion is that no one need run for a bunker when Sharia is mentioned any more than that someone should dive under a desk when the Ten Commandments is mentioned as the basis for American justice.

Islamic Dissidents

While Europe was enveloped in intellectual doldrums and cowering in the shadows from barbarian raiders in the eleventh and twelfth centuries, Islamic scholars were enjoying studious pursuits. One inquiring mind was Abdul-Fath Muhammad al-Karim, known in his hometown of Shahrastan (in today's Turkmenistan) simply as Shahrastani. He was born there in 1186. He returned from a *haji* to Mecca, resided for three years in Baghdad, then returned home where he spent most of his life as an Iman teaching and writing. He died in 1253 at age sixty-seven. I list him here because many of his contemporaries believed him to be of a Shia and therefore heretical.

Shahrastani wrote on all the world's religions and theologies, a monumental history of non-Islamic religions unrivaled until modern times. Indeed, he was personally pious and even-tempered, and this translated into his objective treatment of other religions, extraordinary in any age. At a time when devout Muslims would have been aghast at Indian theological and religious views, Shahrastani apparently viewed Indian religion as a challenge of scholarship and religious interpretation.

When Europe was bathing in the complacency of civil and ecclesiastical rule of Christianity, and awaiting the productive theological analyses of Thomas Aquinas, India was enjoying multiple religious beliefs and practices. The Brahmans denied prophecies because, as they said, if God gave us intellect, why cannot we discover God's benefits on our own. Moreover, how is one to be sure that a divine messenger is valid? The Brahmans are further divided into those who are followers of the Buddha and therefore profess meditation, and those who believe in transference of the soul.

Another group believes in spiritual beings and divine messengers who assume various forms and are ascetic, and they recognize them when they abstain from food, drink, and sex among other things. In addition, there are worshippers of all kinds: of stars, the sun, the moon, trees, water, fire, and idols. Thus, whatever witchcraft and alchemy prevailed in the Middle Ages in Europe, it was certainly not matched by the variety of religious beliefs among the Indians, who, by an accident of geography, would certainly have been condemned as heretics had they lived in Europe.

Averroes (1126–1198)

The Islamic scholar Averroes (Ibn–Rushd) was trained in theology, jurisprudence, medicine, philosophy, and law, was both a lawyer and physician who became the most influential Islamic philosopher of the Middle Ages, and a brilliant dissenter from the orthodox Islamic belief. He served as the personal physician to two caliphs, in Spain and Morocco, and was chief judge in Cordoba where he was born. He died in Marrakech in Morocco in 1198.

He was extremely influential among both Jewish and Christian philosophers in subsequent centuries, more than among his fellow Islamic scholars. He argued that the aim of philosophy was to discover the meaning of religious beliefs by combining reasoning with Islamic truths, a doctrine as dangerous to Islamic theology as it was to medieval Christianity. Averroes attempted to do for Islam what Augustine had done with Plato for Christianity, what Maimonides tried to do with Judaism, and what Aquinas attempted for Christian theology. But because of the collective power of fundamentalist Islamic scholars who thought his views dangerous to Islam, Averroes was banished for a time from the favor of the caliphs but was later reinstated. He scrupulously avoided denying his own faith, but all the time sided with Aristotle in beliefs about truth based on reason often at odds with revelation. However, he claimed that one could know the existence of God with reason and not just revelation, a view Aquinas also held. His main contribution was that faith and reason did not conflict so there was no need for them to be reconciled, an idea the British theologian Anselm had proposed about the same time.

Averroes believed that there was one soul, that it was immortal and it could not be divided into separate bodies. There was no personal soul or personal immortality, a view contrary to both Christian and Islamic theology. He said that the soul is separate in the same way that light is reflected in a mirror, seen in many diverse bodies but is not actually inside any individual body. Aquinas said of him: "For these reasons, Averroes was moved, as he says, to hold that the possible intellect, by which the soul understands, has a separate being from the body, and is not the form of the body."[3]

Averroes wrote that philosophy was a separate discipline from religion and only for the select few, that there was no special divine providence, no individual soul, that matter was eternal, that there are a number in intermediate spirits between God and humanity, and that mystical knowledge is the ultimate aspiration of the soul. For these beliefs his books were burned and he was exiled.

Akbar the Great (1542–1605)

A thousand lunar years after Mohammad's epic journey from Mecca to Medina in 622, Akbar the Great, the Mughal Emperor of India, reflected on his times. He was a man who acted cautiously upon the multireligious diversity of northern India that included Hindus, Muslims, Christians, Sikhs, Jains, Jews, and Parsees. Akbar strove to maintain peaceful coexistence among all his peoples by laying the basis for religious neutrality and secularism in the empire. He wrote that no man should be interfered with on account of religion and that anyone should be allowed to transfer to a religion that pleases him. By such statements, Akbar professed his belief in reason and not dogmatic traditions to address social problems. For example, he concluded that slavery was unjust and released all imperial slaves in 1582. His faith was based on reasoned choice and not on unquestioning adherence. Had he not been a ruler, his tolerant ideas would have easily placed him on the rolls of heretics or in the prisons of his enemies.

Akbar's ideas are relevant because reason, tolerance, justice, and good faith in diverse cultures are not just in the Western tradition. His legal codes laid the foundation for a secular, non-denominational empire in India. Practicing what he preached, Akbar abolished discriminatory taxes on non-Muslims and invited intellectual Hindus into his court. A Hindu general commanded his armies.

Europe during the life of Akbar was conflicted with religious plurality resulting in wars among Christian denominations fighting over theological quibbling we might think ludicrous. Europe, had it known of Akbar's tolerant message, would not have heeded it. In 1592 Giordano Bruno, whom we will read about in the following chapter, was arrested for heresy and publicly burned at the stake in 1600. Had they known about Akbar's religious tolerance, European heretics might have immigrated to India.

Whether as Jew, Muslim or Christian, proposing incendiary ideas in theology was dangerous enough. But even budding medieval chemists were looked on suspiciously. A few brave men tried experiments in alchemy and its futile procedures for changing chemical compounds and, like Roger Bacon described later in this chapter, were accused of magic and witchcraft.[4] So strong was the myth that gold could be manufactured that the court alchemist of the ruler of Egypt was blinded for failing to convert base metal into gold. Europe had neither the technical resources nor the expertise to venture into competitive commercialism. Trying to produce gold that would be marketable worldwide was one of the more questionable experiments. What Europe could do was recruit monks to its hundreds of monasteries for contemplation and subsistence agriculture, and raise an army of peasant conscripts for wars abroad if the pope thought it expedient. Military adventurism into the Middle East was soon to replace superstition as an employment opportunity.

John Leo

A remarkable book appeared in 1550 in Rome, written in Arabic and Italian, that described the geography of Africa. It was written by a man named John Leo, described as a Moor like Shakespeare's Othello. But in the notoriety after the publication of the book, the author could not be found.

He was born as al-Hassan ibn Muhammad ibn Ahmad al-Wazzan in Grenada in the late 1480s prior to the expulsion of the Jews and Muslims known as the *Reconquistada* in 1492 by Ferdinand and Isabella, the Castilian rulers of Spain. The Al-Wazzans fled to Fez in Morocco where the young man later to become John Leo attended a *madrassa*, studied law, and traveled throughout North Africa and into Sudan and to Constantinople with his uncle in the service of a sultan.

He was captured at sea in his late twenties by corsairs of the Knights of St. John (to become the Knights of Malta) and given to the Medici pope, Leo X. After imprisonment he was released after inducements to convert to Christianity and given the name John Leo, or Leo Africanus. When Pope Leo died within two years, John Leo left Rome for Bologna where he compiled a lexicon of Arabic, Latin, and Hebrew. He returned to Rome under the protection of Pope Clement VII and it was during this time he wrote his famous geographical study. When the forces of Charles V sacked Rome in 1527 he fled to Tunis where it is said be reconverted to Islam. He is rumored to have died in his adopted city of Fez.

The details of his life are sketchy. Did he, for example, have a wife and family in Fez when captured? Did he marry a Christian woman while living in

Italy? It is playful to imagine the world in which he lived, and his religious conversion and reconversion as a means of surviving in alternately hostile or friendly environments, using his language, travel, and diplomatic skills as currency to fulfill literary ambitions and earn a living. He lived for seven years as a protégé of the pope but endured in Italy as a scholar, foreigner, and converted Christian. How he would have returned to the Muslim world without disavowing everything that happened to him is not known. The details of the lives of some outcasts and heretics is murky, but lack of biography that does not diminish their heroism. The geography of where one lives most often determines the religion of choice, convenience, or compulsion.

The Crusades (1095–1291)

The cause was blessed, justified by all ecclesiastical and regal authorities, and linked the cross and the sword. Calls for the liberation of Jerusalem set in motion armies of the indigent and hapless whose misfortunes reverberate throughout the Middle East even today as one of the worst examples of aggression, moronic misunderstanding, and religious animosity. And yes, history does seem to repeat itself. According to an esteemed Arab poet during the time of the Crusades, the world seemed divided into two camps: those who had brains but no religion, and those who had religion and no brains. The terse parallel may seem overdrawn but recent history with the science curriculum and struggle among evolution, creationism, and Intelligent Design advocates, and Muslim suicide bombers supplies some evidence for its insight.

I explore the background of the Crusades briefly here because it forms an historical context for the confrontation between Islam and the West today, and is the origin, pretext, and prelude for heroism, heretics, courage, and stupidity in the modern era.

The Crusades disrupted families and the land, diverted significant resources from subsistence agriculture, and depleted the extremely modest educational and cultural life and what little economies that bonded people together in Europe. In the East, the military movement accelerated the ambitions of the Turks who had no interest in Jerusalem, but who eventually did conquer Constantinople in 1453, thus uniting all Muslims under the Ottoman Empire that dominated the region until 1918. Because the Turks had sided with Germany in World War I, triumphant European powers, principally France and Britain, returned to carve up the Middle East, creating the authoritarian nations and sheikdoms that characterize the region now. The present map of the Middle East can be traced to the blunders of the Crusades.

The young and restless, who might have been apprenticed in the arts, trades, crafts, or joined a monastery, suddenly felt a vocation to vow allegiance to a war endorsed by a pope, Urban II, whose motives were more political than pious. Young and old were called from their plows and sickles to wield battles axes and broad swords for the faith. Urban II manipulated restless Frankish princes (he was Frankish himself) and encouraged them to fight an enemy abroad rather than endanger the fragile peace in Europe. He could have called it a Jihad if he had known Arabic.[5] If the precedent of the Nuremberg Trials of the Nazis in 1945 had been a legal guide then, it would have been possible for an international tribunal to bring the pope and assorted kings to trial for crimes against humanity.

There was no biblical authority for recruiting illiterate pilgrims and peasants and turning them into soldiers to war against other religions. But in 1096 the Christian message had been unexpectedly corrupted from loving one's enemies to exterminating them, a motif adopted in the 21st century by scores of radicalized Islamic suicide bombers. Islam, on the other hand, was able to locate several scriptural passages that justified violent responses against those it defined as infidels. Radical members use these proclamations today to fight against Western ideas of secularism and colonialism:

Prescribe for you in fighting, though it is hateful to you. *Koran*, II, 216.

And fight the unbelievers totally even as they fight you totally; and know that God is with the godfearing. *Koran*, IX, 36.

An unusual chain of events, unpredictable in consequences, began the crusader catastrophes. Emperor Alexis in Constantinople had formally requested help from the West in subduing the Turks from south central Asia endangering Christians in what is now Anatolia in Turkey. Had Alexis had any premonition about the ragged armies that passed through Constantinople seeking provisions, knowing they would not be equal to the trained army of the Turks, he would never have sent that letter.

There were several crusades against papal enemies in Europe, the Baltic States, and the Balkans until the fifteenth century and against Muslims in Spain. But the majority of the battles occurred in Asia Minor and Palestine. War fever then unexpectedly erupted in 1096 when Christians began killing Jews in Germany, even though Jews were protected by German imperial degrees. Many thought it easier to kill non-Christians in Europe than to undertake an arduous journey abroad to slaughter them. It was the first pogrom or genocide against Jews in Europe. It would not be the last. The barbarism that had overrun Rome in 410 remained like a dormant virus in medieval Europe, and it emerged like a fully resurrected organism when Pope Urban II ordered the deaths of non-Christians without conducting a feasibility study, or sending any diplomats to work out an amicable solution. He may as well have simultaneously called forth Anubis, the jackal-headed, long-eared Egyptian god of the dead to embalm all the recruits.

The pope's war cries translated into a Christian duty for recruits who signed on to kill for God and to receive penance as a remission of sins towards salvation. Pilgrims who turned back were excommunicated, a double insult.[6] These crude peasants slaughtered their way across a thousand miles of Christian

Europe as they ravaged the countryside for provisions before reaching Constantinople. More died of thirst and starvation, disease and desertion while marching from Constantinople to Jerusalem than were killed by Turks.

The Greek emperors of Constantinople had originally found the hordes of European peasants mislabeled as soldiers merely unpalatable and malodorous. But they soon began to regard the successive waves of adventurers as more intrusive and dangerous than the Turks besieging their dwindling borders. It never occurred to the castoff religious fanatics from Europe, egged on by their esteemed clerics like Bernard of Clairvaux, that reaching Constantinople was the easy part, and that they had to fight their way through the hostile territory of the Turks before ever reaching the gates of Jerusalem.

The Crusades consisted of eight major military campaigns originating in Europe and spanned over two centuries from 1095 to 1291. Peter the Hermit's disorganized and unruly peasant army of 40,000 symbolized what can happen when logistics are lacking. Peter's ill-starred campaign set off without plans or military preparedness. Its enthusiastic but naive adventurers were all killed by the Turks outside Constantinople. The Children's Crusade in 1212 never reached its destination as all were sold by the ships' captains into slavery in Egypt and Tunisia. The fourth Crusade, probably at the urging of Venetian economic interests, captured Constantinople in 1204 and stole, pillaged, raped and killed Muslim worshippers and destroyed the greatest city in the world at the time and never even fought against Muslims. Crusaders seemed to have made no distinction between religious piety and indiscriminate and wanton slaughter.

Crusaders captured Jerusalem in the first Crusade in July 1099, but lost it again in 1187 to Muslim forces under Saladin. European princes and the papacy had grown weary of supporting meager gains so far away. Greater economic challenges existed in their own backyards. Unknown to the Crusaders, Jerusalem had always been a multicultural, multi-religious city, a place where Jews, Moslems and Christians from many eastern sects mingled freely. Moslems had guaranteed the rights of Christians to enter the city and worship. Even today, a Muslim family holds the privilege of opening the doors daily of the Church of the Holy Sepulcher.

Contrasted to the West's barbarity during the Crusades, the Muslim world was the more civilized, erudite, and educated. The Crusades were the worst example of the West's rapine, avarice, and venality cloaked in the symbols of a religious pilgrimage. Moslem leaders, whose word was more binding, whose code of conduct more generous, and whose respect for human rights more compatible with civilized conduct, were the uncontested humane and moral winners in these campaigns between East and West.

The military battles were not as significant and long lasting as were the cultural and educational mix between East and West, the confrontation of Christendom and Islam, and the rediscovery of the high state of Islamic culture in science, mathematics, medicine, art, and even exotic foods. Europe became enriched by this encounter, though that was not its purpose. The Crusaders themselves realized how backward they were compared to Arab cultural tastes.

French pastries and spices today are staple food products in the markets and bazaars of Istanbul as they have been for centuries. The soldiers of the Crusades brought pastries to Europe from the Middle East, as Marco Polo brought pasta from China.

The two heroes from all the campaigns were, for the West, the spoiled and arrogant Richard the Lion Heart of England (English troops played only a minor role in the Crusades), and the Kurd, Saladin the Magnificent for the East. The French king Louis IX, who later was canonized as St. Louis (now immortalized in the city in Missouri), led the last two Crusades, the seventh and eighth, but died of drowning after landing in Tunis in 1270.

> God has laid down for you the religion He ordained for Noah, the one we have revealed to you as we charged Abraham with it also, and Noah, and Jesus, saying: 'Be doers of this religion and do not let yourselves become divided about it.' But those who indulge in false worships, to them your message is too onerous."   *Koran*, Sura 42:13

Through the machinations of Enrico Dandolo, the doge of Venice, the misnamed fourth Crusade, indebted to the Venetians for providing a fleet and provisions for a crusade, resulted in the sack of Constantinople to satisfy the debt. The Venetians sought only the interests of the mercantile republic and had no interest in recapturing Jerusalem, a city that held no economic value. The greater disaster was the indiscriminate destruction of the most civilized city in the world at the time, a metropolis holding more wealth, architecture, artistry, and classical writings than had evaded the destruction of earlier barbarians.

Since all Crusaders were Christian, heretical ideas were necessarily avoided among an illiterate population. But assassinations, murders, pillaging, and rapine were allowed and indeed sanctioned by the highest ecclesiastical and regal authorities. Dissenters who might have created controversy could not be found because few could read or write, so they were replaced with the buffoons and brigands that constituted the Crusaders, many of whom, like the marchers of the first Crusade, were unable to reach Jerusalem when the route was laid out for them. It would have been preferable to chastise heretics instead of massacring both Christians and Muslims in such vainglorious campaigns.

There was no triumph of the Crusades, only a presumptuous explosion of faith devoid of understanding or wisdom. Many participants were courageous but without honor or dignity. Ludicrous ideals were held out as standards of probity and devotion. The Crusades were a fatuous series of offensive military excursions driven by blind faith, self-righteousness, intolerance and massive ignorance, the attributes of an intellectually impoverished civilization. The fact that it lasted nearly 200 years, involving so many saints, popes, kings and assorted nobles, testifies to the depths of the misplaced exercise in religious militarism. The Crusades were to define the Middle Ages in the same way that the Mongols about the same era would define their civilization: barbaric military adventures blessed by deities whose aim was the extension of war over continents. The Crusades are a symbol of the extremes of religion literally as a weapon against unsuspecting Jews and Muslims and indiscriminately against papal enemies in Europe. The violent and radical force in Islam today, the Jihad, resembles the crusade's combative but repugnant spirit, the ideal of a holy war, an oxymoron if there ever was one.

The Rise of the Military Orders
and the Fall of the Templars

As the crusading armies trickled back from Syria and Palestine in the twelfth century, the church reverted to combating heresy in its own backyard. The Order of Dominicans was established to preach the ordained truths of the church and to obstruct heretical ideas. The secular arm of the state instituted legal procedures against those the church deemed antagonistic to faith. By the thirteenth century, the spirit of the Crusades was revived against the Cathars (The Albigensian Crusades, 1209–1229), and inquisitors were established to ferret out the contumacious. When inquisitors found the rebellious and defiant in error, since the church had no power to put anyone to death, the accused were handed over to secular authorities who ordered them burned at the stake. What was less clear is whether the secular power, even a king, could assume the role of judge of heretics without ecclesiastical cooperation. In fact, Pope Innocent III granted the secular courts power to punish heretics in 1207, revealing whose authority was supreme. Thus, the stage was set for the purging of various individuals and even religious military orders. What was clear is that the secular courts functioned as a surrogate of ecclesiastical pleasure.

A medieval knight was a man who had passed through the subordinate classes of a page and a squire. The nonhereditary "Sir" conferred by British royalty survives as a contemporary honorary acknowledgement but can be given to rock stars whose chivalry may be questionable. The symbolism of chivalry exists in fraternal organizations like the Knights of Columbus, a Roman Catholic service group, and in some degree the Masons. Medieval knights were just soldiers usually attached to some member of the major or minor nobility. Their exploits are remembered more for fictionalized accounts in romance novels than in battles in the cause of religion.

The Hospital of St. John, an order that came to be known as the Hospitallers founded in Jerusalem, cared for the sick and poor by managing a hostel and hospital for pilgrims next to the Church of the Holy Sepulcher. Members engaged in military operations and evolved into the Knights of Rhodes and, after 1530, the Knights of Malta. The order emerged from work at a German hospital in Acre during the third Crusade. All these orders had military operations and all were assigned to guard the numerous castles including the extensive Crac des Chevaliers given to Hospitallers in 1144.

But the largest and most notorious was the Order of Templars.[7] The Military Order of the Knights of the Temple of Solomon, eventually known as the "fighting monks" or simply "Templars," was established in Jerusalem in 1119, about twenty years after the capture of the city. Nine poor soldiers who decided to remain to protect pilgrims took a vow before the Patriarch of Jerusalem, Hugues de Payens, a knight from Champagne, who housed them in his palace next to the temple (the Al-Aqsa mosque today). He journeyed to Europe to seek church approval for a distinct religious order.

The Templars were officially recognized in 1129 at the Council of Troyes and members adopted the habit of the Cistercian monks (with the one modification of a red cross on their chests) and the Rule of St. Benedict. They took the traditional vows of poverty, chastity and obedience and an additional vow of protecting pilgrims. They reported only to the pope and not through bishops. There were two classes: knights and the larger group of sergeants or serving brothers. They were not priests nor did they ever choose to become priests, but they did enlist priests as chaplains. As a religious organization the order was allowed to own property without any taxation and this oversight would become its downfall in less than 200 years.

The Templar satisfied both a prevailing religious and military ardor that led to explosive growth. The order attracted men who wanted to be monks seeking a contemplative life, and mercenaries who wanted to fight for a just cause. Only a few actually became priests, fewer still after the Crusades became knights. Most were lay brothers who worked the extensive farms. Thus, the result of the marital consummation of Christianity and militarism were lay members who combined the contemplative ideals of a monk with the valor of a soldier. Charity was expressed in swordplay to earn salvation.

Popes took them under their wings. The papal bull *Omne Datum Optimum* in 1139 approved their rule and gave them papal protection and granted them property taken from the infidels. The castles that stand scattered across the landscape of the Levant are silent witnesses to their wealth and power, which did not enlist applause from the regular clergy.[8]

I have included Templars as dissenters here, although they appear to be more like victims of regal abuse. King Philip IV of France (known as Philip the Fair) had heard rumors of ignoble actions and behaviors that included the denial of Christ, spitting on the cross, obscene kisses, and the encouragement of homosexuality, actions later confessed to by over a hundred members. Philip ordered them arrested, tortured and their lands confiscated. It is hard to believe that the knights were guilty or would have collectively tolerated the more serious of the offenses they were charged with. The confessed actions under torture were less an example of the stamping out of a heresy than that of the King coveting the property and wealth of the order, as Henry VIII did of church lands when he abolished the English monasteries in 1538.[9]

Jacques de Molay (1244–1314) was grand master when Philip ordered the their arrest. De Molay was from the minor nobility, a soldier who joined the order to fight the infidels and spent his life from the age of twenty-one in its service. He managed the order from its base in Cyprus until Pope Clement V recalled him to France. Shortly thereafter, King Philip had all knights arrested and summarily tortured to admit to a series of offences including the denial of Christ. Jacques de Molay confessed to some crimes but not to those against chastity. The knights had peculiar initiation ceremonies that included spitting on the cross and denying Christ. The closest contemporary version of this is hazing at Greek fraternities or high school athletics. Or perhaps the order wished to emphasize the role of obedience as would be true at any military induction. The failure to correct this bizarre ceremony led to its dissolution.

At subsequent papal hearings De Molay repudiated his confession, made under torture he said. He was burned anyway at the stake on an island in the Seine near Paris in 1314, a victim of regrettable circumstances but not likely a heretic. Ironically, King Philip and Pope Clement died the same year.

Other kings did not follow in this persecution. Pope Clement V reacted with dismay and initially with utter contempt for king Philip's hasty actions as more was at stake than the presumption of heinous deeds among some members. The king's actions were a challenge to papal prerogative. As the trial of the Knights Templar lasted over seven years, the power alliance between regal and papal power came to dominate the presumed rights of a religious order, even one that had defended the papacy in battle against the Saracens. In order to maintain peace in the Holy Roman Empire, the Pope had to make the best of an imperfect situation.

By 1311 inquiries had been held in countries of Europe and the Pope convened the Council of Vienne in 1312 to decide the fate of the Knights. They were not allowed to plead their own case, and the council and pope announced the order's abolition. The language and behavior of heretics had been used to exterminate a rival claimant to French royal prerogatives and lands as pope and kings agreed that their power relationship was more important than any religious order, even a military one that had served admirably in war. As history demonstrates, individuals who are neither heretics nor dissenters suffer when authorities seek to maintain or increase power.

That it was deemed necessary to have a military religious order at all demonstrates the futility of the militancy of the Crusades and its twisted religious mission. Once the Crusades were over unofficially in 1291 when the Christian armies lost the Levant, it was difficult to sustain the rationale for any military order regardless of the nobility, status or sanctity of its members.

The Crusade Against Heretics and the Cathars

The campaign against heretics and dissenters arose proportionate to the accumulation of power in the papacy with the willing cooperation of baronial kings in Italy and northern Europe. Prior to the Fourth Lateran Council convened by Pope Innocent III in 1215, it wasn't clear what Catholic belief entailed, even

MAJOR CHURCH COUNCIL STATUTES AND PAPAL BULLS AGAINST HERESY

1179	Third Lateran Council: heretics are anathema
1184	Pope Lucius III: *Ab Abolendum*: severe measures against heresies
1207	Pope Innocent III: *Cum ex officii mostri*, bull giving secular courts power to punish heretics
1215	Fourth Lateran Council excommunicates heretics
1229	Council of Toulouse grants power to seek out heretics even in homes
1231	Pope Gregory IX: appointment of judges against heretics

Source: E. Peters 1980

though the Third Lateran Council in 1179 had produced several canons condemning heretics. In 1184 Pope Lucius III issued the papal bull *Ad Abolendam*, the first major charter against heretics. But none of these actions would have affected well-intentioned but dissident thinkers unless there existed a solid foundation of civil and ecclesiastical power in the papacy, an extensive authoritarian organizational structure between the pope and bishops, cooperation of the civil authorities, and the marriage of canon and Roman law.

The church borrowed Roman laws for treason, and the *inquisitio* procedures for discovering it, and applied it liberally to any Christian religious dissenter. The medieval church, having adopted the bureaucratic organization of Roman civil order by making the pope a kind of emperor at the top of a hierarchy of clerics, linked its ecclesiastical mandate to the legal foundation of Roman society by comparing Roman criminal activity to the Christian idea of sin.

Despite the shaky political unity in Europe between kings, local aristocracy, and the papacy, a multiplicity of heretical beliefs flourished. One of the earliest widespread reform movements emerged from the charismatic Peter Valdes of Lyon about 1175. He preached an extreme form of poverty similar to Puritan Protestantism and dispensed with the ecclesiastical hierarchy and priests, maintaining that laymen could just as easily administer the sacraments. He rejected everything not in scripture, like penance and indulgences, and urged strictness in seeking the poor and simple ways of Jesus. His interpretation of poverty was condemned about the same time as the poverty of Francis of Assisi was promoted. Peter's preaching and ideas spread throughout southern France, northern Spain, and Italy and were discountenanced by ecclesiastics and eventually declared heretical by popes and councils.

The purpose of military crusades against Europeans was to eradicate revisionist beliefs in order to protect the unity of Christianity. Campaigns were undertaken against heretics in Germany in 1232 and Bosnian heretics in 1227 and 1234. By the thirteenth century, crusading emerged as one of the mainstays of the European economy and one of the principal occupations for ambitious and restless young men. The fact that soldiers were directed against other Europeans and not just Muslims did not change the nature or force of the rallying cries against those opposed to the pope or the faith.[10]

CATHAR BELIEFS

Material world ruled by Satan
Physical creation the result of Satan's rebellion
Denial of baptism and confirmation sacraments
Denial of the Trinity
Son and Holy Spirit subordinate to the Father
Denial of Jesus as a man
Repudiation of church hierarchy
Enjoined upon Perfects after initiation (*consolamentum*):
    No eating of meat, eggs, cheese
    Abstinence from sexual intercourse
    Not to lie, steal, kill, or take oaths

Source: Clifton 1992, 8–9

Pope Innocent III in 1208 was persuaded to call for a crusade against European heretics, the Cathars (from *catharos*, Greek for "pure") or Albigensians (from the city of Albi where the heresy was centered) who were Manichees in disguise, people who revived an ancient dualist belief in two gods, one good and one evil. The Inquisition was instituted specifically for condemning them. They controlled much of the southern French countryside and had the support of the Counts of Toulouse and Foix.[11] The fight for the suppression of the Cathars lasted two decades eventually uniting northern and southern France.

The southern French provinces of Provencal from the Mediterranean east of the Rhone and west to Bordeaux were culturally distinct from northern France. The language was more closely aligned with Catalonia and Spain. Although ethnic, linguistic, and cultural identity can be an influence supporting religious separation, the inhabitants of this region considered the wealth of the church at Rome an obstacle to the purity of Christian belief. The dualist religion that sprung from Zoroaster, and at one time combined by the Persian Mani in the second century CE with Christian ideas, was brought to Europe by returning crusaders. It was tinged with Gnosticism as well as a keen asceticism and had widespread appeal.

The drainage of the Garonne River in southern France going upstream from Bordeaux southeastward to Toulouse and then on past Carcasonne and to Narbonne on the Mediterranean has always been a rich and diversified agricultural area, harboring along its contributing tributaries steep valleys lined with cliffs and precipitous limestone walls. By the twelfth century this region produced grains, sheep, wines, and in its urban centers like Toulouse, then with a population of about 35,000, a variety of tradesmen, bankers, merchants, and, of course, heretics.

An increasing urbanized society like this, rich in natural resources, blessed with water and sunshine, attracted a diversity of new industries like weaving and agricultural production and its fair share of illiterate workers. Moreover, the Languedoc (*langue d'oc*) was a region rich in religious pursuits, boasting the addition of twelve Cistercian abbeys between 1136 and 1165. Toulouse had fifteen hospitals by the late eleventh century, seven leper houses, and landed estates and houses of the Knights Templar and Hospitallers. The region also drew, like mercantile goods to a fair, a diversification of ideas that only remotely resembled approved Christian dogma.

Dual Gods and Evil

How should Christians reconcile sin, redemption, and salvation with deities with ulterior motives for humanity and opposed to personal salvation? Why should evil beings care about humans at all? Dual gods with similar but antithetical powers, whether created by one god or self-generated by unknown powers, is one of the oldest spiritual convictions. The concepts of Satan and devils survive today in Judaism, Christianity, and Islam. How an omnipotent god can supposedly allow another created god to exist at all and then challenge it for supremacy confounds logic but certainly not myth. But why there should be twin gods opposing each other in a struggle for humanity is even more of a mystery. Couldn't there be two gods harmonizing the universe instead of fighting over it? The Cathars revived all these ancient beliefs. Because they believed that the material world is held hostage by the evil god they were able more easily to reject materialism and accept ascetic practices in order to achieve transcendental, spiritual realities.

The ancient Greeks were more realistic about their gods and the relations of deities with mortals. In poetry, plays, and epics they simply made gods humanlike with divine powers and created them as both good and evil, just like humans. Zeus had both his magnanimous and agitated moments, copulated with mortal women, deceived his wife Hera, and sent messenger gods (Hermes/Mercury) to disrupt mortals if they angered him. Greeks gods were like family . . . always around and unpredictable even when you didn't want or need them. The Greeks invented spiteful, semi-divine creatures like Medusa with snakes in her hair and the Minotaur. These desperate creatures could be defeated by semi-divine heroes like Perseus or Theseus.

Thomas Aquinas (1225–1274) demonstrated that there can be no evil in God, but that God knows evil things and yet cannot will evil.[12] How then to explain the presence of evil in the world, said the Cathars, except by the existence of an evil God? Aquinas argued that evil was the result of intention and will and contrary to nature. "Therefore evil, since it is the privation of what is natural, cannot be natural to a thing. Hence whatever is in a thing naturally is good for that thing, and it is an evil if it is lacking. Therefore, no essence is evil in itself."[13] Aquinas wrote that there can be no sovereign evil, but in all his scholastic logic he never used the example of Satan.

So the conclusion is that it depends on whether you consider evil to be, like Aristotle and Aquinas, a primary or accidental cause, an essence, the absence of good, or in more contemporary thinking, a value placed on an action, or, like the Manichees and Cathars, an evil God, the source of all material discomfort in the world. The Cathars had not read Aquinas, because they were exterminated if they did not covert or repent about the time of his birth, and probably would not have accepted his strained logic as convincing enough to reverse their beliefs.

Apparently nobody seriously considered that bad faith in men might be the cause of the projection of the abstraction of an evil deity. And no one answered the question of how a spiritual essence, an evil god, would create material essences to struggle over a good god. And yet supposedly intelligent men had permitted the language and content of mythology to morph into theological dogma and disillusioned thinking so rife with such absurdities that they would kill each other over the acceptance of its meaning. The trump cards of the Tarot deck, in which the devil directs the affairs of the world, best symbolize this lingering belief in twin gods.

Dominicans and the Inquisition

The establishment of the Order of Preachers or Dominicans by St. Dominic in 1216 to preach the benefits of the doctrines of Christianity to the unlettered and heretical and to convince them of their errors was a direct result of the Cathar heresy. The papacy had originally thought that the heresy was the result of ignorance that only needed proper instruction for redemption. The papacy was to discover to its consternation that the heresy was entrenched and not swayed by reformist preaching.

Moreover, the creation of the Franciscan Order by Francis of Assisi was promoted as an antidote to the poverty and simplicity Cathars exemplified in their virtuous lives. The Fourth Lateran Council of 1215 clarified theological ambiguities like the doctrine of transubstantiation that had been the source of interpretation since Berengar of Tours (c.1000–1088). He held that the bread and wine of the Eucharist only became divine once consumed, and not at the pronouncement of a priest's words. More about this issue will be covered when we examine other heretics in following chapters.

But the most popular and longstanding institutional development was that of the Inquisition. The law Greeks invoked to condemn Socrates was the failure to worship the gods of the prescribed pantheon. Blasphemy against the gods in classical Rome was associated with state treason, but the absence of an accuser forced an inquiry. When canon law was written for the new university at Bologna, the document was copied verbatim from the fifth law about heretics in the Code of Justinian from the fifth century.

The church reestablished the Roman practice of inquiring (*inquisitio*) into crimes against the state that included religious practices anathema to Roman civil codes. Dominican monks largely presided over these proceedings begun in 1231 by Pope Gregory IX. He ordered that heretics be imprisoned for life or, if they refused to recant, turned over to secular authorities for execution. This usually meant burning at the stake, but local practices might include hanging. Pope Innocent IV added a papal bull (Latin: *bulla* or notice from which we get "bulletin") that permitted torture to obtain confessions. The Franciscans also became heresy hunters, and Europe was divided into regions to smooth the bureaucratic administration of excommunications, torture, confessions, and recantations. Standardized manuals were developed for inquisitorial use. The accused could not have a cleric or a lawyer representing them because helping a heretic placed anyone under suspicion of heresy. The Inquisition continued its practices until the 1400s in most of Europe, but until the 1800s in Spain.

The following is a typical pledge under oath sworn by Barthelemy Amilhac after an inquisition by the bishop of Pamiers on September 11, 1320. He was accused of heresy and of protecting Beatrice, his concubine, also accused of heresy who had fled capture.

> I, Barthélemy, appearing for questioning before you, Reverend father in Christ my lord Jacques, by the grace of God bishop of Pamiers, abjure entirely all heresy against the faith of our Lord Jesus Christ and the Holy Roman Church, and all beliefs of heretics, of whatever sect condemned by the Roman Church and especially the sect to which I held, and all complicity, aid, defense and company of heretics, under pain of what is rightfully due in the case of a relapse into judicially abjured heresy;
>
> *Item* I swear and promise to pursue according to my power the heretics of whatever sect condemned by the Roman Church and especially the sect to which I held, and the believers, deceivers, aiders and abetters of these heretics, including those whom I know or believe to be in flight by reason of heresy, and against any one of them, to have them arrested and deported according to my power to my said lord bishop or to the inquisitors of the heretical deviation at all time and in whatever places that I know the existence of the above said or any one of them.
>
> *Item* I swear and promise to hold, preserve and defend the Catholic faith that the Holy Roman Church preaches and observes.[14]

Barthelemy asked that the sentence of excommunication be withdrawn. His punishment was lifted the following April. He was absolved by the bishop since he had apparently only harbored a woman for his comfort and not heresy.

The Cathar heresy arose as Catholicism struggled to consolidate its religious and secular grip on Europe. Its popularity arose primarily because of a weakness in the doctrinal unity of Catholicism, the receptivity of novel religious ideas, pervasive illiteracy, the opulence of church hierarchy, the careless morality of the clergy, the glacial slowness of church reform, anticlericalism, and the economic difficulties of daily life. As is true in all social movements, it was likely the convergence of a variety of factors that precipitated and sustained it. The intellectual foment it generated within the church and its popularity assisted by aristocrats posed imminent challenges to secular authority and papal privileges like taxation and the defining of orthodoxy. Crushing the movement was the only viable alternative. But the death of the Cathars only lasted until the Protestant Reformation raised new theological issues, dismembered Catholicism in Europe, and led to successive waves of religious wars and bloodshed in the name of God.

Peter Abelard (1079–1142)

Born near Nantes the eldest of four sons of a moderately wealthy father, Peter Abelard was the only one of the boys not to become a soldier. Instead he found adventure in books, learning, and teaching. Abelard received a solid education in his youth and was recognized as an exceptional student at an early age. Although the eldest child, he gave his patrimony to his younger brothers to devote his life to the pursuits of learning. He studied at the cathedral school of Chartres, and then at the University of Paris, and established himself as an illustrious student, challenging his teachers, and staying on at the university to emerge as its preeminent instructor. By the hundreds his students followed him for the rest of his life, even to living ascetically with him when he was defending himself against charges of heresy.

His life roughly corresponds to the erection of Gothic cathedrals, the Norman conquest of England in 1066, the first Crusades, the renewal of philosophy's rediscovery of Aristotle, and the establishment of universities. Clearly, he is an epochal figure, one of the twelfth century's leading French intellectuals in an age of rapid social transformation, and one of the most daring, innovative and enthusiastic thinkers, exactly why he fell afoul of church authorities.[15]

He made significant contributions in theology, logic, liturgy, poetry, and music, but perhaps is best known for his love letters to Heloise.[16] His life was controversial and the power of his political enemies made him a pariah among theologians like Bernard of Clairvaux, one of the chief advocates for the Crusades. Nevertheless, Abelard put his finger on the great debate of the day by challenging the conventionally accepted notion of mental ideas representing transcendental realities, an idea Augustine had picked up from Plato and adopted to Christianity, and in using reason to argue questions of scripture.[17]

Abelard gave prominence to reason and logic in his Latin tract *Sic et Non* (Yes and No) by reconciling various disputes among theologians. He showed that by disagreeing among themselves they could not even agree on the meaning of scripture, and by posing statements from scripture, prophets, psalmists, and theological commentators frequently revealed how they contradict each other.[18] His book did not intend to reconcile the various differences; it only presented them as controversies. The danger to the Christian faith and the church was that by admitting truth is plural and not singular, that dogma might be forever challenged, and thus that human reason might appear to be superior to faith, an ecclesiastically unacceptable idea.

Abelard was summoned to defend himself against the charges of heresy by an ecclesiastical court. The clerical judges were so intimidated by the excellence of his persuasive arguments, that they condemned his works without a hearing. What offended the church authorities most was his insistence that there were no mysteries in faith and dogmas that could not be defended by reason. He was condemned to silence on all theological issues, a judgment upheld by the pope. He retreated to a monastery where he died at age sixty-three, acknowledged by his peers as the greatest intellect of his age.

But Abelard is also justly famous for his notorious love affair with Heloise, the ward of a rich uncle, a canon of the cathedral, who entrusted her to Abelard's education. At seventeen, she was the brightest student in northern France and his pupil. He was forty, not yet a cleric, and was the brightest teacher at the best university, and arguably, the best philosopher of his time. She bore him a son, Astrolabe. Even though they later secretly married, the uncle sent his kinsman after Abelard whom they emasculated.

Ruined physically yet enjoying the sympathy of Paris and the clergy, he took the vows of a monk and withdrew to a thatched hut where he led the life of a hermit. His former students flocked to him. He gave lectures to them for years until he was called to be the abbot of a monastery outside of Paris (St. Gildas). His love for Heloise, who took the vows of a nun and became abbess of a convent, lasted all his life. He wrote for her some of the most beautiful love songs and hymns of the Middle Ages. Their passionate love story, his songs for her, and their love letters have graced romantic literature ever since. They both died when they were sixty-three years of age though he died twenty-two years earlier. They are buried side by side today in the Pere Lachaise cemetery in Paris near the entrance they were placed together in 1813 after 653 years of being buried separately. Flowers appear daily on their tombs.

Roger Bacon (c.1214–1292), Alchemist

> For this cause you must first learn to know the complexion and properties of all things before you do enterprise to make commixtion together in their proper natures, and it is needful that you know the works of nature.[19]

Roger Bacon, an intellectual maverick in the era of the scholastic metaphysics and labyrinthine theology, was one of the first real pioneers since ancient Greeks to promote the importance of scientific principles. He experimented with optics, promoted the inadequacy of logic as a tool of discovery, and encouraged the value of mathematics and scientific experimentation and a reanalysis of classifying knowledge.[20] He was largely unrecognized in his lifetime for his vast learning from Arab scholars, his command of several languages, his grammars of Hebrew and Greek, and his scientific theorizing. At the pope's insistence, he wrote major works on philosophy, grammar, mathematics, geography, chronology, the calendar, music, optics, ethics, alchemy, and logic, and devoted forty years of his life to the sciences and languages. His two-volume masterpiece of more than 800,000 words is the *Opus Majus*, a work of stunning brilliance and scientific prescience.

He was one of the first to recognize the contributions of Islamic scholars to science and philosophy and quoted them often in his works. He was the first to write a Greek grammar for use in Latin and the first Christian, as far as we know, to write a Hebrew grammar book. His inquiring mind really did not know limitations and this attribute alone would have made him remarkable in an age of intolerance and superstition. Because he offended his own Franciscan clerical authorities with his curiosities and blunt manner, he spent more than eleven years in solitary confinement unable to lecture, teach, or write anything. Although he did not succumb to physical death, the deprivation did result in a form of intellectual death since he was unable to communicate with anyone.

Bacon was born into a reasonable wealthy family, probably the son of a local squire in the village of Ilchester, in the era of the Magna Carta of King John, his crusading brother Richard the Lion Heart, and the legends of Robin Hood. He studied at the young universities of Oxford and Paris. He became bored with the Aristotelian logic of the Parisian school after receiving his MA in 1241. From an approximate five-year sojourn at the University of Paris, he returned to Oxford as a faculty member in 1247 and devoted himself to writing books on experimental research. Like Einstein, he did not conduct scientific experiments, confining himself to theories. He entered the Franciscan Order in 1257 but may not have actually become a priest, only a lay brother or friar.

Oxford University

The city of Oxford is entwined with the university and in many ways is still a classic example of a medieval city. You can saunter down streets named Blue Boar, Bear Lane, Magpie Lane, Shoe Lane, even Dead Man's Walk. The Bear Tavern on Blue Boar Lane dates from 1242 and undoubtedly Bacon visited it. The Saxon Tower dates from c. 980 and is the oldest structure in the city. St. Michael's Church at the foot of the Tower is mentioned *The Doomsday Book* (1086) as the priests owed tax payments to the Norman conquerors. The stained glass window medallions over the altar in St. Michael's date from 1290 when Bacon was still alive. The residence where Bacon lived is now under a shopping mall.

Off Cornmarket Street is an entrance to the Gold Cross Inn, dating from 1183. A performance of Shakespeare's *Hamlet* was first held in 1593 in the courtyard. Shakespeare often stayed in the inn when traveling between London and his home in Stratford. Oxford University began with the founding of St.

Edmund's College in 1190. The first university library dates from 1320, more than a century before the printing press was invented. The Bodleian Library at Oxford, containing 6.5 million volumes, was originally the library of Humphrey, Duke of Gloucester, a great-grandson of John of Gaunt whom we will encounter in a later chapter. His benefaction of books was from 1439–1444. The medieval manuscript room of the library is still called Duke Humphrey's Library. Duke Humphrey was regent to the young Henry VI. Humphrey was a poor ruler but an excellent patron of Renaissance learning.

Bacon's Ideas

Bacon's thinking was well in advance of his era, but it was about 200 years later before his accomplishments were rediscovered. For example, the close proximity of Spain to India appears in a fifteenth century book, *Imago Mundi* (the Image of the World), by Pierre d'Ailly. But the passage is lifted, almost verbatim, from Roger Bacon's *Opus Majus* and can be found in a letter Columbus wrote to Ferdinand and Isabella of Spain in 1498. An obscure passage in a work of Bacon's formed the speculative argument for what was navigational suicide by undertaking a voyage that was, in fact, unrealizable in its day, sailing from Spain to China, unless there existed an intervening and as yet undiscovered continent.

Bacon insisted on the necessity of referencing original authorities as the foundation for a critical review, an amazing insight for a scholar of the 13th century.[21] Many during Bacon's time thought these inquires witchcraft. Not until Lavoisier (1743–1794), examined in a later chapter, did modern chemistry, and the specific naming of chemical substances come into its own. Bacon was accused of studying alchemy which most thought was conjuring up black magic or evil spirits.

Bacon believed that science must use mathematics to confirm experiments, an idea unheard of at the time. He said that logic was useless unless its conclusions could be confirmed by scientific experiments. In the thirteenth century this was heresy. He is the first scholar to make the transition from philosophical speculation to mathematical methods in modern scientific inquiry. Experiments had indeed taken place among ancient scholars like Aristotle. But Bacon is the first to extract the method of experimentation and signal its importance as a separate discipline for verification. Bacon's writings on optics led to the discovery of the telescope in 1571.

Many feared that in studying Bacon they would incur the enmity of the ecclesiastical authorities. They were right. He was opposed by members of his own Franciscan order. He was apparently friendless, regarded suspiciously, had restrictions placed on him by superiors, and found it nearly impossible to carry out his scientific experiments. Bacon writes about his ordeal: "My superiors and the friars kept me on bread and water, suffering no one to have access to me, fearful lest my writings should be divulged to any other than the pope and themselves."[22] And what were these ideas? Motorized carriages, flying machines, and gunpowder, already known to the Chinese for centuries. Experimental ideas such as these would not appear again until Leonardo de Vinci 200 years later. Roger Bacon was a dangerous example of intellectual independence at the time, but a model for it today.

Bacon criticized the corruption of his age, attacked authority, and argued for conducting scientific experiments, all the time protesting his allegiance to the church. But he soon incurred the enmity of religious authorities after accusations of experimenting with light and optics, gunpowder and magic. Serious charges brought against him were based partly on envy and partly on ignorance. He was imprisoned for "suspected novelties," although the exact charges and trial are unclear. There is some evidence he was convicted for astrological beliefs.[23] He died under mysterious circumstances when he was in his seventies. It wasn't until the sixteenth century, when scientific suggestions he had made were actually discovered, that his influence spread, a perfect exemplar against ignorance and superstition.

> Many in consequence wavered in their faith, or rather failed entirely in it, and, abandoning the sacrament of Christianity, became apostates.[24]

By 1250 many soldiers who had not necessarily been the most devout began to despair as their defenses were besieged and provisions scant. Matthew Paris reports on the probable words they said as their faith disintegrated. "What does our devotion profit us? What advantage do we gain from the prayers from religious men and the almsgiving of our friends? Is the law of Mahomet better than that of Christ?"[25]

Heretics Condemned

Pope Lucius III at the Council of Verona in 1184 and Pope Innocent III at the Fourth Lateran Council in 1215 proclaimed decrees that legislated the prosecution of heretics. The Synod of Toulouse called for the extirpation of heretics, the Cathars especially, and permitted citizens to seek them out in suspicious houses, rooms, and hiding places, even forests. The synod further forbade the laity to possess books of the Old or New Testaments and allowed only devotional works such as psalters and breviaries. To complement the ecclesiastical pronouncements, secular laws were passed upholding the religious decrees and prescribing even more severe punishments for failure to comply.

Trial records describe these proceedings. Men like Amalric of Bena, a professor at the University of Paris, was condemned posthumously in 1210. Joachim of Flora was condemned because he was a mystic. Ortlieb, a Strasbourg magistrate, was condemned by Innocent III in 1216. In the year 1250 the bishop of Lincoln deprived a clerk named Ralph of his benefice because of incontinence. When Ralph refused to yield it, the bishop excommunicated him. After forty days the bishop asked the sheriff to take him prisoner. But because the Sheriff was a friend of Ralph, he delayed detaining him, so the Bishop excommunicated the sheriff too. The sheriff appealed to King Henry III who was perturbed because these excommunications infringed on his secular powers. The King in turn appealed to the pope, Innocent IV, and with the payment of some money, obtained a letter that proclaimed that bailiffs of the kingdom had to plead their cases before him and not church officials. The clear distinction between secular and ecclesiastical judicial authority was thus established as an historical but expeditious precedent.[26]

About 1040, Berengar of Tours, as noted earlier, questioned the Eucharist and said that the holiness of the host was only sanctified after its consumption. Since the central doctrine of the Eucharist had never been officially defined, the Fourth Lateran Council in 1215 promulgated the doctrine of transubstantiation by decreeing that the sacrament was the Body and Blood of Christ after the priest spoke the words, "This is my Body." The philosophical principles cited were Aristotelian, particularly the concepts of substance and accidents. The "accidents" of the bread (like its size, color, etc.), the council proclaimed, were mystically transformed into the "substance" of Jesus, but without that substance being tangible. The doctrine was a marvel of linguistic and philosophical ambiguity that managed to confound logic and physics while maintaining the perpetual suspension of natural laws for words spoken aloud by ordained clerics over unleavened bread. The explanation has not been updated based on molecular structures, nor further clarification been offered of how the same spiritual presence repeatedly turns into material reality and back again, and all this simultaneously in various parts of the globe.

As the church became more inelastic in its authoritarianism, its power was exercised in suppressing unorthodox persuasions, and less in reforming its beliefs to accommodate intellectual diversity. Moreover, it stretched its authority into both spiritual and temporal matters. The English medieval historian Matthew Paris, who had access to privileged documents and the ear of the royal court, throughout his narrative vents his animosity toward the papacy for its venal ways.[27] He is especially critical of the papacy for extracting money and only rarely attributes this to the necessity of supporting the crusader effort. For example, he notes a papal directive from 1234 that extracts a twentieth part of all church revenues to the redemption of the Holy Land and binds everyone to this taxation under pain of excommunication. The directive declared that the church would protect their property during their sojourn, forbid creditors to collect interest on loans, and even postpone interest on debt owed to Jews, and then excommunicates pirates who raid ships going to the Holy Land.

But it was the reform movement in religion that dissipated European religious domination, as we shall see in the following chapter, but not before other social movements were also denied a hearing. By the late Middle Ages, the church had turned into an anti-intellectual defender of a limited religious code that inhibited social intercourse and the free exchange of ideas. The church preferred the contentment of righteous absolutism to the discontent of allowing freedom of thought.

The medieval church had neither method nor inclination to channel heresy or social dissent into favorable outcomes. Its sole recourse was suppression. As a result, tiny pockets of dissenting voices, many perhaps ignorant of what orthodoxy was, and others rationalizing the absurdities of papal initiatives like indulgences, reacted with occasional invective, caricature, or subtle logic hoping to stimulate legitimate reform and not militant antagonism. Since there were no socially defined outlets for alternative views, normal societal tensions erupted over any perplexing religious disagreement. Many of these disparate issues would eventually emerge as separate faiths, bursting out when Christianity fragmented during the Protestant Reformation into evangelical faiths, mystical beliefs, biblical literalists, and religions suspicious of clerical hierarchies and arcane liturgies.

CHAPTER TEN
LATE MEDIEVAL REFORMERS
AND INTELLECTUAL DISSENTERS

It is impossible to understand medieval heretics outside the context of the absolute domination of the Catholic Church, of feudalism and the aristocracy, and the pervasiveness of superstitions. Heresy meant political isolation and social ostracism for anyone bold enough to think independently or to challenge ecclesiastical authority, and imprisonment and death for those who actually did. Individual heresies have come and vanished over the centuries but the church lumbered on with campaigns crushing dissent. By the late Middle Ages heresy described countless individuals who challenged conventional rituals or doctrines. Periodically, their burned ashes blew in the wind reminding everyone of the dangers of insubordination.

There were three principal issues motivating notable clerics like Wycliffe and Hus, and selected members of the aristocracy and a few royals. This symbiotic relationship between the aristocracy and ecclesiastics is relevant for framing the discussion about how heretics lived in this era. Men who only sought church reform became the objects of opprobrium and were also condemned for heresy because questioning the authority of the church was tantamount to heresy. The sexual practices among the clergy were more tolerated than the venality of the papacy. The main issues or reformers were:

- The growing wealth and extravagance of the church and papacy
- The concentration of papal power and influence even in secular affairs, and the corresponding growing influence of national kingdoms
- The questioning of unresolved doctrinal issues like the granting of indulgences and transubstantiation

The increased income of the churches and monasteries was largely caused by the expansion of wealth among the mercantile classes. New wealth prompted the growth of cities. Moreover, the feudal aristocracy continued to provide for ecclesiastical and monastic enrichment. Yet increased population after the 1348–1350 plague of the Black Death, volatile economic cycles and the uneven distribution of wealth created growing protests from peasants and even from reform-minded clergy and literate laity. The zeal and popularity of clerical reformers like Wycliffe and Hus, and the popular movements they generated, threatened both nobility and ecclesiastics. A tenth of all income generated in England, a national tithe, was forwarded to the papacy.

The bureaucracy of the judiciary grew as papal and inquisition trials and secular courts administering death penalties attempted to control widespread dissent. Judicial proceedings, such as those where laymen brought property suits against clerics, were administered by the courts of bishops and not by the secular arm of government. Kings and their secular courts sought to diminish or eradicate papal control over clerical benefices.[1] A few remarkable, scholarly men rose to challenge the church on some or all of these issues and were predictably silenced. But their challenges were not forgotten and within a century would be revived again, coalesced in the teaching of Martin Luther with the backing of the German nobility, resulting in the permanent division of Christianity into multiple denominations.

An ordinary person was subject not only to the king's laws but those of the church regarding life events like birth, marriage, death. and morality. Secular clergy, priests and their clerks, were attached to a bishop who controlled a diocese. Franciscan friars and Dominican preachers and all monastic clergy answered only to the pope for discipline and the rules of their order for behavior. Ecclesiastical courts administered uneven justice to miscreant friars. Bishops were both religious and secular leaders, since they ruled property and served as chancellors and diplomats for kings, some even as generals of armies, as well as managing spiritual concerns. Often, the king nominated a gifted statesman for a bishopric and the pope consented. Hence, clerical avarices, such as extortion in the probate of wills, of which bishops had a monopoly, were more noticeable than priestly pieties. It was indifference to the spiritual care of faithful worshippers that especially agitated men like Wycliffe who sought to eliminate the secular offices of all clergy.

Does the authority of scripture determine what one believes and how one behaves? Or is it the authority of the pope and bishops to decide how people attain salvation and whether their actions are spiritually meritorious or not? The answer for Wycliffe, Hus, and Tyndale was scripture. What began as the reform of the papacy and church policies morphed into a rejection of the Papacy and the reinterpretation of vague doctrines and ritualistic practices. The Protestant Reformation has roots, not in the Augustinian German priest Luther or England's Henry VIII, but in the priestly minds of the English John Wycliffe and the Czech John Hus in the fourteenth century.[2]

John Wycliffe (c.1328–1384)

The initial impulses for systematic ecclesiastical and doctrinal reform came from John Wycliffe who studied and taught philosophy and theology, and was later master at Balliol College at Oxford and then rector at parish churches. His central belief was that mankind's persistence in a state of grace, and the power of the scriptures, are the main forces governing conduct, not belief in ecclesiastical power. Wycliffe and his followers translated the Bible from St. Jerome's Latin Vulgate into English so the laity could read and understand it. These beliefs in the power of the scriptures and personal conscience made him popular with the masses but got him indicted, but never convicted, as a heretic. Today we might call him a good Lutheran.

He extolled the virtues of poverty as a condition of the priesthood and abhorred priests serving in secular offices.[3] He believed that clerics should be tried in secular courts. Wycliffe did not believe that the pope had authority over individual consciences but that individuals answered to God alone, and did not need an ecclesiastical intermediary. This key idea, combined with the necessity for any person to read the Bible in his own language and interpret it according to his own purposes, formed the backbone of subsequent Protestant beliefs.

Wycliffe had a puritanical eye focused on clerical misuse of money. His book on simony argued forcefully against the selling of any worldly goods or services that would benefit the pope, bishops, monasteries, or clergy. Similarly, he argued against endowments granted to churches and monasteries. For many centuries it had been a custom to bequeath land or money to monasteries to secure masses and prayers for the souls of donors. However pious the motives of the rich donor, claims were made against the monastery or church by descendants who did not feel such devotion, and who had been deprived of the estate of a father or grandfather. Wycliffe wanted the land or funds to return to the classes who donated them but really desired to relieve the taxation on the poor. No one in this desperate age apparently considered using the disputed funds or land to establish a college, hospital, or other public institution. Wycliffe had preached and published tracts in Latin for the secularization of church property and this alone gained him countless enemies. But compared to the corruption, chicanery, slander, venality, bribery, and even assassination that characterized secular life everywhere, Wycliffe's emphasis on poverty, simony, endowments, and papal taxes seem tame.

Wycliffe could not incite pet topics on the episcopate in its own dioceses without response. Accordingly, the archbishop of Canterbury, Simon Sudbury, and the bishop of London, William Courtenay, had decided to indict Wycliffe as a heretic in 1377 and set a trial for him at St. Paul's. Wycliffe came accompanied by four friars from Oxford to assist in his defense and with John of Gaunt who was accompanied by several of his soldier bodyguards.[4] When a dispute broke out between the duke and Courtenay about whether Wycliffe should stand or sit during the proceedings, and when the dispute carried over among uncontrollable spectators, Wycliffe and his sympathizers thought it prudent to withdraw and the disgraced assembly broke up in confusion. Wycliffe gained new popularity with the public.

John of Gaunt was the fourth son of Edward III and his Belgian queen, Philippa of Hainaut, a part of the Plantagenet family dynasty. They named their children after the places where they were born. John was born in 1340 in Ghent, where English wool was spun into cloth, near Philippa's landed estates. Ghent in England was pronounced "gaunt," and hence his name. John campaigned with his older brother Edward (1330–1376), known as the Black Prince from the color of his armor, and accompanied him in two great victories at Crecy and Poitiers. Edward never became king because Edward III reigned for over forty years and the son died when he was forty-six years old. Edward's young son would reign as Richard II from 1377-1399, an accession John of Gaunt did not oppose. John of Gaunt, as duke of Lancaster, would marry three women, enjoy innumerable mistresses, and have nine children with his wives. His eldest son became King Henry IV.

CHRONOLOGY OF JOHN WYCLIFFE

1328?	Born at Wiclif-on-Tees
1345	Student at Oxford
1358	Master of Balliol College, Oxford
1361	Receives Master's degree
1361	Rector at Fillingham
1363	Granted leave to study at Oxford for degree in theology
1372	Doctorate in theology
1374	Rector of Lutterworth; royal ambassador to Bruges
1377	Trial at St. Paul's: Pope Gregory XI issues bulls against Wycliffe and asks him to come to Rome; he refuses
1378	Trial at Lambeth: appears before Gloucester Parliament
1380	English Bible translation begins; condemned at Oxford
1382	Blackfriars Synod condemns him
1384	Pope Urban VI summons him to Rome; Wycliffe dies

John of Gaunt often heard Wycliffe preach at the royal court and admired his view about the state having power over the church so he protected him. Gaunt sent Wycliffe on a diplomatic mission to Belgium and supported him for over a decade until he became disillusioned with Wycliffe's indictments and switched his patronage to the Carmelites. Gaunt had become more conservative in his later years while Wycliffe never relinquished his radical religious bent.

In 1378, Pope Gregory XI ordered Oxford authorities to try Wycliffe. This was an obvious political move by the pope whose image was tarnished by the failure of the conclave at St. Paul's to come to terms with this papal and episcopal irritant. At the time about half the Oxford faculty supported Wycliffe and planned to defend their privileges against ecclesiastical intrusion. Moreover there was rising antipapal sentiment among royalty and the populace. The general public was incensed that papal tax collectors were assessing the earnings of humble workers to fight the pope's war against his Florentine enemies while English shores went undefended from her European enemies.

The bishops assembled at Lambeth Palace on the south banks of the Thames River across from Westminster Abbey. Upon receiving a letter from the widow of Richard II deprecating no condemnation of Wycliffe, and hearing a crowd declare outside that it would not tolerate an inquisition in England, the assembled bishops wisely deferred any decision. Once again, Wycliffe, with royal help and favorable crowds of followers, adjourned to his country rectory where he wrote voluminously in turgid and numbing prose. Never again in England would a papal commission have any substantive authority. The absence of papal authority paved the way for local ecclesiastical courts and secular laws to prosecute heretics in England.

The year 1378 was also definitive because it produced the Great Schism in the church when rival popes were claimants for the papacy. The spectacle of one pope excommunicating a rival pope was repellent to Europe and appalled Wycliffe who turned his vindictive prose against the papacy itself.

In 1380 while at Oxford Wycliffe concluded that the doctrine of transubstantiation was false. The church did not formally commit to this doctrine until the Council of Trent in 1518. Transubstantiation is the belief that Christ's body and blood are transformed at the command of a priest from the bread and wine. The doctrine from the Last Supper was explained in Aristotelian terms: that the substance of the bread and wine is transformed while the accidents remain. Wycliffe logically argued that material accidents cannot exist without a material substance and be replaced by a divine accident. His argument went to the heart to Catholic ritual. His views would become the prevailing Protestant doctrine. His argument showed that admitting accidents as real without a substance was suspicious in faith and revolting in reason, an attempt to justify something incomprehensible in nature.[5] Such manifest heresy could not go unanswered.

Peasants' Revolt

In 1381 the Peasants Revolt stunned England and resulted in bloodshed—the archbishop of Canterbury, Sudbury, was murdered—and extensive massacres and property damage ensued. The peasants or serfs were not slaves but tenants on the land of manorial lords. Lords of the manor and serfs each had distinct rights. Peasants had their own family plots to cultivate and were not subject to eviction. But they also had to work part-time for the lord of the manor, generally on specific days, to fill the lord's granaries and help pay his taxes. Barons and lords often hired additional workers to plow the fields and reap the harvests. The Black Death decimated the labor force. But the desire for freedom from serfdom, falling wages for non-peasant workers and rising prices for commodities, also propelled the 1381 revolt. The rioting galvanized Wycliffe to raise social consciousness about the plights of the poor.

The Peasants Revolt has to be understood by the calamity of the Black Death that preceded it, a disastrous sweep of infectious pestilence that decimated a third to a half of Europe's population. The dire economic consequences depleted labor and resulted in ruined agricultural economies. Hygiene and sanitation was poor anyway, but when the parasite invaded in 1348—and it returned periodically until 1464—it did not spare the clergy. Hence, many unqualified clerics were promoted in haste to replenish depleted ecclesiastical ranks. It was difficult to discern whether the intervention of the Black Death, which did not discriminate between classes, occurred because of God's wrath on ecclesiastics, or because of God's justice against heretics like Wycliffe.

The precarious life of the peasant was most affected when parents lost children, manors lost owners and tenants, and prices rose everywhere as wages declined, all a recipe for economic collapse. Some serfs demanded freedom instead of increased wages. Feudal barons wanted lowered taxes. As the government sought its share of the diminishing revenue for foreign wars, a hated poll tax in 1380 brought new discontent and prepared the way for a full-scale revolt. The growing recruits to the Peasant Riot in 1381 swept through villages and invaded the homes of landlords, lawyers, government workers, and the specially hated tax collectors. Rioters opened jails and dungeons and freed prisoners and ransacked the homes of the rich. They were particularly assiduous to destroy the rolls and charters describing feudal laws and the bondage of serfs, and the archives of lawyers who recorded deeds of servitude. The rebellion was squelched but with great loss of life on both sides. Richard II abrogated the verbal promises he had made to the leaders of the insurrection, restored order, reinstated the landowner laws, and tried and executed more than 110 of the leaders.[6]

Abjuring the silence necessary to avoid clerical arousal and revolt, but siding with the peasants seeking justice, Wycliffe raised his voice in tract after tract against clerical and church abuses perpetuating his reformist views and keeping church revolt active from his parish safe-haven at Lutterworth. He castigated the clergy and especially the mendicant orders for preaching poverty but not living it. His pen lacerated the clergy for its abuses, the popes for their wealth, and misguided doctrines like the mass, purgatory, and indulgences for their false premises.

Both church and state united in their temporary disagreements to put down this disastrous rebellion. As a result, Wycliffe lost his royal support. Wycliffe's chief adversary Courtenay was made archbishop of Canterbury who replaced the murdered Sudbury and moved quickly to silence Wycliffe. A special committee found ten heretical and fourteen erroneous conclusions in his works and the Archbishop had Wycliffe's writings banned at Oxford.

He reserved his most potent vehemence for the papacy. The autocratic rule and wealth of the popes had been institutionally ingrained by the fourteenth century. Bishops and abbots were appointed by the pope and generally transferred about a third of an annual income to him. Additionally, a tenth of any papal benefice was sent to the pope, and vacant benefices, sometimes left vacant by popes deliberately, had all of their incomes sent to Rome.[7] Occasionally, popes asked for special remittances from kings. The wealth of the papacy irritated Wycliffe and he protested that popes should be as poor as Christ and set an example of poverty for all Christendom.

Calls for Church Reform

Calls for church reform were compounded by the rivalries among claimants and dissension about the papacy itself. In 1305 a severe disagreement between Pope Boniface VIII and France's King Philip IV led to the election of a French pope, Clement V, a former archbishop of Bordeaux. Pope Clement V moved to Avignon in 1309 for his personal safety and in effect transferred the Vatican to his residence, a period of history known as the Avignon Popes when rival claimants vied for the triple tiara. Clement's successor was John XXII, a former bishop of Avignon, elected by the Sacred College at the time dominated by French cardinals. Gregory XI returned the papacy to Rome in 1376 but only after the papal travesty scandalized generations of Catholics who heard about popes acting like kings, events that gave reformers like Wycliffe ample cause to inflame universal repugnance for papacy politics, wealth, and usurpation of peasant earnings.

The buying and selling of church offices was a practice known as simony, a word whose origin is found in the actions of Simon Magus in *Acts* 8:5–25 in which Simon seeks to purchase the spiritual power of the apostles. Wycliffe wrote a book on its practices arguing that the church cannot make a claim to temporal powers or material possessions.[8]

If we review all his major ideas about the worldliness of the clergy, the necessity for the individual to relate to God personally without the need of clergy, the denigration of the pope as head of the church, the rejection of indulgences, the spreading of the church's wealth to all God's people, and the denial of the doctrine of the Eucharist, we find all the seeds of the Protestant Reformation. Wycliffe's ideas became the basis for what Henry VIII accomplished a half century after Wycliffe's death in 1538 when he dissolved all the monasteries and confiscated their estates. Wycliffe inadvertently laid the foundation for the rise of the sovereignty of the divine right of kings and nationalism.

Wycliffe was sincere to a fault and whatever his motives there is no question that he was morally earnest in his convictions and unconcerned about preferential treatment or preference. There is no hint in him of ambition for secular or ecclesiastical office. His life was exemplary and gave no one cause to injure his piety. He was unafraid to speak his mind, and he spit invective against the superstitions of the times like the worship of relics, clerical extortion of marriage fees, and the selling of offices. In advocating for the sovereignty of God he nevertheless confronted face to face the sovereignty of the church. This supreme act of courage endeared him to reformers everywhere.

In 1382 he suffered the first of his paralytic strokes and hence was unable to answer the papal summons to Rome. He had a second incapacitating stroke in 1384 and died that year. Because he was never excommunicated he was buried in consecrated ground. When this was revealed, the Council of Constance in 1428 ordered his bones to be disinterred, burned, pounded into dust, and scattered in the nearby river.

John Hus (1373-1415)

The village of Husinec near the Czech border with Bavaria has not had a more illustrious son than John Hus, one whom Czechs are still proud to claim as a martyr, even if he was burned at the stake as a heretic because of a combination of ecclesiastical pique and political scheming for doctrines the church had not formally defined.

Hus was a staunch follower of Wycliffe, and his preaching and writings testify to how closely he modeled his doctrinal statements on him. He derided clerical abuses as Wycliffe did and thereby drew the enmity of unworthy clerics. Hus questioned whether Christ was in the Eucharist, ridiculed the sale of indulgences and clerical offices, and had unkind words for the pope and his office. Hus was a transplanted Wycliffe, a doctrinal clone of the first Protestant and a true religious renegade.

By 1389 Hus was attending the University of Prague, then one of the most renowned institutions of higher learning in Europe, and the first college in central Europe. It was founded by Emperor Charles, King of Bohemia, in 1348 with a charter from the Apostolic See. The language of instruction was Latin as it was for all universities in Europe. Rectors of late medieval universities, unlike college presidents today, had police powers not just jurisdictional authority over faculty and students.[9]

John Hus received his bachelor's in divinity in 1394 and his master's in 1396. He never received a doctorate. He was ordained a priest in 1400 and became rector of the university in 1402 at the young age of twenty-nine. But about this time he discovered Wycliffe whose articles were being debated in the European academic community.

The Bohemian archbishop found the talents of the young Rector useful and entrusted him with a mission to a small Bohemian town to investigate the case of the appearance of supposedly bloody wafers used for Mass. Hus discovered that the priests were fraudulently proclaiming miracles and exposed and discredited them drawing their personal animosity. He frequently preached against the simony and corruption of the clergy and rich priests and a few bishops, many of whom were German and not Czech who had purchased their benefices. A few of the more venal clergy would remain his implacable enemies and take revenge on him during his trial.

Multiple Popes

Since 1378 a great schism persisted as rival popes at Avignon and Rome competed for the claim to papal legitimacy. On March 25, 1409 a Council of Pisa was convened, attended by four patriarchs, twenty-two cardinals, eighty bishops, representatives of 100 absent bishops, eighty-seven abbots with the proxies of those who could not attend, forty-one priors and generals of religious orders, and 300 doctors of theology or canon law from the universities of Oxford, Paris, and Cologne. None of the rival popes came although they were summoned.

The Council of Pisa deposed both popes, declared the Holy See vacant, and unanimously elected a new pope, Alexander V, who completed the tragedy by promptly dying. His successor was an ignoble man, John XXIII. (As he was not acknowledged as a true pope, the titular name was appropriated by the first Polish pope, Angelo Giuseppe Roncalli, 1881–1963). Europe now had the scandalous situation of having three wandering popes each claiming to be the authentic descendant of Peter's power. Kings throughout Europe wondered whether they should give allegiance to any pope. King Wenceslaus of Bohemia wanted to observe neutrality between the rival popes, but the Archbishop and the university opposed him. This is when Wenceslaus appointed Hus rector of the university.

By 1411 Pope John XXIII, the lone Roman pope, summoned Hus to appear before the papal court then in Bologna to answer certain charges. When Hus failed to appear, the presiding cardinal of the commission pronounced the penalty of excommunication and informed the Czech archbishop, who then had the proclamation of excommunication read in all the churches and ordered Hus's books burned. Fortunately, Hus was in favor with King Wenceslaus and Queen Sophia and the king protected him from arrest.

The king ordered the archbishop in the summer of 1411 to indemnify those whose books about Hus had been confiscated and burned. The Archbishop ignored the order. The king then sent magistrates to confiscate the estates and property of the archbishop and clergy to indemnify the owners. The Archbishop retaliated by excommunicating the fifty or so magistrates and town officials who participated in the property confiscation. The archbishop then placed the whole town under an interdict, which meant that no religious services, no masses, confessions, preaching, or burial ceremonies could be performed.

Sensible minds soon prevailed. The king was asked to arbitrate the stalemate and the archbishop relented, the interdict was lifted and committees appointed to hear grievances. The following September the archbishop died. Hus was once again summoned to appear before a papal commission during the Council of Constance (1414–1418). His attendance would prove fatal.

Hus and the Council of Constance

At one time or another in its four years the Council of Constance had in attendance twenty-nine cardinals, three patriarchs, thirty-three archbishops, 150 bishops, 100 abbots, fifty provosts, and 300 doctors of theology. It was estimated that 5,000 monks and friars were present and about 18,000 ecclesiastics. The occasional visitors must have included a fair share of storytellers, charlatans, mountebanks, thieves and prostitutes, variously reckoned from 50,000 to 100,000. Innkeepers and hostels owners would have been pleased at the influx of paying visitors. One of the prelates in attendance from France was Pierre Cauchon, Bishop of Beauvais, and former rector of the University of Paris, who would be chief prosecutor in the trial of Joan of Arc in 1431.

The council's main decision in 1413 had been to condemn the writings of Wycliffe. But its deliberations and activities soon centered on the simmering controversy lingering since 1378 of multiple popes each claiming divine rights. Council members thought that it would be best for Christendom if all three popes voluntarily resigned. The Council of Pisa had deposed all the popes in 1409 but none had voluntarily resigned, nor had any attended the council's proceedings. The Council of Constance, as participants at Pisa had done, first declared that as a sitting body it was the voice of the Holy Spirit, and that it superceded even papal authority. It compelled the abdication of Benedict XIII and summarily deposed John XXIII who, sensing his predicament and loss of political support, fled to northern Germany for protection. Gregory XII voluntarily resigned. The council effectively concluded the deterioration of the image and scandal of the church in Europe and stamped again the dictates of the Council of Pisa.

Hus arrived at Constance on November 3, 1414, to plead his case before a tribunal that was reluctant to grant him a hearing. His Bohemian enemies had assembled and arranged to have petitions placed on the cathedral doors outlining accusations against him drawn, or so it was said, from his book *De Ecclesia*. Spies placed around his residence were soon replaced by armed guards. Then Hus was arrested and imprisoned in a Dominican monastery.

King Sigismund wanted Hus declared guilty and did not want him to return to Bohemia even though the king had granted him a safe conduct pass, which he subsequently revoked. The king wanted to abort the Hussite movement hoping it would collapse after Hus's death. Hus's friends meanwhile circulated petitions requesting his release, and Hus belatedly realized that he had been invited to Constance under false pretenses. Depositions of witnesses were taken in Hus's cell while he was ill. Hus addressed letters to the population of the city pleading his case. Then, unexpectedly, Hus was removed and imprisoned in the tower of a medieval prison outside the city walls and chained to a post where reputedly he was tortured.

The papal commission to investigate Hus ended when the suspect pope, John XXIII, fled the city. New commissioners were appointed and visited Hus in prison and found him physically and psychologically weak. The commission published a list of forty-five articles from Wycliffe's works condemning Wycliffe as heretical. As similar statements were found in Hus's works, this formed the basis of his condemnation too. Hus was not granted a hearing to any charges.

During his prison hearings and formal trial innumerable accusations were presented primarily directed at his doctrinal statements like predestination and transubstantiation. Even the most ardent Christians could not deny the prevalence of simony and immorality among the clergy. But attempting to alter church practices or policies was as difficult then as parliamentarian or congressional calls for reform today.

Hus's enemies maliciously doctored or falsified statements from his writings to make them appear more insidious and heretical than they were. Hus courageously refused to recant the authentic statements attributed to him, such as his claim that unworthy priests could not administer the sacrament, knowing his prestige would be diminished among his followers.[10] During his public trial, held in the cathedral of Constance, Hus heard the reputed heretical statements attributed to him read out. He was not allowed to respond to the articles. Even unidentified witnesses had testimony admitted. Sentences were passed almost immediately and the first sentence ordered all his books burned. The second sentence declared him a manifest heretic who was to be delivered over to secular authorities for punishment. His ecclesiastical garments were removed and a paper hat with the words *hic est heresiarcha* (here is an heresiarch) inscribed on it was placed as a mark of derision on his head. A large army of about 3,000 militia, accompanied him outside the city where he was stripped of all his clothes, tied to the stake with cords, and a rusty chain strapped around his neck. Faggots were placed around his feet and straw piled to his chin. Flames consumed him within the time it takes to recite two Hail Marys. He was convicted, essentially on false testimony, for what he wrote and said and not for his pious, virtuous, and blameless behavior. The arrogance of power had triumphed over a just man.

After his execution, followers spread his message as a part of a wider, more radical movement in opposition to Catholic orthodoxy, especially in rural areas. These Hussites denied purgatory, infant baptism, the intercession of saints, images and relics, and confession. They upheld various views of the Eucharist that in general denied the real presence of Christ in the consecrated bread, and allowed lay preaching and popular interpretation of the Bible, both under the guidance of the Holy Spirit. The denial and reinterpretation of Catholic ritual, doctrines and modes of belief was the origin of the differentiation of Christianity into multiple denominations. The Reformation had begun.[11]

Cecco d'Ascoli (1257–1327) and Astrology

Cecco d'Ascoli was professor of astrology at the University of Bologna, a poet, mathematician, and early naturalistic observer, the only person known to have been condemned and killed for his writings on astrology. Cecco had been asked to desist teaching when his views became widely known. He was found guilty in 1324 of offenses against the faith, fined seventy crowns and required to do penance. In 1326 the charges were more serious and he fled to Florence where he became a court astrologer. But ecclesiastical justice caught up to him and he was burned at the stake in 1327 for heresy at the age of seventy. If authorities had only waited a couple of years he might have died of prostate cancer thus saving the cost of a trial.

There is no existing documentation about the exact nature of his offense. Since inquisition trials were held in secret it is possible that his trial and condemnation either were not recorded or do not survive. Some commentators claim that he applied astrology to Christ's life, arguing that if Christ was a man his rule would fall under the stars. The contrary argument is that if Christ's fate was determined by the stars, how could God be omnipotent? The scholar Albertus Magnus, who died in Cologne in 1280 where his empty tomb can still be seen, proposed that God used the stars so mankind could decipher his intentions. The church canonized him in 1931.

Though astrological influences had largely been rejected centuries earlier by prominent authorities as without merit, astrology held center stage with theology in the medieval intellectual debate. Cicero and Lucretius had spoken out against astrology as irrational and magical. Augustine had argued most forcefully against astrology as a vestige from the pagan past.[12]

What is it about astrology that holds such strong appeal? It appeals to universal appetites for prophecy and knowledge of the future. It is obvious that the sun controls vegetative life with its heat and energy, and that the gravitational pull of the moon effects tides and women's menstrual cycles. Gravity binds us to the earth and the sun's light allows life to flourish, and we commonly accept that as humans we fall under the laws of physics. It seems logical then that the stars combined in some conjunctive pattern would have some influence in the governance of human lives. And it is that belief where we can see where astrology and religion can so easily intersect. It was a short step from that to believing, as many early Christians did, that the planets and stars were the residences of spirits.

Praise him sun and moon, praise him all your stars and light. Psalm 148

Medieval intellectual playfulness extended to other pursuits that sought to reveal nature's operational secrets. If the stellar harmony of the spheres spoke truths about humanity, perhaps the metals of the earth corresponded in some way with the planets and stars and shared in their substantive nature. Thus was born alchemy. Roger Bacon studied this medieval science too and both he and Cecco sought the mysteries of material composition under astrologically propitious moments. For churchmen all this was borderline heresy, an idea proposed by the devil. Wasn't it possible that a man, like Dr. Faustus in Marlowe's play, could use magic to summon demonic powers?

Cecco wrote several love sonnets to Becchina, a shoemaker's daughter in 1291.[13] His other poems written in his thirties touching the common themes of love and death were rough, uneven, often not very poetical, and filled with a pessimistic perspective about life. His sonnets in fact yield a partial insight into his sour personality. Here is an example of his curious poetical utterances, a sonnet in which he argues for certain horrors for everyone who hates their fathers shortly after his lost his own father:

> No one provoke such ire as this must raise . . .
> Scourge each man who his sire's good name gainsays
> And if by chance a handful of such rogues
> At any time should come into our clutch
> I'd have them cooked and eaten then and there,
> If not be men at least by wolves and dogs . . . [14]

He admired and cultivated a friendship with Dante only to fall out with him later, and in one sonnet castigated Dante for apparently censuring his homage to Becchina. On the other hand, Dante was known to be opposed to astrology and had figures in hell with their heads turned around for vainly trying to predict the future. This opposition alone could have caused Cecco's wrath.

Dante Alighieri (1265–1321) wrote one of the most celebrated epic poems ever penned, *Comedia*, later to be known as *The Divine Comedy*, but chose the wrong political party, the White Guelphs. When his party lost political power and influence in 1301, Dante was exiled, his property confiscated, and he was condemned to be burned at the stake if he returned to Florence. He lived his life in exile and died in Ravenna. I do not profile him at length because he only chose the wrong side in politics though he suffered much of the same fate except death of those who died for their principles.

Marcilius (Marsiglio) of Padua (c. 1275–1342)

Marcilius was an Italian scholar who served as rector of the University of Paris, the most illustrious university in Europe at the time. When Louis IV of France sought legal assistance to wage legal discourse with Pope John XXII, he found Marcilius handily in the same city. Marcilius published *Defensor Pacis* (*The Defender of the Peace*) in 1324 and it proved to be a political firestorm. He claimed that the singular cause of civil strife was the claim of the papacy to absolute power, and that both the pope and the priesthood are subject to government and secular law. His reply to critics in *Defensor Minor* (c.1339–1340) restates many of his arguments. His political theory is not the equal of Aristotle's *Politics*, but together with Machiavelli's (1469–1527) *The Prince*, his works form the background of modern political science.

Marcilius argued his cases cogently and with evidence from scripture and other classical precedents, just like a legal brief. His abundant quotations show a man who had access to a considerable library. His arguments read like judicial interpretations and reveal his early training as a notary and lawyer who came from a family of lawyers and judges. We praise these ideas today because they extol equality of rights and acknowledge the sovereignty of the people, and they redefine and limit ecclesiastical, especially papal, authority. He viewed the law as the supreme authority in temporal affairs. The spiritual needs of the people should be conducted by clerics not engaged in binding or loosing what belongs in the realm of secular law, and this extends to popes.[15]

The non-theological intellectual debate of the late Middle Ages, particularly as law became a staple subject in the universities and gained broad acceptance, was about the respective powers between the temporal and spiritual realms. The revival of classical learning, and the political writings of Aristotle and Cicero for example, helped clarify political theory and the role of law in human affairs. The Bible was the sole authority for spiritual powers. But the papacy claimed to have jurisdiction in both spiritual and seculars matters, arguing that since the spiritual is superior that it ought to rule over temporal affairs too. Marcilius's unique turn of this argument is that reason governs the law, faith governs the spirit, and that spiritual power has its place but no claim over the secular. He believed that the collective power of the people was better able to manage religious affairs than the priesthood. In an age when kings and popes fought for power and authority over people's affairs and land, Marcilius with his bold pen decimated the idea of papal and ecclesiastical supremacy over secular authority.

Popes and leaders like bishops and abbots of monasteries had broadened the understanding of the concepts of church and spiritual prerogatives (*sacerdotium*) to encroach on the strictly political concepts of state, secular, and temporal dealings (*regnum*). Papal claims of universal hegemony agitated kings and secular authorities alike. Marcilius's argument had a favorable reception among the laity and not just anticlerical extremists. Clerics in general believed that the higher spiritual authority granted them through God's favor control over secular affairs. Marcilius reintroduced the crucial distinction between spiritual and temporal authorities and separated religious and political powers, the divine and the human, and then introduced the power of the people (*universitas*) as the common institutional authority. He went further and noted that it was the prerogative of the secular legal authority to appoint, depose, or punish a pope, not the other way around.

Marcilius's contentious but logical, legal ideas overturned the medieval ecclesiastical authority structure by advocating that the temporal affairs of the church are subject to the secular authority. That statement alone could not have been ignored. But when he stated that Peter had no more authority than the other apostles, was not the head of the other apostles, and that God did not ordain anyone his vicar on earth, this idea the pope had to condemn. Marcilius concludes in *Defensor Pacis*: "The decretals or decrees of the Roman or any other pontiffs, collectively or distributively, made without the grant of the human legislator, bind no one to temporal gain or punishment."[16]

CONDEMNED IDEAS OF MARCILIUS

- No priest or church assembly can claim personal property.
- Spiritual power does not imply coercive punishment of persons or property in this world.
- Neither priests nor the Pope has power to command the faithful to fast or forbid labor on certain days.
- Popes cannot absolve persons from a vow with another person or with God, including the marriage contract.
- Spiritual power was never intended to extend to apostolic successors.
- The supreme human legislator is the community of humans and their rulers.   Source: Marsiglio 1993

Pope John XXII wrote in the bull *Licit iuxta*: "We declare by sentence the above mentioned articles (he listed five) . . . to be contrary to Sacred Scripture and enemies of the Catholic faith, heretics, or heretical and erroneous, and also the above mentioned Marsilius and John (Marcilius's companion, John of Jandum), will be heretics—rather they will be manifest and notorious arch-heretics."[17] Marcilius had to flee Paris and find refuge in Germany under the protection of the emperor.

Marcilius was able to remain in the employ of King Louis as his lawyerly skills were exemplary and valued. His condemnation did not result in either trial by the Inquisition or death by secular powers. Today we are accustomed to the concept of popular sovereignty he proposed, revived fully in the Enlightenment under Hume, Locke, and Rousseau and incorporated into the foundation of American jurisprudence. Its wisdom has been established. But such an idea in the late medieval period challenging papal authority was heretical and anathema.

Saint Joan (1412–1431)

Mix together a young warrior woman, a war of more than a hundred years between two perennial national enemies, religious leaders with a belief in sorcery and a warped view of heresy, and an unrealistic dress code for women, and you can partially begin to understand the life and times of the Maid of Orleans. The romantic legends about her still inflame French nationalism and patriotic religious panting and have outlasted the nineteen years of her abbreviated life. The common belief is that her actions were miraculous and sanctioned by God and that the spirit voices she unhesitatingly obeyed were true. The less charitable view is that maybe she was neurotic, but certainly an opinionated adolescent contemptuous of her elders and insufferably intolerant toward informed advice from military officers, prelates, and statesmen. Anyone who has raised teenaged daughters can identify with adolescent rebelliousness.

By the time young modern women of her age would be entering college and deciding what to do with their lives, Joan would be dead at age nineteen. She had forced herself upon royalty, persuaded them of her resourcefulness, formed and commanded a determined army when she was seventeen, faced down adversaries with uncommon physical valor, and conducted herself with dignity in a trial before her male enemies.[18] She was truly a remarkable young woman, a feminine prototype of moral courage. We can only imagine her accomplishments had she lived a full life.

The Hundred Years War

Her short military experiences occurred in the middle of the Hundred Years War, lasting from 1337 to 1453, a war about feudal English principalities and titles in France. When William conquered England in 1066 he never relinquished his lands in France. When subsequent generations could not produce heirs, battles ensued between France and England over rival claims by cousins, nephews, or daughters in closely related dynasties in both England and France. Marriages were always arranged to solidify territorial claims. English society was shaped over the following three centuries by incessant wars on French territory.

Aquitaine was the largest and wealthiest region in southwestern France, and Eleanor of Aquitaine (1122–1204) one of its richest women. She became duchess at fifteen when her father died on a pilgrimage. She married Louis VII and went with him on the second crusade, a militarily mismanaged expedition. She later had the marriage annulled after the birth of two girls and married the philandering and much younger Henry II of England, who sired numerous bastard children and who encouraged, if he did not order, the death of Thomas Becket, the archbishop of Canterbury.

They would have four sons, Henry, who would die young, Richard I (the Lionhearted), Geoffrey, and John, all of whom would rebel against their father as their ambitions for French lands and titles exceeded paternal love and loyalty. Richard and John would become king. In her late seventies Eleanor became a nun, having outlived all her children except for John, dying when she was eighty-two years old.

The possessions of Henry II, the French King of England, the first of the Plantagenet line (or Angevin, after Anjou in west central France) included Aquitaine, Maine, Anjou, Brittany, and Normandy, or about half of what is today France. Rival claimants in France, discontented dukes and counts that included Henry II's own sons, sought their own sovereignty. They were claimants who did not want to be bound by mere conjugal couplings, or the weddings of noble sons and daughters that interfered with their prerogatives. The mood in France when Joan was born was for independence from England.

The English would win victories at Crecy (1346) and Poitiers (1356), and then the French in a following generation would recover them. The English would return to France, as did the celebrated Henry V, and win decisively at Agincourt in 1415 and dictate terms of the Treaty of Troyes (1420), which included Henry's marriage with the daughter of the French king insuring that the future royal would be king of France and England. This in effect disinherited Charles, the dauphin, who fled to Bourges in central France. Henry V died in 1422. His successor, the duke of Bedford, resumed the prosecution of the war by besieging Orleans in 1428 hoping famine would starve out the inhabitants, a common military tactic. In 1429 when English victory appeared imminent at Orleans, Joan suddenly appeared.

Voices and Visions

The events of Joan's life have been popularized in novels, plays (Shakespeare's *Henry VI*, G. B. Shaw's *Saint Joan* among others), celebratory poems, and movies. As a young girl she began hearing voices, wireless communications from the saints Michael, Catherine, and Margaret, that told her to go the dauphin (later Charles VII of France) to aid him. Her father, Jacques D'Arc, a prosperous farmer in Vaucouleurs in northeastern France along the Meuse River, was understandably opposed. To forestall her, he promised her hand in marriage. To preserve her virginity she had promised to saints, she fled to an uncle.

Why these voices did not speak directly to the dauphin is not revealed. She boldly presented herself and the story of her visions to the regional captain who apparently succumbed to her forceful presence and persistence if not her charms and sent her to Chinon, about 450 miles distant, accompanied by six soldiers to see what the dauphin thought of this visionary woman. Try to imagine Joan, that wisp of a teenager meeting her nobility in the grand ballroom, trying to convince him of the validity of her voices. She was then seventeen years old.

Charles (1403–1461) was twenty-six when he met Joan. He was the eleventh child and fifth son, a rare male survivor among his numerous siblings. Charles insisted prior to their meeting in Chinon that a panel of distinguished prelates convene at Poitiers, the capitol of Aquitaine, to examine her audacious and suspect claims. The examination lasted three weeks and found no fault in her personal behavior or integrity. Charles granted the interview and accepted her as a military commander, bypassing the normal military training program, if there was one. The besieged French were so desperate they accepted the offerings of a teenage girl as their military savior. Apparently French troops needed motivational therapy more than military leadership because with her as commander they succeeded in raising the siege of Orleans and defeated the English at outposts along the Loire and at Patay. This must have caused undue anxiety among the English troops who hadn't recruited a female military leader since the native British Boadicea who rebelled against the Romans.

After the victories, Joan insisted that Charles journey to Reims to be crowned king as her voices had predicted. His coronation as Charles VII was the cause of suppressed French exuberance and English puzzlement and anxiety. But Joan was eager to keep the English on the defensive militarily. Charles procrastinated perhaps to savor citizen enthusiasm for his elevation to the kingship as he slowly rode through villages, and to bargain for concessions by advancing treaties with the English for ending the conflict, a prisoner to his vanity. This was not Joan's style and she chaffed at his dallying because the impetus of the military drive was diminishing and possibly lost, and the English regaining strength from weakened positions.

Capture, Trial, Execution

While she was on a campaign in Compeigne on May 23, 1430, the gates of the city were inextricably closed as she and her small band were in retreat from an excursion and sought entry to the city. Historians debate whether or not she was treacherously betrayed. She was dislodged from her horse by the advancing English and captured. The feared maid was in enemy custody, a fate her voices had predicted for her, but not the day nor the hour. Officials of the Holy Inquisition at the University of Paris were eager to get her before them as so much of what she had said, they thought, smacked of heresy.

She was in the custody of John of Luxembourg, a count of Ligny who was in the employ of the English duke of Burgundy, and who had the prosperous option of selling Joan to the English or ransoming her to Charles VII. John's older brother Louis was a cardinal and chancellor of England. Joan would be in his custody for four months. Charles VII made no attempt to seek her release possibly believing that she would no longer be useful in war and had no advantage in peace, since she had no political or economic power base other than popular acclaim. Finally, for a simple payment of 10,000 crowns John of Luxembourg sold her to the English.

All Europe knew the political overtones of her captivity. The English held a woman, a prisoner of war and an international celebrity who had defeated them in several battles. Were her military successes a sign that the English had no legal claims in France? She was wildly popular among the French and had secured the coronation of a French king thus vitiating The Treaty of Troyes by which no Frenchman was to inherit the kingship of France. She was a virgin and personally blameless. Could she be tried on heresy because she heard voices commanding her to kill English? (She never actually killed anyone in battle.) Exposing her as a witch, fraud, or heretic would by implication cast doubt on the legitimacy of Charles VII. The war between the French and English was not over with Joan's capture. It would continue for another twenty-two years, until 1453. The political motivations and ramifications were as much on stage as Joan herself was on trial.

In May 1431 she was taken to Rouen, then a sympathetic English city in French territory, and placed on trial that lasted from January 9 to May 30. An inquisition was legally based on canon, not civil, law. Canon law had its origin in Roman law and was reintroduced for ecclesiastical purposes in the twelfth century and thereafter adopted for nearly all trials. The judge, not a prosecutor, brought the charges and convened other judges. There was no twelve-person jury. At Joan's trial there were twenty-five officials who were notaries, or experts in theology or law. Her chief accuser and judge was Pierre Cauchon, bishop of Beauvais, an ambitious, and unscrupulous academic and greedy prelate (he held many benefices) who had negotiated Joan's sale to the English. There was no defense lawyer. Trial officials sought to have her tried as a sorceress, invoker of demons, or witch, anything but a prisoner of war, which is in fact what she was.

Neither the judge nor the tribunal charged her with a crime. Joan was held as an enemy of war when, given the composition of the court, she should have had the protection of women jailors and been treated humanely. Instead she was shackled day and night in leg irons and three men slept with her at night to guard against her escape. The chief benefit is that a trial record has been preserved which gives us a complete snapshot of her life.[19]

She was brought before impertinent men who thought her insolent for defending her rights as a woman, and who rode, fought, and won decisive victories in battle. The court document proudly records its bias and how shocked the judges were for: "utterly disregarding the honor due the female sex, throwing off the bridle of modesty, and forgetting all feminine decency, wore the disgraceful clothing of men, a shocking and vile monstrosity." The recording of such drivel would be ludicrous were it not to become much of the trial record. She was questioned several days, March 15, 17, and 24 in that spring of 1431 just on wearing men's clothes, and the judges would not allow her to hear mass unless she changed into women's garments.

Her claims of private revelations from celestial beings dominate the trial proceedings, and indeed all of Joan's short life. A passage by Paul in *I Corinthians* (12:10) notes that all have access to the Spirit but in differing manifestations. Thus, the church had scriptural authorization for calling upon God based on the discernment of spirits. It's easy to snigger at the notion of Joan's private revelations, but there were several notable female visionaries in the fifteenth century, and the church canonized two others besides Joan: Bridget of Sweden (1303–1373) and Catherine of Siena (1347–1380).

But there are also scientific explanations. Hearing voices is one symptom associated with a brief psychotic disorder that includes hallucinations and delusions in which patients refuse to relinquish the truth of their belief even when confronted with contradictory evidence. A child hearing voices is not abnormal. Such a condition in adults, however, is associated with schizophrenia, very rare in children, but affecting about one in every 100 adults. Joan might have had a persistence of a normal childhood condition of hearing voices and seeing images that lasted through her adolescence. If Joan had other developmental disorders, this too could have complicated and focused her belief in a primary symptom—hearing voices. It's possible too that she had a touch of clairvoyance, or psychic abilities or mystical powers, and attributed such mental perceptions to God's intentions for her mission.

On May 30 1431 bishop Cauchon violated the procedural rules of the tribunal by not handing her over to civil authorities for death, but directly to the executioner. She was led into the square of the Old Marketplace where she first had to hear an oration against her, a kind of mini-death in itself. In the presence of about 800 men at arms she was burned alive at the stake. Charles VII later called for a new trial with the approval of the pope. Many of those who had been involved in her initial trial and villagers who had known her in her home village were called as witnesses. Her trial was nullified in Rouen in 1456.

She was unblemished in her personal life and admired by her troops, qualities absent enough in military and political life in any age. She was uneducated, but as mistress of the farm her father owned she was not a mere working serf. She had charisma, enormous self-confidence, and conviction. It's possible she was cleverer than history has imagined her, and that her voices were not delusional or hallucinatory but a clever political stratagem by a shrewd country girl to gain the attention of powerful clerical and aristocratic forces by tapping into the superstitions of the times.

It was her challenge to church authority rather than her victories on the battlefield that got her tried, for placing her private revelations above the authority of the pope and clerics, and unbelievably, for wearing men's clothes. But ultimately, the English could not allow a mere girl to lead French armies against their troops. National pride overrode feelings of putting a French peasant girl to death. She was unafraid of authority figures and felt perfectly justified in her bold actions. Her spirit voices did not rescue her from internment, but that does not diminish the strength of her character, the unusual accomplishments she made, or high standards of integrity she held in her short life.

Joan's simplicity, honesty, and moral courage are silhouetted against an age of turpitude, religious authoritarianism, papal schisms, and battles for land using the questionable standards of the chivalric code and warrior ethos as cosmetic covers for ambition, greed, and religious dogmatism. Her virtues shout at us across the centuries and transcend all ages. If she were alive today, she would be a marine.

She was proclaimed a saint in 1920 by Pope Benedict XV, likely to appease the nominally Catholic French and irritate the irredeemably Protestant English.

William Tyndale (1494–1536)

Why would anyone want to kill someone who only wanted to translate the Bible into the native language? What would prompt authorities to kill a man for only wishing to have those uneducated in Latin able to read God's word in the vernacular? Asking such questions is to presume that reason might prevail over faith, sensibleness over superstition, or sanity or madness. To advocate and promote death for a mere translator seems perverted. Yet countless heretics, many of whom were clerics, and many who claimed they were only following their consciences, were hanged or burned after first undergoing torture.

After graduating from Magdalen College, Oxford, and serving for a few years as a parish priest and then a tutor to a landowner's children, Tyndale became determined to translate the scriptures into English. His argument for an English Bible was rational if poorly received.

> The sermons which thou readest in the Acts of the apostles . . . were no doubt preached in the mother tongue? Why then might they not be written in the mother tongue . . . the manner of speaking is both one; so that in a thousand places thou needest not but to translate it into English, word for word . . . A thousand parts better may it be translated into the English, than into Latin.[20]

Tyndale sought the assistance of Cuthbert Tunstall (1474–1559), Bishop of London, friend of Thomas More (profiled later) and Erasmus, an esteemed member of Henry VIII's inner circle of diplomats and statesmen. Tyndale audaciously asked to live in the lord bishop's residence while translating the New Testament. It was an outrageous request because the translation would have been automatically prohibited—a provincial law known as the Arundel Constitution of 1408 forbade the translation of the Bible into English—and because Tyndale assumed that he, a young priest whose only employment thus far had been as a tutor to a family's children, could live indefinitely as a guest with the bishop of London. Tunstall was courteous in declining. Just a few years later, when Tyndale did translate and publish the New Testament, Tunstall pursued him with all the vigor of an indignant prosecutor.

Tyndale found a sympathetic and religiously reform-minded rich merchant named Humphrey Monmouth who let him live in his house while he translated from the Latin Vulgate.[21] There was no hope the book would ever be published in England. London had only seven printers, all tightly regulated. No book could even be brought into England without episcopal permission, and no book published without the consent of censors. Still, Lutheran books were smuggled into England at an alarming rate.

The arguments against an English translation at the time were that unauthorized persons might mistranslate certain crucial passages thereby altering the original intent, or that their commentaries and marginal notations on selected passages might be doctrinally incorrect. Opposition leaned against unauthorized translators.

However, the issue of biblical translation was more complicated than in which language it is read. A more fundamental question was: Who has the right to interpret scripture, the church or just any scholar? Thomas More held that only the clergy can interpret scripture, and only they can decide on the methods of interpretation. Tyndale supported the view of Martin Luther that the authority of the Bible was more preeminent than the authority of the church, a fundamental difference that still divides Catholics and Protestants. This basic difference in religious authority defined the sixteenth and seventeenth centuries and over time fertilized the fields of Europe with the blood of its separate adherents.

And Tyndale did in fact translate words differently and these differences encapsulated his view of the preeminence of the scripture over the church's assumed priority to interpret it. For example, the official translation of the Greek word *ecclesia* was rendered as "church." Tyndale translated it as "congregation" (closer to its original Greek meaning of an assembly), implying that the power of faith was in the hands of the community of believers and not the ecclesiastical hierarchy. (The Arabic *umma* of Islamic believers has a similar meaning of assembly of the people.) Likewise, he translated the Greek *presbuteros* as "elder" rather than "priest," a difference central to the Presbyterian denomination. But these two word differences revealed Tyndale's downplaying of the church's emphasis on its episcopal structure, and his own accent on the people's right to their own beliefs and consciences after reading God's words.

But there was more than just scriptural translation in Tyndale's criticism. He was intensely critical of the pope, church councils, and bishops. "When the bishops and abbots and other great prelates had forsaken Christ and his living, and were fallen down before the beast, the vicar of Satan, to receive their kingdom of him . . . "[22] For example, the county of Gloucester, Tyndale's home county, was in the diocese of Worcester. Four Italian priests had managed to acquire it in succession. In 1521 Pope Leo X gave the office to Guilio de Medici, an illegitimate son of one of his relatives, the archbishop of Florence, who would eventually become Pope Clement VII. This was approved by Henry VIII in 1523. Cardinal Thomas Wolsey (1473–1530) exercised his patronage and received the revenues of this bishopric on behalf of his ecclesiastical Italian brother, who was not too strict in the accounting of revenues.[23] Such were the excesses of benefices and papal patronage executed through local cardinals and absentee bishops. Honorable people were scandalized by the system.

So knowing the dangers of his bold translating ambitions in England, and his criticisms of church abuses, Tyndale discreetly sailed for Hamburg in April 1524. He carried either money or letters of credit from accommodating English merchants to pay for the expenses of his publishing venture. He would remain on the continent for the rest of his life, the next eleven years, actively hounded by heresy hunters for nine of those years.

He contracted with a printer in Cologne to compose his translation. Cologne was then a bustling mercantile city with easy access by cargo ship through the Rhine River to English ports for smuggled, illegal Bibles and circulating Lutheran tracts. But drunken printers gave away Tyndale's scheme to Cochlaeus, a friend of Tunstall, the bishop of London, and a notorious Bible-hunter, then visiting Cologne. Tyndale got wind of the attempt to capture him and fled upriver to Worms, then a safe Lutheran city, with several plates of typeset where he located a new printer. His New Testament, the first ever in the English language, appeared in 1526.

The New Testament had been perverted in the vernacular by a perfidious follower of the Lutheran sect, according to Tyndale's detractors. Copies had been smuggled into English villages where they sold briskly at hefty markup prices. Anne Boleyn owned a copy. Smugglers and merchants alike were well rewarded. Confiscated copies of Tyndale's translation were burned at St. Paul's Cross in London. In a rare incongruity, English Catholics were burning the book on which their faith was based and written in the language they spoke.

TYNDALE'S LIFE EVENTS

1494	Born in Gloucestershire
1510-1515	BA, MA, Magdalen College, Oxford
1515-1520	Cambridge, Teaching as a Priest
1521	Schoolmaster in Gloucestershire
1523	London
1524	Germany; Translating Scriptures
1526	6000 Copies of the New Testament Printed; English Copies Burned in London
1526–1534	Biblical Writings
1534	Hiding in Antwerp
1535	Arrested
1536	Tried, Defrocked, Strangled and Burned

But meanwhile, printers, smugglers, and booksellers all profited. Printers in Germany, Belgium, and Holland published authors like Luther as well as books attacking him. Clever printers publishing heretical books gave false addresses and printing names to avoid detections. Heresy, like prohibition in America in the 1920s, was suddenly good business.

Besides the translation of the Bible and commentaries on selected scriptural books and the Gospels and Epistles, Tyndale's other writings, like *The Parable of the Wicked Mammon,* are commentaries more thick with devotion than theology. In *A Brief Declaration of the Sacraments* he denies the doctrine of transubstantiation, that the Eucharist contains the real body and blood of Christ: "Even so I deny the body of Christ to be any more in the sacrament than God was in the golden calves . . ."[24]

Other documents, like *The Obedience of a Christian Man,* are essays that could duplicate for sermons. Tyndale in this long essay brazenly suggested that a person's allegiance should not be to the pope, but first to the king, God's real chosen representative on earth. The doctrine of the divine right of kings thereby received a religious boost. But how one rationalizes that a king is God's appointed, which has no scriptural authorization, and yet condemn a pope who apparently has some scriptural authority is puzzling.

Alarming as these accusations were during Tyndale's lifetime by 1538, when Henry VIII had confiscated all monastic property in England and disbanded its members, Tyndale's reforms of clerical abuses had succeeded in a way he could not have imagined. Although the literacy rate in Europe and England was low, these attacks on the church were popular and widely read, and even Henry VIII, encouraged by his then-mistress Anne Boleyn, mother of Elizabeth I, who favored Tyndale' writings, was familiar with them.

It was an age of extreme religious agitation, men of orthodoxy, like Thomas More, knew these subversions could lead to large-scale civil conflict. The evangelical Thomas Muntzer in Germany, who fell out with Luther but believed he was God's designated representative, had raised a rabble of 8,000 inspired souls to do battle with priests and godless rulers. Over 5,000 of his followers were slain by the armies of German princes. When he was caught hiding in an attic, he willingly signed a confession and recantation, but was beheaded anyway. Self-proclaimed prophets and evangelicals could be demented, but their charisma tended to attract the gullible and foolish. The enmity of authorities was directed at men like Tyndale because he fueled this intemperance and occasional open uprising against the church.

But this was also an age when Luther and other reform-minded budding Protestants challenged myriad church beliefs like miracles, images, pilgrimages, praying to saints, the papacy, and indulgences. The spread of these ideas with the new technology of printing making ideas widely known, captivated ordinary people and fed an unstoppable tide of reactionary religious interpretations.

After the death of Cardinal Wolsey, Thomas Cromwell became lord secretary to Henry VIII. Cromwell was an earl but born the son of a tradesman in humble economic conditions and was sympathetic to Tyndale's writings. In 1530 he sent Stephen Vaughan as a secret agent into Europe to find Tyndale and offer him safe passage back to England, probably at the request of Anne Boleyn. Vaughan met with Tyndale on two or three occasion in a field outside Antwerp. Tyndale was moved by Cromwell's offer on behalf of the king but suspicious that the clergy would revoke the privilege and arrest him as a heretic.[25]

Thomas More, who described Tyndale as a "hellhound in the kennel of the devil," devoted his nights in writing attacks against this enemy of orthodoxy. From 1530 to 1533 More wrote over a half million words in refutation of him, including *A Dialogue Concerning Heresies*, one of the world's most extensive religious rebuttals. More's voluminous tract was a desperate attempt to counter the spread of what he thought were heretical ideas. His condemnation reads like a set of bad sermons, minus Tyndale's crafty wit and pathos, literary style, or scholarship. Here's a sample in the original Elizabethan spelling of More's ponderous style.

And surely the thynge y mad Arrius, Pelagius, Faustus, Manicheus, Donatus, Eluidius and all the rabel of the olde heretyques to drowne them selfe in thos dampnable heresyes was nothing but hyghe pryde of theyr lernynge in scrypture wherin they followed theyr owne wyttes and lefte the common fayth of y catholyke chyrche prefeerrynge theyr owne gay gloses before the right catholyke fayth of all Cryswtes chyrche whcihe can neuer arre in any substancyall point y og wolde haue vs bounden to byleue.[26]

More was a pit bull on behalf of Catholic orthodoxy and the papacy when he attacked heresies with inelegant, rugged, almost unreadable prose. He used the full weight of his legal authority as chancellor of the king when condemning heretics to death when he actually captured them. He had suspected heretics imprisoned, often illegally, in prison cells on his property where he also had a whipping post used to loosen the tongues of suspected heretics his agents caught.

Tyndale was eventually betrayed by Harry Philips, who presumably was an agent employed by Thomas More. Philips posed as sympathetic to Tyndale's cause and led him outside his safe house, the home of the English merchant in Antwerp where he was seized. After a secret trial before a commission that defrocked him as a priest, he was mercifully strangled before he was burned at the stake, aged forty-two, a martyr to language and the imbecilities of theological equivocations and political paranoia. In colossal irony, his translation became the basis for the King James or Authorized Version of the Bible in English in 1611. But by then England was firmly in the Protestant fold. Vindication of this magnitude is welcome, but only if you are alive to enjoy it.

A summary of the ideals of his life can be concluded with the closing of a letter he wrote in 1533 to another condemned heretic and his confederate, John Frith, then imprisoned in the Tower:

Fear not the threatening, therefore, neither be overcome of sweet words; with which twain the hypocrites shall assail you. Neither let the persuasions of worldly wisdom bear rule in your heart; no, though they be your friends that counsel you.[27]

William Tynsdale is a transitional figure between the high Middle Ages and the Renaissance, a bridge between the end of the domination of the Catholic Church and the beginning of Protestantism. He lived in a time of geographical discovery and religious turbulence, when not only communities but whole countries were turning against Rome. Henry VIII took over control of the church in England and sided with Luther's reasoning about the importance of the Bible against the authority of the church, and the power of faith over that of good works. Everyone thought of Henry as a Protestant, though he acknowledged until his death that he was only a reformist Catholic. The political entity known as the Holy Roman Empire dissipated because of a massive popular religious revolution fueled by morally courageous heretics and the wide dissemination of their ideas through printing.

Girolamo Savonarola (1452–1498)

If you had lived in Florence in the latter part of the fifteenth century, like Michelangelo you would have gone early to the Duomo, Florence's magnificent San Marco cathedral begun in the thirteenth century, to reserve a seat to listen to the impassioned sermons of Savonarola, the firebrand, eloquent Dominican preacher who could alternately make you weep and sigh. His preaching for moral purity, realized in his own austere practices, was extremely zealous against the worldly behaviors of his time. He was a medieval man at the beginning of the Renaissance exemplifying a stern morality just when art, literature, the classics, and the rediscovery of the joy of living were beginning to be welcomed in European civilization.

The Medici Family

Savonarola lived during a tumultuous time in Florence when the Medici family held power. The Medici family ruled Tuscany and personified the easy-going morality of fifteenth century Italy, and almost single-handedly fostered the humanistic Renaissance revival. They were not just any ruling family but became one of Europe's most powerful and richest dynasties. Beginning with Cosimo Medici about 1400 the family nurtured every major Italian artist. Michelangelo, Leonardo de Vinci, Galileo, Raphael, Donatello, Filippo Brunelleschi, Botticelli—all received patronage from the family. The offices for Cosimo's extensive family holdings and civil administration were laid out on either side of a street with a corridor linking the two buildings next to the Arno River. Today this is the Uffizi (the "offices"), one of the world's most treasured museums of Renaissance art.

Lorenzo Medici (1449–1492) was a contemporary of Savonarola and was horrified by Savonarola's turn to what he perceived was the religious Dark Ages, full of justice for sins, God's retribution for extravagances, and woes upon the rich whose money supported the arts. Religion was not his strong suit. Giovanni Medici, the second son of Lorenzo Medici, became Pope Leo X (1475–1521). He instituted the sale of indulgences to support his extravagant lifestyle thereby incurring the simmering wrath of Martin Luther who sparked the religious revolt that divided Christendom. Giovanni's nephew, another Medici, succeeded him as Pope Clement VII. It was Clement who induced Michelangelo to complete his painting of the Sistine Chapel in the Vatican. Savonarola infuriated the Medici family.

Savonarola's downfall began because he preached against the ostentatious and unholy lifestyle of Pope Alexander VI (1431–1503), Rodrigo Borgia who fathered seven children. But history is kinder and more sympathetic to Alexander's memory. Even his contemporaries saw his youthful indiscretions as forgivable, even in a pope. He was not extravagant in his personal life as were later popes. He did manage the affairs of the Vatican with superb administration and, if he did sell cardinals' hats and other benefices, he kept the revenues of the Papacy balanced.

Rodrigo Borja (which he later respelled as Borgia) was born in Xativa in Spain January 1, 1431. His uncle became Pope Calixtus III, and with his education at Xativa, Valencia, and Bologna, his handsome appearance and cheerful grace and manners, presented himself easily for ecclesiastical advancement. He was made a cardinal at twenty-five and the following year vice-chancellor of the Vatican Curia. He would not become a priest until he was thrity-six years old. Cardinal Rodrigo's wife, Vanozza de Catanei, bore him four children of which Cesare (afterwards known as Caesar Borgia) and Lucrezia Borgia are the most illustrious. Rodrigo took the name of Alexander when elevated to the Papacy. He used the full weight of his office to enrich his children who followed his mentoring in military, diplomatic, and personal matters. Alexander had to contend with warring factions within the Papal States and with invading armies, like that of Charles VIII of France. Alexander saw Savonarola, not so much as just another angry preacher, but as a consummate instigator of the affairs of state in Florence.

The combination of Savonarola's invectives against the corruption he saw in Florentine society, among the Medici princes and courtiers, and in the immorality and simony in the papacy and curia, pitted his ascetic demeanor and railings against the most powerful antagonists of the day. When he welcomed the invasion into northern Italy of the French king Charles VIII, and pleaded with the king to restore a democratic republic that would extinguish the rule of the Florentine rich, he sealed his fate with the rulers and the people of Florence and the papacy. Charles VIII of France, at the invitation of the duke of Milan, entered Italy with an army bent on conquering the kingdom of Naples. Thereafter, Savonarola's enemies multiplied. Many sought his outright death but cooler heads lobbied for his preaching silence, expulsion from Florence, or excommunication. In the end, he was not only silenced and excommunicated, but hanged and burned after a staged but secret trial. Death for him was foreordained by the authorities, but torture was liberally applied during the trial itself on trumped-up charges of heresy and schism. Subsequent printed trial proceedings were severely edited or forged.[28]

Savonarola became a lightning rod for Florentine religious revival, a combustible mix of piety and devotion, anticlericalism, wealth, civic pride, and democracy, and an emergent humanism that tested the limitations of Catholic endurance. Florence was a city of churches but also of prostitutes and an extensive secular life. He appealed to the most pious side of the Florentines but managed to alienate the worldly, the rich and powerful, and, most of all, the papacy and Pope Alexander VI against whom Savonarola directed his vituperation as the embodiment of simony and moral turpitude.

Savonarola was tortured with two of his companion friars on charges of schism and heresy, having visions and prophecies, and causing disorder in Florence. Pope Alexander VI sent absolution to the condemning and executing authorities. The friars were led barefoot and unfrocked on May 23, 1498 to the Piazza della Signoria where they had inspired the bonfires of the vanities. They were hanged from a gibbet and the young were allowed to stone them as they died. They were then burned to ashes that were scattered in the nearby Arno River.

In summary, the majority of those described in this chapter did not have to wash clothes in the river, milk the cows, clean stables, or hunt their food. For the most part they were scholars, academics, lawyers, or clerics, the information people of their age. They had the luxury of leisure to write their opinions or preach their cause or rebellion. Besides those who just wanted to reform church practices or doctrines, others sought relief, diversion, or entertainment in more bizarre activities—witchcraft, alchemy, tarot readings, or stargazing. A few bold enough to assert their independence were able to challenge the occult, superstitions, the ignorance of institutions and individuals, even translations of the Bible. Some of the facts and people may be centuries old but the religious dilemma facing modern thinkers and dissidents remains.

By the time of Martin Luther, the papacy and some princes were in full body armor dressed to persecute the spread of multiplying reformed sects. These in turn were arrayed against each other in equally intolerant frames of mind, believing any of their dogmas was also unworthy of critical examination. Protestantism had unveiled the more obvious absurdities of Catholicism only to maintain rudiments of Christianity equally revolting to reason.

CHAPTER ELEVEN
RENAISSANCE DISSENTERS

The intellectual choices for a budding academic in the sixteenth century were unappetizing. One could side with the humanists who favored Christian commentaries on Aristotle, or follow the less popular Neo-Platonists who tended to extol mysticism. Academic subjects were logic, scholastic philosophy, theology, law, and church painting. Trade occupations were more plentiful, though long service as an apprentice was necessary. For careers beyond the trades there were merchants, physicians, lawyers, monks, and a few professors.

But inquisitive minds with access to expensive books could not venture too far with unauthorized ideas since the church was punitive with critics. Bernardino Telesio (1509–1588), for example, a vociferous critic of metaphysics who declined an archbishopric offered by the pope, pointed out the wonders of experimental science and knowledge derived from the senses. His book expanding on this novel idea, *De rerum natura iuxta propria principia* (On the Nature of Things according to their Own Principles), was placed on the Index of Forbidden Books in 1588, but greatly influenced other Renaissance thinkers like Francis Bacon and Giordano Bruno.

Lorenzo Valla (1406–1457) was a priest and serious scholar of rhetoric who taught at Padua, Rome, and Naples. His systematic investigations into textual authenticity rattled the civil and clerical establishments. He was tried but cleared of heresy by an inquisition in Naples, and another time had to flee for his life from Rome. Later, he was apostolic scribe to Pope Nicholas V, secretary to Callixtus III, and retired as canon of the Lateran Basilica in Rome, the city of his birth.

Valla was the first to examine critically the *Donation of Constantine* that reputedly recorded the conversion of Constantine and gave to the then pope Sylvester I (312–335) territorial principalities to him and all his successors. Valla exposed this document in *De Falso Credita et Ementita Constantini Donatione Declamatio* (1440) as a forgery fabricated between 750 and 850. By exposing the forgery he legally deprived the pope of lands. Valla believed that all such documents should be examined with a critical eye, especially those claiming spiritual genuineness. He was equally critical of Aristotle and Scholastic methods and argued in favor of classical and not clumsy church Latin.

This spirit of textual criticism was dangerous but would empower another generation eager for irreverent intellectual challenges. The church would retaliate with the usual punishments of torture and burning at the stake. Nevertheless, the spirit of criticism would carry over from texts to church practices, against the pope and eventually the church itself, laying the beginnings of the Reformation. The most notorious heretic of this age was Bruno.

Giordano Bruno (1548–1600)

He is blind who does not see the sun, foolish who does not recognize it, ungrateful who is not thankful unto it, since so great is the light, so great the good, so great the benefit through which it glows, through which it excels, through which it serves, the teacher of the senses, the father of substances, the author of life.[1]

Bruno satisfies the classic definition of a heretic. He became a Dominican monk and then priest, was indicted by the Inquisition, fled the monastery, lectured for over fifteen years throughout Europe to enthusiastic and critical audiences, wrote poignant and insightful books and pamphlets which antagonized Roman clerical authorities, was eventually captured through guile, imprisoned for eight years, tried by the Inquisition, and burned at the stake in Rome.

Bruno was arrogant and quarrelsome but he defended human dignity and the right to think freely by offering alternatives to Catholic orthodoxy. He persuaded everyone of the power of reason, to have intellectual thoughts accepted even if they violated dogma. Bruno not only synthesized previous philosophies of natural science from the ancient and medieval worlds, he enriched its vitality with new insights, emboldened with lively dialectics that defied superstition and supernaturalism. He has been described at his worst as a youthful hothead, intemperate, and indiscreet. But at his best he wrote some of the most stylistic prose and insightful views of anyone in that illustrious era.

Science, Reason, and Faith

The theory of Copernicus in *De Revolutionibus Orbium Coelestium* in 1543 had a profound and lasting impression on Bruno's thinking. Copernicus's revolutionary cosmology, and Bruno's elaboration of its implications, fueled interest in mathematics and astronomy in the following decades and helped accelerate Western civilization out of the medieval era. Decades after Bruno's death, Galileo, with the aid of the telescope, would provide the evidence for the Copernican theory and Bruno's theories of natural science. Bruno proposed, daringly for his day, that the universe is infinite and has no center and no circumference. Bruno was a theoretical astrophysicist prior to the technological advances that allowed scientists like Johannes Kepler to collect evidence supporting evolving these new cosmological theories.

The central question Bruno raised in an era of radical dogmatism was whether intelligence and faith, revelation and reason, even speculation and facts, could coexist. The answer was painfully obtained in 1600 at the height of the Renaissance and it was a definitive No. But the question is still relevant today for anyone who lives in the theocratic Islamic world or any religious fundamentalist society.

Giordano Bruno was born the son of a soldier in the village of Nola in the Campagnia region of Italy near Naples, the birthplace of Octavius Caesar (Augustus) and Marcus Agrippa, and was a contemporary of Elizabeth I of England with whom he met and conversed.[2] At fifteen he entered a Dominican monastery that once housed Thomas Aquinas. Within a decade he grew skeptical of certain church doctrines and practices. His emphasis on reason, which he perceived as a kind of revelation, was a rejection of preconceived ideas. His mind at this early age became freed of syllogisms and dogmatic assumptions. He felt unfettered to pursue new ideas without fear and the threat of ecclesiastical retaliation, conceding no restraint on his intellectual activities. By 1576 at age twenty-eight he renounced his monastic vows and wandered a nomadic existence throughout northern Europe for the next 15 years.

He stayed only temporarily in northern Italy, first in Noli near Genoa where he taught boys grammar, before arriving in Venice and then Padua in 1576, where fellow Dominicans suggested he wear the friar's habit to arouse less suspicion. While in Geneva he published a vicious attack on a professor of philosophy by exposing what he believed were twenty errors contained in the professor's lecture. Since the professor was a close friend of the rector of Geneva University and a translator of the Bible, Bruno and his publisher were arrested. The printer had to pay a fine but Bruno had to answer before a theological committee where any arguments he advanced, following an apology, were received cordially but unconvincingly. Geneva would not become a permanent residence.

Fleeing to Toulouse, he earned his doctorate in theology at the university and acquired a teaching post. The doctorate conferred the distinction of teaching at any university in Europe. Religious wars at this time in France caused him again to move north to Paris. There he gave thirty lectures, one each on the divine attributes according to Aquinas, and gained instant notoriety, even getting the attention of King Henry III of France who questioned him about his ideas on memory. Bruno had a tenacious memory, and he wrote two treatises on mnemonics.

His writing style was humorless and vituperative. His writings won him few friends but scores of enemies all his life. He couldn't just write what he thought because errant ideas could get an author imprisoned and tortured. So Bruno, like Galileo, had to couch everything in allegory. The popular narrative form was a dialogue, imitating Plato, so that the author, if questioned about a purported heretical intent, could claim that he was being philosophical and not strictly theological. This literary but ill-intentioned ruse didn't work for either Galileo or

Bruno. But Galileo only suffered house arrest for the rest of his life, while Bruno was incinerated.

> Can you be convinced that we will be summoned, interrogated, judged, and condemned less frequently for our idle works than for our idle words?[3]

The Inquisition did not have access to an Interpol service throughout Europe or it could easily have found Bruno. He would not have been difficult to track even for a private detective as he left enemies in every city he visited. His arrogance alienated many students, faculty, and even hosts who allowed him to dwell in their homes. Today psychoanalysts might diagnose him with a moderate personality disorder, or physicians as suffering from a nutritional deficiency. It's more likely he was insolent, impatient with incompetence, and had an ability to easily grasp and analyze what others could not. In others words, he was an intellectual snob.

Bruno's Satires

Bruno satirized Christian symbols and theology under the guise of classical myths. In the following passage from the last five pages of *The Expulsion of the Triumphant Beast*, he does so with the Nicene Creed's dogma of the trinity using the example of the Centaur, part man and part beast. It was for such allegorical concoctions that prompted the authorities to bring him to trial and condemn him. This was the only writing of Bruno's cited by the Roman Inquisition.

> Now what do we wish to do with this man inserted into a beast, or this beast imprisoned in a man, in which one person is made of two natures and two substances concur in one hypostatic union? Here two things come into union to make a third entity . . . But the difficulty in this lies, namely, in deciding whether a third entity produces something better than the one and the other, or better than one of the two parts, or truly something baser. I mean, if the human being has been joined to an equine being, is there produced a divinity worthy of the celestial seat, or rather a beast worthy of being put into a flock and into a stall . . . ? I want to believe much more still, that a man is not a man, and that a beast is not a beast, that a half of a man is not a half man, and that a half of a beast is not a half beast, that a half man and a half beast are not imperfect man and imperfect beast, but rather . . . a god.[4]

The mighty Jove is the hero of this extended allegory and he has convened a council of the gods, a celestial senate. The discussion among the gods begins with the purging of certain vices as the deities assigned to the stellar realms, and their replacement by the virtues. Borrowing from Greek folklore Bruno anthropomorphizes every abstract virtue and gives each the power of speech. A modern reader finds this narrative tedious, but the discussion about the position and motion of the stellar bodies conforms to Bruno's theory of the heavens. Despite its lumbering Latin style, there are passages of sheer brilliance and a freshness of insight rarely seen in literature of this period. Here is a sample:

> Because just as divinity descends in a certain manner, to the extent one communicates with Nature, so one ascends to Divinity through Nature, just as by means of a life resplendent in natural things one rises to the life that presides over them.[5]

Calling *The Expulsion of the Triumphant Beast* heretical does not do justice to the intricacy of its design, its vast scholarship, or the subtlety of its persuasions. I do not see it as a metaphor for the purging of society. The Inquisition easily could have perceived this book as a symbol of the purging of the clerical hierarchy, or even the replacement of revealed religions for a natural religion. I think that is what Bruno intended.

Prior to modern understanding about the role of genetics in the development of life, Bruno, although he was speaking of the soul as the motivator and animator, penned this novel idea for his times in *The Cabala of Pegasus*:

> Sebasto: So you maintain steadfastly that the soul of the human is no different in substance than that of the beasts? And they do not vary except in representation?

> Onorio: That of the human is the same in specific and generic essence as that of flies, sea oysters and plants, and of anything whatsoever that one finds animated or having a soul, as no body lacks a more or less lively communication of spirit within itself.[6]

Within his dialogues are predictable sarcasms administered to philosophers and pedants. *The Cabala of Pegasus* is devoted to a satirical explanation of academicians and individuals as dolts. An Ass is the primary protagonist in the dialogue and gains entrance to the academy with the help of Mercury where he lectures those who supposedly have knowledge. This form of writing is what passes for humor in the Renaissance and is similar to the clever plays of Aristophanes, and may be an imitation of Apuleius' *The Golden Ass*, the first novel from the first century. Bruno's main point is that Aristotle's philosophy is passé and those who slavishly espouse it asinine. But Bruno is not always consistent and it's worth noting that his book *Cause, Principle and Unity* is an exposition of the main ingredients of Aristotle principles, like substance and accidents, potency and act, originating from Aristotle's *Metaphysics*.

Bruno took delight in carrying out a vendetta on academicians, particularly the dons of Oxford, and against those who disagreed with him whom he consistently characterized as fools and hypocrites. His London dialogues display a frustration in his academic non-acceptance in circles he periodically inhabited. His disdain against his colleagues not only would not have secured him tenure but got him formally dismissed from Oxford and kept him constantly on the move throughout the European academic world.

He quickly became appraised of his hopeless predicament after his arrest in Venice in 1592. He alternately argued at his trial that he was only expressing philosophical truths and that if he had been in error he humbly repented. Like Galileo a few decades later, when faced with the seriousness of the charges against him, he would lie and feign repentance. There had been a time when the church had condoned a wide range of the interpretation of religious views. In fact, in the sixteenth century only five persons out of 1,565 who had been tried by the Inquisition in liberal Venice had been executed. After Luther and the advancement of Protestantism, all that changed as the church became more defensive and aggressive in its treatment of those who strayed from dogma. Pope Clement VIII meted out the severest measures against those accused of heresy. The Roman Inquisition was not the liberal Venetian Inquisition.[7]

LIFE OF GIORDANO BRUNO

1548	Born at Nola near Naples
1563	Enters Dominican monastery at fifteen; reads voraciously
1576	Abandons monastery, flees to Rome, then other cities
1577	Venice; writes first book, *De segni de Tempe* (lost)
1578	Geneva
1579-1581	Toulouse, where he receives doctorate in theology
1581	Paris: series of thirty lectures; writings on memory; meets with King Henry III; leaves Paris because of religious wars
1583	Oxford; attacks Oxford theologians for their views on Aristotle, declared persona non grata
1583	London: resides with French Ambassador
1585	Ambassador recalled to France, Bruno follows but finds his presence in Paris unwelcome
1586	Germany: universities of Marburg and Wittenburg
1588	Prague
1589	University of Helmstedt, Frankfurt am Main
1591	Offer from Venetian nobleman to come to Venice
1592	Imprisoned in Venice, transferred to jail in Rome in 1593
1600	Burned at the stake

Claims against the accused by the Inquisition were drawn up by the tribunal, but the names of accusers were never disclosed so that the person indicted never knew who initiated the proceedings. There were no public records as all proceedings were in private, and all who testified did so under an oath of silence.[8] The inquiries never focused on the contributions of a philosopher or scientist to the advancement of knowledge, but whether or not anything in the writings contravened scripture or church teachings. Allegory had been a proven literary device since early Christian times to avoid heretical charges for those writing suspect theological or philosophical ideas. This clearly did not work in Bruno's case, but there were few alternative writing styles for real heretics.

Bruno was transferred from Venice to Rome in February 1593 through aggressive diplomacy from Rome and subtle threats. For the next six years he was effectively ignored and lingered in prison. Finally, the Roman office issued a statement excommunicating him and ordered his books burned and prohibited. He was then released to the civil authorities on February 16, 1600, a standard practice as ecclesiastical courts might condemn someone to death but never actually carry out executions. The church didn't want blood on its hands.

At 5:30 a.m. on February 19th Bruno was led in chains clothed in a white robe decorated with crudely drawn devils to the Campo di Fiori. He responded to the taunts of the crowd as he was led to the stake with quotes from his writings. A long metal spike was driven through his left cheek emerging through his right check and pinning his tongue, and a second spike was driven through his lips. Both rendered him silent. He was wrapped around a post with a thick rope while faggots were piled up to his chin. A torch was placed at his feet and when the fire was extinguished the remaining bits of his body were hammered into powder and his ashes thrown to the wind so no relics would remain for followers to collect.[9]

It's enough to accept that geniuses really are different from the rest of us. They only want to have us treat them with respect if not awe and outright adulation at their productions or pronouncements. Bruno was born about 200 years too early. Intellectuals in the Renaissance had to function in a very narrow intellectual milieu as conditions were not always favorable to the expression of original ideas. It was only when the feudal and claustrophobic traditions of the church broke down, and political upheavals and religious wars subsided, that creative men of letters and science would win grudging acceptance and not be automatically classified as heretics. In Bruno's day that percolating intellectual environment was confined to the aristocracy and a few enlightened professors and clerics, and its limited distribution of ideas sustained by a few wealthy patrons. Bruno's wanderings through Europe seeking an audience for his ideas and safety from prison and death are symbols of every intellectual in any epoch.

Thomas More (1478–1535)

It took the Catholic Church 400 years to sanctify Thomas More because there are parts of More's life and writings, especially his written and personal attacks against heretics, that are troubling, and not just because of mind-numbing prose in rambling tracts defending Catholic orthodoxy.[10]

More gave his life for his religious beliefs as a dissenter to King Henry VIII, his former boss. He is a courageous example of an English Renaissance humanist who was an eminently successful London lawyer, diplomat, a man of letters and historian, a courtier and civil servant who became lord chancellor of England. Henry VIII had him killed for not supporting his divorce. Together with Desiderius Erasmus, he was a powerful exponent of the spirit of humanism, of using classical works to promote learning and Christian virtues, and as one of the founders of a modern educational system sponsoring secular learning. He is remembered for his deep religious piety, his contribution to literature, his attacks on heretics, and his acute legal mind. He was a layman not a cleric.

More was born the son of a prominent lawyer, judge, and court administrator, Sir John More, who exerted a profound influence on his life, and whose status and position accelerated Thomas's early benefits. Thomas himself would soon exhibit his own academic brilliance, personal charm, integrity, and administrative competence. He attended St. Anthony's school in London from about six to twelve years of age studying Latin grammar and letters, rhetoric, mathematics and music, learning to sing and play the flute.[11] Afterward, his father arranged for him to become a page in the home of lord chancellor and archbishop of Canterbury, John Morton, later Cardinal, and the most powerful man in England after the king.

At age 14 he went to Oxford University during Columbus's first voyages of discovery, but left before taking a degree. He then entered the study of law at Lincoln's Inn in London and was made a barrister. He continued advanced law studies for several more years while practicing law in London. By 1504 he was a member of Parliament, and in 1510 under-sheriff of London acting as a judge. In 1509 Henry VIII ascended the throne at seventeen years of age. More was made Ambassador to Holland in 1515, the year his most famous work, *Utopia* was published in Latin he wrote during protracted diplomatic negotiations with the Dutch over commercial trade issues. He became speaker of the House of Commons in 1523 and Lord Chancellor in 1529. He was beheaded in 1535 on the order of Henry VIII for treason after a perjured trial rather than to swear to Henry's supremacy over the Church in England, but ostensibly for his refusal to acknowledge Henry's divorce from his wife Katherine of Aragon.

More and Henry VIII

The adult life of Thomas More is connected inextricably with the life and times of Henry VIII. More attracted the attention of the young Henry because of his successful law practice in London, and the young king lured the reluctant More into his service at court. His education in rhetoric, his extensive law experience, his swift legal decisions as a judge, and his pleasant disposition, wit and learning made him skilled as a diplomat and statesman, first as royal secretary and later as lord chancellor. He kept the ciphers for secret correspondence, checked warrants and made appointments, made diplomatic missions to France, and witnessed royal documents. One of his duties was to draw up a plan for educating the king's illegitimate son, Henry Fitzroy.[12] His deep piety made him detached from corruption and, though clever in the formality, secrecy, and machinations of the court and knowledgeable in the ways of the world, unmoved by the spectacles of power.

By 1527 Henry wanted to divorce his wife Katherine. The pope had granted a special dispensation for this marriage in 1503 when Henry was only eleven years old, the year following Henry's brother Arthur's untimely death. By 1527 Henry wanted to have the marriage annulled claiming that the special papal dispensation to marry was illegal. His real reason was that Katherine was not producing any male heirs and because Henry had fallen in love with Anne Boleyn.

But in 1529 Henry needed a strong chancellor, respected by the people, and Thomas More accepted with private reservations. More resigned in 1531 because of growing political tensions between Henry and the Papacy and Henry's marital difficulties. Thomas Cranmer, the compliant archbishop of Canterbury, declared the marriage with Katherine invalid, paving the way for Henry to marry Anne Boleyn in 1533. The pope promptly excommunicated Henry. Cranmer was later paid for his services with beheading in 1556 under the orders of Queen Mary I (1516–1558), or Mary Tudor, Henry's very Catholic but estranged daughter by Katherine of Aragon.

The English clergy accepted Henry as the head of the church in England, and repudiated the pope's authority in the realm. Thus was satisfied in deed an idea that had medieval roots in Marcilius of Padua, John Wycliffe, and William Tyndale, all of whom were disenchanted, as was the general populace, with papal irregularities, intrusion in affairs of state and taxation.

Henry got the Parliament to pass the Act of Supremacy declaring himself, and not the pope, leader of the church in England, and the heirs of Anne Boleyn the legitimate claimants to the throne. Elizabeth I was the daughter of Anne and Henry. Anyone not taking an Oath of Allegiance was in fact found treasonable, as was More, who was imprisoned in the Tower of London in 1534 and beheaded in 1535, claiming in his final words that he was "the king's good servant, but God's first."

Utopia

More's major literary work is *Utopia*, a Greek word which means "no place." It is a moralistic treatise similar to *The Meditations of Marcus Aurelius*, concerned with virtue and righteousness in human life. It was satirical and an inspiration for Jonathan's Swift's stories about the Lilliputians in *Gulliver's Travels* (1726). *Utopia* is set in an imaginative location at a time in history when new continents were actually discovered. It reflects More's views on Christian ethics for a just society, drawing on classical and biblical sources, Paul, and Augustine. He owes a large intellectual debt to Plato's *Republic*.

He discusses the absence of money and the abolition of private property where all goods are held in common. Gold and silver are used to make chamber pots. This Christian, socialistic view of society and good sense among the leaders and the people prevails throughout the text. He discusses how the Utopians wage war, care for their sick, conduct their various religious customs, even how marriages are arranged. *Utopia* is a prime example of Christian humanism. Yet

More's ironic humor, the vision he had of the world of a kind of monastic, communal order and Christian piety also shine through in these pages.

The twin pillars of the influences on him of religion and humanism are illustrated by two quotes:

> For they never discuss happiness without combining the rational principles of philosophy with principles taken from religion. They think any inquiry concerning true happiness weak and defective unless it is based on religion. [13]

> Of all the pleasures they especially embrace those of the mind, for they esteem them most highly, thinking they arise from the exercise of the virtues and from the consciousness of a good life. [14]

Like Erasmus, More was a passionate advocate for humanism. He argued for classical learning in *Letter to Oxford* when some professors were suppressing all secular learning, even the learning of classical Greek. He writes: "But I have no doubt that prudent men like yourselves will easily devise your own plan to suppress those disturbances and impertinent factions and that you will make sure that all types of learning will not only be safe from derision and mockery but will also be valued and honored."[15]

The Clash Between Church and State

More is a symbol of the clash between religious and civil authorities over the power to govern spiritual matters. He was disturbed by Luther's rupture and was asked by London's Bishop Tunstall to write a response. *A Dialogue Concerning Heresies* (1529) is a religious polemic in rebuttal to the challenges of Luther and Tyndale, but regrettable in laborious prose and burdensome sentences.[16] He argues for a firm belief and obedience in all things to the church with bluntness and without equivocation. He says the church cannot err. "And therefore syth the chyrche byleueth that we sholde worship them (the saints) that kynde of byleue can be none errour but must nedes be trewe."[17] The book was intended as an educational text for both clergy and laity to refute Lutheran ideas point by point. He studiously avoided any vigorous advocacy for the papacy, as that route was politically dangerous in Henry's England.

As a politician, he was keenly sensitive to the potential for radicalism in the emergent Protestant movement Luther initiated, and the disturbing religious convulsions it generated among readers. Thousands of heretical books were finding their way into English homes and libraries. More wrote constantly at night for a couple of years after long days at the office. The effects of fatigue, laborious repetition, and a lack of studious reflection and careful editing show through in these pages. In these books he was so dedicated to refuting heretics that his enthusiasm for upholding orthodoxy overcame his sense of style and solicitude for his readers. He was quite earthy and descriptive of heretical offenses and of those who perpetrated them. More was not a teaching divine or priest, nor was he trained in theology, as were Luther and Tyndale. In this long-winded rebuttal, More exhibits none of the subtlety, logic, theological sophistication, or readability of Tyndale's arguments or Luther's stout prose style.

He used salty but not obscene language to describe heretics. The kinder view is that he was just entertaining his audience.[18] The view I favor is that he really did perceive his heretical enemies as vermin and insects bred from the devil. But its self-righteous tone and combative, religious certainty detracts from the awe felt for his otherwise personal courage standing up to Henry VIII.

It's enough to know that as a judge and high court official More raided businesses with his agents searching for heretic books, gave orders for accused heretics to be tortured, many on the grounds of his house in Chelsea, and if he condemned them, witnessed their executions. Henry VIII had the official title of "Defender of the Faith" given by Pope Leo X in 1521 for his book against Luther. But More was the judge and enforcer of the faith.

More supported the heavy sediment of prevalent Catholic practices like indulgences, and in his personal life showed the strength of will to put his life where his mouth and pen were. Although he was at ideological odds with his opponents, like the long dead but still influential John Wycliffe or More's contemporary William Tyndale, all demonstrated the same kind of gritty heroism in defense of their beliefs. Wycliffe was somewhat fortunate to have died of natural causes before he could be burnt at the stake, though his corpse was desecrated years later. For their fearless valor, More was killed ostensibly for treason and Tyndale for heresy. If they were opponents today they would be arguing their cases on primetime TV.

HERETICAL IDEAS IN MORE'S ENGLAND

Questioning free will & salvation
No veneration of, or prayers to saints (or relics)
Questioning the validity of miracles
No physical presence of Christ in the Eucharist
No sacraments
No purgatory
Discrediting of pilgrimages
Salvation through faith alone
Questioning the role and legitimacy of the papacy
In favor of the laity's interpretation of the Bible
In favor of the translation of Bible in the vernacular

Ironically, had not Henry VIII persuaded Parliament into passing the Act of Supremacy in 1534 making him titular head of church and state in England, More's idea of reviving the inquisition in England against heretics might have prevailed. Although Catholicism was revived temporarily under the rule of Mary

Tudor from 1553 to 1558, the separation of England from Rome effectively allowed civil society to regain a separate legal system without ecclesiastical interference. More won the battle as an example of moral courage, but lost the war against church reform and religious identities separated from the papacy. The more complete liberation of the individual from prescribed religion, and the development of human rights protecting an individual's right to religious beliefs and practice, would have to await later philosophies of freedom and popular revolutions.

More was deeply committed to his religious principles and the rule of law even to death. His works reflect his Christian ideal of society. His personal courage and religious fortitude are symbols of magnanimity even to martyrdom.

Johannes Kepler (1571–1630)

The home life of children is influential in determining who they are and what they become. The man featured here had a rotten home life. The boy's grandfather had been a furrier and mayor of the town, but was arrogant, obstinate and short-tempered. His grandmother, according to the boy's own words, was fiery, extreme in her hatreds, violent, lying, jealous, a bearer of grudges. All offspring seem to have been dysfunctional.

The boy's father had no trade or craft, was a wanderer, full of malice, who narrowly escaped imprisonment for murder. He changed his religious affiliation in order to join the army. His aunt was burned alive as a witch. His mother, a gossip, quarrelsome with a bad disposition, was accused of consorting with the devil. She narrowly escaped burning at the stake. She underwent an extensive trial for practicing witchcraft when she was in her seventies. His surviving brother was an epileptic and had a psychopathic streak. The boy himself was sickly much of his life and nearly died of smallpox when young. His schoolmates disliked him because he was good in studies. He returned their enmity.

But when he was only twenty-four years-old, because of the fame of his teaching and academic brilliance, he was appointed professor of mathematics and astronomy at Gratz in Austria. The boy was Johannes Kepler, arguably the most significant astronomer and mathematician of his age.

But unhappy as his childhood was, I include him as a dissenter because in his adult life, having been excommunicated from the Lutheran church by a peevish pastor, and having fought his mother's witchcraft trial for years, eventually getting her sentence suspended for lack of evidence, he refused to convert to Catholicism when the emperor offered him a very tempting stipend and position. In this defining act of refusal for religious principle during the Thirty Years War, and toward the end of his life when he needed the money for his family, he set an example that is as magnanimous as his scientific and mathematical achievements, and for which he is little known.

Kepler had been a restless student who emerged in adulthood as a prodigious scholar whose patience and endurance made him complete his life's work of formulating the first exact laws of nature. His findings still govern our view of the universe. Kepler confirmed Copernicus's theory using the mathematics from the Danish astronomer Tycho Brahe. His own observations and calculations paved the way for Isaac Newton's theory of gravity, having nearly stumbled upon a gravitational theory himself. He did his calculations and arrived at his laws without analytic geometry, not yet invented by Descartes, and without calculus, later to be developed by Gottfried Wilhelm Leibnitz and Isaac Newton, and without the aid of computers.

He spent four years calculating the orbit of Mars testing seventy different hypotheses. At twenty-six he published his defining work, *Mysterium Cosmographicum* (1596), in which his thinking evolved from merely theoretical speculation to empirical science by enunciating the first laws of nature. He believed that there must be some "force" coming from the sun that governs the revolutions of the planets, anticipating Newton's explanatory laws of gravity. Kepler concluded that the orbits were elliptical, one of his crowning intellectual achievements and his First Law.

Kepler's great accomplishment is that he helped unite astronomy and physics that had had a rupture for 2,000 years. In him we can witness an age in which antiquated concepts about the nature of the world are probed, and new concepts and terminology to explain the nature of the universe are invented. His achievements, embracing geometry, astronomy, epistemology, music, and even astrology, were acknowledged by all future scientists. Following a lifelong obsession to unlock nature's secrets and using all the available resources of all known knowledge had not been attempted since Plato and Aristotle. But his scientific accomplishments should not blur his personal distinction on behalf of his religious principles and turning down monetary emoluments if he would only convert to Catholicism. He never did.

Rene Descartes (1596-1650)

That all at present known is almost nothing compared to what remains to be discovered.   Descartes, 1637

Descartes overthrew the belief that only faith was the way to gain knowledge. He proposed instead that an individual's thoughts, initiated by doubt as a method, gave access to knowledge, thereafter known as the Cartesian method. Thoughts, not faith, could answer a person's questions about God, self, free will, and knowledge. Descartes is the first modern philosopher who re-established Plato's philosophical worldview that a person is composed of two parts, mind and body, though this idea had become a rock of theology. But more significantly, he held as probably false everything that was merely questionable. He found so many opinions and opposing sides voiced for most truths, that he concluded that everything was false that was only probable. He did not favor the idea that one had to choose the truth of anything from the presentation of opposing views. Doubt borrowed from the Greeks became his instrument for gaining new knowledge, another rational perspective from the faith-driven scholastic method.

But it is impossible to neglect his mathematical genius. He was one of the first, along with Pierre Fermat his contemporary, to show how the calculations of arithmetic are related to the operations of geometry. This simple relationship had occurred to Archimedes centuries earlier. But Descartes went further in his study *Geometrie* to show how a geometric point in space could be determined by the expression of two or more algebraic coordinates to locate a number of points that hypothetically form a curve. We still use his graph where the x or horizontal line is positive, and the y or vertical line is negative below the x line. He was the first to use the first letters of the alphabet to represent known mathematical quantities, and the last letters of the alphabet to represent unknown ones.

Like Kepler, Descartes was not killed for his ideas, but his life was in danger in his final days and he fortunately died a natural, though preventable, death in Sweden. Had he lived in Italy, I believe he would have been tried and condemned. Geography and the politics of religious or national parochialism can define a person's allegiance, or indictment for heresy.

To understand Descartes' popularity during his own day we must first understand the series of crises that perplexed the seventeenth century about religious thought, skepticism, reason, and the nature of truth, all brought about by the liberating thought of the Protestant Reformation and the bloody confrontation known as the Thirty Years War between Catholics and Protestants. For a growing number of mentally restless men religion and its increasing fragmentation into denominations of religious truth did not explain the natural world. In an era of new scientific discoveries and explorations, neither faith nor scripture answered how the world works.[19]

Rene Descartes was the son of an upper-middle-class lawyer and regional councilor in Brittany. His mother died thirteen months after his birth while delivering another infant son who died soon afterward. He was raised by a maternal grandmother. When he was ten he entered a Jesuit college where he resided for the next eight years. For the rest of his life he remained indebted and loyal to the Jesuits, and maintained correspondence with many of them, though he rejected his early scholastic training except for mathematics. He entered the University of Poitiers in 1614 and graduated in canon and civil law in 1616. He then entered army service in Holland as a training consultant, some suggest as a spy. He left the Dutch army for the army of Emperor Maximilian in 1619, where he studied math, music, mechanics, all of which could have military utility, and natural philosophy, which was to define all his subsequent work and establish his permanent reputation.

After army service he lived in Paris sustained by a modest inheritance from the sale of his title (*signeur*) and his father's estate. But though a devout Catholic, he moved to Protestant Holland where he felt safer in the discussion and publication of his ideas some of which, in the highly charged religious mood of the day, were dangerous to the clergy and its supporters. His sustainable financial resources allowed him to continue his investigations all his life without interruption, accompanied by a valet and a number of servants, and without the need of a university appointment or any employment.

He never married but in 1634 took a mistress—his only known liaison—who bore him a daughter who died when she was only five.

Descartes' first and lasting academic love was mathematics, and as a young scholar he wrote a study on geometry and invented analytic, or problem-solving algebra. He proposed that algebra, the way of calculating magnitudes, be applied to geometry, the study of extensions. His conclusion was that all truths could be subjected to the rigors of calculation. Unlike law where juries must decide a case beyond a reasonable doubt, mathematicians must have certitude. Euclid's *Geometry* today is as certain as it was when Euclid wrote it. The certainty of mathematics is what Descartes was seeking for laws of the mind. But in philosophy there are no certainties. He gave math to philosophy while viewing life philosophically.

Descartes also wrote on music, physiology, optics, cosmology, and the psychology of the emotions, demonstrating his wide-ranging interests. He had for years been writing a treatise on physical science, known in his day as natural philosophy. However, when Galileo's work *Dialogue on the Two Chief World Systems* was condemned in Italy, though published in Protestant Holland, and Galileo forced into house arrest, Descartes immediately realized that he must either abandon his own similar work or write a persuasive preface demonstrating metaphysical reasons for making his work legitimate in the eyes of church authorities. Galileo's condemnation effectively closed intellectual debate in southern Europe. As a result, creative development moved from Italy to northern Europe and Protestant countries where such speculations were more favorably received and where the long arm of the papacy could not reach with impunity.

Thinking and Doubt

This "preface" became the famous *Discourse on Method*, an acknowledged classic in epistemology, or the study of the theory of knowledge. This work begins the history of modern philosophy, and was to serve as a foundation to his work on theories of the natural order in nature. He wrote it in 1629, in a first-person style and in very readable French, but did not publish it until 1637. The church placed it on the Index of Forbidden Books in 1667.

"Since I am thinking," Descartes says, "I must exist." He might just as well proclaimed that "we breathe therefore we are." But that mundane pronouncement, to show the power of the consciousness of existence and expressed so pithily, would have relegated animals to the same stature of humans. That was an idea that would have to await later scientists. To show such favor would have been acceptable to animals but an injustice to humans. As a Catholic Descartes could not, and would not have admitted, that "mind" and "God" might be in themselves, like his x's and y's in algebra, representations of other abstractions or unknown realities. Besides, it would be too contentious for theologians to accept that animals had souls, though not have been for Aristotle who thought they did.

And if I exist, Descartes continued, then this idea of God I have must have been put there by God and therefore God exists. The idea of fixed ideas, of the mind's possession of implanted ideas, so to speak, still lingered from scholastic philosophy. The danger to the church of this kind of speculation was that Descartes placed the existence of God in a person's reason and not in external reality. But his conclusion is also a non sequitur, because the idea of God could have arisen from consciousness itself, from culture, education, religious indoctrination, almost any other external stimulus. The conclusion from this fault in Descartes' thinking is that if any idea exists, it could have been put there by God, and that therefore I do not have my own ideas. This in turn questions the existence of human free will.

He began his famous *Discourse on Method* with the following observation:

> Good sense is, of all things among men, the most equally distributed; for everyone thinks himself so abundantly provided with it that those even who are the most difficult to satisfy in everything else, do not usually desire a larger measure of this quality than they already possess.[20]

What Descartes wrote throughout his essays, and anticipating David Hume in the following century, was that we should doubt the senses because they frequently present us with false or confusing information. We should begin anew to discover what principles about ourselves appear to be universally true. "I know how very liable we are to delusion in what relates to ourselves."[21] In fact, he says, we should use doubt itself as a method for discovering truth.

Descartes wanted to separate his notion of science from pseudo-sciences like astrology and alchemy, and apply the rigors of mathematics that he hoped would disassociate real knowledge from claptrap. He suggested that we can know nothing with certitude, not from evidence of the senses or logic since both can be wrong and are potentially illusory. But then he said that the only single certainty he had, and which he cannot doubt, is himself doubting. If he thinks he doubts, he exists, and that is the one clear and distinct idea he knows for certain. It is clear because it is obvious to everyone. It is distinct because it does not follow from logical premises in a syllogism favored by the scholastics. Here is that famous passage:

> As I observed that this truth, I think hence I am, was so certain and of such evidence that no ground of doubt, however extravagant, could be alleged by the skeptics capable of shaking it, I concluded that I might, without scruple, accept it as the first principle of the philosophy of which I was in search.[22]

His establishment of this criterion would appear to negate the authority of both church doctrine and scripture. Here was a man claiming to be Catholic proposing an intellectual challenge to the authority of faith itself. Descartes was faced with ecclesiastical absolutism where even theory could not stray far from dogma. Descartes made philosophy accessible to the reading public, and in his vernacular French not in Latin.

Descartes was the first since the Greeks to espouse the philosophy of doubt, as opposed to rationalistic thinking and authoritative dogmas. Others would later maintain that the method of doubt was not just to be used once in a lifetime in the search for truth, but could be used over and over again as a refutation of absolutism in knowledge. Descartes revived Platonic, metaphysical "clear and distinct ideas," thoughts that Roger Bacon tried to overturn with his emphasis on science and empirical inquiry. Princess Elisabeth of Bohemia, profiled in another chapter, put her finger (and mind, so to speak) on Descartes' dilemma: the necessity of explaining how the immaterial mind and the material body can possibly relate to each other.

Descartes' appeal was to all bickering Protestant religious groups. But his rationalism challenged and undermined the authority of the church because it claimed that individual reason, beginning with self-awareness, was the final appeal to truths about mental realities and nature and not the dogmas of the church. Thereafter, the authority of the self, an incipient form of individualism, would stand larger than religious authority. The mind is free, and this conclusion comes not from a logical syllogism but from one's own implicit and undeniable sense of consciousness.

So many of his writings were incomplete at his death because the climate of the times urged caution in publishing controversial works. The Calvinists too in Holland were threatened by his ideas. Descartes was both a genius exploring new intellectual adventures in math, science and philosophy, riskily proclaiming doubt as a method of finding truths, but was also a practicing Catholic who did not seek to disturb the clerical authorities or upset his religious convictions. The dualism of Descartes was not only his proposition between the body and the mind, but between truths compelling him through reason, and his obedience to religious faith as he believed in it.

DESCARTES' MAIN WRITINGS

1618	*Composition on Music*
1626	*Rules for the Direction of the Mind* (published posthumously)
1630–33	*The World* (published posthumously & incompletely)
1637	*Discourse on Method*
1637	Geometry
1641	*Meditations on First Philosophy*
1644	*Principles of Philosophy*
1647	*The Description of the Human Body* (published posthumously)

The individualism of modern philosophy and the mathematical precision of all sciences, both of which define the modern epoch, were born with Descartes. It is rare to find a person so dedicated to his pursuit of "quiet" (his term), or the continual pursuit of greater knowledge that he believed made for happiness on earth. The search after him begins for more far-reaching theoretical and universal principles. With Descartes the Middle Ages comes to an end, the Renaissance blossoms, and doubt and mental concepts become an integral part of philosophy.

Baruch "Benedict" Spinoza (1632–1677)

Of all the things that are beyond my power, I value nothing more highly than to be allowed the honor of entering into bonds of friendship with people who sincerely love truth.[23]

As Spinoza walked out of a theater, an unknown man brandishing a knife jabbed at him. As Spinoza leapt away, the knife's point missed his person but pierced his coat, a souvenir he kept with him un-mended for the rest of his life. The incident was a cautious but essential reminder of the threats that attend ideas that challenge popular wisdoms and ingrained superstitions.[24] Spinoza fits the profile for this book because he was excommunicated from his synagogue, which makes him a Jewish heretic, did not convert to Christianity, and had his life physically threatened for his beliefs.

The outlines of his relatively short life in Amsterdam or even where he was born are spare, as were his modest living conditions and frugality in food. But his influence was lasting and profound. He died of tuberculosis when only forty-five years-old, likely aggravated by silicon dust from grinding lens for a living. He changed his name from Baruch to Benedict when he ceased being a Jew although he never became a Christian. His ancestral Jewish family immigrated to Holland from Portugal, and prior to that from Spain, escaping the persecution and the forced conversion to Christianity imposed by the Inquisition and Ferdinand and Isabella in 1492. Spinoza went beyond petty doctrinal quibbles with his radical theological ideas, and for his scholarly pains was excommunicated by his Jewish congregation in 1656.

He published two major influential books. The first was *Tractatus Theologico-Politicus*, published in 1670, and officially prohibited in 1674.[25] He argued in this treatise that not only were biblical writings questionable, but that the church should be subordinate to the state, an idea championed by Marsiglio of Padua, Wycliffe, and Tyndale, as we saw, and Thomas Hobbes in *Leviathan* in 1651. The subtitle reveals more of Spinoza's principal ideas than the title itself: "A Critical Inquiry into the History, Purpose and Authenticity of the Hebrew Scriptures, with the Right to Free Thought and Free Discussion Asserted, and Shown to be not only Consistent but Necessarily Bound up with True Piety and Good Government."

Like Descartes, who wanted to cleanse his mind of presuppositions and start anew with a fresh look at finding knowledge, Spinoza "resolved to examine the Scriptures anew, in a spirit of entire freedom and without prejudice, to affirm nothing as to their meaning, and to acknowledge nothing in the shape of doctrine . . . "[26] His principal conclusions in the *Tractatus* after reexamining the Bible sent tremors through Western religious communities and reverberates still. Here are the main features.

- That spiritual knowledge can be derived from natural understanding and not from prophets.
- That interpretation of faith is everyone's prerogative.
- That liberty of conscience needs to be protected by the state.

These conclusions would in time become the staple of liberal Protestant and some Jewish theologians, and embedded in the First Amendment of the U.S. Constitution. But in the seventeenth century they were extremely contentious.

The second major work was *Ethic*, published posthumously in 1677. Its purpose was to separate faith and belief from philosophy, and to highlight reason as the method for finding God. Spinoza found God in nature, which he considered God's perfect revelation, and not scripture, which he thought too bewildering and subject to multiple interpretations.[27] His decision not to publish *Ethic* during his lifetime because of its incendiary contents was probably deliberate, although it must clearly have pained him not to witness its circulation.

Spinoza believed that God and nature are interchangeable, the infinite presented to us in the forms of spirit and matter. He thought that God's substance was nature, a pantheistic notion considered blasphemous at the time, even by Calvinists. Asian philosophers like Lao Tze (c. 604 BCE) had made similar claims about the infiniteness of nature but without the idea of God. Alexander Pope would find God in nature and leave that romantic philosophy buried in the poetic legacy of William Wordsworth, Percy Shelley, Lord Byron and John Keats to leaven the literature. Poets could express pantheism but not be considered heretics, so no church or court did them harm. There is also here a touch of mysticism that Spinoza might have absorbed from the teachings of the Kabbala he would have learned in his early education.

Spinoza argued that miracles are sacrilegious because they contradict nature and also reason, what he called "the true testament of God's word." He said God is one substance but composed of two major attributes, thought and extension, ideas that mirror logic and geometry, another legacy of Descartes. These may not be God's only attributes but they are the only ones we can know. After meeting with Spinoza, Leibniz concluded that Spinoza's God was incompatible with orthodox belief. Leibniz certainly took his cue from Spinoza's bold assertions to continue the break from religious rigidities and stale theological thinking.[28]

Ethic contains the mental acrobatics of scholastic philosophy tinged with math, long and tedious discussions of the mind, emotions, the nature and attributes of God, freedom of will, and ethical behavior formed deductively, just like in logic and geometry. It is useful to recall that he was writing in the days when particle physics and microorganisms were unknown. The concept of substance, for example, was a philosophical abstraction derived from Aristotle used in explaining biblical ideas about the nature of God, and religious practices like the transformation of the bread into the body of Christ in the Mass. But in other ways Spinoza's creative thinking and philosophical originality do not defer to Jewish or Christian theology. It is in this sense that his courageous convictions make him unique in the intellectual marketplace.

He was conscious of how far his ideas departed from religious persuasions. In his polite refusal to accept a professorship of philosophy offered to him on February 16, 1673, he declined to give public instruction as he did not know the limits of freedom in developing his philosophy nor what disturbances of his ideas might be to established religion. He had already experienced how volatile men were in their dispositions toward religion while he was leading a solitary life. He could readily imagine what controversy he would cause in the public arena.[29]

Indeed, his mild and unpretentious disposition argued against controversy: He was interested only in promoting what he thought was the truth. Here is what he wrote to his good friend Ludowijk Meyer who had written a preface to one of his books:

> I should like all men to be able easily to persuade themselves that these are published for the good of all men, and that you, in publishing this little book, are mastered simply by the desire to spread the truth, and that you are doing all in our power to make men, in a kindly and friendly way, to take up the study of true philosophy, and to pursue the good of all. This everyone will easily believe when he sees no one is hurt, and that nothing is put down which can be even slightly offensive to anyone.[30]

Spinoza's radical but innovative ideas rocked the theological and ecclesiastical establishments and pumped new vitality into philosophy that had been so linked throughout the Middle Ages with theological equivocations and petty artifices. He wrote in Latin and was proficient in mathematics, and he was so greatly influenced by Descartes that he used geometry, logic, and reason to explain God and ethics, the kind of methodology of deductive propositions that Euclid used to describe geometric principles, and Newton the physical universe. It's a clinical, detached, and tedious prose almost to insensibility, but rigorous in deductive logic. Entering Spinoza's cerebral world is traversing backward into an intellectual mindset, like crawling back into Plato's cave, that even few philosophers care to enter. Nevertheless, his bold departure from the scriptural and theologically acceptable set him apart as an authentic dissident. His excommunication made him a religious and social outcast. His ideas made him a European religious pariah except among those few who saw and acknowledged his creative genius.

Voltaire disputed Spinoza's initial premise, that there existed a universal necessary Being called God, from which all existence could be deduced. Spinoza's abstract generalizations stretch the limits of metaphysics in the bold attempt to blend philosophical terms with religious principles of belief, a feat that proved more dangerous to faith than to philosophy.

Voltaire (1694–1778)

He was born Francois Marie Arouet on November 21, 1694, the son of a notary, and like Descartes educated by the Jesuits with whom throughout his life he maintained a peculiar fondness. He changed his name to Voltaire, partly because of his hatred for his father who saw him as worthless. By the time he was thirty, through felicitous affiliations and by dint of his lively wit expressed in poetry, successful plays, histories, clever epigrams, and satires, he became a guest of Parisian and Prussian royalty.

Prior to the French Revolution there was no social equality in French society. Only families that could trace their nobility back farther than 300 years were allowed to hunt with the king and serve in high government positions. It was an exclusive aristocrat's world. Clever intellectuals like Voltaire, whose family came from the working class, were tolerated for their amusing qualities but never really fully admitted into the closed circle. He spent nearly a year in his early twenties incarcerated in the Bastille for writing satirical verses about the aristocracy.

I include him here not because of his testy personality and character flaws but for his courage in defending his own rights when he was assaulted (he was imprisoned before he could fight an aristocrat in a duel), for personal justice and the freedom to write, for defending the rights of others, for lending money to the poor without interest, for establishing schools, employing more than 100 workers on his estate at Ferney, and because ecclesiastical, aristocratic, and civil authorities sought to arrest and imprison him for his satirical writings in which he used over 108 different pseudonyms to cloak his identity.

In his mid-twenties he had bested wits with an aristocrat named August de Rohan-Chabot. Offended, de Rohan had his bodyguards beat Voltaire outside the door of his residence. None of his aristocratic friends would help Voltaire or do anything to upset a fellow aristocrat. Voltaire began to take up fencing lessons but was arrested after a cardinal, the uncle of de Rohan, appealed to the king to stop a probable duel. In 1725 Voltaire was thrown into the Bastille, and then after two weeks, exiled to England where he spent the next two years learning English.

When he returned from exile in England in 1728 he discovered that the city government of Paris had defaulted on municipal bonds. To help alleviate the investment losses among its most wealthy citizens, the city offered a special lottery to which only the owners of the worthless bonds could apply. Why the city's financial experts didn't just make payments of the money they had and give so much to all investors is unknown. When Voltaire heard this news, he and fellow investors ingeniously decided to purchase all the bonds in advance from all the investors, realizing that the bonds were coupons for winning a lottery, and that if he and his allies held all the tickets, one would assuredly win. Voltaire amassed a fortune that sustained him all his life and he wisely invested in businesses like grain and paper manufacturing.[31]

Shortly afterward Voltaire wrote *Letters from the England Nation*, a delicious set of descriptions about English manners, and religious differences between France and England that was satirical enough about all things French to be condemned by French censors. Copies were discovered in the offices of Voltaire's printer, who was promptly incarcerated in the Bastille, and orders sent to arrest Voltaire, who barely escaped to the military camp of his friend Duke Richelieu, a descendant of the famous Cardinal under Louis XIV, who sheltered him.

Voltaire and Emilie du Chatelet

When he met the Marquise Emilie du Chatelet (1706–1749) in 1733, all caution for cavorting with a woman of royalty evaporated. Both Voltaire and Emilie had numerous love affairs during their lives. But their affair was noteworthy for being literally a meeting of the minds. Here was a woman worthy of his wit and acumen, someone with whom he found physical and mental attraction, an uncommon chemistry of love. It was less important that she was married and a mother. He was Europe's best-known author and she a woman of significant means and high intelligence. They had a fifteen-year relationship.

Emilie, the marquise du Chatelet, was a woman of incomparable talents who, with her husband, Marquis Florent-Claude du Chatelet, whom she married in a formal arrangement when she was nineteen, lived in a landed estate in Circy in Champagne, and at a townhouse (still existing in Paris). Voltaire often resided in both residences, but mainly at Circy. After Emilie gave birth of a boy and a girl by the time she was twenty-seven, and fulfilling the standard conventions of the day among the royalty, she and her husband agreed to lead separate lives.

Emilie had a lively singing voice, was the lead actress in Voltaire's plays, and played the harpsichord. As a young student she mastered Latin, English, German, and Italian and studied Flemish when living in Brussels. She translated Sophocles *Oedipus Rex* from Greek into French. But her first love was mathematics. She used her acute knowledge of math to conduct scientific and astronomical experiments. Voltaire did not have a mind burning for science but tolerated it in order to be engaged in study with her. Together they studied the Bible, metaphysics, and astronomy, interspersed with animated discussions about poetry, art, politics, and the theater. She wrote a book on Leibniz and translated Newton's *Principia Mathematica* into French from the original Latin because she found the English version faulty.[32] She published *Institutions de Physique* about Leibniz in 1740. Her translation and commentary on Newton became crucial for later developments in physics and mathematics, though recognition for her contributions was slow and neglectful.

Their affair over many years was passionate, and their love of knowledge and separate wealthy status gave them abundant opportunity to read, write, and experiment together fulltime. Like all lovers they had predictable fallouts over the years, then reconciliations. As Shakespeare keenly noted in *A Midsummer's Night's Dream*, "The course of true love never did run smooth." Voltaire's self-servicing ambition often outran his good sense, and Emilie's volatility and gambling overshadowed her sensible practicality. Both were exceptionally intelligent and this fueled their amorous desire, literary creativity, and scientific intensity, but clashed with their temperamental personalities.

Zadig (1747) is Voltaire's famous novel, composed while he was hiding from authorities, that is part autobiography about his love for Emilie and their joint projects, and part philosophy of his opinions about life and destiny.

After one of their more pugnacious separations, and while visiting the court of Stanislaus, king of Poland, she fell in love with Marquis Jean-Francois Saint-Laurent, a minor poet, when she was forty and he thirty. She would become pregnant by him. Returning to her home castle of Circy, she induced her husband to return from his command of his troops at Dijon and remain with her for a few weeks. Thus, all but she and Voltaire, who was party to the plan, were convinced that the new child would be his legitimate heir or heiress.

She gave birth on the night of September 3, 1749 to a girl, and died September 10 from infection because of the labor. She was only forty-three-years-ago, perhaps the most accomplished woman of the eighteenth century. The infant girl died shortly afterward. Her daughter Francoise Gabrielle Pauline, had married an Italian nobleman and moved to Naples. She never saw her parents again. Emilie's son, Louis-Marie Florent, became Louis XVI's ambassador to England but was guillotined during the French Revolution.[33] Her grandson died in prison and this ended the lineage.

Voltaire was beside himself with grief at her death. He consented in 1750 to join the court of Frederick, King of Prussia, himself something of an intellectual who sought enlightened company at his court in Potsdam. But by 1753, besides the balls, plays, operas, dinners, and the pension, he quickly became disenchanted and then came the inevitable falling out with his regal sponsor. He wandered disconsolately throughout southern Germany and France until he came to reside in comparative literary freedom among the Swiss and his retirement until his death in 1778.

Voltaire's Writings

He and Emilie connived to take into their confidence Jeanne Poisson, Louis XV's mistress—who became known thereafter in history as Madame de Pompadour—so they could have access to the court's proceedings. Madame de Pompadour made Voltaire royal historiographer and he was admitted to the French Academy as a return favor.

It is as an historian that he created authentic masterpieces like *Siecle de Louis XIV* (1751) and his seven-volume *Essai sur l'historie generale et sur les moeurs et l'esprit des nations* (1756), the first attempt at a history of civilization. The following selection is from one of Voltaire's minor works, an example of his cleverness, and what made him so popular among his throngs of avid readers throughout Europe and the irritating bane of the authorities.

A fictional Egyptian princess, Amasidia, grieves for her lost love until she recognizes him in a field tended by an old woman sorcerer. He has been changed into a white bull and it is soon revealed that he is Nebuchadnezzar (c.605–562 BCE), a real Babylonian king who defeated the Egyptians in Syria becoming the undisputed master of all of western Asia. Thus does the acerbic, skeptical, and witty Voltaire open his short story, *The White Bull*.

Historically, Pharaoh Necho defeated Nebuchadnezzar years later. Ever the military man jealous of his conquests, Nebuchadnezzar then turned to crush the revolt in Judah and destroyed Jerusalem in 586 BCE. These historical events are turned upside down as Voltaire seeks to de-mythologize real characters, making fun of prophets clad in ragged clothes, elevating reputed biblical enemies to a divine status. Nebuchadnezzar as a white bull becomes a divine Apis bull in Egypt where he is adored, even though in reality he was Egypt's dreaded enemy and conqueror. He is later reincarnated as a mere mortal king. Voltaire's clever prose is easy reading and ingeniously creative. The last line of *The White Bull*, chanted by the Babylonians, is "Long live our great king, who is no longer an ox."[34] It's a clever satire, so characteristic of Voltaire's writing style, unsurpassed until Jonathan Swift and Mark Twain.

In his final decades he alternately lived in four residences in and around Geneva to escape whichever authorities might be pursuing him. He finally settled in Ferney and improved the estate by converting it into a profitable working farm with more than 100 employees. It was complete with barns, poultry yards, sheepfolds, wine-presses, fruit houses, 500 beehives, and a colony of silkworms. By 1770 he was manufacturing watches and clocks, jewelry and silk hose from his silkworm production and selling his commodities throughout Europe. When he entertained or held plays the guest list often extended from sixty to eighty people.[35]

He has been classified as a philosopher but left no logical intellectual edifice, no coherent argument for a rationale of human life. *The Ignorant Philosopher* attempts to answer metaphysical life questions like existence, free will, eternity, dependence, soul and spirit, reason and thought, justice and truth. This short book is a series of abbreviated essays each of which he could have written in the time it takes to finish a crossword puzzle at breakfast, a document where he asks more questions than he answers, and criticizes the intellectual icons of the day, like Spinoza, Descartes, Leibniz, Hobbes, and Locke.

His clever indictment of Leibniz's "best of all possible worlds" and philosophical synopsis is the novel *Candide,* perhaps Voltaire's most popular satire. [36] This readable novel illustrates how Voltaire was unafraid to ridicule, not just the church, but the more illustrious philosophical icons of his day and take them to task for being impractical in human affairs. The protagonist, Dr. Pangloss, is an incurable optimist who refuses to change his rosy outlook on life after a chain of unbelievable calamities, never considering a revision of his unduly rosy perspective on life. *Candide* is a satire on the absurdity of philosophies like those of Leibniz, or poetic ones like Alexander Pope ("God's in his heaven; all's right with the world"), than of the foibles of men in an uncertain and precarious existence in the real world. It is also likely his own pessimism after the loss of Emilie, the love of his life.

He was wealthy all his life, speculating and investing. He did not just leech from royalty. With his profits he loaned money at high interest rates to French nobility, German princes, and dukes, from all of whom he often extracted particular favors of protection from censoring authorities, usually from the publication of a slanderous or anti-establishment book or pamphlet he popularized. He was often accused of writing slanderous and illegal tracts that he just as frequently denied. He was thus able to purchase, from debts owed, his continuing freedom from official sanctions.

Voltaire gave a lesson in critical inquiry by forcing reconsideration of the figures and fables in the Bible, the impact of Chinese and Indian literature, and the absurdities of the literature of his own time. He gave readers a taste for style as they read some of wittiest, humorous, and flowing narratives ever written. And it all came effortlessly from his pen, always illuminating a truth, spontaneous and often bitingly impudent. He extolled human freedom and liberty above all other humane virtues, and favored public programs that enriched people's lives and advanced the cause of humanity. He wrote against superstition, false ideologies, prejudice, and sanctimonious pretense and conveyed an enlightened skepticism.

In 1776, two years before his death, the Americans launched their independence and war against English oppression, which they gained in 1781 with the defeat of English forces at Yorktown with the help of the French fleet. In 1789 the French began their own revolution from royal domination. Although Voltaire never formulated a political theory, he remained in favor of a monarchy and distrusted democracy that he thought would embolden the idiocy of the masses. But he would have applauded the social transformation that recognized peoples' inherent rights and freedoms, a political goal in which his ideas likely played a significant role. In a previous century, he could easily have become one of those burned at the stake. All the tributes and eulogy his genius merited, even from literary and clerical enemies, was justified.

His satirical poetic excesses and sarcasm mirrored his adversarial personality against pedantry, superstition, and mediocre minds. Clergymen denounced him to the police for his licentiousness. The aristocracy felt the sting of his pen.

His wit made his arrogance palatable, and his freethinking ideas guaranteed him wide readership throughout Europe.

And he pilloried everything Europe held sacred. Besides his deprecations against rival scholars, he satirized the church, clerics, revelation, theology, prophets, resurrection, miracles, messiahs and matter. He was the consummate anti-cleric in an era of French atheists, who devoted his life to making fun of the pretentious and the preposterous, while discussing religion with the more liberal members of the Calvinist religion in the highly literate city of Geneva. He lived long enough to alienate all but his literate philosophical and theatrical friends, one cardinal and several bishops, and a sprinkling of the aristocracy of Europe. He was hypersensitive and did not enjoy any sarcasm toward him that he so easily directed toward others. Until his later years he professed a belief in God calling himself a theist.

Friends had convinced him to journey to Paris in 1778 after a twenty-eight-year absence and he was feted like a king on arrival. But at eighty-three he fell ill and died after a few months on May 30, 1778. An estimated 100,000 formed the funeral procession. His remains were laid next to Descartes and Mirabeau in the Pantheon in Paris. In 1814 his bones and Rousseau's were stolen—clerics were suspected— and burned with quicklime on a vacant lot.

CHAPTER TWELVE
TWO QUEENS, ONE PRINCESS

The Protestant Reformation in Europe began as a revolt against the abuses of the church. But within decades the unity of Europeans was shattered by battles among the nobility for land, between princes for power, and between kings and popes for autonomy and hegemony. New alliances were formed as older ones collapsed and arrayed themselves along the lines of religious persuasions— Catholic, Lutheran, Calvinist, Anabaptists, Quakers, and various emerging denominations. England had Anglicans and Puritans. Scotland became Calvinist and Presbyterian. Suddenly, there were multiple paths to salvation appealing to the oppressed and disenchanted or merely the confused. Even the devout had to choose sides judiciously. A person could only practice faith safely if living in a realm where the prince, king, or queen was of the same religion. The choices between Catholic and sundry Protestants led to religious tribalism and devastating confrontations like the Thirty Years War, one of the bloodiest and most costly wars in European history until the twentieth century, ending, as most wars do, a meaningless conflict as confused and futile in its conclusion as it was in its beginning. The theology of charity yielded to imperial lusts for power and territory and the pugnacious righteousness of new dogmatisms.

In this religious maelstrom there lived two queens and one princess who put their faith, so to speak, in religion as the key to defining their lives. Mary, queen of Scots, lost her head over her claim to the throne of England in part because of her religion. Christina, queen of Sweden, abdicated her throne and her Lutheranism to become a Catholic. Elisabeth, princess of Bohemia, lost her lands but kept her Calvinism, and would not become a Catholic to become Queen of Poland. Instead she entered a Protestant abbey and became its abbess. Each of these strong-willed and intelligent women believed that their faith was more important than their royal status.

Renaissance female royalty were educated and groomed for leadership, diplomacy. and statecraft, even though not all of those groomed actually lived to reign. Princesses in the line of succession had appointed tutors who taught them languages from an early age—French, Spanish, and Italian, and later in adolescence, Latin and Greek and occasionally Hebrew. Princesses were taught music and dance and domestic skills like weaving. They learned riding, archery, games, and sports. Princes too would receive the same kind of education but be trained additionally in the military crafts of war and the manly arts of hunting. Thus, suitably prepared through rigorous education, expectant rulers could more fluidly assume the duties of a king or queen, and to converse and negotiate with their international counterparts who would have had similar preparations.

Mary Stuart, Queen of Scots (1542–1587)

She became queen before she was a year old. She married three times. She was widowed in France when she was eighteen. Her second husband, Henry Stuart, Lord Darnley, became King of Scotland. He helped plan her overthrow with rebellious clan nobles and was one of the plotters who conspired to kill her male secretary. Henry was in turn assassinated when he was twenty-one. They had a child who became James I of England. Her third husband, Bothwell, by some accounts raped her and then married her to secure the throne for himself. A battle of the clan nobles left him, Henry, defeated and her, Mary, without defenses. She was abducted and imprisoned in Scotland. She escaped to England, trusting in her cousin Elizabeth to help restore her to her rightful throne. Elizabeth imprisoned her for nineteen years then had her beheaded.

She died a broken woman aged only forty-four, a victim of incessant court intrigue, rival nobles, international politics, and religion. She was a heretic to her people in Scotland, a Catholic ruler in a Protestant country, and in England. Throughout her short life, however, she preserved her integrity, adhered to her faith, trusted too much in her relatives and even in her son, and not enough in her instincts for survival in a cutthroat world. Her courage is her lasting badge of honor.[1]

She was beautiful, statuesque, and overly compassionate to her people. She was Queen of France and Scotland with a legitimate claim to the English throne, because her great-grandfather had been Henry VII of England. Scottish clansmen and nobility killed her Italian secretary in her presence, and then captured and imprisoned her in Lochleven castle in the middle of a lake from which she heroically escaped. She fled to England believing that her cousin Elizabeth would reinstate her on the Scottish throne and let her son replace Elizabeth when she died, thus uniting the two kingdoms. Mary put her trust in the presumed compassion of her royal cousin but in doing so exposed her naivete about regal succession, foreign policy, politics, and religious differences.

Queen of Scotland and France

Mary was born December 8, 1542, at the palace of Linlithgow in West Lothian, Scotland, the same year her father James V of Scotland died. The following September, aged only nine months, she was crowned queen of Scotland in Stirling Castle. By the age of five the Scottish Parliament gave her in marriage to the future king of France in a treaty that also included mutual defense against the English. There would be perils to establishing foreign defense policy on the lives of children in marriage, pawns in the dynasty game of international alliances.

From the time Mary was six until she was nineteen, she was acknowledged Queen of France in waiting, betrothed on April 19, 1558, in the new great hall of the Louvre, and formally married on April 24 at Notre Dame Cathedral. Her fourth cousin Francis was sickly and psychologically unsuited to marriage, if not life itself. He had a chronic respiratory infection that kept him pathetically weak and, it is said, without normal emotional responses.

In 1559 young Francis II was solemnly crowned king of France at Rheims. The following year he was dead. Mary had lost her childhood companion and intimate friend. Only eighteen herself, she was now a widow and Queen Dowager of France. They had no children. She was, however, still queen in Scotland. But in her long absence her country had turned fiercely Protestant under the leadership of John Knox, while she was a staunch Catholic and now a foreigner.

Nevertheless, she returned to Scotland to take possession of her Scottish throne. She would honor and tolerate the Scots' practice of Protestantism, while keeping her own Catholic rituals private. Catholic priests had by then either been killed or driven from the realm. Among her first decisions was to issue a proclamation that tolerated religious practices that noted, in part, that no one should disrupt any public worship, including hers, under pain of death. She was a Catholic sovereign ruling over a Protestant people and, unlike her aunt Mary Tudor, had no intention of changing the religion of her subjects.[2]

But in England, conditions were quite different. She was likely unaware that her personal religious tolerance would not be as much of an issue as that of Catholics in Spain, France, and Austria might use her as a symbol to restore Catholicism. Under similar circumstances, many would have switched religious affiliations to become ruler. Because Mary did not renounce her faith, she is recognized here for her moral courage.

Many are of the opinion that it would be more equitable for a people to choose a husband for a queen than that a queen should choose a king for a people. But if a Scottish queen like Mary was going to select a suitable candidate, her choice would be complicated by the international power politics and national alliances of the sixteenth century, and reconciling differences between her Catholicism and Scotland's Protestantism. Her lethal fault was that she wanted to succeed Elizabeth as queen of England. If Mary were to choose a Catholic for a consort, her allegiances to her subjects would be jeopardized and the succession of a Catholic heir imperiled in Protestant Scotland. If she chose a Protestant for a companion, her private life would be complicated, and the religion of heirs compromised.

Mary and Henry Stuart

In the end, Mary chose as husband Henry Stuart, Lord Darnley (1545–1567), who was also, like Mary and Elizabeth, a great-grandchild of Henry VII. His mother was a descendant of Margaret Tudor, daughter of Henry VII and sister of Henry VIII, making him a legitimate contender for the English throne, which is why as a male heir Elizabeth and England feared him. He was Catholic, born in England, and therefore, even according to Henry VIII's will, could not be debarred as a foreigner from succession. Elizabeth had him confined temporarily for pressing his claim, but she eventually relented and released him when he was nineteen in 1565 and gave him a passport to journey to Scotland.

He was tall, handsome, and athletic. His height favored Mary as she was often taller than most of the men she encountered in her life. While he was convalescing from an illness and she was nursing him, she fell hopelessly in love with his youthful attractiveness. She wed him and Henry Stuart became her second husband. But when he was not sick he was a libertine and profligate, spoiled and ambitious, without the temperament or character to lead. After he became king, he was often hunting with his cronies days at a time, neglecting state business documents that needed his signature with Mary's. Had he not been murdered he would have died of syphilis.

Mary relied on the services of David Riccio, her Italian secretary as he was more cultivated and educationally appealing than any choices for that office among her Scottish courtiers. The Protestant clan lords suspected he was her lover and plotted to abduct her and her unborn child, kill Riccio, and install Henry as king, even though he was nominally a Catholic. The whole conspiracy had the flavor of a bad movie, but stupid enough for a court assassination. Several of these deluded conspirators, including Darnley, came into her apartments where she, her attendants, and Riccio were gathered for supper. Thugs appeared and caught hold of Riccio, took him into a nearby hall and stabbed him as many as sixty times. Mary, then pregnant, felt she had been threatened with her own life too, and that her husband was an accomplice. She never trusted him again.

Mary did not miscarry over this horrific incident and gave birth to James VI of Scotland (and James I of England) in 1566. Mary used the occasion of his birth to effect a feigned reconciliation with Darnley. By 1567 it was clear to all that Darnley had been a coconspirator against Mary. Other members of the nobility were now plotting to kill him. Whether Mary was partisan or even knowledgeable about this plot is open to interpretation.

Kirk O'Field was a manor house in Edinburgh Mary and Darnley often frequented. Mary did not sleep there the night Darnley was killed. The clumsy conspirators chose explosives as their weapon of choice. They placed so much gunpowder in the downstairs room so that the entire house of 60 feet by 37 feet was blown apart. Darnley, waking in the middle of the night when he heard commotions and saw so many men gathering noisily outside, fled in his nightgown. Later, he and a page were found in the garden far from the house dead from strangulation. Several minor characters were captured and executed for this assassination but no members of the nobility. Mary had all the symptoms of a nervous breakdown as she suspected her life was again at extreme risk.

The suspected chief conspirator had been James Hepburn, fourth Earl of Bothwell (1535–1578) and sheriff of Edinburgh.[3] Mary had called upon him in 1565 when he was in France to join her in putting down a rebellion by her half brother, the Earl of Moray. Thereafter, Bothwell was her faithful companion. He was brought to trial for the murder of Darnley on April 12, 1567, but the trial was a judicial farce and he was acquitted. He divorced his wife, abducted Mary, possibly raped her, and then compelled her to marry him as her protector. They were married days after Bothwell divorced his wife. The Scottish aristocracy were incensed. They never waited long to take vengeance when one clan member attempted to take power over the others.

There is historical controversy about how Bothwell convinced (or coerced) Mary to marry him, and whether or not she consented as a means of liberating herself from adversarial members of the nobility. Mary and Bothwell were married May 15, 1567, in a Protestant ceremony. Bothwell was apparently honest and loyal to her and, had he survived, might have been her best advocate, protector, and most able administrator. Aristocrats met May 1, 1567, in Stirling intending to free Mary and her infant son from Bothwell's clutches. After the marriage Mary cried and some say threatened suicide. Once free of him in England she sought a divorce.

The marriage was so unpopular that within weeks Mary would eventually be forced to abdicate. Bothwell, his estate and titles having been forfeited, fled for his life when his forces were defeated. He went first to the Orkney Islands, then to Norway where he hoped to raise an army to put Mary back on the throne. Instead he ran into friends of his former Scandinavian mistress, then creditors eager to collect on past debts. Finally, he fell into the hands of the king of Denmark who threw him in a dungeon where he died after ten years, probably insane.

In 1565 Mary had been a beautiful, energetic woman. Within two years, and certainly by the end of 1567, she was a broken woman, twice widowed, once because of a murdered husband, prone to illness and anxieties, plagued by conspiracies and murders in her presence, uncertain of her future and that of Scotland. Her only consolation was that her son, James, was crowned king of Scotland at the tender age of thirteen months. She was held in confinement in Lochleven Castle until her escape as a Catholic queen fleeing to a Protestant country and to her cousin, Elizabeth, whom she believed would restore her rightly on her throne and allow her to succeed Elizabeth. She repudiated her Scottish abdication once she was free of her imprisonment in Lochleven.

Queen Elizabeth I

If two blood-related queens meet to decide who should rule, the outcome is going to be less of a catfight and more a fight to the death. If one had only been a man, they could have married and that would be an end to it, although this might have initiated new indignities in the bedchambers. Of course, if one had been a man, there would not be any need for a queen at all except to acquire heirs.

Elizabeth (Tudor) (1533-1603) **was** the only child of Henry VIII and Anne Boleyn. She was fourteen when her father died. Elizabeth's younger brother, Edward VI (1537–1553), feeble son of Henry VIII and his third wife Jane Seymour, succeeded his father as King and reigned from 1547 to 1553. Edward died an agonizing death when he was only fifteen. Under Edward and his protectorate the government became Protestant. Elizabeth was imprisoned in the Tower for a short time when her older half-sister, Mary Tudor, was queen from 1553–1558.[4] Mary Tudor was the daughter of Henry VIII and Katherine of Aragon. As Queen Mary she reinstated Catholicism as the religion of choice in the realm and prosecuted Protestants. She was stubborn like a Tudor, but unlike her father or younger sister, had little political good sense. Religious identification became literally a matter of life and death.

Elizabeth was twenty-five when she was crowned queen of England after Mary Tudor's death in 1558, and there was controversy from the first about her legitimacy and claim to the throne. Moreover, there had been a succession of early Tudor deaths:

- Arthur, Henry VII's eldest son (1486–1547) and older brother of Henry VIII, died at fifteen.
- Henry VIII's bastard son Henry Fitzroy, by his mistress Elizabeth Blount, died at seventeen
- Henry VIII himself died at fifty-five
- Edward VI died at fifteen
- Mary Tudor died at forty-two

Elizabeth's longevity as queen did not look promising. The average age of mortality for these selected Tudor royals was twenty-eight, and Elizabeth was already twenty-five. No one imagined in 1558 that Elizabeth would reign for forty-five years, among the longest and most successful monarchical reigns in English history. One thing was certain—England would remain Protestant while she was queen to prevent further religious dissension, foreign entanglements, and possible civil war.

Roger Ascham, Elizabeth's tutor, tells us that Elizabeth was one of the best scholars of her time, reading daily in Greek, and she knew Latin, Italian, French, and Spanish, and thus was able to converse with foreign ambassadors in their own language. She read history all her life. She had great physical stamina combined with her father's love of hunting and the chase. Her hunting lodge still stands in Essex. She knew archery, dancing, and music, and had a carefully crafted, calculating political mind. The plays of Shakespeare enthralled her and he wrote many on her behalf and dedicated nearly all of them to her. However, he would not dare write about the tragedy of Mary, Queen of Scots, though that hypothetical play might have been one of his most dramatic if not politically popular in England.

Elizabeth was too politically astute to be fooled either by members of her conspiratorial court or the machinations of foreign powers seeking her hand in marriage and the alliance of her kingdom. She deftly counterbalanced the Puritans within her realm, and the Catholic countries abroad, especially France, Spain, and Austria. She used her eligibility for marriage as a bargaining tool to pit France, Spain, and Austria against each other, keeping them guessing about her intentions. She married no one, forsaking husband and family for the security of England.

Elizabeth emerged from her troubled childhood and adolescence scarred by personal misfortune. Consider her upbringing. Her father divorced her mother, and then had her beheaded for presumed adultery. She lived with a succession of four step-mothers, one of whom, Catherine Howard, was also beheaded for adultery. Both the child's younger half-brother and older half-sister by law had supreme control over her life. Her half-sister had her imprisoned in the Tower for presumed conspiracies. Several relatives and friends had been put to death for religious or political reasons against the royal will. Elizabeth was certainly schooled, if not traumatized, from an early age in the essential art of personal survival.

Elizabeth symbolized an age when religious affiliation was supreme, and where, if one hoped to live long, one's religion was the same as the monarch's. By means of a keen intelligence, subtle diplomacy, and judicious beheadings and imprisonments, Elizabeth managed to keep peace in her realm and the dogs of war at bay for a half century by outwitting everyone duplicitously, and outliving her rivals at home and enemies abroad. Her death in 1603 ended the House of Tudor.

Mary in Elizabeth's Custody

Against this background of religiously tempestuous England, the chaotic life of the Tudors, and the persona of Elizabeth herself, entered Mary, Queen of Scots, a Catholic and legitimate claimant to the throne of England and Elizabeth's cousin, riding on horseback into England seeking Elizabeth's help and only wanting to succeed her as England's queen. Understandably, she was permanently kept for the next two decades in various castle keeps.

Of the variety of insalubrious castles in the Midlands over nearly two decades, Tutbury Castle was the worst; Sheffield and Lodge were not as bad. She was both hostage as a queen and a symbol of the political battle over alliances and the Catholic/Protestant divisions in Europe and in England. Elizabeth clearly saw her, though she was a cousin, as a threat to her own rule. Had Mary been a Puritan she might have been welcomed as Elizabeth's successor. As a Catholic, she had the potential of rallying Spain and France against England, and fostering England's possible occupation by foreign troops, and a civil religious war within England even without foreign invasion. Her personal virtues were at stake as much as her royal status and religion, and the power she symbolized both for foreign intervention and internal discord. There were several plots, all with Mary's approval, to overthrow Elizabeth and place Mary on the throne. But they were all aborted. Mary was trying to get out of confinement; Elizabeth was trying to keep her from claiming her throne.

Mary's saddest heartbreak was with her son James, now installed as king of Scotland though she, having repudiated her abdication, stated she was still queen. From infancy James had been led to believe that his mother was an adulterer and conspirator in the murder of his father. James had been raised a Protestant and Elizabeth was his godparent. Elizabeth had signed a treaty with James and had sent him money as a token of this alliance. Mary realized too late that her only child and son had deceived and betrayed her while she was held in custody and had no intention of seeking her release in England.

Mary was constantly in communication in the 1580s with her French and Spanish allies, secretly hoping that her friends in Spain and her relatives in France would seek to get her released, or at least exiled to safety. Elizabeth and her spymaster Francis Walsingham (1530–1590) were so alarmed at Mary's influence abroad that they decided to concoct a scheme that would provide evidence for her treasonous conspiracy. Walsingham was an intelligent, skillful diplomat and statesman and Elizabeth's trusted chief of staff. He was educated at Cambridge and in the law at Padua as a Protestant during the Catholic reign of Mary Tudor. He ran an extensive network of agents and was able to decipher and read Mary's coded messages intended for the French ambassador, thus providing him evidence of Mary's schemes.

All the scheming came to a head with the plot of Anthony Babington, a committed Catholic, wealthy, naïve, and impetuous. He hatched a plan to rescue Mary with the aid of supporting Spanish troops, kill Elizabeth, and place Mary on the throne of England. Walsingham's agents had intercepted the messages between Babington and Mary who had agreed to the plot. By apparently admitting to a plan to assassinate Elizabeth, she sealed her fate.

Mary believed she had been incarcerated illegally. She had never been indicted for any crime or stood trial for anything. Now she was to be tried for an act of treason that had been arranged and guided by Francis Walsingham. An Act of Association had been passed by Parliament in 1585 specifically with Mary in mind, and it provided for the execution of any conspirators. It was an ingenious piece of legal maneuvering so that Elizabeth would have no royal challenges to her claim by making it treasonous even to claim so.

And if any such detestable act shall be executed against Her Highness's most royal person, whereby Her Majesty's life shall be taken away . . . that then every such person, by or for whom any such act shall be executed, and their issues being any wise assenting or privy to the same, shall by virtue of this Act be excluded and disabled for ever to have or claim, or pretend to have or claim, the said Crown of this Realm, or any other Her Highness's dominions, any former law or statute to the contrary notwithstanding. And that all the subjects of this Realm, and all other Her Majesty's dominions, shall and may lawfully, by virtue of this Act, by all forcible and possible means pursue to the death every such wicked person, by whom or by whose means any such detestable fact shall be in form hereafter expressed denounced to have been committed, and also their issues being any wise assenting or privy to the same, and all their aiders, comforters and abettors in that behalf.[5]

Mary's request had been to succeed Elizabeth as queen of England after her reign if she survived her. For Walsingham and Cecil, Elizabeth's chief councilors, a strict policy of Protestantism would simply not incorporate a Catholic Mary as that could lead to civil war. On the other hand, the English succession mattered for Mary, not because of the restoration of Catholicism, but as an essential component for a settlement with England to insure domestic stability in Scotland. While imprisoned in England Mary was unaware that her son James had already achieved reasonable political stability, to the degree that was possible at all in Scotland. James did succeed Elizabeth, making the Act of Association, the legal basis for Mary's execution, redundant at Elizabeth's death in 1603.

Mary had neither secretaries to prepare for a capital offense nor legal counsel when she was summoned to trial. No one apparently thought to question how it was possible, diplomatic niceties aside, that a foreign head of state could be incarcerated for years, then brought to trial in a foreign country for a capital offense. She was a queen, the daughter of a king, a cousin of the reigning queen, and had come to England on her own with Elizabeth's assurance of aid against enemies. For all this she was imprisoned. As queen she would not submit to others, nor to the laws of a land that was not hers. Elizabeth saw her elimination differently: as the prevention of a possible intervention by France or Spain in England, or a civil war between Catholic and Protestants.

Mary Stuart unknowingly originated the Stuart dynastic line that lasted from 1603 to 1714, when Elizabeth left no heirs and Mary's son James (1566–1625), king of Scotland, also inherited the English throne, uniting England and Scotland for the first time. His most lasting legacy may be the King James translation of the Bible first appearing in 1611. Shakespeare wrote *Macbeth* specifically for him.

MARY STUART TIMELINE

1542	Born at Linlithgow Palace
1543	Crowned Queen of Scotland
1548	Mary sails for France
1558	Mary marries Francis II of France in Notre Dame
	Mary Tudor dies; Elizabeth crowned queen of England
1560	Francis II dies; Mary is dowager queen of France
1561	Mary returns to Scotland
1565	Mary marries Henry Stuart, Lord Darnley
1566	David Riccio stabbed in front of pregnant Mary
1566	James VI (James I) is born; Elizabeth I is a godparent
1567	Darnley is murdered; Mary abdicates in favor of James
1567	Mary marries Bothwell, her abductor; Scottish lords led by her half-brother Lord Moray defeat her and Bothwell;
1567	Mary imprisoned in Lochleven Castle
1568	Mary escapes to England; Elizabeth imprisons her
1569	Abortive attempt to marry the Duke of Norfolk; Elizabeth imprisons Norfolk in the Tower, he is released, then executed for instigating a plot to rescue Mary
1573–1586	Various plans to marry and plots to rescue Mary
1586	Trial at Fotheringhay Castle
1587	Execution

Mary's trial began October 15, 1586, in a room directly above the great hall of Fotheringhay Castle outside Peterborough about sixty miles north of London. This massive castle was built around 1100. Today not even ruins exist; just small mounds of grass on private lands. Her secretaries who had testified in writing to the tribunal against her did not appear in person to testify at her trial, a situation Mary thought illegal. Her son James, enthroned in Scotland, never intervened to advocate for his mother's reprieve or leniency.

Elizabeth took months to sign the death warrant, perhaps feigning grief at having to do so, or just weighing the international consequences. But she had no compunction when she not so subtly suggested to Mary's warden that he relieve her of the onerous task of condemning Mary by assassinating Mary himself. Mary was spared a private assassination, which she feared in her last days, because this Puritan warder, Paulet, who had made Mary's life miserable and humiliating under his care, declined. He wrote in his response that such an odious deed was not in his conscience, and he did not want a blot on his posterity to shed blood without law or warrant. Elizabeth responded petulantly saying that such men proclaimed great zeal for her safety but would not perform murder for it. After Mary's execution, Elizabeth brazenly sent Sir Robert Carey as an emissary to Scotland to explain to James that she, Elizabeth, had not personally authorized the execution and was grief-stricken when it was carried out. She lied.

Mary was beheaded inside the castle on February 8, 1587. Her crucifix, writing book, jewels and small articles of possession, bloodstained clothes, and the block on which she had laid her head were burned in the courtyard. Mary's son, James VI of Scotland, became Elizabeth's successor as James I of England. Thus began the House of Stuart in 1603, the reign under which the first English town, Jamestown, was founded, while the colony, Virginia, was memorialized after Elizabeth, the Virgin Queen. Mary's remains were eventually entombed in Westminster Cathedral in London.

Meanwhile, the mighty Spanish fleet and its accompanying soldiers, which Mary had hoped might rescue her from incarceration, were being readied so King Philip II (1527–1598) could ravish English coasts, revenge the death of Mary, make England Catholic, and so that Philip (after whom the Philippines are named) could claim his right to the English throne. Philip had been husband of Mary Tudor, and therefore king of England until she died in 1553. The Spanish Armada was defeated in 1588 through a combination of lack of the heavy ships' maneuverability, bad weather, lack of supplies, and, some said, God's will.

Queen Christina of Sweden (1626–1689)

A few monks like Francis Borgia (1510–1572), the Duke of Gandia in the province of Valencia in Spain who became a Jesuit, abandoned lives of luxury, power, and nobility to pursue religious ideals. Christina of Sweden is among such heroic figures, certainly not a nun, but a high-strung, intelligent woman, disdainful of those of lesser station, possibly neurotic, a self-aggrandizing ex-queen. But her numerous character flaws do not diminish her sacrifice in her youth: to renounce a throne and follow a religious imperative. I include her here for her youthful sacrifice, but not for a life of sacrifice.

Christina of Sweden, like Queen Mary her counterpart in Scotland about a century earlier, was crowned queen as a child because of the death of her father, Gustavus Adolphus, killed in Germany fighting as a Lutheran for the Protestant cause and the recovery of land during the Thirty Years War.[6] His military intervention into Germany is relevant to understanding his daughter's conversion. At the time Sweden's hegemony included Finland, parts of northern Poland and Germany, and the Baltic states.

The Thirty Years War (1618–1648)

Religion in the seventeenth century was made the instrument of peace, politics and war, as today it often still is. The Thirty Years War was complicated by dynastic succession, territorial acquisition, and religion, but was assuredly a power struggle against the Hapsburgs' rule and the idea of a Holy Roman Empire. Though France, Austria, and Ireland remained predominantly Catholic, other northern European countries were Protestant. By and large, Catholics lived in southern Germany, in the Rhineland, Bohemia, and Bavaria, and Lutherans in northern Germany, Scandinavia and the Baltic states. But there was a scattering of Calvinists, Unitarians, and even secretive nonbelievers everywhere.

King Gustavus Adolphus of Sweden, the Lion of the North, raised an army of 40,000 Swedish and Saxon troops in 1630, concluded an alliance with the crafty diplomat Cardinal Richelieu in France, and re-conquered central Germany for the Lutherans in 1631. Both militaries ravaged and burned towns and indiscriminately slaughtered defending militias and mercenaries and urban inhabitants who harbored them. Mercenaries were raised in Sweden, Spain, Bohemia, and France and fought on German soil with no allegiance except to their pocketbooks.[7]

Near Leipzig, Gustavus with 25,000 troops met the formidable Catholic general Wallenstein with 40,000 men. Gustavus succumbed in the battle when a bullet struck his bridle arm, another his horse, and another entered his back. The death of the king of Sweden did not end the conflict but did hasten the crowning of Christina. Within decades, central Germany was in ruins, its cities burned, agriculture plundered and then destroyed, and millions of new graves dug. The population of Germany decreased by a half to two-thirds, and the influence of religion declined throughout Europe, though Calvinism was recognized as a separate denomination, a pyrrhic victory.

The Young Queen

Christina's physical appearance—fair complexion, long hair, a slight figure with a serious mien—belied her strong resolve and complex personality. She wore men's clothes, rode and swore lustily like a man, was skillful at sports, and neglected most feminine ornaments except for wigs. She scorned the idea of marriage, like Elizabeth in England, because it would rob her of her independence, and because a future husband would want to become king. But her failure to marry, after promptings and solicitations from her councilors to produce an heir, and her aversion to the sight and thought of birth, induced at least one of her biographers to speculate that she may have been lesbian.[8]

She collected art as well as philosophers, poets, and scholars.[9] Toward the end of her life in Rome she had in her possession over 160 sculptures, innumerable urns, columns, and decorative artifacts, and paintings by Titian, Rubens, and Raphael.[10] She founded several colleges, corresponded with the leading scholars in Europe, brought John Comenius and Rene Descartes to Sweden, honored poets, imported printers, sent Swedish students to Arabia to learn Asian scholarship, and encouraged scientists. Descartes came to escape persecution and to find patronage. Christina, who did not sleep more than a few hours a night, required him to teach her lessons three times a week beginning at 5 a.m. In January 1650, in Stockholm, this did not suit Descartes' late-sleeping habits well and he caught an infection and died after only a month instructing her.

She took poor care of her health in her younger years, worked too hard, did not sleep enough, and ate too many greasy, salty, highly spiced foods. Accordingly, she had recurrent fevers, fatigues, pains, headaches, and faints. Her Swedish physician, Bourdelot, made sensible treatment recommendations and her health improved dramatically. She was so indebted she made him her court favorite.

She would offend nearly everyone when she abandoned Lutheranism to become a Catholic, realizing that she would have to relinquish her throne and her country. It was illegal to be a Catholic in Lutheran Sweden. She would also be besmirching her father's heroic defense of Protestantism if she even considered converting to Catholicism. She first considered such a move in 1645, made a vow in 1648 to quit everything and become a Catholic, and began the first overt steps toward conversion in 1651. She gave several reasons to her Senate for abdicating: that she thought that the country needed a man to lead in times of war, and that she needed time for peace in her personal life. No one believed her, and privately and publicly questioned her motives.

She had sent a Jesuit as a private courier to Rome in 1652 for other Jesuits to come and discuss her conversion. Two Jesuits came in secret disguises with false names and ciphers to use for coded messages. Francesco Malines came from a noble Piedmont family and was professor of theology at Turin, well versed in languages and mathematics. Paulo Casati was professor of mathematics and Theology at Rome. Christina's code name was Don Teofilio, which means God-lover.

She had the unenviable task of negotiating the passage of her Catholicism and abdication under the ruse of diplomatic and trade affairs with foreign dignitaries and Italian visitors. The whole conversion adventure took years and involved secret negotiations with the Jesuits in Italy, delegates from Spain acting on behalf of Philip IV of Spain, a diplomat from France, a Count from Italy, and Cromwell's minister to Sweden's court. Christina thought the Spanish courtier was acting for the king when Philip IV, who was coyly suspicious of Christina's ulterior motives, only sent him to Sweden as an envoy. Christina was cannily using her conversion to conclude a treaty with Spain. But she was keenly aware that after her abdication she would need political support wherever she was. She wanted to insure that her finances were secured for her exile. By November 1652, the Jesuit General had approved her conversion.

She abdicated June 6, 1654, by removing her crown herself, discarding royal insignia and clothes, and said her goodbyes, but not without seeing to it that the council provided her with adequate income and preserving her rights to be queen. She attended the coronation of her cousin, Charles Gustavus, crowned Charles X, then slipped out of the city, cut her hair short, changed her name, dressed like a man and, in the company of four carefree men, absconded to Denmark. She was twenty-eight years old.

It is at this juncture that we look for what she relinquished, though it is not possible to discover absolutely her motives. She abandoned the city, palace, and surroundings of her girlhood and all her Swedish friends forever. She left her admiring subjects. She gave up crown, privileges, honors, notoriety, and dignities, all that most people seek and fight to obtain. It is for this act of sublime renunciation, in the springtime of her life, that she most merits esteem. For the next thirty-five years she would live in exile, a puzzle to Sweden, her former subjects, and the whole Protestant world.

Christina may have thought she was safe once away from Sweden but she was being tracked by every intelligence agency in Europe. Oliver Cromwell as lord protector in England, for example, was worried that Christina might make contact with the exiled Charles II. After the beheading of Charles I in 1649, the Puritan commander was obviously anxious that no royal assist another fellow royal, like Charles II who would eventually return to England after Cromwell's death, or even, more horrible to consider, that she might contemplate marrying him. Other governments were intrigued by the idea of a queen on the loose, so to speak, marriageable and still able to make alliances with their enemies, or concords that might jeopardize special interests. She settled in Antwerp, then Hamburg, in palatial homes and resumed a round of merry parties, meeting foreigners and visiting dignitaries, and attending social events.

Her abdication was one thing; her conversion another. She was an ex-queen immediately vexed by loss of considerable finances and access to staff who could satisfy her demands. Her accustomed lifestyle became more diminished and funds came erratically. Moreover, converting to Catholicism in the seventeenth century in Europe held its own difficulties and her new freedom and ex-royal status did not permit her many choices in announcing her conversion to an unwelcome world. She completed a secret conversion to Catholicism ceremony in Brussels, and a more public one in Innsbruck. A public announcement, however, made in a Catholic country like The Netherlands, at the time under Spanish dominion, or in Catholic Austria under the Hapsburgs, was not as precarious as would be travel through Protestant countries, noticeably accompanied by an entourage of about 250 attendants.

Self–Exile in Rome

She had decided to live in Rome, likely choosing it as her destination city because the pope, then Alexander VII, was not only the vicar of Christ but head of the papal states. Thus, while she lived in Rome no other king or queen would be in the city to challenge her regal residential supremacy. She was welcomed into all the northern Italian cities she entered and finally in Rome with all the pomp and circumstance her station dictated. She initially resided in the Vatican at the pope's insistence, a very special privilege, until moving into the Farnese Palace, even today one of the grandest buildings in Rome. Farnese Palace was begun in 1517, redesigned 1534, modified under Michelangelo, beginning in 1546, and completed in 1589, so it was relatively new when she occupied it. Today it houses the French Embassy.

While in Rome and Paris she enthusiastically attended all the celebrations, the balls, banquets, plays, hunting parties, and carnivals and flung herself wholeheartedly in the whirls of gaiety.

For eight years she had surreptitiously prepared for her abdication. But within months of arriving in Rome and in exile, she was in Paris concluding a treaty with the wily Cardinal Jules Mazarin, Louis XIV's chief minister, to become queen of Naples, at the time held by the Spanish, though the French did have a tenuous claim.[11] The French were prepared to give Christina the loan of an army and the opportunity to rule another province. She was also personally motivated by revenge because the Spanish had not helped her once she abdicated as they had promised. But why she would want to become queen again is puzzling. It turned out to be a phantom crown. Her need for money to support her lifestyle and her considerable staff once she abdicated was distressing to her economically and possibly psychologically.

While residing in Paris to negotiate with the French, and to obtain loans and funds from her cousin Charles Gustavus in Sweden, she discovered, through intercepted messages, that one of her closest confidantes had betrayed her intentions to the Spanish. She immediately had him summarily killed by her guards the same day. Parisians were appalled. Soon all Europe had a new perception of the exiled queen. Christina had clearly not thought through the ramifications of her impulse. The tragic affair placed the French in an awkward situation since secrecy was no longer possible: A visiting court official had been killed in a palace of the king of France. Christina should have allowed Cardinal Mazarin to handle the episode for her. The French plan to install her on the throne at Naples was now stillborn, and the French were eager to rid themselves of her royal presumptions and her embarrassing presence. Pope Alexander VII was incensed and understandably altered his views of this new convert living under his protection.

She returned to Rome in March 1659. By then she was in love. The object of her affection was Cardinal Decio Azzolino, a man of considerable talents, not wealthy or from an illustrious family, but one of the brightest intellects among the cardinals. She fell for him from their first meeting. She, among one of the most independent women known in the age, suddenly was a slave to love. But she had made herself a liability to others. Azzolino, however, remained a friend and there is no record of any intimacy, though they did use un-decoded ciphers in their long correspondence. When she arrived in Rome he found her a new residence, the Palazzo Riario, and assumed control of her administrative affairs and the hiring of her staff.

At the death of Alexander VII in 1667, the cardinals elected Clement IX as pope and he was favorable to Christina, even to supporting her futile attempt to become queen of Poland in 1668. He was pope only two years but was one of the most beloved. While in Hamburg celebrating his election to the papacy and negotiating with the Swedes for more money from her landed estates in Pomerania (part of today's northern Germany and western Poland ceded to Sweden at the conclusion of the Treaty of Westphalia in 1648), she indelicately hung banners and had masses and *Te Deum's* sung in honor of the pope's election. Hamburg, a Protestant city, took unkindly to these Catholic gestures and one night a mob threw rocks, broke most of her windows, and stormed her residence. She ordered her guards to open fire on the attackers and they killed eight and wounded scores.

She lived in a tumultuous age of political and scientific revolutions and literary and intellectual invigoration. Cromwell rose to power after the death of a king, Charles I, and the age saw the restoration of the English crown under Charles II, while Louis XIV, the Sun King, shone on all with renewed regal authority. John Bunyan and John Milton were writing memorable poetry, John Dryden, Daniel Defoe, and Jonathan Swift glorious prose, and Moliere penned plays that still tickle the fancy. Isaac Newton reconstructed the laws of the universe on his own initiative and made principles that made it all seem so sensible and predictable. Thomas Hobbes, John Locke, Gottfried Leibniz, and Baruch Spinoza upturned the tables of philosophy. Christina was enlightened about notables of her day, keeping abreast of movements and significant political events when she wasn't actually meddling in them.

In later years in Rome she founded the Accademia Reale, today's equivalent of a think tank, in which she actively engaged. The academy sponsored lectures, papers presented by serious scholars, and discussion groups meeting once a month.

It's possible her conversion was a search for personal liberation, to find a less demanding culture than icy Sweden to give full rein to her comfortable lifestyle. I believe in her later years she also sought to break free from the rigidities of Catholicism by entertaining a mystical side. Quietism was a heretical cult practice that preached that a devotee had to find personal absorption in the divine through meditation, and that sinful actions were the work of the devil thereby absolving individuals from personal responsibility.[12] She followed this religious fad for years. Her tutor in this mystical exploration, Miquel de Molinos, was condemned as a heretic by the Roman Inquisition. Her autobiography reveals a deep religious belief, though she probably did not have a full adherence to all Catholic dogmas. But there is compelling evidence that her sentiments were not just cosmetic.

She had a rare genius and her independent spirit and royal birth allowed her to pursue her dreams and crazy schemes. She was a captivating and at times pathetic figure, cutting a large political swath through the heart of Europe and into the hearts of some and the pocketbooks of others. She had a queenly arrogance, but was not as cynical as Louis XIV. She appeared frivolous and full of levity to those who knew her, flaunting social conventions with a flighty temperament, and exhibited a lax carelessness in her personal appearance. She wore men's clothes and men's shoes, a wig and large hat, and apparently often deliberately presented herself as disheveled so as to show her disdain for ostentatious dress. One shoulder was higher than another, a defect from birth. Her eyes were her most memorable feature, described as blue and fiery. In her declining days she was chubby and shabby.

Her behavior often resembled a spoiled and undisciplined adolescent, and she swore like a sailor. She dissimulated when she found it necessary, even revealing state secrets if she thought it would benefit her personally. She penned a book of maxims and pithy sayings of varying degrees of originality, many of which she did not honor in her own life, and began, but did not complete, her autobiography of forgettable prose. She was extravagant in her personal life. She too often inserted herself into the power politics of Europe where her presence complicated rather than resolved issues.

But she dazzled and charmed everyone, especially the sophisticated royalty, aristocrats, diplomats, and scholars she met. But secretly, and not just because of her superior horsemanship, she desired to lead an army like Joan of Arc or her father. Had she not chosen to convert to Catholicism she would have remained neutral in religious matters and would have formed a simple faith for herself without pretensions.

She died April 19, 1689, aged sixty-three, and was buried in St. Peter's, a special honor accorded only three other women in history. Cardinal Decio Azzolino, the man she loved above all others, died two months later.

Elisabeth von der Pfalz, Princess Palatine (1618–1680)

Holland was a divided country in the seventeenth century. Northern Holland, revolting against the repression of the Spanish conquerors, was fighting to retain its Protestant independence, and southern Holland was struggling to retain a Flemish Catholic identity. While Newton was revising views of the universe and Descartes exploring differences between the mind and body, Rembrandt, Vermeer, Franz Hals, Jan Steen, Jakob van Ruisdael, and Peter Paul Rubens, all painting in Holland during this age with so many other illustrious artists, were reflecting new artistic perspectives in colorful portraitures, landscapes of pictorial realism, and still life. These Dutch painters, except for Rubens, relied less on religious themes than did Italian Renaissance predecessors, and instead immortalized ordinary people and domestic life in landscapes and stills, and in portraits the burghers and their families rich enough to purchase paintings that would become some of the world's most priceless art works.

In the midst of this flourishing artistic world lived my next heroine, Elisabeth, Princess of Bohemia. The difference in spelling, often found in her references, is deliberate and distinguishes her from so many others of the same name. Her grandfather was James Stuart (James I of England), son of Mary, Queen of Scots, and Anne of Denmark who converted to Catholicism from Lutheranism in the 1590s.

Bohemia is today roughly the size of Hungary and the Czech and Slovak republics. Protestantism gained a strong foothold there about the time of John

Hus. Many who rejected Catholicism also instigated treason against the hereditary nobility. Thus the region became the site for the Thirty Years War beginning in 1618. During this long war involving France, Spain, and Sweden, Bohemia lost 75 percent of its population, from 3 million to 800,000. The nobility were executed or banished, and their property confiscated. What citizens remained either left the region or rejoined it as Catholics.

From headquarters in Vienna, the House of Habsburg and its Emperor Ferdinand ruled the Holy Roman Empire stretching from Poland to Portugal. Elizabeth, mother of our heroine, was the daughter of James I of England. She married Frederick, a Calvinist, and immediately found herself inconveniently embroiled in a revolt against the Catholic Habsburgs that attempted to recover lands for Catholics that even the law of the empire had recognized as Protestant. Ferdinand's imperial envoys sent to negotiate the dispute were unceremoniously thrown from the windows of the royal palace in Prague. Arrogant Czech nobility offered Frederick the throne, he accepted, and the Thirty Years War began as Habsburg troops occupied Bohemia.

At the beginning of these hostilities was born Elisabeth von der Pfalz on 26 December, 1618, in Heidelberg, the daughter of Frederick and Elizabeth Stuart, Princess of England. She was the third child and the eldest girl of their thirteen children. Her father and family were routed out of their home and principality. The family fled to Amsterdam and then to The Hague where they lived in exile. Elisabeth remained with a grandmother until she was nine and then joined the family in The Netherlands. The family was in desperate financial circumstances though not so much that Elisabeth had to hire herself out as a laundress.

When she was only fifteen Poland's Catholic king, Ladislaus IV (1595–1648) offered her a marriage proposal that included her conversion to Catholicism. She was determined not to become a Catholic, so that proposition was rejected, a courageous act on her part that did not redeem her family's fortunes, but has earned her a place as one of my heroines.

But the family had its share of tragedies. Three of her other brothers would leave to fight on the side of their uncle, Charles I of England, then engaged in England's civil war with Cromwell. When Cromwell won, Charles I was beheaded in 1649. Her oldest brother downed in 1629 in a boating accident and her father Frederick's inability to save his son made him clinically depressed. Three years later her father died on the battlefield when she was only fourteen. Her brother Edward converted to Catholicism, a personal betrayal in the Calvinist family. Another brother brazenly killed in the street a man who had bragged of an affair with Louise, their younger sister, further damaging the family's reputation. Her mother had recklessly spent the family's fortune and Elisabeth had become permanently estranged from her.

She demonstrated early in her childhood a love of books and learning, to the astonishment of her siblings. It was this scholarly trait that endeared her to many of the leading intellectuals of her day.

Correspondence with Descartes

But she is best remembered for an absorbing friendship and extensive corre-spondence with Descartes, one of the premier intellectuals of the age, when she was twenty-four and he forty-seven. To a contemporary culture symbiotically linked to the technology of hand-held visual communication, writing letters might seem like a pedestrian and simplistic form of relating to someone. But unlike deleted text messages, letters have a more lasting quality especially if they contain a warmth and stylistic quality that makes the emotional impact en-riching and timely. The writing of letters is a disappearing if not extinct art. Twenty-six letters of her to him survive written in a florid but extremely literary style and full of remarkable discernments. Their correspondence is the intersec-tion of her youthful, ambitious inquiry and his intellectual self-importance.

In May 1643, Elisabeth wrote to Descartes with uncommon philosophical prescience and insight:

> How can the soul of man determine the spirits of the body, so as to produce voluntary actions (given that the soul is only a thinking substance). For it seems that all determination of movement is made by the pulsion of a moving thing, so that it is pushed by that which moves it, or, by the qualification (qual-ity) and figure (shape) of the surface of that thing. For the first two conditions, touching is necessary, for the third extension. For the one, you exclude entirely the notion that you have of the soul; the other seems to me incompatible with an immaterial thing. This is why I ask you to give a definition of the soul more specific than that in your Metaphysics, that is to say of its substance, as sepa-rated from its thinking action. For even if we suppose the two to be inseparable (which anyway is difficult to prove in the womb of the mother and in fainting spells), like the attributes of God, we can, in considering them separately, ac-quire a more perfect idea of them.[13]

How can the mind move the body if it is immaterial? Descartes answered unsatisfactorily, as he admitted in a response. Once you propose that an individ-ual is composed of two or more different substances, one material and one im-material, you have to describe how they are related. But Elisabeth with the pre-cision of a stiletto instantly perceived the philosophical weakness of Descartes' dualism. In a follow-up letter a month later, on June 20, 1643, she pleasantly lets him know directly that she has been brushed off and that he has not answered her inquiry. Here was a woman with a delicate writing style slinging barbs at the leading intellectual of the day for his casual dismissal of her question.

She was equally uncompromising with him with the topic of God's will. To invoke God's will in any misfortune, when she knew that it was too often the negligence and stupidity of men that caused human suffering, was no consola-tion. Does Descartes really believe that God controls everyone's free will? She upbraids him—"I am not persuaded by arguments . . . it seems to me repugnant to common sense . . . "—for not answering these human dilemmas to her satisfaction either. She was never satisfied by abstract arguments unrelated to experience.

This was heady stuff for a young woman whose mental abilities obviously exceeded the majority of her contemporaries. In this and all her letters she conveys the ease and style of court etiquette with the reasoning ability of a practicing philosopher, touched with a gentle rebuke. Descartes quickly realized he was not corresponding with just any member of the royalty or a dilettante seeking stimulating epistolary companionship, but an intellectual equal. Descartes' respectful and sometimes insipid and flattering responses to his new correspondent equivocate in his answer about the union of body, mind and body. It apparently never occurred to him that the body might have unique abilities that we associate with mind, and that these might not be separate entities at all. But to say so publicly would have invited instant condemnation, and Descartes was too cautious to admit such a proposition even theoretically.

ELISABETH'S TIMELINE

1618   Born at Heidelberg.
1619   Frederick her father becomes king of Bohemia. Before she turns two, he loses his throne, lands, and possessions. The family flees to Germany.
1627   She rejoins her parents living in exile in Holland. She is tutored in court etiquette, scripture, mathematics, history, the sciences, and languages (French, English, German, Dutch, Latin, and Greek).
1631   Her father dies.
1636   She decides not to marry.
1642   She reads Descartes' *Meditations on First Philosophy*.
1643   She writes to Descartes posing philosophical objections. The correspondence lasts until his death in 1650.
1645   Her brother, Edward, renounces Protestantism, becomes a Catholic and marries Anne of Gonzaga.
1646   While in Germany she seeks a return of her lands from Queen Christina.
1649   Christina of Sweden invites Descartes to Sweden; Descartes accepts in part to plead Elisabeth's case.
1650   Descartes dies in Sweden.
1667   Elisabeth enters a Protestant convent at Herford in Westphalia.
1680   She dies as abbess after a long and painful illness.

No mere admirer, but an understanding reader of his metaphysics and math, she would test him again and again in subsequent letters and private meetings with questions about algebra, physics and chemistry. These were not love letters, as they might have been, though some letters were discussions of the emotions, but expressions of key ideas between two intellectuals.

On September 13, 1645, she wrote him a sentiment that can easily summarize her own life. "Birth and fortune force me to use my judgment promptly in order to lead a life sufficiently difficult and free of prosperity to prevent me from thinking of myself, just as if I were forced to trust in the rule of a governess." [14] She returned to Germany in 1646 as talks began to end the Thirty Years War, though it would take another two years, until 1648, for the Treaty of Westphalia to conclude the final negotiations that conflicted Europe. Her older brother returned to rule over a much smaller territory of Palatine.

In 1667 she entered a Protestant convent at Herford in Westphalia. She eventually served as Abbes, overseeing about 7,000 people, and farms, vineyards, mills and factories. She offered refuge to members of all religions, such as William Penn, the founder of Pennsylvania, Robert Barclay, and other Quakers. Her consummate love of learning, her works of charity, her rejection of the national conflicts inherent in marriages between royals, and of worldly comforts means she is welcomed into my consortium of heroines.

CHAPTER THIRTEEN
ENLIGHTENMENT DISSENTERS

Two epochal moments in the eighteenth century summarize that defining century: the overlapping of the French revolution and the Enlightenment movement. The Revolution liberated people from monarchy and feudal servitude, and the Enlightenment liberated freedom of thought and expression from medieval suppression. Both had broad consequences for personal and social liberties and are now central to Western democracies. There may be more heretics in Western societies but they are not legally persecuted for their ideas or religious views as they once were. We can honor the memories of a chosen few who made the period crucial for helping with the establishment of the fundamental rights of freedom of religion, speech, the press, assembly, and to petition the government for a redress of grievances. The French and American Revolutions are linked as the foundations of the liberation of human freedom and expression.

The French Revolution

The French Revolution occurred because of a convergence of royal extravagance, accumulated national debt, the simmering resentment of the peasantry—the backbone of the agricultural economy—the lingering feudal system of the taxing authority rights of the aristocracy, their property, and entitlements, and the indolence and tithing privileges of the church. It was all a ready recipe for revolution.

To forestall insurrection in France in 1789, the king, Louis XVI, and his councilors decided to call representatives to Paris—a meeting of the Estates General. This combined group was named after the French *etats*, but consisted of defined feudal orders or social classes. These included delegates from the First Estate, the aristocracy, the Second Estate, the church, and the Third Estate that the common classes of people elected in their provinces. They came to discuss the nation's dire financial situation and social grievances. It was the first time in history any king had asked for advice from the people. He would lose his head as a result.

The nobility and clerical delegates did not want to meet with the commoners, delegates from the Third Estate, and so they conferred in separate rooms.
The question of representation immediately arose as a procedural voting issue.

A Summary of the Rights of Man
Approved by the National Assembly of France, August 26, 1789

Men are born and remain free and equal in rights. Social distinctions may be
founded only upon the general good.

The aim of all political association is the preservation of the natural rights of
man. These rights are liberty, property, security, and resistance to oppression.

The principle of all sovereignty resides essentially in the nation. Nobody nor
individual may exercise any authority which does not proceed directly from the
nation.

Liberty consists in the freedom to do everything which injures no one else;
hence the exercise of the natural rights of each man has no limits except those
determined by law.

Law can only prohibit such actions as are hurtful to society. Nothing may be
prevented which is not forbidden by law, and no one may be forced to do anything not provided for by law.

Law is the expression of the general will. Every citizen has a right to participate
personally, or through his representative, in its foundation.

No person shall be accused, arrested, or imprisoned except in the cases and according to the forms prescribed by law.

As all persons are held innocent until they shall have been declared guilty, if
arrest shall be deemed indispensable, all harshness not essential to the securing
of the prisoner's person shall be severely repressed by law.

No one shall be disquieted on account of his opinions, including religious views.
The free communication of ideas and opinions is one of the most precious of the
rights of man. Every citizen may, accordingly, speak, write, and print with freedom, but shall be responsible for such abuses of this freedom as defined by law.

The Third Estate had a majority of delegates duly elected in the provinces
but was to be allowed only one vote equal to the others. The Third Estate protested, but the king could not have allowed the common people to outvote his
main supporters, the nobility and the church. Universal adult suffrage had been

instituted but not allowed to function. So Members of the Third Estate formulated their own constitutional agenda, called themselves the National Assembly, took to the streets, tore down the Bastille, and shook the throne of Louis XVI and the aristocracy to its foundations. The idea of popular sovereignty, once just a rallying cry of enlightened liberals like Rousseau, took foothold as the people's rule in France as it had America.

The intoxicating ardor of those July days in 1789 toppled the pillars of the old regime, declared for new ones in the Rights of Man, and then turned on itself. The National Assembly abolished all hereditary privileges and titles, proclaimed a constitution with the king's consent, and then executed aristocrats and administrators who had not already fled abroad.

The National Assembly passed a Declaration of the Rights of Man in August 1789 and the summary above shows how its ideas influenced the American Bill of Rights in 1791, the first Ten Amendments to the U.S. Constitution. Had the British prevailed in the American Revolution I would instead be profiling George Washington, Thomas Jefferson, James Madison, Ben Franklin and others who would have been hanged as traitors.

The Enlightenment

The Enlightenment was just as revolutionary in the arena of ideas and its effects equally permanent.

For centuries Europeans had traversed through the wilderness of medieval superstitions, a venture that was too prolonged and intellectually sterile. A few brave individuals, driven only by independence in thought and not impelled by gold, ambitions, or imperial aggrandizement, began the explosion of ideas that resulted in the canon of Western civilization. Beginning in the latter part of the eighteenth century the Enlightenment unleashed the shackles of authoritarian domination of the altar and the crown and opened new worlds of literary, scientific and artistic freedom. The publication of one series of books, the first encyclopedia, is synonymous with the origin of this fecund period. The *Encyclopedia* popularized and helped categorize knowledge. Its authors and editors were unanimous in rejecting regal and ecclesiastical authority and tainted tradition, and extolled experience, reason, and evidence. The *Encyclopedia* ushered in a novel concept not heard since the Greeks—that ideas are the pre-eminent authority, not kings or titled aristocrats and ordained clerics. The thirty-five volumes of *L'encyclopedie, ou Dictionnaire raisonne des Sciences, des Arts et des Metiers* whose first volume appeared in 1751, was largely the accomplishment of Denis Diderot, a prototype of the stand-alone dissenter, an authentic hero.[1]

Denis Diderot (1713–1784)

I allow everyone to think as he pleases, provided I am allowed to think as I please.[2]

Diderot, a literary bohemian who edited and wrote most of the first encyclopedia, was a novelist, playwright, and art critic who epitomized the Enlightenment in France. He did not live to witness the revolution, but had he lived long enough he would have certainly been beheaded. The authorities had him imprisoned in 1749 for writing a licentious novel, and the French *Parlement* outlawed his encyclopedia, though it became too popular to be totally suppressed. He refused to live abroad to escape censorship. Catherine of Russia purchased his library, enjoyed his company and gave him a pension. His principal occupation was to defend himself against his detractors and advance his nonconformist beliefs. He is included here among dissidents because he courageously maintained his unauthorized license to write as he chose in the face of dangerous royal and government displeasure and torrential public opprobrium, though he did not forfeit his life for this privilege. He had the sophistication and subtlety to cut through transparent sophistry and jargon. He insisted on intellectual self-reliance and independence even in the face of authoritarian threats.

His single most important contribution was the *Encyclopedia*. Its final version in 1777 included thirty-five volumes of which Diderot, in the twenty-six years he devoted to it, contributed twenty-eight volumes. The complete set was expensive to produce and to own so rich patrons had to be located who could sponsor it. Several thousand donated. The whole production effort was an engine of propaganda to counter religious orthodoxy and social traditions. From time to time printers were persecuted, its publisher periodically jailed and then released. No copies were ever found to be burned so discreet were the agents in alerting printers in advance.

Diderot was a subtle atheist who had a sister who was a nun said to be mad and who died in her late twenties, and a brother who was a priest, thus confirming that opposing religious persuasions can exist in siblings. Among his fellow literary giants whom he knew and most of whom he persuaded to write articles in the *Encyclopedia*, were Rousseau, Montesquieu, Voltaire, Abbe Etienne Condillac, D'Alembert, and Baron D'Holbach. Diderot was a literary equal to them all. In his lifetime he received acknowledged praise from Voltaire (who did not give it easily), Goethe, Thomas Carlyle, and grudging esteem from Rousseau. Diderot's writings, and those of his like circle of authors, challenged the status of the old order in the days leading up to the French Revolution, and sharpened satirical pens, like Moliere's, to portray the ostentatious frivolity and pompousness of the age.

His talents and writing interest ranged over a rich variety of topics from physiology and psychology, to gender issues, comparative grammar, dramatic arts, and education. He wrote fiction and nonfiction, plays, newsletters, pamphlets, dialogues, and critical reviews.

Rousseau, that quarrelsome misogynist, certainly desired the destruction of the *ancien regime* and would have done anything to hasten its overthrow. Voltaire was more reform-minded and would have accepted a government ministry had he been in favor with the royals, aristocracy, or church. Diderot, on the other hand, was less captivated by a political cause and was too genuinely amiable to form lasting hatreds. Nobody wanted to elevate Diderot to any political stature and yet he was the forerunner who championed intellectual freedom that gave the revolutionary movement its impetus.

He married Antoinette Champion, a woman of limited education, but rumored to possess other attractive attributes, who gave him several children but only one daughter who survived to adulthood.

Diderot's Writings

The Conversation with D'Alembert (*La Reve de D'Alembert*), written in 1769, is Diderot's explanation of his beliefs that were so controversial that it was not published until 1830. *La Religieuse* (*The Nun*), written in 1760 but not published until 1796, twelve years after his death, is equally scandalous with its tales of secrecy, torture and a lesbian mother superior.

One can quibble over whether or not Diderot was a real philosopher, as some claim that he was only a synthesizer of the ides of others. But one essay, *The Conversation* (1769), in the form of a dialogue outlines his principal motifs that include evolution, or the idea that organisms evolve from one species to another, arguments against believing in one Intelligent Being, the mutation of organic particles, and notes satisfying sexual tendencies. For example, in one statement about evolution, he wrote:

> There is not more than one substance in the universe, in man, in animals... A canary is made of flesh and a musician of differently organized flesh. But the one and the other have a same origin, a same formation, the same functions, and the same end.[3]

Darwin could not have expressed that idea more poignantly or pithily. Each of these topics could form the basis for an article in contemporary leading scientific journals or literary or aesthetic magazines. Diderot was a materialist and his personal philosophy expressed in this one essay establishes his credentials as one of the leading outspoken intellectuals of his age or any age. His *Conversation of a Philosopher with the Marechale de* *** is an argument against the principal teachings of Christianity and solidified his atheism. But the point here is not about his atheism but his bold stand in favor of intellectual freedom in an age when the publication of such ideas merited prison or worse.

Similarly, his book titled *Jacques the Fatalist* (1778), which Diderot claimed was not a novel, satirizes what he calls Destiny, but which is really about free will. The book's rambling set of dialogues, his favorite form of narrative, has no actual plot but is a series of random incidents that appear bizarre and purposeless, and that is the whole point. There is no plot to life either. Even conversations have a chaotic quality. The whole book is a philosophical comment on the lack of free will. Throughout the book, Jacques the protagonist keeps repeating whenever something strange happens that "It must have been written up above . . . " At other times, he is more explicit as when he says: "We believe that it is we who control Destiny but it is always Destiny that controls us."[4]

In Lisbon on February 1, 1755, an enormous earthquake felled the roof of a large church killing hundreds inside attending Mass. This one event led Leibniz to question Divine Providence and Voltaire to write a satirical poem and feature the event in *Candide*. Diderot makes reference to the same event in this work, thus symbolically noting that providence, free will, fate, and destiny were all his themes.[5] Like Voltaire, D'Alembert, D'Holbach, and other atheists of his generation, Diderot dispensed with the theological foundations of ethics and morality.

Though Diderot spent only three months in prison in 1749 for writing one licentious novella, *Les Bijouox Indiscrets,* he continued writing what he thought but never published for fear of government retaliation and possibly prison or exile. His pension in 1765 from Catherine the Great of Russia gave him the freedom to write without royalties for the last nineteen years of his life.

By late 1783 and early 1784, Diderot had fallen seriously ill with multiple maladies including gallstones and lung inflammations. He had quit his infidelities and he and his wife settled in to a mutual exhaustion from recriminations. He died July 31, 1784, age seventy-one, of coronary thrombosis at his dining table after a hearty meal. Because of the imprecations of friends and not his religious beliefs, he was buried in the Church of St. Roch in Paris from which his body later mysteriously disappeared.

Philip-Augustin Caron de Beaumarchais (1732–1799)

> I should never have completed my mission but for the generous, indefatigable, and intelligent exertion of M. de Beaumarchais, to whom the United States are, on every account, more indebted than to any other person on this side of the ocean.[6]

If it were not for footnotes to opera guides, few would appreciate that Rossini's loveable opera *The Barber of Seville* and Mozart's delightful adaptation of *The Marriage of Figaro,* an attack on the privileges of the nobility, were first composed by this dramatist and man of courage. He was primarily a dramatist but became a wealthy adventurer, patriot, statesman, spy, and supporter of liberty. From 1774 to 1777 Beaumarchais was a secret agent for the French monarchy and provided supplies and arms to the American Revolution. He was imprisoned several times, narrowly escaped the guillotine in 1792, but never ceased advancing the cause of human dignity, liberty, and justice, which merits his profile here.

Inventor and Entrepreneur

His initial encounter with injustice and betrayal was when he was twenty. His inquisitiveness and curiosity as a watchmaker apprenticed to his father compelled him to investigate the merits of designing a smaller, less weighty, and cumbersome pocket watch. Through diligent reading of technical manuals and experimenting with his own money, he designed a new escapement for watches and showed it to a master watchmaker, a member of the guild named Lepaute who turned out to be unscrupulous and conniving.[7] When Lepaute saw what young Pierre-Augustin had designed he presented it to the French Academy of Sciences as his own invention. Insulted and chagrined, Beaumarchais brought a complaint to the minister of the royal household, the official referee in matters involving the guilds. He wrote a letter to a newspaper presenting his documented version, showing his written designs, sketches and calculations, and soon Paris was abuzz about the scandal. The Academy agreed and concluded that Beaumarchais was the inventor. Suddenly, the young man came into prominence for honesty, intelligence, and courage.[8] Louis XV was impressed and when told that Beaumarchais could make a watch small enough to fit on a lady's finger, immediately ordered one for Madame de Pompadour. Several courtiers lined up to order watches thus improving the financial state of the Caron household that included three marriageable sisters.

Through a combination of good luck and insight, he managed to enter the court by purchasing an entrée, a post in the royal court pantry services, from an aged friend. Actually, it was the wife of the friend who initiated friendship with him that soon became an affair of the heart. When the old man died, Beaumarchais married the widow, six years older than himself. She unexpectedly died herself soon thereafter. He then added the new name Beaumarchais to his family name, probably after *bois-marche* as walks in the woods were then fashionable. He had not validated inheritance privileges with his marriage and so gained nothing after her death.

His inventiveness then turned to musical instruments and he made an improvement to the pedals of the harp. When this additional invention became widely known he was asked to give music lessons to the four unmarried and bored daughters of King Louis XV, a sweetheart task he did without remuneration once a week for years.

A rich banker friend, a board director for the military school, asked him to intervene to the king in securing support for the school. For this lobbying favor the banker gave him 60,000 francs of bank stock, his total financial interest in the school. The wealthy financier, Joseph Paris-Duverney, corresponded with him for ten years. Over 600 letters in code survive, still not deciphered.

Such adulation at court and with powerful allies and friends attracted the notice of rivals and enemies, and so in March 1763 a Chevalier provoked him into a duel. Public opinion even then did not condone duels but did accept the defense of one's honor. Though not an excellent swordsman, Beaumarchais managed to put his sword into his opponent's chest. He told the King's daughters about it, who told their father and the matter was hushed up. But rumors and insinuations against his character continued.

Within five years, though talent, inventiveness, cleverness, charm, and skillful stock manipulation, he had risen in court circles, mingled with the leading intellectuals, purchased a noble title and gained a fortune. His wealth allowed him the luxury of writing plays that illustrated his supple intellect and wit. Two remain as the epitome of musical comedy: *The Barber of Seville* (written while he was in Spain in 1764–65 in a noble but vain attempt to convince the suitor for his sister's hand to marry her) and *The Marriage of Figaro* (1785). Figaro was a satirical and derisive attack on nobles, royal power and privileges, suborned justice, and the censorship of literature. He continued to revise it for differing audience tastes over the years. Napoleon was said to have remarked that it launched the revolution.[9]

Beaumarchais and Two Revolutions

In 1775 he was sent to England as a special emissary to report on the growing crisis between England and the American colonies. He predicted the success of the American revolt and recommended to the king a secret campaign to aid Americans as a way of weakening England, France's perennial enemy. He established a company and began buying and outfitting ships loaded with weapons and provisions and recruiting experienced French officers, like the Marquis de Lafayette, for the American army. His heirs were not reimbursed for his personal losses to the American cause until 1825, and then only with a reduced amount of his real costs excluding inflation.

The French Revolution was, like its American cousin in the same decades, an overthrowing of the abuses of regal power. It was also the beginning of the end of the disenfranchisement of peasants who suffered from excessive taxation to the state and nobility, tithes to the church, and the intermittent ravages of war. There were precious few institutions through which individuals could air grievances. It was relatively easy to kill a king. It would be much more difficult to unleash and then rein in the caged emotions of the peasantry who sought revenge for centuries of historical wrongs.

Besides the rising hostility of the peasants, there was the increasing wealth of the mercantile class. This educated middle class had most of the nation's money but little access to political power. The aristocracy had all the privileges, but only some of the country's wealth. And the government was hopelessly in debt in 1787. Louis XVI continued to increase the court's expenditures and the interest on the debt expanded. The nobility spent the taxed money the middle class and peasants earned. The American rallying cry that emboldened the revolution in the colonies, "No taxation without representation," had a loud echo in

France. The American Revolution, and its constitutional prerogatives and sound defeat of the English, had its own motivation among the French for a similar upheaval by 1787.

This social bourgeoisie movement rooted in economic imbalances used peasant bitterness to rise against the excesses of the French upper classes, the riches of ecclesiastics, and disaffection of the church in general, and then to eliminate the monarchy, though that was not its original intent. The French Revolution caused all European royals to sleep uneasily in their beds after the guillotine deaths of Louis XVI and Marie Antoinette. In 1792 the French clergy were asked to choose between excommunication or death. The more devout chose death. Some revolutions are more revolting than others.

Courts were assembled in haste, with a nod from the judge who had no legal precedents to follow, and aristocratic and clerical defendants became victims and were turned over to executioners. About 2,000 clergy thus met their fate. Beaumarchais had hastily fled that same month but was eventually captured, imprisoned, and released through the help of a friend, Mademoiselle Ninon, otherwise known as Amelie Houret, then his mistress, but shared with others in that privilege. Because she was in alliance with the revolutionists, she saw to his release. Two days later every prisoner he was with in prison was executed. He fled to the countryside, then to Holland, England, and Hamburg before returning to Paris three years later after the Reign of Terror in which an estimated 50,000 were executed.

The popular slogan of Liberty, Fraternity and Equality still stirs patriotic sentiments among the French, especially when they sing the patriotic *Marseillaise*. But it was dangerous folly to criticize the liberties of the revolution when murderers were hailed as patriots. There was more fratricide than fraternity in the Reign of Terror from 1789 to 1793 as ordinary citizens took their revenge on the bourgeoisie. No aristocrat was accorded a fair trial with equal justice, as lethal retribution was the reigning ideology. Defense lawyers were eventually eliminated to speed sham trials. Louis XVI was executed in Paris on January 21, 1793. By 1794 over 900 death sentences were passed by the tribunal monthly. The ruler who sanctioned this revolutionary terror, Maximilien Robespierre, so alarmed his remaining enemies with his insolence and atrocities that he himself was arrested and guillotined in 1794.

Beaumarchais said he was in favor of the French Revolution, but only after it began. Ordinary French citizens did not believe him because of his purchased aristocratic status. And yet, he was a popular playwright and his literary success and his many well-placed bourgeoisie friends, rather than his purchased title, may have saved him from mob frenzy. He must have thought that if he could unite politics and art he might save France.

He was an entrepreneur, in the original meaning of the term, but also a capitalist before the Marxists invented that description. While in Spain he proposed several outrageous business plans to Spanish ministries, who did not respond positively to any of them. The most ignoble scheme was to transport large numbers of African slaves on French ships to Spanish American colonies. He purchased and exploited an extensive tract of forested land near Chinon for its timber. His marriages invariably resulted in monetary gains to him. In short, his life provided an illustration of how multifaceted a man's life can be. His successes ran to unusual success as an inventor, music teacher, businessman, playwright, courtier, government diplomat, and spy, traits very similar to his American contemporary, Benjamin Franklin.

He was said to have a volatile personality. He was a manipulator exploiting the naive weaknesses in the aristocracy to his own selfish advantage by bilking the French government, particularly King Louis XVI, of funds supposedly earned from secret missions. It is easy to ridicule him for this display of arrogance and greed. We can't dismiss him as a madman but certainly as a miscreant about whom one should remain skeptical, but not as a man dangerous to personal injury, unless challenged to a duel.

His persistent dedication to the cause of personal liberties remains as the hallmark of all his other, less worthy qualities. He certainly defended himself in court against his multiple adversaries, but he also defended with his own coin the rights of those who needed to be free of oppression. He was personally generous to those in need and gave money freely to those who sought his help. His aristocratic title and his wealth nearly got him executed, but his popularity as an artist and his strong voice in favor of human freedoms prevailed. That's enough of a legacy for one lifetime. Perhaps it is best to let a man who knew him well to describe himself (in a document he submitted to the Commune of Paris) and let that serve as the summation of his personality.

> Who was I, then? I was merely myself, and myself such as I have remained, free among the fettered, serene in the gravest dangers, braving all storms, doing business with one hand and waging war with the other, as lazy as a donkey yet working unceasingly, the butt of a thousand slanders, but happy within myself, as I have never belonged to any coterie, be it literary, political or mystic, never paid court to anyone, and have therefore been rejected by all and sundry.[10]

He died in his bed the early morning of May 18, 1799, of a cerebral hemorrhage. The dream house he had built in 1787 within sight of the Bastille was demolished in 1818, and his bones transferred to Pere-Lachaise Cemetery in north Paris in 1822 after his tomb in the garden of his home was smashed. As with so many others, cruel justice comes in succeeding generations with the desecration of a gravesite of the perceived villain.

Antoine Laurent Lavoisier (1743–1794)

> We ought, in every instance, to submit our reasoning to the test of experiment, and never search for truth, but by the natural road of experiment and observations.   Lavoisier in *Traité élémentaire de chimie*, 1793

The father of modern chemistry was one of the most renowned men of his day, an authentic man of science and independent investigator of natural phenomena. He died during the criminal excesses of the Reign of Terror led by Robespierre in 1793–94 when popular revolutionary fervor turned ugly and thousands were executed under the judicial rubric of treason. Accused of profiteering by the committee of the Reign of Terror, he was, tried, convicted and guillotined.

But throughout his life he studiously quantified his extensive chemical experiments, thereby substantiating claims of verifiable reliability. He first proposed the essential role of oxygen in organic life by studying the role fire played in combustion and its interaction with air. He made contributions to French economic thought and was an economist before that term was widely known, pioneered the role of science in agriculture, and achieved renown as a geologist, chemical genius, humanitarian, and notable public servant. It takes but a moment to cut off a head, but hundreds of years to develop a scientist as meticulous and theoretically brilliant, as one observer noted.

He had inherited a significant fortune from his mother, and he invested it in a private consortium that collected taxes on tobacco and salt and other customs' duties. His wealth allowed him to be self-employed all his life, and he devoted it to scientific experimentation.

Lavoisier was born into a wealthy family and attended college for seven years studying all the major sciences of the day, mathematics, botany, chemistry and astronomy.[11] He received a baccalaureate in law in 1763 and passed the bar but never practiced law. He was elected to the Academy of Sciences in 1768 when he was only twenty-five. When he was twenty-eight he married thirteen-year-old Marie-Anne Paulze, and her collaboration in his work proved to be dynamic, supportive and constructive all his life. They had no children, but their mutual love and collaboration proved the strength of the commitment. As a linguist and skilled draftsman she learned English, which he did not read, and drew the thirteen copperplate illustrations in *Traité Élémentaire de Chimie* (*Elements of Chemistry,* 1789), his classic chemistry textbook.

This text offered new theories and first proposed the law of conservation of mass. It contained a list of the known elements, or substances that could not be further broken down, and these included oxygen, nitrogen, hydrogen, phosphorus, mercury, zinc, and sulfur. Lavoisier underscored the need for careful observation and experiment. He tried to arrive at the truth by linking facts and to suppressing reason, which he thought an unreliable instrument of science.

He studiously did not want to clutter his text with acknowledgements of what other experimental researchers had done, not because he didn't appreciate their efforts, but because he wanted to disclose fully the results of his experiments. The first part contains his method and the arrangements of proofs he intends to follow. The second part consists of the tables and the nomenclatures, and the third part of all the operations connected with today what we understand by modern chemistry. He sent a personal copy to Ben Franklin who had personally witnessed a few of his public experiments in Paris.

LAVOISIER'S SCIENTIFIC CONTRIBUTIONS

Law of Conservation of Mass
Co-Discoverer of Oxygen and Hydrogen
Recognized the nature of Combustion
Disproved Theory of Phlogiston
Introduced metric system
First to quantify experiments
First Periodic Table of Elements (33 elements)
Improvements in the production of gunpowder

His first scientific studies were in geology and he and a colleague traveled for months all over France collecting rock samples, noting the markings of stratification in the rock formations, and making measurements of elevations. He came to the conclusion in 1766, intuitive for its day, that the earth had undergone a succession of epochs marked by the advancement and retreat of the sea. His subsequent investigations were improved lighting for the street lamps of Paris and the nature of mineral waters.[12]

By 1785 Lavoisier had presented experiments to the members of the Academy of Sciences that water, thought to have been an irreducible element since ancient times, was in fact a compound of two gases: oxygen (his coined term) and "inflammable air," which we know as hydrogen. He added conclusions he had not published previously especially on combustion and fermentation. He was careful to note that in experimenting, no matter how precise one thinks the instruments, that the possibility of abstraction is necessary. He recognized that analysis was as much a part of scientific research as the simple operations of the laboratory.

At the height of his research prominence he was able to conduct chemical research from 6 to 8 a.m. and again from 7 to 10 p.m. During the day he was engaged in his business dealings, with the gunpowder administration and meetings of the academy. As the French Revolution gathered political impetus, Lavoisier became active and was chosen as a representative of the provincial assembly of Orleans where he owned a country estate. He wrote schemes for charitable foundations, trade, agriculture, insurance for the elderly, and tax reform.

He was elected to the Commune of Paris and served in the National Guard. These administrative bodies were not local legislatures, but councils or assemblies that articulated people's needs to royal officials and ministers who then made the laws in the name of the king. Lavoisier was on the executive committee of the Orleans provincial assembly and he actively drafted proposals and reports on taxation, debt refinancing, welfare, mineral resources, and agriculture.[13] These committees were truly representative and not just assemblies appointed by the king as they had been in the past. He was actively involved in the election process of local committees.

Lavoisier argued that the king's power was limited to the consent of the people. In this vision he was politically advanced, which is why he initially supported the revolution and its ideals with limitations on the monarchy and with its representation from all segments of the population. But it would only be a short leap of reason to abolish the French monarchy altogether, as indeed America had rid itself of an English king. By 1792 the monarchy was abolished and Louis XVI guillotined in January 1793.

But it was his service on such committees as a government agent and a minor but still a member of landed nobility that forged his enmity with citizen authorities. Peasants assuming power in the new regime did not need the landed aristocracy to inform them of their needs. They misread Lavoisier, the lifelong public servant, scientist, and moderate revolutionary, and instead only saw him as a dreaded adversary because he owned an estate near Blois, had financial holdings in tax collections, was director of the Discount Bank and the Academy of Sciences, both abolished, but above all as a symbol of the old power structure.

He and his father-in-law, Jacques Paulze, were imprisoned, summarily tried on May 8, 1794, and executed together that afternoon. He was fifty-one years-old.

Jean-Antoine-Nicolas Caritat, Marquis de Condorcet (1743–1794)

Caritat was born on September 17, 1743, in Ribemont. His father, a member of a minor military nobility, died shortly afterward. He attended the Jesuit school at Reims when he was eleven and the University of Paris at fifteen. He did not follow in the family military tradition and remained in Paris deciding on a career in science.

From his early twenties he was a recognized man of genius. He submitted *Essai sur le calcul integral* to the Academy of Sciences in 1765, his third paper submission to the academy. It was instantly hailed by qualified mathematicians for its brilliance. At twenty-six years of age he was elected to the academy and became friends with some of the leading thinkers of the era. Within four years of joining he was its permanent secretary. He wrote papers on philosophy, math, science, social problems, education, and constitutional issues. Yet despite his wide-ranging accomplishments, he is generally regarded as one of the lesser lights of that illustrious age. I have chosen him here because even though like Lavoisier he enunciated the liberal philosophy that impelled the revolution he too died from its excesses.

In the spirit of the times, but in advanced thinking for the age, he saw democracy as encompassing universal suffrage and universal education, the sharing of wealth, programs of national insurance, and equal rights. His short book, *Sketch for a Historical Picture of the Progress of the Human Mind* (1795) is among those critical documents composed from prison like Boethius's *Consolations of Philosophy*, or Martin Luther King's *Letter from a Birmingham Jail* (1963). Condorcet's treatise was composed while in hiding from the authorities of the Reign of Terror. Such an exercise written while imprisoned certainly focuses the mind. His essay emphasizes the perfectibility of human nature, a naïve, idealistic, liberal theme among romantic poets and optimistic philosophers typical of his times.

> The rough and stormy passage from a crude state of society to that degree of civilization enjoyed by enlightened and free nations is no way a degeneration of the human race but is rather a necessary crisis in its gradual progress towards absolute perfection. [14]

It was a theme with echoes from his previous writings, notably his reception speech at his admission to the academy in 1782. He elaborated on this theme in *The Nature and Purpose of Public Instruction* (1791) where he wrote: "It is the duty of society to promote the discovery of speculative truths as the sole means of advancing the human race to the successive degrees of perfection . . ."[15]

His sketch is full of the corruption, treachery, ignorance, and irrationality of humanity through the centuries, a common liberal, romantic theme. His claim is that these human imperfections have evolved and that his time was the beginning of the impetus toward human perfection. This theme is part of his wider idea of the inevitability of progress. He never did reveal any understanding of social evolution, how one epoch developed from another, but insisted that progress was uniformly positive and linear and that history was littered with the debris of misfortune and superstition. Like most of his contemporaries, he sought emancipation from the past so that enlightenment policies could move the masses toward equality. Nevertheless, despite its argumentative limitations, his sketch represents the times and is one of the first studies in intellectual history.

He could not foresee that another revolution, the Industrial, would be needed to redistribute property and wealth so that equality could be realized. The new capitalists, the barons of industry, were merchants, traders, and speculators who became wealthier than former aristocrats, but who exploited natural resources and laborers as much as had feudal lords. Democratic governments protected new landowners with laws founded on the sovereignty of property rights as assiduously as they had former church privileges or the hunting grounds of kings.

Condorcet's most ambitious paper described how the mathematics of probability could enlighten social and political matters. The eighteenth century is the origin of the development of the social sciences and the demonstration of how mathematics could be used to enhance understanding of social issues. The strength of logic was that it was based on the relation between two verbal statements in order to draw a conclusion. The beauty of probability theory is that it concludes with certainty from the calculation of actual events.

Essay on the Application of Mathematics to the Theory of Decision-Making (1785) was written for a non-technical, popular audience. Like Anne-Robert-Jacques Turgot (1727–1781), from whom he obtained his inspiration, he believed that the moral sciences, as they were then known, could have the same conclusive certainty as the physical sciences, and that this new understanding would elevate humanity toward perfection.[16] The use of logic, or syllogistic thinking, and reason can lead to vague results and often error. Condorcet expanded on this argument in a paper in 1793, *A General View of the Science of Social Mathematics.* He was convinced that the useful application of mathematics would reduce error and prejudice in decisions. He specifically noted math's usefulness to climate, customs, election results, maritime insurance, life annuities, mortality rates, even lotteries.

Condorcet's "calculus of probabilities" is today's probability statistics. It is so widely used in polls and data collection and analysis we forget that it is only a tool used systematically in the past century. Statistics is a math instrument that gathers facts and then determines certain values of the group. The most familiar measure is the average or arithmetic mean. Sampling techniques yield excellent estimates of the occurrence of an event within close error ratios, usually 3–5 percent. Insurance rates are premised on such calculations.[17]

His descriptions of the usefulness of mathematics are more persuasive than many of his other papers because he can be precise and use fitting examples. Other papers, like those on the emancipation of women and on education, are more argumentative and rhetorical, more florid in style, like a lawyer pleading a case before a judge or jury. All his well-argued prescriptions for social improvement were grounded in the goal of progress toward human betterment, which appears to be a tautology. "The revolutions," he writes in the paper on education, "brought about by the general advance of the human race towards perfection must certainly lead to reason and happiness."[18] But revolutions like that in France do not automatically lead to reason or happiness. While his motive may be excessively altruistic, the mechanics of implementation in any society are imperfect because they involve human fallibilities.

Condorcet on Education

After the revolution of 1789, there was not only a liberation of monarchical rule, but a freedom to express new ideas that solidified human and civil rights long denied or neglected in political and social life. Formal education demanded new principles and Condorcet rose to propose his views.

CONDORCET'S KEY IDEAS
ON PUBLIC EDUCATION (1791)

Society is obliged to provide public instruction
    For equal rights
    To reduce inequality
    To increase useful knowledge

Society is obliged to advance the occupations
    To maintain equality among practitioners
    To make occupations more useful
    To diminish the danger of some occupations
    To accelerate their progress

Society is obliged to provide education to promote human perfection
    To afford everyone the opportunity to develop talents
    To prepare new generations in the culture
    To prepare nations for change

Public Instruction needs to:
    a) teach each individual according to capabilities,
    b) to insure proper subject matter knowledge,
    c) to prepare students for occupational knowledge

Instruction must be equal for men and women

His ideas on education, expressed in his 1791 paper *The Nature and Purpose of Public Instruction*, reads like a contemporary education reform bill. The fact that it makes reasonable good sense does not make it politically acceptable. The table is a partial outline of a few of his key ideas he presented before the Legislative Assembly in 1792. Napoleon, however, did include Condorcet's educational scheme in his reorganized government plan when he came to power. We accept many of these educational propositions today because so many have been adopted. But during his day scarcely one child in a hundred had access to even a comprehensive elementary education. Ignorance, he noted, keeps people from understanding and exercising their rights.

As he had stated so many times in previous publications, his outline for an education plan was grounded on the necessity for equality. The rules of a society help to reduce, he argued, the inequalities found in many individuals, and public instruction entails some dependency on society but also reduces inequality between individuals. Common men can better realize and exercise their natural rights with a proper education and begin to mitigate social and economic gaps.

More important, it is indispensable to continue one's education beyond formal schooling and throughout the life span. If one does not continue to improve intellectually after schooling, to strengthen knowledge acquired, to correct errors and prejudices, one would have diminished and perhaps vitiated the education previously gained. "It is not enough for education to form men. It is also necessary for education to maintain those it has formed, enlightening them, safeguarding them for error, preventing them from relapsing into ignorance."[19]

He stated, but did not elaborate upon, the need to identify the objects of instruction, what books should be used for each subject and the most useful forms of instruction, what teaching methods should be included, and what kind of teacher selected. His premise was that the instructional methodological and personnel choices should be appropriate to the conditions. But he also wanted to limit the powers of the public authority so that it, or any institution it established to administer education, did not itself become tyrannical and self-perpetuating. And he advocated for the equality of women to an equal education.

The revolutionary mood gave him liberty to champion all human rights and he became most effusive over constitutional principles, the bedrock of modern societies. He desired above all a rational plan for political decision-making and representation from the body politic. Regrettably, neither his education program nor constitutional plans he presented to the Committee on the Constitution in 1793 were ever adopted. Both were lost in the struggle for power among the political parties partly because his long essays were a scholarly argument for a constitution and education plan, not an outline for the mechanics for operation. His analysis was laudable but was unhelpful to legislators trying to decide how a republican democracy should proceed in executing its powers.

Condorcet was imbued with a lively intellect, an engaging writing style, and humane ideals. He fortunately lived when the expression of free ideas temporarily flourished. But in the last two years of his life rulers in France attempted to thwart what they perceived were counter-revolutionary tendencies. The result was the Reign of Terror. Lesser men like Robespierre, who had more oratorical skills than intelligence, ruled and executions became the principal activity of the state. France approached as close to anarchy as a state could be without dissolving itself. Nearly all of the heads of the most brilliant minds of the age were either decapitated, deposed, or exiled, and their glorious ideas, ambitions, and schemes silenced. But ideas do not die as men do. The citizens of Paris were to discover to their dismay that monarchs are not the only ones capable of insane butchery. Once released of its bondage maniacal mobs, sanctioned by demagogic leaders, sought unholy refuge in the most despicable forms of violence.

Unwilling to presume further on the benevolence of his patron, Condorcet left his hiding house disconsolate and wandered the outskirts of Paris until he asked for food at an inn where his dress and demeanor aroused suspicion. He was arrested and found dead in his cell the following day of a blood clot according to the medical examiner. Once the Convention found and read his *Sketches*, they ordered 3,000 copies printed at state expense and distributed throughout France.

For all the exaltation of Enlightenment values and principles, the eighteenth century was still an era of intolerance, cruelty, and torture. For example, Jean-François de la Barre (1745–1766) was a knight, but his minor aristocratic status could not save him from religious intolerance. On August 9, 1765, the wooden crucifix on a bridge in Abbeville was vandalized. The local bishop asked parishioners, under threat of excommunication, to reveal all they could about the incident to civil judges. Some parishioners accused three young men, not about vandalizing the crucifix, but for not removing their hats when a Catholic procession had passed on the bridge. One of those accused was La Barre whose bedroom was searched and three prohibited books, including Voltaire's *Philosophical Dictionary*, were found. He was tortured into confessing his alleged crimes, and then sentenced by the Paris Parliament to be tortured again. He was beheaded and his body thrown into flames along with his copy of Voltaire's book. The National Convention reversed his conviction in 1794.

After a decade of liberation from monarchy but not tyranny, and from class struggles, foreign wars, political volatility, runaway inflation, lawless tribunals, senseless executions and periodic massacres, everyone in France was weary of revolution. The various authorities—the Assembly, the Committee of Public Safety, The Commune, The Convention, The Directorate—passed laws but never forged a constitution. The French Revolution severed the heads of a King, Louis XVI, and a queen, Marie Antoinette, aristocrats, dissenters, and revolutionaries alike, and a campaign of terror fed by war abroad and inflation at home, made dictatorship inevitable. Enter Napoleon Bonaparte who took the unleashed violence of the revolution into the rest of Europe.

EPILOGUE

Men who are sincere in defending their freedom, will always feel concern for every circumstance, which seems to make against them; it is the natural and honest consequence of all affectionate attachments, and the want of it is a vice. But the dejection lasts only for a moment; they soon rise out of it with additional vigor, the glow of hope, courage and fortitude will, in a little time, supply the place of every inferior passion, and kindle the whole heart into heroism. Thomas Paine, *The American Crisis*, IV, Sept. 12, 1777, 148 of *Collected Writings*

This biographical parade has been a partial anatomy of heroism. More people have been indecisive, timid, fearful, and spineless than bold in the face of antagonism or adversity. There have been moral leaders who could have spoken out against atrocities and did not. Pope Pius XII and several members of the hierarchy were silent from 1939 to 1945 against two of the most criminal, murderous regimes in history—the Nazis in Germany and the Stalinists in Russia. The silence of the Catholic Church, even in so-called Catholic countries during these war years, may not have eliminated human extermination but we will never know for sure.

Who will ever know about the unrecorded acts of fortitude from secretive police states like Russia during the days of Stalin, or of Erich Honecker in East Germany from 1945 to 1989, or Kim Jong Il in North Korea, or any of the totalitarian and repressive regimes in Africa?

By providing the background of individuals of valor from different historical eras, I intended to demonstrate that acts of human courage and sacrifice have not changed. State control over human freedoms and rights has always sought to quash voices raised in protest to restrictive policies. Whether the Roman curia, the emperor, the pope, the Roman Catholic or Orthodox Church, the king who ruled by divine right, theocratic states, autocrat governments with total military power, empowered Muslim imperatives, or democratic governments who silence dissidents with administrative and legal restrictions, imperial powers always attempt to silence those emboldened enough to question their authority, prerogatives, or policies.

I hope the reading experience has been personally uplifting because the repetition of suppression by religious and governmental fascism and authoritarianism is likely to be depressing without a few examples in every generation of uncommon valor. These "enemies of the state" were not plotters of insurrection or conspirators seeking to subvert the government. They were competitors in the world of ideas, those who dared to defy a sacred convention, uncompromising autocrat, or a religious imperative, like insulting a dead prophet, or writing lines of poetry mocking a living king.

But individual deeds of heroism do not imply that the actors are saints either. I have tried to point out that an act of heroism may define a person's legacy but not necessarily a whole life. A high government official may be in everyone's opinion a "good man," but he may yet one day lie before a court to protect his boss and go to jail. His one act of perjury will follow him for the rest of his life no matter what other significant accomplishments he did. The same is true for a few of those selected here.

A few of these figures may not have been people who would have been on your Christmas card list or whom you would have invited to dinner, but they would have been people you would have liked to have met and spoken to, even for a few moments, to get a true sense of their commitment.

The greatest, but not the only, threats to liberty and human freedoms have come from religious authoritarianism and intolerance. Zealous religious fanatics have killed themselves to silence dissidents or perceived enemies of their faith. We tolerate the insane who use religion as their protection, while sending to asylums those who make no such claim on religion. Despite improved economics, access to higher education, and increased living standards, intractable faith has become its own self-sustaining force. All monotheistic religions are surging in numbers and fundamentalist, inflexible beliefs are generating new heroes and heroines against the rigidities of dogma. The twenty-first century is a clash between believers who have no doubts about the certitudes of their faith, and their opposition to other faiths, or those with no standard religious faith. The purpose of any critical examination like this is not to pass judgment on a specific religious belief, but to challenge dogmatism and analyze the multiple contexts of religious belief where heroism is germinated.

Prior to the emergence of monotheism, independent Greek thinkers were threatened with death or exile because they challenged belief in multiple gods or the mythology of deities. Once monotheism, whether Christianity in the West or Islam in other parts of the world, and religious truths became linked to secular rule, adherence to dogma or religious rituals became the standard for civil order. I have been in countries where to eat during daylight hours in a Muslim country during the holy month of Ramadan in violation of the imposed fast is enough to get you thrown in jail. Heroic men and women have always stepped forward to confront conventional thought, beliefs, or practices, placing their lives in jeopardy to voice alternative views.

Henry VIII wrote a long essay refuting many of Martin Luther's propositions and attacks on the papacy. In gratitude the pope named him, in a designation still used by British royalty, *Defender of the Faith*. America today is engaged in a similar controversy over religion, secularism, and science. Religion flourishes on college campuses more than it has in decades. However, the more religiously devout students have become, the less willing they seem to be to engage in a critical analysis about faith or how it interacts with science. Professors who might suggest social science or literary interpretations of religious texts have been subjected to threats and intimidations.

The Islamic world today allows little or no religious freedom and finds scriptural validity for shunning social contact, and even acts of violence toward so-called infidels, similar to the punitive impositions during medieval Europe, or the Massachusetts Bay Colony in the 1680s, or the Holy Roman Empire in Europe until the eighteenth century. The subjugation of faith in God, according to religious fundamentalists of all stripes and in all ages, is equivalent to restricting the varying paths, and the manners, rituals, and beliefs that individuals seek to experience the divine.

Totalitarianism today, like absolute monarchy in past centuries, has a methodical tedium in crushing of dissent even ordinary citizens might resist passively. But even democratic governments manufacturer slogans, preferably favoring nationalism, that act as sleeping pills to squelch public debate, to lull the electorate into nodding to its policies. Legal freedoms in democratic societies will ultimately protect individuals, but not from harassment or intimidation.

Outcasts, heretics, dissidents, and renegades by definition will always be social pariahs, whether they lived in ancient Athens or Rome, Christian Constantinople, medieval Paris, Elizabethan London, or today's Tehran, Pyongyang, or Riyadh. The more odious and stubborn are the ways of humans, the more courageous the heroes and heroines who rise above inhumanities. An historical examination of religious fervor, current laws against minority religions, and the close association of religion and state governance promote crackdowns on all independent behaviors.

It's relatively easy to navigate through life when faced with no threats, without fear, and without incessant warfare or communal eviction, as is true today in some parts of Africa. But occasionally individuals can find themselves stuck in a compromising situation where the tide of opinion runs against the swell of good sense and the morally preferable. At such moments it takes courage to withstand rejection by the majority without appearing to be self-righteous. Finding the strength within at that critical time is what makes some people special.

The medieval Islamic scholar Ibn Arabi offered an insightful alternative to religious expediency using the metaphors of religion.

> My heart is a pasture for gazelles and a convent of Christian monks,
> A temple for idols and the Ka'bah of pilgrims,
> The Tablets of the Law in Torah and the Book of Qur'an.
> I follow the religion of Love, wherever loves takes me,
> There is my religion and my faith.
> Muhyiddin Ibn Arabi, 1165–1240, in *The Interpreter of Desires*

Many religious fundamentalists, certainly Muslim suicide bombers, are willing to die for their faith, or to protect their faith from corrupting influences, particularly the secularism of Western societies. There appear to be fewer individuals whose principles are so ethically but not religiously strong that they also sacrifice their lives for what they believe. In this study I have tended to profile not martyrs, or those who consider themselves martyrs, but instead those who stand for an independent cause or idea. Here are saints like Joan of Arc and Thomas More, but also reform-minded clerics outside the mainstream who challenged an autocratic religious belief or practices, like clerics Kaj Munk who faced down despotic occupying armies. Edith Stein, who happened to be a nun, died because of her Jewish heritage. Spinoza was excommunicated from Judaism, did not become a Christian, but was treated as an atheist.

Today, organizations like Human Rights Watch and Amnesty International are dedicated to protecting universal human rights. Such associations help alert the world community against inhumane treatment, and seek to bring offenders to justice by exposing human rights violations. These groups want to abolish the death penalty, oppose wartime abuses, denounce torture, stop violence against women, and end the proliferation of arms. Every day there are victims of discrimination and systematic abuses: trade unionists, lawyers, and judges who face death threats, and journalists who expose corruption. My study is really incomplete as new heroes and heroines, prisoners of conscience, can be found daily on the websites of Amnesty International and Human Rights Watch.

History to a civilization is what memory is to an individual. People with Alzheimer's disease or amnesia are disoriented, lost in the present, and unable to know where they are because they can't remember where they've been. So it is too with a civilization or society that has lost its way and can't remember to correct in the present mistakes learned from the past. Trepidation in confronting injustice is made sturdier if one can step back out from time and grab from the past a tough ethic, to get out of one's immediate experience and learn about the problems that never change and make that a part of one's inheritance. Learning about these individuals can help restore the relevance of history. The young may be lucky if they stumble upon such wisdom early in life. The rest of us have to read history and the classics more thoughtfully.

The cheapening of language, the vulgarity of entertainment, the debasement of civility, and the glorification of violence are just a few of the traits that have corrupted modern culture. The knowledge of history allows us to make better adjustments in our own lives and society.

Unborn outcasts and heretics will come from the same contexts they have in the past: authoritarian governments vs. the individual dissident, the polarizing and extremist relationships between science and religion, and the individual who stands brazenly and defiantly in the face of a race riot, ethnic cleansing, or the dominance of one religion over another.

Somewhere in the catastrophe and debris of armed brutality are individual acts of kindness and courage that will never be known. In an isolated part of an urban conflict, in a lonely stretch of desert, in a thick tropical forest, someone is defending honor, human dignity or saving the life of another while placing one's own life in peril. Like the Muslim ceremony of stoning the devil during the Haj in Mecca, we would prefer a symbolic act to take out our collective hatred on evil. But that rarely happens. Education cannot prepare us for the kind of sacrifice that leads one to give up life for a principle, cause, or higher purpose. Living moral courage requires extraordinary will power, though few heed its whispered inner voice. When someone does listen, everyone deserves to honor and esteem the heroic example that results as all humanity is thereby ennobled.

APPENDIX A
ORIGIN OF THE JESUS LEGEND

Publicus Sulpicius Quirinius (ca. 50 BCE–22 CE) was born less than noble. But through imperial loyalty, diligence, a solid military career, and estimable character, and a model of duty and honor according to Tacitus, he rose to become a Roman senator, then consul and governor of Syria during the reign of Augustus and during the early lifetime of Jesus. The prefect of Jerusalem, like Pontius Pilate, answered to the Governor of Syria. Quirinius is mentioned in the *Annals* of Tacitus, the *Tiberius* of Suetonius, Strabo's *Geography*, and Josephus' *Jewish War* and *Antiquities*. Indeed, we know more about him from official documents and historians than we have extra-gospel evidence of Jesus.

Luke notes (2:1–3) that a census of the whole world was undertaken during the reign of Caesar Augustus. However, censuses under Roman policy were only undertaken when a new province was added or a king was deposed, as Herod Archelaus was in 6 CE when the Roman census described in Luke supposedly occurred. Moreover, from 23 BCE to 17 CE there was no "Cyrinus" (in Greek, *Kurinou*) that Luke notes listed among Roman documents as Governor of Syria or in Pamphylia-Galatia.[1]

Luke writes that this census was the cause of Mary and Joseph leaving Nazareth and journeying to Bethlehem. But Matthew, who didn't write about a census, wrote that Jesus was born during the reign of Herod the Great who died in 4 BCE. The Roman census did not occur until ten years later, in 6 CE. Either we have here a huge chronological disparity uncharacteristic of any trustworthy historian, or a misplaced historical event to satisfy a mythical revelation, to confirm a biblical prophecy that that Jesus would be born in the city of David to highlight his kingship claim.

According to legend, Jesus had a miraculous birth, appeared from the face of a rock on December 25 while nearby shepherds heralded his birth. Immediately, he was hailed as a god who would bring about the people's salvation, a god of justice, truth, and light. He performed many miracles while on earth. He ate sacred meals with his followers, chiefly bread and wine, symbolizing flesh and blood. After his death he ascended into heaven and is scheduled to return on the final day to judge the living and the dead. If this legendary story sounds familiar, it is because the heroic legends of ancient literature, many only recently discovered, have been repeated in the gospels, just like events from this legend of the Persian deity Mithras.

The birth of Jesus has amazing parallels with Mithras that cannot be ascribed to coincidence alone. In a bas-relief found in the crypt of St. Clements in Rome, Mithras emerges from a rock under the shade of a sacred tree, on a birthday celebrated on December 25th, and in such humble beginnings only shepherds witnessed and heralded his miraculous entrance into the world. Mithras embodied the sidereal powers of the empyrean, the highest heaven beyond the planets, the true paradise symbolized by fire and light. In Luke's story about the birth of Jesus, a star appears symbolizing fire and light. Magi, who are after all Persian magicians, appear at Bethlehem to offer homage.

After a last supper shared with chosen companions, Mithras ascended into the heavens where he constantly protects his faithful devotees who piously serve him. The services included ritualistic washing with ablutions in a catharsis of purification (like Jesus washing the feet of the apostles), abstinence from certain foods, to choose good over evil, to resist the prince of darkness.

Followers of Mithras believed in the immortality of the soul and the resurrection of the body after death. Mithras will descend to earth and banish evil once and for all, separate the good from the bad, and offer believers the divine beverage, bull fat with consecrated wine, and then all souls will enter life everlasting. Readers of the early gospels would have been familiar with Mithras since he became the most widely venerated deity among Roman soldiers. Thus, for readers of Matthew and Luke who describe the birth of Jesus, the legend of Mithras is repeated and Jesus is simply a symbolic reincarnation of the ancient god. Matthew and Luke revisit the most ancient literary legend of one of the oldest deities and recreate the story of his origin in the person of Jesus.

APPENDIX B
CHURCH COUNCILS

The first eight recognized church councils attempted to determine what was orthodox and what was heretical. The Eastern Orthodox Church (Greek, Slavic, and Russian rites) as opposed to the Roman Catholic or Latin church, recognize only the first seven councils to Nicaea II. The first few councils met with, and sometimes without, imperial approval. After Constantine's first council at Nicaea, councils were most often summoned by the emperor and often debated his agenda. The pope, the bishop of Rome, did not attend the defining Council of Nicaea in 325.

There is lingering scholarly debate about whether an assembled group of bishops constitutes a synod or a council and exactly whom the assembly represents and whom the decisions effect. When emperors summoned bishops to assemble this usually represented a council even though there was often unequal representation from all regions. There has been further discussion about how many bishops were necessary for a quorum and what rules governed proceedings.

Synods in the early history of the church were regional congregations of bishops and at various times met at Constantinople, Palestine, or North Africa but were not representative church councils. They often met to condemn heretics or to set policy. In the last thousand years all councils have been held in Western Europe and have further defined church morals, discipline, and rules. The Second Lyons Council in 1274 and Ferrara-Basel in 1431 and 1438 tried unsuccessfully to reconcile the schism between Eastern Orthodox and Western rites of the Catholic Church. The Council of Trent in 1545, occasioned by the Protestant Reformation, attempted to correct and confirm beliefs and practices that had not previously been elaborated on.

There are twenty-one recognized Catholic Church councils. There are a third less unrecognized church councils, and fourteen alone that met in the fourth century, many convened by emperors. The decisions of these councils often contravened earlier council decisions thus calling into question what the doctrines of the church were, and how they were initially formulated. A few councils met to condemn the decisions of previous councils, thus calling into question the divine inspiration supposedly accompanying decisions made by such congregations.

Here are the officially recognized Roman Catholic Church councils.

YEAR   COUNCIL
325   Nicaea
381   Constantinople
431   Ephesus
451   Chalcedon
553   Constantinople II
680   Constantinople III
787   Nicaea II
869   Constantinople IV
1123   Lateran I (Ironically, the Church of the Lateran in Rome is named after Lateranus, the Roman god of the hearth. Cf. Arnobius, *Against the Nations*, Book III, 6. Hence, five Roman Catholic Church councils, nearly one quarter of all recognized councils, can be said to be under the name if not the auspices of a Roman deity.)
1139   Lateran II
1179   Lateran III
1215   Lateran IV
1245   Lyons I
1274   Lyons II
1311   Vienne
1414   Constance
1431   Basel & Ferrara-Florence (and in 1438)
1512   Lateran V
1545   Trent
1869   Vatican I
1962   Vatican II

The nonrecognized church councils include:

YEAR   COUNCIL
327   Nicomedia
334   Tyre
336   Constantinople
338   Alexandria (declared the council of Tyre invalid)
342   Antioch (Emperor Constantius ignores the homoousian issue and deposes Patriarch Athanasius)
343   Serdica (assembles but never formally convenes)
351   Sirmium (prohibits non-scriptural terms in defining creedal statements)
353   Arles
359   Ariminum (more than 400+ bishops delete "substance" (*ousia*) and "consubstantial" from the Creed and state that the fathers at Nicaea

were acting "without proper reflection" because scripture does not contain such distinctions)

359	Seleucia
360	Constantinople (rejects Nicene conclusion and forbids further creeds; condemns all enemies)
360	Paris (Gallic bishops condemn blasphemies of Council of Ariminum, excommunicate all who disagree, reaffirm Nicene Creed)
362	Alexandria (Egyptian bishops reaffirm Nicene Creed after Arian Emperor Constantius dies)
364	Lampsacus (Hellespont bishops declare 360 Council of Constantinople invalid and reaffirm Nicene Creed)

NOTES

Chapter 1

1. R. Duncan, *Selected Writings of Mahatma Gandhi* (Boston: Beacon Press, 1951), 115; G. Ashe's superb biography, *Gandhi* (New York: Stein & Day, 1968).

2. Duncan, *Selected Writings*, 112.

3. Ashe, *Gandhi*, 44.

4. Duncan, 241.

5. Ibid., 53.

6. Ibid., 167.

7. J. M. Washington, *A Testament of Hope: The Essential Writings of Martin Luther King* (New York: Harper & Row, 1986), 219.

8. Parts of the civil rights movement began much earlier. The historic presidential directive Executive Order 9981 that ended racial segregation in the military was signed on June 26, 1948, by a president whose grandfather had been a slave owner, and who is not generally known as a civil rights advocate. President Harry Truman was appalled by violence against black World War II veterans. In 1947 Truman had created a commission to end lynching, poll taxes, and to begin an integrated military, not achieved until the Korean War in 1950, the first war in which blacks and whites fought together in integrated units. Southern Democrats killed Truman's attempt to get legislation passed by Congress, but not his orders to the military in which he stood constitutionally as commander in chief.

9. M. L. King, *The Measure of Man* (Philadelphia: Fortress Press, 1988); D. L. Lewis, *King, A Biography* (Urbana; University of Illinois Press, 1978); C. Carson and K. Shepard, *A Call to Conscience: The Landmark Speeches of Dr. Martin Luther King, Jr.* (New York: Warner Books, 2001).

10. Washington, *Essential Writings*, 297.

11. M. Friedly and D. Gallen, *Martin Luther King, Jr., The FBI File* (New York: Carroll & Graf Publishers, 1993).

12. Stanley Levison, a New York lawyer and King confidante, actually did King's income taxes. Hunter Pitts "Jack" O'Dell ran the New York office of the SCLC. Both men had had affiliations with the Communist Party in the 1950s, but it is unclear whether either was actually a party member. Nevertheless, these connections caused consternation in the FBI. President Kennedy was informed and notified King in a private conversation of the former Communist affiliations of these two men. King believed that the past association did not mean they were active and kept them in his confidence.

13. Carson and Shepard, *A Call to Conscience*, 85.

14. D. Sharpes, "Mandela One More Politician Caught in Country's Struggles," *Standard-Examiner*, July 15, 1990, D3.

15. Donald Woods, *Biko* (New York: Paddington Books, 1978).

16. *Japan Times*, May 27, 2006, 13.

17. A. H. Ali, *The Caged Virgin, An Emancipation Proclamation for Women and Islam* (New York: Free Press, 2006). Cf. also C. Caldwell, "Daughter of the Enlightenment," *NYTM*, April 3, 2005, 26–31.

18. I. Buruma, *Murder in Amsterdam, The Death of Theo Van Gogh and the Limits of Tolerance* (New York: Penguin Press, 2006), 245.

19. M. Simons, "A Critic of Muslim Intolerance Faces Loss of Dutch Citizenship," *NYT*, May 16, 2006, A8.

20. Buruma, *Murder in Amsterdam*, 245.

Chapter 2

1. Orhan Pamuk, "Freedom to Write," *New York Review of Books* 53 (9) (May 25, 2006): 6. Pamuk won the Nobel Prize in Literature in 2006.

2. Human Rights Watch (http://www.hrw.com) monitors abuses and activities against human rights in all the world's countries. Five Iranian writers were murdered in 2005.

3. L. Petersson, *Deserters* (Copenhagen: Danish Resistance Museum Publishing, 2005), 20.

4. W. Herbstrith, *Edith Stein* (New York: Harper & Row, 1985) is instructive and filled with quotes and letters from her and those who knew her. For her spiritual writings see J. Sullivan, *Edith Stein, Essential Writings* (Maryknoll, NY: Orbis Books, 2002). For a discussion of her philosophy, cf. A, MacIntyre, *Edith Stein, A Philosophical Prologue, 1913–1922* (New York: Rowman & Littlefield, 2006).

5. "A Top Dissident Refuses to Give In," *Economist* (December 8, 2005): 56.

6. S. Fowler, "Turkey, a Touchy Critic, Plans to Put a Novel on Trial," *NYT*, September 15, 2006, A4.

7. http://nobelprize.org/peace/laureates/1991/kyi-bio.html

8. http://www.commondreams.org/views03/1211-03.htm

9. http://nobelprize.org/peace/laureates/2003/ebadi-bio.html. Cf. "Ten Questions for Shirin Ebadi," *Time*, May 15, 2006, 6.

10. http://www.memritv.org/Transcript.asp?P1=1050.

11. J. M. Broder, "Muslim's Blunt Criticism of Islam Draws Threats and Some Hope," *NYT*, March 11, 2006, A1. See also A. W. Wafa, "Kabul Judge Rejects Calls to End Trial of Christian Convert," *NYT*, March 24, 2006, A3.

12. I. Fisher and E. Povoledo, "Italy Grants Asylum to Afghan Christian Convert," *NYT*, March 30, 2006, A12.

Chapter 3

1. E. S. Gaustad, *Roger Williams* (New York: Oxford University Press, 2005), 103ff.

2. Virginia is named after Elizabeth (the virgin Queen) and Jamestown after James I. The King James Version of the English translation of the Bible occurred during his regal tenure although he had no part in its translation.

3. Gaustad, *Roger Williams*, 5ff.

4. Ibid., 12–13. He was not officially redeemed from the Bay Colony's sentence of expulsion until 1936 when the Commonwealth of Massachusetts officially apologized and revoked the order.

5. A charter from Parliament for Providence Plantations with help from Oliver Cromwell. It was not until 1663 that he was able to obtain a royal charter from Charles II.

6. T. Paine, *The Crisis*, no. 4, 54. Paine's biography by A. J. Ayer, the well-known British philosopher, *Thomas Paine* (New York: Atheneum, 1988), combines his life with the controversies about his major writings. Eric Foner's *Tom Paine and Revolutionary America* (New York: Oxford University Press, 1976) emphasizes Paine's influence on America.

7. Ayer, *Thomas Paine*, 9.

8. T. Paine, *Collected Writings*, ed. E. Foner (New York: Library of America, 1995), *Common Sense*, 33–34.

9. Ibid., 21.

10. Ibid., 34 and 43.

11. *The Crisis*, no. 1, 47.

12. In the seventh essay; ibid., 196.

13. Ibid., 211. In a letter to Henry Laurens.

14, A. Cobban, *A History of Modern France, Vol. 1: 1715–1799* (London: Penguin Books, 1957), 162ff.

15. T. Paine, *Agrarian Justice Opposed to Agrarian Law and to Agrarian Monopoly Being a Plan for Meliorating the Condition of Man by Creating in Every Nation a National Fund* (Paris: W. Anlard, 1797). Online services for this and other documents of his from the British Library and Library of Congress are available at: http://galenet.galegroup.com.ezproxy1.lib.asu.edu/servlet/ECCO.

16. Paine became furious with Washington for not interceding with the French to rescue Paine from prison and wrote him a testy letter after he returned to the United States. Washington's motives are unknown but he probably thought Paine expendable and did not want to jeopardize relations with the French. Similarly, Jefferson refused Paine's offer of diplomacy with the French even though Jefferson could easily have consented since many French eulogized Paine for his efforts at their revolution. (Cf. Ayer, *Thomas Paine*.)

17. The Treaty of Guadeloupe Hidalgo at the close of the war in 1848 gave the United States California, Nevada, and parts of Colorado, Utah, Arizona, and New Mexico. The Mexicans realized the danger they were in when Gen. Stephen Kearny and his army of more than three hundred men captured Santa Fe in August 1846. Capt. Cooke left Santa Fe with his Mormon battalion of 340 men headed to California. The United States then purchased additional territory from Mexico (the Gadsden Purchase) in New Mexico and Arizona in 1853 to rectify the U.S. southern boundary of where the border is today.

18. Geronimo, *Geronimo, His Own Story*, ed. S. M. Barrett (New York: Ballantine Books, 1970).

19. E. R. Sweeney, *Cochise, Chiricahua Apache Chief* (Norman: University of Oklahoma Press, 1991).

20. Ibid., 195.

21. See Red Cloud's Farewell Address, July 4, 1903, http://www.bigisland.com/~stony/redcloud.html.

22. Ibid.

23. Willa Cather (1875–1947), the famous Pulitzer prize–winning novelist noted for, among other works, *O Pioneers!* (1913), *My Antonia* (1918), and *Death Comes to the Archbishop* (1927), graduated from Red Cloud High School in Nebraska on June 13, 1890.

Chapter 4

1. For material on these polls and accompanying articles cf.: CBS Broadcasting, Poll: "Creationism trumps evolution," CBS News, November 22, 2004; Pew Forum on Religion and Public Life, *Public Divided on Origins of Life* (Washington, D.C.: Pew Research Center for the People and the Press, 2005), National Academy of Sciences, http://www.nationalacademies.org.F. Newport, "Third of Americans Say Evidence Has Supported Darwin's Evolution Theory," *Gallup Poll*, November. 19, 2004.

2. C. Darwin, *The Autobiography of Charles Darwin and Selected Letters*, ed. F. Darwin (New York: Dover Publications, 1958), 29.

3. A good introductory book for a study of evolution is Ernest Mayr's *What Evolution Is* (New York: Basic Books, 2001). A more thorough examination is Richard Dawkins' *The Ancestor's Tale, A Pilgrimage to the Dawn of Life* (London: Phoenix Books, 2004). For the life of Darwin I have relied principally on his autobiography. See also J. Browne, *Charles Darwin. Vol. 1, Voyaging* (London: Jonathan Cape, 1995).

4. C. Darwin, *On the Structure and Distribution of Coral Reefs* ed. J. W. Williams (London: Walter Scott Publishing Co., ca. 1890), 181–82.

5. C. Darwin, *The Descent of Man and Selection in Relation to Sex*, 2nd ed. (London: John Murray, 1888), 156. For descriptions of alternative theories to natural selection, see P. J. Bowler, *The Eclipse of Darwinism* (Baltimore: Johns Hopkins University Press, 1992).

6. W. W. Howells, "Skull Shapes and the Map: Craniometric Analyses in the Dispersion of Modern Homo," *Peabody Museum Papers* (1989) 79:1–189. On the human genome see G. M. Church, "Genomes for all," *SA* 294 (1) (1989) 2006:46–55.

7. R. Cann and A. Wilson, "Mitochondrial DNA and Human Evolution," *N* 325, (1987): 31–36.

8. S. A. Tishkoff, et al., "Convergent Adaptation of Human Lactase Persistence in Africa and Europe," *NG*, December 10, 2006.

9. J. N. Wilford, "For Neanderthals and Homo Sapiens, Was It De-Lovely?" *NYT Science*, February 15, 2005, D4.

10. D. Serre, et al., "No Evidence of Neanderthal mtDNA Contribution to Early Modern Humans," *PLoS Biology* 2 (3) (March 2004).

11. A. Harmon, "Couples Cull Embryos to Halt Heritage of Cancer," *NYT*, September 3, 2006, A1.

12. Horace, *Book III*, Ode XXIX.

13. D. K. Sharpes and M. M. Peramas, "Accepting Evolution or Discarding Science," *Kappa Delta Pi Record* (Summer 2006): 156–60.

14. C. Zimmer, "A Fin is a Limb is a Wing: How Evolution Fashioned its Masterworks," *NG* 210 (5) (2006): 126–27.

15. M. T. Cicero, "On the Nature of the Gods," in *Brutus, On the Nature of the Gods. On Divination. On Duties*, trans. H. M. Poteat (Chicago: University of Chicago Press, 1950), 227.

16. Boethius, *The Consolation of Philosophy*, trans. V. E. Watts (New York: Penguin Books, 1969), 50.

17. M. S. Donovan and J. D. Bransford, ed. *How Students Learn: Science in the Classroom* (Washington, D.C.: National Research Council); and C. Scott, "Stand by Science," *Edutopia* 1 (4) (2005): 52–54; A. Hart, "Judge in Georgia Orders Anti-Evolution Stickers Removed From Textbooks," *NYT*, January 14, 2005, 16ff. Cf. also M. Malikow, "Engaging Students in Controversial Issues," *Kappa Delta Pi Record* 42 (3) (2006): 106–8.

18. S. Negri, *Kartchner Caverns State Park* (Phoenix: Arizona Department of Transportation, 1998), versus T. Vail, *Grand Canyon: A Different View* (Green Forest, AR: Master Books, 2003).

19. C. Darwin, *The Descent of Man, and Selection in Relation to Sex*, 2 vols. (London: John Murray, 1871).

Chapter 5

1. F. Fernandez-Armesto, *Civilizations* (London: Macmillan, 2000), 138ff.

2. Margot Adler, *Drawing Down the Moon, Witches, Druids, Goddess Worshippers, and Other Pagans in America Today* (New York: Penguin/Arkana 1986); Scott Cunningham, *Wicca, A Guide for the Solitary Practitioner* (St. Paul, MN: Llewellyn Publications, 1996); M. Gaskill, *Witchfinders, A Seventeenth-Century English Tragedy* (Cambridge, MA: Harvard University Press, 2005); M. K. Roach, *The Salem Witch Trials, A Day-by-Day Chronicle of a Community Under Siege* (Lanham, MD: Taylor Trade Publishing, 2002); and T. M. Luhrmann, *Persuasions of the Witch's Craft* (Cambridge, MA: Harvard University Press, 1991). Books about religion like Rabindranath Tagore's *The Religion of Man* (London: Unwin, 1988), and Mircea Eliade's prodigious work of scholarship, *A History of Religious Ideas* (Chicago: University of Chicago Press, 1978), were also helpful.

3. Eliade, *History of Religious Ideas*, 265–67.

4. C. S. Clifton, *Encyclopedia of Heresies and Heretics* (New York: Barnes & Noble, 1992), 79–80.

5. W. Durant and A. Durant, *The Renaissance* (New York: Simon & Schuster, 1953), 527.

6. M. Gaskill, *Witchfinders*, xiii.

7. Ibid.

8. Roach, *Salem Witch Trials*, xx.

9. Two books are notable: R. Plimpton, *Mary Dyer, Biography of a Rebel Quaker* (Boston: Branden Publishing, 1994), and E. S. Brinton's fictionalized biography, *My American Eden, Mary Dyer, Martyr for Freedom* (Shippensburg, PA: Burd Street Press, 2003). Remember Patience Whipple, a young girl of twelve when she made the journey on the Mayflower, has a diary of the events of the initial Puritan crossing and the first days of the settlement. Cf. Kathryn Lasky, *A Journey to the New World, The Diary of Remember Patience Whipple* (New York: Scholastic, no date).

10. Later, settling near New Amsterdam (later New York), Anne, together with fourteen members of her immediate family, were butchered in 1643 by Indians. Her youngest daughter, Susannah, was held hostage by the Indians for over two years and when released spoke only the native Indian language.

11. At the time William, son of William and Mary Dyer, captained small supply ships, and he had made a separate diversion to help free his mother. He would later become the seventh mayor of New York City.

12. Shelter Island was so named because it protected the Quaker community at the time but not because it was a safe haven for boats. The Quaker boats were always tied up stern first at the docks for quick getaways from Puritan authorities.

13. P. Boyer and S. Nissenbaum, *Salem Possessed, The Social Origins of Witchcraft* (Cambridge, MA: Harvard University Press, 1974), 10–11.

14. E. Goldscheider, "Witches, Druids and Other Pagans Make Merry Again in the Magical Month of May," *NYT*, May 28,2005, A11.

15. Euripedes, *The Bacchae*, vol. 1, trans. R. Potter (London: A. J. Valpy, 1832), 5.

16. R. Tagore, *The Religion of Man* (London: Unwin Paperbacks, 1931, 1988), 56ff.

Chapter 6

1. J. Maringer, *Gods of Prehistoric Man* (New York: Alfred A. Knopf, 1960). To project backward in time to make survival and ritualistic activities religious and spiritual, "is the key to the religious and spiritual life of ice-age man" that Maringer claims. But this is to superimpose modern religious beliefs on ancient hominids. But Maringer goes even further and without supporting evidence to claim that "the men of the last ice age buried their dead evidently believing in a physical afterlife." But burying the dead could have simply been a health problem unrelated to religion to avoid the stench of a rotting ancestor. (73)

2. I. Wunn, "Beginning of Religion," *Numen* 47 (4) (November 2000): 417–52.

3. *The Hymns of Orpheus*, 1993, 63. The Derveni Papyrus, discovered in 1962 and written in ca. 420 BCE, contains the theogeny of Orphic mysteries. It was found near Thessaloniki carbonized among funeral pyre ruins and is one of the oldest surviving Greek papyri, a primary document illuminating the religious and philosophical developments in the fifth and fourth centuries BCE. Even today some Greeks from Thessaloniki living within the shadow of Mount Olympus gather in a meadow to perform ancient rites honoring Zeus. A bearded man in a sleeveless yellow tunic officiates at a ceremony christening a young infant by throwing some grain into charcoal burners and, after dipping flowers in water, sprinkles the crowd. If these rituals—the incense at the

Mass, the sprinkling of holy water on the faithful by the priest, the eating of bread and wine, and the "mysteries" of the sacraments—sounds Christian it is because the ceremony was first an ancient Greek ritual. The movement's purpose is twofold: to increase awareness of Greece's ancient past, a world based on philosophical and scientific knowledge and not an apocalyptic vision, and to curb the power of the Greek Orthodox Church in a country where church and state are not separate. The clergy and church facilities in Greece, for example, are paid from general tax revenues. If this appears to be like a new age movement, then its seekers join a long list of those who want to return to a past and ethos that exist only within a framework of Christian rituals. (B. Carey, "For the Worst of Us, the Diagnosis May Be 'Evil,' *NYT*, February 8, 2005, D1–4).

4. W. Burkert, *Babylon, Memphis, Persepolis. Eastern Contexts of Greek Culture* (Cambridge, MA: Harvard University Press, 2004).

5. J. B. Bury et al., *CAH*, vol. 3 (New York: Macmillan, 1925), 102–8. Greek literature and the Bible and gospels have parallel themes, stories, and allegories that are directly traceable to Mesopotamian legends. There are countless affinities and similarities between Sumerian, Babylonian, and Akkadian epics and Homer, just as there are between the Bible and gospels and Homer. Apsu and Tiamat in the *Enuma Elish* recur in the *Iliad* as Oceanus and Tethys. Gilgamesh's voyage to find Utnapishtim is paralleled in Ulysses' voyage in *The Odyssey*. Endiku's ghost appearing to Gilgamesh is similar to the psyche of Patroklos appearing to Achilles. The female deity Ishtar becomes enraged in *The Epic of Gilgamesh* as does Aphrodite in the *Iliad*. Homer imitates the patient Ninsun in *Gilgamesh* with Penelope in *The Odyssey*. The gods are immortal in *Gilgamesh* as they are in the *Iliad*. Hera takes an oath by "heaven and earth" in the *Iliad* (15.36) as does Yahweh in Deuteronomy (4:26). These parallel themes, allusions, and allegories may seem trivial in individual instances, but taken together they constitute a compelling argument for scribal imitation.

6. G. S. Kirk et al., *The Presocratic Philosophers*, 2nd ed. (Cambridge: Cambridge University Press, 1983), 363.

7. Ibid., 366.

8. H. Arendt, *The Life of the Mind* (New York: Harcourt, 1978), 129–51.

9. For the Asian mind and religion, the inner meaning was not a God of cosmic identity but a God of the human personality. "The Super Soul which permeates all moving things, is the God of this human universe, whose mind we share in all our true knowledge, love and service, and whom to reveal in ourselves through renunciation of self is the highest end of life," R. Tagore, *The Religion of Man* (London: Unwin, 1988), 15.

10. Socrates to Theaetetus in Plato's *Theaetetus*, ed. I. Edman (New York: Modern Library, 1956), 506. Protagoras was born in Abdera in Thrace, lived in Athens, and was asked by Pericles to write a constitution. But of his life and career we know little, not even where he died, although legend says he drowned off the coast of Sicily. The main source for Protagoras is Plato, who lived in the following generation and who used his ideas extensively in two dialogues, *Protagoras* and *Theaetetus*. Other sources are Sextus Empiricus and Diogenes Laertius, both of whom wrote centuries afterward, so it is likely there is more fiction as fact.

11. Kirk, *Presocratic Philosophers*, 313.

12. J. Gernet, *A History of Chinese Civilisation*, vol. 1 (London: Folio Society, 2002), 88ff.

13. B. Watson, *Hsun Tzu, Basic Writings* (New York: Columbia University Press, 1966).

14. Twenty years after the discovery of the Zoroastrian book *Avesta*, Mozart composed *The Magic Flute* in 1791 with a hero he named Zarastro.

15. W. Durant and A. Durant, *The Age of Faith* (New York: Simon & Schuster, 1950), 178–202.

16. F. C. Grant, *Ancient Roman Religion* (New York: Liberal Arts Press, 1957), 162.

17. Durant and Durant, *Age of Faith*, 314.

18. A. S. Pease, *M. Tullis Ciceronis De Natura Deorum* (Cambridge, MA: Harvard University Press, 1958). ("Haec fere dicere habui de natura deorum, non ut eam tollerem sed ut intellegeretis quam esset obscura et quam difficiles explicatus haberet," 1224).

19. Grant, *Ancient Roman Religion*, xx–xxi.

20. http://www.thelatinlibrary.com/arnobius.html

21. E. K. Gazda, ed., *The Villa of the Mysteries in Pompei, Ancient Ritual, Modern Muse* (Ann Arbor: University of Michigan Museum of Art, 2000), 63. Plutarch became the head priest at Delphi the last twenty years of his life. C. J. Gianakaris, *Plutarch* (New York: Twayne Publishers, 1970).

22. *Plutarch's Moralia*, trans. C. King (London: George Bell & Sons, 1889), 258ff.

23. R. Turcan, *The Cults of the Roman Empire* (Oxford: Blackwell, 1996), 10ff.

24. J. B. Rives, *Religion and Authority in Roman Carthage from Augustus to Constantine* (Oxford: Clarendon Press, 1995), 96–99.

Chapter 7

1. The Phoenician in the *Heroikos*, early third century by Philostratus, in J. K. B. Maclean and E. B. Aitken, *Flavius Philostratus: Heroikus* (Atlanta: Society of Biblical Literature, 2001), 21.

2. An inscription with this designation was found over a Marcionite church in southern Syria dating to the late fourth century and may have referred to the Christ God of the gospels, the real God according to Marcion, and not the Greek term that referred to the Messiah promised by the Jews. Designated name changes were common. Gaius of the Julii clan became "Caesar"; Jesus of Nazareth became "Christ."

3. "*Tanta religio, et ea magna ex parte externa*," according to Livy. See Book 25, 1, 1–8 and Book 29, 14. See also F. C. Grant, *Ancient Roman Religion* (New York: Liberal Arts Press, 1957), 51ff. Cicero as augur in 53 BCE was a judge over cases involving religions, piety, ceremonies, fidelity to oaths, temples, shrines, and sacrifices as he describes in *The Nature of the Gods*, Book 1, 14. See also Grant, 87ff. For a study of such club groups and their variety in Carthage see J. B. Rives, *Religion and Authority in Roman Carthage from Augustus to Constantine* (Oxford: Clarendon Press, 1995), 204ff.

4. R. S. Wilson, *Marcion, A Study of a Second-Century Heretic* (London: James Clarke & Co., 1933); and cf. E. C. Blackman, *Marcion and His Influence* (London: SPCK, 1948).

5. E. Gibbon, *The Decline and Fall of the Roman Empire* (New York: Penguin Books, 1952), 314. The library at Alexandria established by Ptolemy, the first Greek ruler of Egypt, was the largest in the ancient world containing over a half million manuscripts. It was partially burned during the war in 47 BC. The libraries at Pergamun and Ephesus were also respected, though not as extensive in the number of its collection. The first library in Rome was not built until 40 BCE, followed by the great library of Octavian destroyed in 80. Calling them public, as we understand that term today, is a misnomer since books were not loaned out but only open to aristocrats and scholars. Private libraries, like Cicero's, Atticus or Varro or that of emperors, also contained important texts. Augustus founded two libraries in Rome, and Tiberius and Vespasian each started one. Vespasian collected items from the library at Jerusalem. Herculaneum like Pompeii had been buried by the eruption of Vesuvius in AD 79. The Villa of the Papyri, which appears to have been the seaside retreat of Calpurnius Piso, the father-in-law of Julius Caesar, in ancient Herculaneum, is the largest Roman villa ever found. It was partly and

imperfectly excavated in 1752–1755. Among the deposits archaeologists discovered the only intact library of texts from classical Roman times, more than 1,800 carbonized papyri rolls. Among the partial texts translated, most are of Epicurean philosophy, the popular intellectual pastime of Roman literati.

6. "Senatus Populusque Romanus Divo Tito Divi Vespasiani Filio Vespasiano Augusto," reads the inscription on the Arch. Titus is one of the seven kings mentioned in Revelation 17:9–11 where the "whore of Babylon" is a symbol of Rome.

7. P. McKechnie, *The First Christian Centuries* (Downers Grove, IL: InterVarsity Press, 2001).

8. I. M. White, *From Jesus to Christianity, How Four Generations of Visionaries and Storytellers Created the New Testament and Christian Faith* (San Francisco: Harper San Francisco, 2004), 295. It was a dilemma also described by Justin Martyr.

9. Philostratus, *Life and Times of Apollonius of Tyana* (New York: AMS Press, 1967). Cf. Maclean and Aitken, *Flavius Philostratus: Heroikus*; and G. R. S. Mead, *Apollonius of Tyana, The Philosopher-Reformer of the First Century A.D.* (New Hyde Park, NY: University Books, 1966).

10. Writing against Marcion in the third and fourth centuries were Justin Martyr, Irenaeus, Rhodon, Tertullian, Hippolytus of Rome, Epiphanius, and Ephraem. Marcion's own work, *Antithesis*, has not survived nor have writings favorable to his position. See White, *From Jesus to Christianity*, 408–11.

11. Eusebius quotes Irenaeus's *Against Heresies*. Eusebius, *The History of the Church from Christ to Constantine*, trans. G. A. Williamson (New York: Dorset Press, 1965), 163.

12. "Israel's ancient literature can be viewed increasingly as evolving out of the genres of kindred literatures." F. M. Cross, "The History of Israelite Religion," *BAR* 31 (3) (2005): 45. Cf. also D. K. Sharpes, *Lords of the Scrolls, Literary Traditions in the Bible and Gospels* (New York: Peter Lang Publishers, 2005).

13. Numenius, *Numenius Fragments*, trans. E. des Places Paris: Societe D'Edition Les Belles Lettres, 1973), 53.

14. Tertullian, *Q. Septimii Florentis Tertulliani Opera Omnia* (Wirceburgi: In Officina Libraria Staheliana, 1780). The argument against Marcion runs from 295 to 606 in my 1780 edition. Tertullian would have rhetorical fun making buffoonery out of Marcion's proclamations about two gods, one of the Old and one of the New Testament in his first two books against Marcion. But Tertullian would be on shakier ground in Book III when he tried to justify messianic prophecies from the Bible and where he ventures into theological speculation and allegory stretched with dubious hypotheses while projecting his own millennium message. His assumption in Book V that there is an obvious direct link and felicitous unity between the prophecies of the Bible and the activities recorded in the gospels is unconvincing.

15. T. D. Barnes, *Tertullian, A Historical and Literary Study* (Oxford: Clarendon Press, 1971).

16. The main Tertullian works cited are Tertullian *Q. Septimii Florentis Tertulliani Opera Omnia*, and *Tertullian's Prescription against hereticks; and the apologeticks of St. Theophilus Bishop of Antioch to Autolycus, against the malicious calumniators of the Christian religion, translated from their respective originals, with notes and preliminary dissertations* (Joseph Betty, Oxford, 1722). Also Eighteenth Century Collections Online. Gale Group. http://0-galenet.galegroup.com.library.lib.asu.edu:80/servlet/ECCO and Tertullian. *The Treatise Against Hermogenes*, trans. J. H. Waszink (Westminster, MD: Newman Press, 1956).

17. Tertullian, *Q. Septimii Florentis Tertulliani Opera Omnia*, vol. 2, 287, and the tract, *Adversus Hermogenem* continues to page 327. Among Christian apologists in the second century, where only fragments of references to their works remain, are Quadratus,

Aristides, Justin Martyr, Tatian, Melito, Claudius Apollinaris, Athenagoras, Theophilus, and Minucius Felix. See White, *From Jesus to Christianity*, 376–77.

18. Known from documents found among a large deposit of medieval manuscripts in the Cairo Genizah in the late nineteenth century. "For the apostates let there be no hope, and may the arrogant kingdom be uprooted speedily in our days, and may the Nazarenes and the heretics perish in a moment and be blotted out of the Book of Life, and not be inscribed with the righteous." McKechnie, *First Christian Centuries*, 87ff. Cf. also W. Durant and A. Durant, *Caesar and Christ* (New York: Simon & Schuster, 1944), 596–619.

19. P. Johnson, *A History of Christianity* (New York: Atheneum, 1976), 43.

20. C. Saumagne, *Saint Cyprien Eveque de Carthage "Pape" d'Afrique* (Paris: Editions du Centre National de la Recherche Scientifique, 1975), 112; and P. Hinchliff, *Cyprian of Carthage and the Unity of the Christian Church* (London: Geoffrey Chapman, 1974), 5–19, 88–90.

21. *Plutarch's Moralia*, trans. C. W. King (London: George Bell & Sons, 1889), 83. As a young student I was first introduced to Plutarch through John Dryden's (1631–1700) translations.

22. Maclean and Aitken, *Flavius Philostratus*, 19ff.

Chapter 8

1. Julian, *The Works of Emperor Julian*, vol. 1, trans. W. C. Wright (London: William Heinemann, 1913), viiff. Also see W. Durant and A. Durant, *The Age of Faith* (New York: Simon & Schuster, 1950), 10ff.

2. Ammianus Marcellinus, *The Later Roman Empire (A.D. 354–378)* (New York: Penguin Books, 1986), 88.

3. Ibid., 209.

4. Durant and Durant, *Age of Faith*, 12.

5. Marcellinus, *Later Roman Empire*, 61.

6. Ibid., 485 n.

7. Ibid., vol. 2, 418–19.

8. Julian, *Works of Emperor Julian*, 151.

9. Ibid., 205.

10. Ibid., vol. 2, 453.

11. Ibid., 297–339

12. Ibid., 303.

13. Marcellinus, *Later Roman Empire*, 279.

14. Julian, *Works of Emperor Julian*, vol. 3, 117.

15. Ibid., 123. In a letter to Atarbius.

16. Ibid., 127. In a letter to Hecebolius.

17. The Septuagint Greek in Exodus 33:20 reminds us that God says we cannot see his face (*prosopon*), although in another biblical contradiction Genesis 32:30 records that Jacob saw God "face to face" (*prosopon pros prosopon,* or in later passages *prosopon kata prosopon*), as did Moses in the same phrase repeated in Exodus 33:11, Numbers 12:7–8, and Deuteronomy 34:10. The Hebrew equivalent word, *paniym*, is close to the Greek *prosopon*. In Ezekiel 39:29: "Neither will I hide my face [*paniym*] any more from them: for I have poured out my spirit upon the house of Israel, says the Lord God." A strange metaphor occurs in Genesis 2:6 where the scribe describes the "face (*prosopon*) of the earth." Indeed, angels also have faces according to Acts 6:15.

18. Hebrews 9:24. In Hebrews 1:3 Paul uses the Greek *hypostasis* to refer to the person of Jesus. Are we to infer that *hypostasis* and *prosopon* are interchangeable? Scholars concede that Origen (ca. 185–254) may have been the first to discuss three

hypostases. Didymus of Alexandria (ca. 310–395) used the formula of "one substance and three persons" (*mia ousia, treis hypostaseis*). The Latin term *substantia* did not have the subtle distinctions or the fine tuning of the Greek word for substance (*ousia*) and could be too easily confused for the Latin meaning of "person."

19. Nestorius, *The Bazaar of Heracleides*, trans. G. R. Driver and L. Hodgson (Oxford: Clarendon Press, 1925), 166.

20. Ibid., 160.

21. Ibid., 95.

22. A. R. Vine, *The Nestorian Churches* (London: Independent Press, 1937). Babai, the first patriarch of a Nestorian church, declared in the late fifth century that the churches he regulated in Persia (including what is today Iraq) would simply be designated as the Church of the East, completely independent of Christian churches in the Roman Empire. Since Persia had been an enemy of Roman subjugation, Persians had been reluctant to entertain Christians perceiving them as a Roman influence. But when Nestorianism was condemned in the West and Christians were fleeing persecution and seeking refuge in Persia, the government thought it expedient to welcome the new religious movement that Rome opposed. The condemnation of Nestorians in the Roman Empire stimulated the movement in Persia. Political persuasion more than theological conviction contributed to the expansion of heresy. The dynasty ended when the Arabs overran Persia in 651.

23. Ibid., 131ff.

24. J. Ferguson, *Pelagius, A Historical and Theological Study* (Cambridge: W. Heffer & Sons, 1956).

25. Chaucer's tragedy of Hercules in the "Monk's Tale" of the *Canterbury Tales* is drawn from Boethius's work. See M. Gibson, *Boethius, His Life, Thought and Influence* (London: Basil Blackwell, 1981); G. O'Daly, *The Poetry of Boethius* (Chapel Hill: University of North Carolina Press, 1991); and Boethius, *Consolation of Philosophy*, trans. J. C. Relihan (Indianapolis: Hackett Publishing, 2001).

26. F. Fernandez-Armesto, *Civilizations* (London: Macmillian, 2000), 445.

27. Gibbon writes of him: "From the earth Boethius ascended to heaven in search of the Supreme Good; explored the metaphysical labyrinth of chance and destiny, or prescience and free-will, of time and eternity; and generously attempted to reconcile the perfect attributes of the Deity with the apparent disorders of his moral and physical government." E. Gibbon, *The Decline and Fall of the Roman Empire*, in *Great Books of the Western World*, ed. R. M. Hutchins (Chicago: Encyclopedia Britannia, 1952), 645.

28. L. G. Westerink, *Damascius, Traite Des Premiers Principes*, vol. 1 (Paris: Societe D'Edition Les Belles Lettres, 1986), xix and n1.

29. Especially chapter 15 of *The Alexiad of Anna Comnena*. Anna Comnena (1083–1153) is considered the first female historian. She was the daughter of Alexis I, Emperor in Constantinople, who wrote the history of the first crusade. For more information, see www.fordham.edu/halsall/basis/AnnaComnena-Alexiad15.html. Cf. S. Runciman, *The Medieval Manichee, A Study of the Christian Dualist Heresy* (Cambridge: Cambridge University Press, 1947), 63–93.

Chapter 9

1. The pointed arch appeared two centuries in the Middle East before it appeared on gothic churches in Europe. Arabs first used the magnetic needle for navigation and invented the astrolabe, a device Columbus used. The Alhambra in Granada in southern Spain is the epitome of a breath-taking explosion of shape, pattern, and color, the highest expression of architectural achievement of Arab civilization in Europe. The most exquisitely beautiful building in the world is in Agra, India, the marbled Taj Mahal, a mausoleum for the Sultan Shah Jahan and his favorite wife, Mumtaz Mahal. The scholar

Al-Birundi accurately determined longitude and latitude. The twelfth-century scholar Avicenna's work, *Canon*, an encyclopedia of medical knowledge, was required of all medical students in Europe until the seventeenth century. Arab doctors divided hospitals into wards for different diseases, a technique still used today. Europe got the decimal system after Arabs discovered it in India about 750. Arab scholars introduced the zero into the numbering system. Algebra, zenith, zero, almanac, orange, sugar, sofa, satin, coffee, and others are Arabic words. Europe had forgotten Greek, and so at places like Toledo and Cordoba, Greek and Greek texts, Hebrew and Arabic books were re-introduced and translated into Latin. Crusaders returned to Europe with sesame, cloves, rice, melons, dates, lemons, pepper, ginger, and coffee, previously unknown in Europe. Islamic artists raised woodcarving, glass-blowing, jewel-making, tile-glazing, and rug-making to new aesthetic levels. Arabs gave the West the guitar in all its various forms. (V. B. Mann, *Convivencia, Jews, Muslims, and Christians in Medieval Spain* (New York: George Braziller, 1992).

2. S. H. Nasr, *Science and Civilization in Islam* (New York: Barnes & Noble Books, 1968). Also Cf. M. Fakhry *M. Averroes (Ibn Rushd), His Life, Works and Influence* (Oxford: Oneworld, 2001). For a description of Islamic cultural contributions see D. K. Sharpes, "An Inquiry into Values of Islamic Fundamentalism," *Journal of Value Inquiry* XXI (1987): 309–15.

3. T. Aquinas, *The Summa Theologica*, vol. 2 (London: Burns, Oates & Washbourne, 1920), 147.

4. R. Bacon, *Speculum Alchymiae, The True Glass of Alchemy* (London: William Cooper, 1683); and R. Bacon, *Opus Majus*, trans. B. Burke (Philadelphia: University of Pennsylvania Press, 1928).

5. J. Riley-Smith, *The Oxford Illustrated History of the Crusades* (Oxford: Oxford University Press, 1997).

6. The language of the Second Council of Lyons in 1274 conveys some of the religious ethos that condemned those who helped the Saracens directly or indirectly and those who assisted the papacy in its campaigns. It even permitted slavery as an appropriate response. "Furthermore, since corsairs and pirates greatly impede those traveling to and from that Land, by capturing and plundering them, we bind with the bond of excommunication them and their principal helpers and supporters. We forbid anyone, under threat of anathema, knowingly to communicate with them by contracting to buy or sell. We also order rulers of cities and their territories to restrain and curb such persons from this iniquity; otherwise it is our wish that prelates of churches exercise ecclesiastical severity in their land. We excommunicate and anathematize, moreover, those false and impious Christians who, in opposition to Christ and the Christian people, convey to the Saracens arms and iron, which they use to attack Christians and timber for their galleys and other ships; and we decree that those who sell them galleys or ships, and those who act as pilots in pirate Saracen ships, or give them any help or advice by way of machines or anything else to the detriment of Christians and especially of the holy Land, are to be punished with deprivation of their possessions and are to become the slaves of those who capture them . . . Those who refuse to comply shall be most strictly compelled to do so by a sentence of excommunication against their persons and an interdict on their lands, unless the malice of the wrongdoers is so great that they ought not to enjoy peace . . . We therefore . . . unto all those who undertake this work of crossing the sea to aid the holy Land, in person and at their own expense, full pardon for their sins about which they are truly and heartily contrite and have spoken in confession, and we promise them an increase of eternal life at the recompensing of the just. To those who do not go there in person but send suitable men at their own expense, according to their means and status, and likewise to those who go in person but at others' expense, we grant full pardon for

their sins." See the following website for more information: http://www.geocities.com/Heartland/Valley/8920/churchcouncils/Ecum14.htm

7. M. Barber, *The Trial of the Templars* (London: Folio Society, 2003). Cf. also A. Demurger, *The Last Templar, The Tragedy of Jacques de Molay Last Grand Master of the Temple* (London: Profile Books, 2005).

8. Ibid. The papal bull, Milites Templi, in 1144 awarded indulgences to any benefactor of the Templars. Thomas Aquinas grappled philosophically, and unsuccessfully, with the convoluted theological issue of when crusader indulgences became effective. In 1145 Milicia Dei gave the Templars papal permission to build chapels and bury their dead in churchyards.

9. Ibid., 80–81.

10. Two noteworthy texts on the Cathars are S. Runciman, *The Medieval Manichee, A Study of the Christian Dualist Heresy* (Cambridge: Cambridge University Press, 1947), and M. Barber, *The Cathars, Dualist Heretics in Languedoc in the High Middle Ages* (Harlow, Essex, England: Longman, 2000). Runciman describes Gerbert of Aurillac, whom he says was Archbishop-Elect of Reims, as suspicious of heresy. He fails to note that Gerbert, a brilliant investigator and mathematician, actually became Archbishop of Ravenna and later was Pope Sylvester II, hardly a heretic.

11. "Attack the followers of heresy more fearlessly even than the Saracens—since they are more evil—with a strong hand and a stretched out arm," wrote Innocent III in March 1208. Milton's *Paradise Lost* poetically describes the battle in heaven between the forces of God and Lucifer waged with cannons, the latest in firepower in the seventeenth century. The Great Satan does not win, but the struggle exemplifies the forces of evil frequently ascribed by American presidents to nations opposed to their policies.

12. T. Aquinas, *The Summa Contra Gentiles*, vol. 1 (London: Burns, Oates & Washbourne, 1924), 84–86, 155–58, and 203–4.

13. Ibid., vol. 3, 16. Aquinas uses arguments from scripture: "God saw all the things that he had made, and they were good" (Gen. 1:31), and "He has made all things good in their time" (Eccles. 3:11). Perhaps had Aquinas had considered this passage in Job 9:16 where the prophet proclaims: "The earth is given into the hands of the wicked; he covers the faces of its judges. If it is not he, then who is it?" as the passage implies there might be evil God.

14. English translation © 1996 by Nancy P. Stork, of trials from 1318 to 1325, available online at http://www.2sjsu.edu/depts/english/Fournier/amilhac.htm Others brought to trial during these years included Agnes Francou (member of the sect of the Poor of Lyons), Arnaud Gélis (drunkard and prognosticator), Baruch (Jew baptized under threat of death), Béatrice de Planissoles, Grazide Lizier (widow and priest's concubine), Guillemette Battegay (widow), Jacqueline den Carot (scoffer), and Navarre Bru (widow).

15. P. Abelard, *The Story of My Misfortunes* (New York: Macmillan, 1972). See also B. Radice, *Abelard and Heloise, The Story of His Misfortune and the Personal Letters* (London: Folio Society, 1977).

16. C. Frayling, *Strange Landscape, A Journey Through the Middle Ages* (London: BCA, 1995); and H. R. Loyn, *The Middle Ages, A Concise Encyclopaedia* (London: Thames & Hudson, 1989).

17. N. Cantor, *The Civilization of the Middle Ages* (New York: Harper Perennial, 1993).

18. B. Boyer and R. McKeon, *Peter Abelard, Sic et Non, A Critical Edition*, vols. 1–6 (Chicago: University of Chicago Press, 1976).

19. Bacon, *Speculum Alchymiae*, 127; Bacon, *Opus Majus*,; and J. H. Bridges, *The Life and Work of Roger Bacon* (London: Williams & Norgate, 1914).

20. J. S. Brewer, *Fr. Rogeri Bacon, Opera Quaedam Hactenus Inedita* (London: Longman, Green, Longman, & Roberts, 1859). Also useful is the biography by Brian Clegg, *The First Scientist, A Life of Roger Bacon* (London: Constable, 2003).

21. A. G. Little, *Roger Bacon, Essays on the Seventh Centenary of his Birth* (Oxford: Clarendon Press, 1914).

22. Brewer, *Fr. Rogeri Bacon*, xciv.

23. P. L. Sideldo, "The Condemnation of Roger Bacon," *JMS* 22 (1) (1996): 60–81.

24. M. Paris, *Matthew Paris's English History from the Year 1235 to 1273*, vol. 2 (London: Henry G. Bohn, 1853), 175.

25. Ibid., 336.

26. Ibid., 336–37.

27. Ibid., 88. For a sample of the invective cf. Matthew Paris: "For the evil name of the papal court, the stench of which exhaled its foul smoke even to the clouds" is a common enough description found throughout his history (Ibid., 48).

Chapter 10

1. To receive a benefice, normally bestowed for life, there were procedures specified in canon law in which clerics received an income, generally derived from property donated to the church, for prescribed duties like saying Mass. Though unknown in America, the practice is still common in Canada and Europe.

2. From roughly 1300 to 1500 Europe was grounded in feudalism and ecclesiastical privileges. To understand this period, consult Langland's *Piers Plowman* and Chaucer's *Canterbury Tales* for an understanding of the peasantry who constituted about 75 percent of the population, who would be subject to the lord of the manor or castle, and/or subservient to the bishop. The Peasants' Revolt of 1381 testified to the legal and taxation abuses they suffered. For an understanding of the economic and political history of the period see the chronicler of the age Matthew Paris, *Matthew Paris's English History from the Year 1235 to 1273*, vol. 2 (London: Henry G. Bohn, 1853); and G. M. Trevelyan, *England in the Age of Wycliffe* (London: Longmans, Green & Co., 1912). N. Cantor's, *The Last Knight, The Twilight of the Middle Ages and the Birth of the Modern Era* (New York: Free Press, 2004), is a good read centered around the life of John of Gaunt.

3. On the other hand, priests were one of the few literate classes in society for kings to recruit able administrators.

4. John of Gaunt (1340–1399) became Wycliffe's regal protector. John was the fourth son of Edward III, the brother of Richard, the Black Prince, and held the title of Duke of Lancaster. In 1377 he acted as viceroy for the aging Edward and, though unpopular because of his war losses in France, ruled England until 1386. He was Geoffrey Chaucer's patron, gave him a pension, a rented house in London, and posts as collector of customs and two ambassadorships, one each to France and Italy.

5. Wycliffe's fuller explanation occurs in his *Tractatus de Apostasia* probably written in 1383. Cf. J. Wyclif, *Tractatus de Apostasia*, ed. M. H. Dziewicki (London: Trubner & Co., 1889), 58ff. "Et illa communis fictitia qua dicitur quod sacramentum eukaristie sit accidens sine subjecto, et nimis heretica; quod autem non sit accidens patet alibi; et quod non sine subjecto, et per consequens tunc no habet deum vel humanitatem Christi ad quemlibet eius punctum; quia utrumque istorum necessario et subjectum: deitas, relationi racionis, et humanitas omni generi accientis" (59). "It's a heresy to call the Eucharist first a sacrament and second an accident without a subject. I have proved the first point elsewhere. If there is no subject there is no substance; if there is no substance, there is no God, and no manhood of Christ in any of its parts."

6. W. Durant and A. Durant, *The Reformation, A History of European Civilization from Wyclif to Calvin 1300–1564* (New York: Simon & Schuster, 1957), 39–45. Papal

documents, letters, and council renunciations about Wycliffe, Hus, and others are in E. Peters, *Heresy and Authority in Medieval Europe, Documents in Translation* (Philadelphia: University of Pennsylvania Press, 1980).

7. J. Stacey, *John Wyclif and Reform* (Philadelphia: Westminster Press, 1964), 34. In 2006 Benedict XVI dropped the title patriarch of the West, first proclaimed in 642. But popes still retained all other titles including bishop of Rome, vicar of Christ, successor of the prince of the apostles, supreme pontiff of the universal church, primate of Italy, archbishop and metropolitan of the province of Rome, sovereign of Vatican City, and servant of the servants of God.

8. "For when someone in exchange for money performs a service or ministers in an office in which the Holy Spirit is conferred, he not only makes money his god but sacrifices both persons to the idol he serves." J. Wyclif, *On Simony*, trans. T. A. McVeigh (New York: Fordham University Press), 41.

9. Count Lutzow, *The Life and Times of Master John Hus* (London: J. M. Dent & Co., 1909). I drew about Hus largely from this biased, convoluted prose but comprehensive biography. Hus's principal work is *Tractatus de Ecclesia*, ed. S. H. Thomson (Cambridge: W. Hefer & Sons Ltd., 1956).

10. The belief that unworthy ministers cannot dispense worthy sacraments originated in the fourth century with Donatus, examined in an earlier chapter. The Synod of Arles condemned this schism in 314. But followers of the movement established their own church hierarchy and within a few years their numbers exceeded that of the other faithful Christians, with each city having opposing bishops. Augustine wrote against this schism that vanished totally with the Islamic invasion a couple of centuries later.

11. J. B. Russell, *Dissent and Order in the Middle Ages, The Search for Legitimate Authority* (New York: Twayne Publishers, 1992), 93.

12. P. Whitfield, *Astrology, A History* (New York: Harry N. Abrams, 2001), 123. Among the notable medieval proponents of a natural study of astrology were Robert Grosseteste, Roger Bacon, Albertus Magnus, and Thomas Aquinas.

13. Dante Gabriel Rossetti, *The Early Italian Poets*, ed. S. Purcell Berkeley: University of California Press, 1981), 264ff.

14. Ibid., 273.

15. Marsiglio of Padua, *Writings on the Empire, Defensor Minor and De Translatione Imperii*, ed. C. J. Nederman (Cambridge: Cambridge University Press, 1993). Cf. also A. Gerwirth, trans. and ed., *Marsilius of Padua, The Defender of Peace, The Defensor Pacis* (New York: Harper Torchbooks, 1967).

16. Gerwirth, *Marsilius of Padua*, 427.

17. Peters, *Heresy and Authority in Medieval Europe*, 230–31.

18. R. Pernoud and M-V. Clin, *Joan of Arc, Her Story* (New York: St. Martin's Griffin, 1999). On the psychiatry of her voices see D. B. Smith, "Can You Live with the Voices in Your Head," *NYTM* (March 25, 2007): 49–53.

19. Her trial from which we learn nearly everything about her is D. Hobbins, trans., *The Trial of Joan of Arc* (Cambridge, MA: Harvard University Press, 2005).

20. S. K. Greenslade, *The Work of William Tindale* (London: Blackie & Son Ltd., 1938), 39. Cf. also the lively biography by B. Moynahan, *William Tyndale: If God Spare My Life* (London: Abacus, 2002).

21. Humphrey Monmouth was released from the tower when no evidence could be found against him. He would later be sheriff of London and escort Thomas More to the scaffold. Cf. Moynahan, *William Tyndale*, 121.

22. Greenslade *Work of William Tindale*, 152.

23. W. Tyndale, *Doctrinal Treatises and Introductions to Different Portions of the Holy Scriptures* (Cambridge: University Press, 1848), xviii.

24. Ibid., 381–82.

25. Moynahan, *William Tyndale*, 229ff.

26. T. M. C. Lawler, G. Marc'Hadour, and R. C. Marius, *The Complete Works of St. Thomas More*, vol. 6, parts 1 & 2 (New Haven, CT: Yale University Press, 1981), 153.

27. Ibid., lix.

28. L. Martines, *Fire in the City, Savonarola and the Struggle for Renaissance Florence* (Oxford: Oxford University Press, 2006). Lest we forget that these heretical ideas in the late Middle Ages about the role of scripture and who can interpret its meaning, we should recall the contemporary example of Nasr Hamid Abu Zayd, born in 1943 in Egypt, an Arabic and Islamic scholar living in exile in The Netherlands because of his arguments in favor of hermeneutics, the interpretation of the Koran in its historical context. He received his PhD in Islamic studies in 1981 and was a professor at Cairo University until fundamentalists prompted an Islamic court to convict him of apostasy. Based on this decision, a similar court ruled his marriage invalid because a Muslim woman cannot be married to an apostate. Since 1995 he lived in exile in Holland with his wife at both the University of Leiden and Utrecht. In 2005 he received the Ibn Rushd prize for Freedom of Thought in Berlin.

Chapter 11

1. From G. Bruno's, *The Expulsion of the Triumphant Beast* (*Spaccio de la Bestia Trionfante*), written in 1564, in A. D. Imerti's translation (New Brunswick, NJ: Rutgers University Press, 1964), 69. Cf. G. Bruno, The *Cabala of Pegasus* (New Haven, CT: Yale University Press, 2002) and *Cause, Principle and Unity, Essays on Magic* (Cambridge, UK: Cambridge University Press, 1998).

2. His real first name was Filippo and his monastic given name was Giordano. For his writings or books about him, cf: G. Bruno, *The Expulsion of the Triumphant Beast*; C. Turnbull, *Life and Teachings of Giordano Bruno, Philosopher, Martyr, Mystic* (Philadelphia: David McKay, 1913); and: I. L. Horowitz, *The Renaissance Philosophy of Giordano Bruno* (New York: Coleman-Ross, 1952):and D. W. Singer's classic study, *Giordano Bruno, His Life and Thought* (New York: Henry Schuman, 1950). P. Johnson, *The Renaissance* (London: Phoenix Press, 2000).

3. Bruno, *Expulsion of the Triumphant Beast*, 110.

4. Ibid., 268–69

5. Ibid., 236.

6. Bruno, *Cabala of Pegasus*, 56.

7. Cardinal Robert Bellarmine, Jesuit personal theologian and counselor to Clement VIII, former professor of theology at the University of Louvain, was present at Bruno's trial in Rome. Just fifteen years later in 1630 he would preside over the trial of Galileo. Bellarmine was canonized in 1930 by Pope Pius XII. More than a half century later, Pope John Paul II would officially apologize for the trial of Galileo and repudiate its results.

8. Papal bull against heretics originated with Pope Innocent III in *Cum ex officio nostri* in 1207, and later inquisitions established by order of Innocent IV in 1250 in the papal bulls *Cum negotium* and *Licet sicut acceptimus*. The first inquisitions were directed against the Cathars in southern France. The notorious Spanish Inquisition effectively operated on its own without Roman involvement. Cf. E. Peters, *Inquisition* (New York: Free Press, 1988).

9. White, *The Pope and the Heretic*, 159–60.

10. For writings of More attacking heretics cf. L. Schuster et al., eds., *The Complete Works of St. Thomas More*, vol. 8, parts 1 and 2 (New Haven, CT: Yale University Press, 1973).

11. P. Ackroyd, *The Life of Thomas More* (London: Vintage, 1999).

12. Ibid., 202.

13. More, *Utopia*, in *Complete Works of St. More*, 47.

14. Ibid., 52.

15. D. Kinney, ed., *The Complete Works of St. Thomas More*, vol. 15 (New Haven: Yale University Press, 1986), 149.

16, T. M. C. Lawler, et al., *The Complete Works of St. Thomas More*, vol. 6, part 1 (New Haven, CT: Yale University Press, 1981), 162ff. The style is in Renaissance English, but even in translation gains nothing in sonorous or easy-to-follow prose.

17. Ibid., 239.

18. J. Jones, *Thomas More* (Boston: Twayne Publishers, 1979), 86ff.

19. G. Rodis-Lewis, *Descartes, His Life and Thought* (Ithaca, NY: Cornell University Press, 1998). Cf. F. S. Gaukroger, *Descartes, an Intellectual Biography* (Oxford: Clarendon Press, 1995).

20. Descartes, *A Discourse on Method* (London: J. M. Dent & Sons, 1941).

21. Ibid., 4.

22. Ibid., 27.

23. B. Spinoza, *The Correspondence of Spinoza* (New York: Russell & Russell, 1966), 146.

24. M. Stewart, *The Courtier and the Heretic, Leibnitz, Spinoza, and the Fate of God in the Modern World* (New York: W. W. Norton, 2005), 33ff.

25. *Tractatus Theologico-Politicus* (London: Trubner & Co., 1862). There were multiple prohibitions and edicts against either the reading or publications of Spinoza's works by church authorities.

26. Ibid., 26.

27. B. Spinoza, *Ethic*, trans. W. H. White (London: T. Fisher Unwin, 1894).

28. Stewart, *The Courtier and the Heretic*, 209.

29. In Spinoza's *Correspondence*, letter 48. Cf. also W. Durant and A. Durant, *Our Oriental* Heritage (New York: Simon & Schuster, 1963), 631.

30. Ibid., 135.

31. D. Bodanis, *Passionate Minds* (New York: Crown Publishers, 2006), 62.

32. K. Frenkel, "Why Aren't More Women Physicists?" *SA* 296 (2) (2007): 90–92.

33. Bodanis, *Passionate Minds*, 292–93.

34. "The White Bull," in Voltaire, *The Best Known Works of Voltaire* (New York: Book League, 1940), 96–118. Cf. A. Maurois, *Voltaire* (London: Thomas Nelson & Sons, 1932); Voltaire, *Philosophical dictionary* (New York: Viking Penguin, 1972); and J. Morley, *The Works of Voltaire*, vols. 1, 23, 41, 41 (limited edition of 190 copies in 42 volumes, edition 39) (Paris & London: E. R. Dumont, 1901).

35. G. Lanson, *Voltaire* (New York: John Wiley & Sons, 1960), 116. This slender volume was first published in 1906.

36. Voltaire, *Candide or optimism* (New York: W. W. Norton, 1966); and *Candide and other writings* (New York: Modern Library, 1956).

Chapter 12

1. Antonia Fraser, *Mary Queen of Scots* (New York: Random House/Delta, 1969).

2. By 1562 Catholics and Huguenots were at war in France after the Duke of Guise fired on a Protestant prayer meeting. The St. Bartholomew's Day Massacre began later, on August 24, 1572, and lasted for months. Tens of thousands of Huguenots died in the prolonged violence.

3. The actresses Katharine Hepburn and Audrey Hepburn were descendants, though not immediately related to each other.

4. Less than a week after Edward's death on July 6, 1553, Lady Jane Grey (1537–1554), also a great-granddaughter of Henry VII, was proclaimed Queen of England through the instigation of her supporter the Duke of Northumberland who had been

Regent to Edward VI. Mary Tudor, however, as Henry VIII's eldest daughter, was the rightful heir to the throne according to Henry's will. Jane Grey was queen for nine days. Mary Tudor and her followers rode into London and imprisoned Jane Grey, her husband, and father in the Tower of London. They were later executed after a second uprising in their name. The death of a cousin for claiming the right to the throne had set a precedent Elizabeth would follow over thirty years later.

    5. http://ccat.sas.upenn.edu/~jmcgill/association.html. Winston Churchill's synopsis of Mary in *A History of the English-Speaking Peoples*, vol. 2 (London: Cassell & Co., 1956) is short but readable.

    6. S. Stolpe, *Christina of Sweden* (New York: Macmillan, 1966); and G. Masson, *Queen Christina* (New York: Farrar, Straus, & Giroux, 1968).

    7. W. Durant and A. Durant, *The Age of Reason Begins* (New York: Simon & Schuster, 1961), 562ff.

    8. Masson, *Queen Christina*, 84ff. Masson cites love letters written to one of her favorite women, Ebba "Belle" Sparre, later in her life as evidence, and that they shared a bed frequently throughout their lives.

    9. S. Gaukroger, *Descartes, An Intellectual Biography* (Oxford, Clarendon Press, 1995), 412ff.

    10. The halls of her palace were filled with art stolen from the Emperor Rudolph's collection in Prague specifically seized for her. These spoils of war remain in Stockholm. Cf. Masson, *Queen Christina*, 121ff. Most of her sculptures from Rome are in the Prado in Madrid. Christina left everything at her death to Cardinal Azzolino, who in turn left his estate to his nephew from whom these treasures were purchased by Philip V of Spain.

    11. Later in her life, in 1668, she sent agents to Warsaw inquiring about her candidacy for the Polish throne. It was a misguided quest but reveals her hopes of returning to financial security.

    12. Quietism among Catholics, Pietism among Protestants, is a form of religious mysticism practiced among Hindus and Buddhists.

    13. http://www.macalester.edu/~adupay/ElizabethViews.htm. Also A. Nye, *The Princess and the Philosopher, Letters of Elisabeth of the Palatine to Rene Descartes* (Lanham, MD: Rowman & Littlefield, 1999), 9–10. For the French see L. Petit, *Descartes et la Princesse Elisabeth, Roman d'amour Vecu* (Paris: Editions A. G. Nizer, 1969), 57–59.

    14. Ibid. "Si ma conscience demeurait satisfaite des prétextes que vous donnez à mon ignorance, comme des remèdes, je lui aurais beaucoup d'obligation, et serais exempte du repentir d'avoir si mal employé le temps auquel j'ai joui de l'usage de la raison, qui m'a été d'autant plus long qu'à d'autres de mon âge, que ma naissance et ma fortune me forcèrent d'employer mon jugement de meilleure heure, pour la conduite d'une vie assez pénible et libre des prospérités qui me pouvaient empêcher de songer à moi, comme de la sujétion qui m'obligerait à m'en fier à la prudence d'une gouvernante." http://www.ac-nice.fr/philo/textes/Descartes-Elisabeth/Descartes Elisabeth.htm#ED13091645 Cf. A. Nye, *Princess and the Philosopher*.

Chapter 13

    1. We are familiar with the purpose of an encyclopedia today but an argument was needed for explaining the first one to a literate audience in the middle of the eighteenth century. It could not be the work of one man, like Samuel Johnson's *Dictionary of the English Language* that appeared in 1755, since no one man could know everything. "Quand on vient a considerer la matiere immense d'une distinctement, c'est que ce ne peut etre l'ouvrage d'un seul home . . . Je ne peux convenir de ce principe, je ne crois point qu'il soit donne a un seul homme de connatitre tout ce qui peut etre connu . . .,

Diderot, *Les Pages Immortelles de Diderot*, choisies et expliquees par E. Herriot (Paris: Editions Correa, 1979), 84–85). It would take time and many hands would be involved in its composition: "Concluons donc qu'on n'executera jamais un bon vocabulaire sans le secours d'une grand nombre de talents, pace que les definitions de noms ne diffent point des definitions des choses, et que les chose ne peuvent etre bien definiies our decrites que pare ceux qui en ont fait une longue etude." (Ibid., 87).

2. D. Diderot, *Dialogues*, trans. F. Birrell (Port Washington, NY: Kennikat Press, 1971), 177.

3. Ibid., 35.

4. D. Diderot, *Jacques the Fatalist and His Master* (New York: Penguin Books, 1986), 44.

5. Ibid., 57.

6. Silas Deane, reporting to the Continental Congress, November 29, 1776, in W. Durant and A. Durant, *Rousseau and Revolution* (New York: MJF Books, 1967), 922.

7. An escapement is a small, notched wheel in a watch with metal teeth that control the regularity of the intervals of the movement.

8. G. Lemaitre, *Beaumarchais* (New York: Alfred A. Knopf, 1949), 21–5. Others, such as J. Sungolowsky, *Beaumarchais* (New York: Twayne Publishers, 1974), and A. Ruskin, *Spy for Liberty* (New York: Pantheon Books, 1965), are inferior.

9. In addition to *The Barber of Seville* (1775) and *The Marriage of Figaro* (1785), he wrote four other plays: *Eugenie* (1767), *Les Deux Amis* (1770), *Tarare* (1787), and *L'Autre Tartuffe* (1793). Hugh Thomas's *Beaumarchais in Seville* (New Haven, CT: Yale University Press, 2006) is a lively retelling of the Spanish adventures in 1764–1765.

10. F. Grendel, *Beaumarchais, The Man Who Was Figaro* (New York: Thomas Y. Crowell, 1977), 294. "Qu'etais-je donc? Je n'etais rien que moi, et moi tel que je suis reste, libre au milieu des fers, serein dans les plus grand dangers, faisant tete a tous les orages, menant les affaires d'une main et la gueree de l'autre, parsesseux comme un ane et travillant toujours, en butte a mille calumnies, mais heureux dans mon interieur, n'ayant jamais ete d'aucune coterie, ni litteraire, ni politique, ni mystique, n'ayant fait de cour a personne, et partant repousse de tours." Cf. C. Borgal, *Beaumarchais* (Paris: Editiones Universitaires, 1972), 4.

11. The College des Quatre Nations (named for the places where the medieval students came from) was founded by Cardinal Mazarin, who donated his extensive library to it in his will, and was also known as College Mazarin, a part of the University of Paris.

12. H. Guerlac, *Antoine-Laurent Lavoisier, Chemist and Revolutionary* (New York: Charles Scribner's Sons, 1975). Lavoisier's text, first published in 1776, is *Traite de Chimie Elementaire, Theorique et Pratique* (Brussels: Canongette et Compannie, 1829).

13. A. Donovan, *Antoine Lavoisier, Science, Administration, and Revolution* (Oxford: Blackwell, 1993), 242ff. Agriculture was the chief industry. France had a population of nearly 25 million in 1784 and all but 2 million lived in the countryside. Cf. W. Durant and A. Durant, *Rousseau and Revolution*, 927ff.

14. A.-N. Condorcet, *Sketch for a Historical Picture of the Progress of the Human Mind*, trans. J. Barraclough (London: Weidenfeld & Nicolson, 1955), 24. His predecessor in this kind of work was likely Turgot's Latin discourse, commissioned by the Sorbonne, *Progrés Successifs De L'ésprit Humain* (1750) that outlined Turgot's philosophy of history who also argued that human societies pass through cycles of barbarism and civilization. Cf. J. S. Schapiro, *Condorcet and the Rise of Liberalism* New York: Octogon Press, 1963).

15. K. M. Baker, *Condorcet, Selected Writings* (Indianapolis: Bobbs Merrill Co., 1976), 111.

16. Turgot was *contrôleur général* (minister of finance) under King Louis XVI from 1774 to 1776. He had a deep influence upon Adam Smith, who was living in France in the 1760s. Many of the concepts in Smith's *Wealth of Nations* (1776) are drawn directly from Turgot.

17. Probability theory was first discovered by Blaise Pascal in 1654 but he only calculated from games of chance and never thought of the math theory as socially adaptable.

18. Baker, *Condorcet, Selected Writings,* 115.

19. Ibid., 117.

Appendix A

1. I. M. White, *From Jesus to Christianity, How Four Generations of Visionaries and Storytellers Create the New Testament and Christian Faith* (San Francisco: Harper San Francisco, 2004), 34.

GLOSSARY

Academus	A local Athenian god
Amen	meaning "so be it;" derives from Amun, Egyptian god
Apatheia	freedom from passion; self-control
Apocalypse	revelation
Apocrypha	non-canonical early Christian books
Apostasy	standing apart, deserter
Apostle	representative
Aramaic	Semitic language related to Hebrew
Arête	virtue; a combination of goodness, excellence & virtue
Atheist	not a god-believer
Basileia	kingdom
Basileus	originally, King
Basilica	palace, but more commonly a large building
Bishop	overseer
Blasphemy	evil speech
Canon	guideline; straight edge
Catholic	universal
Charisma	special gift
Christ	Anointed one (with oil) (see Messiah)
Deacons	ministers or servants
Devas	Hindu word for divinities (English = devils)
Dike	justice, law
Dynamis	power
Christos	The Anointed One (see Messiah)
Ecclesia	assembly (see synagogue)
Ecstasy	literally, out of oneself
Eirene	peace
Epinoia	creative consciousness
Episcopus	overseer; bishop
Eschatology	study of a vision of a divine utopia
Eucharist	gratitude; to show favor
Eudaemonia	literally, good demons; a state of well-being
Evangel	good news or gospel (angel = messenger)

Exegesis	to explain; text interpretation
Gnosis	knowledge
Hairesis	heresy, choice
Heterodoxy	different opinion
Historia	inquiry
Homoeusian	similar in substance
Homousian	consubstantial = of one substance with
Horkos	an oath (literally, a fence)
Hubris	pride, insolence
Hypostasis	to stand under; a foundation or support
Infidel	non-believer
Kabbalah	tradition (mystical Judaism)
Kurios	Lord
Laos	the people (English = laity)
Logos	thought, reason
Martyr	witness
Messiah	Anointed One (Hebrew)
Mishnah	to repeat and study; interpretations of the Torah
Moira	fate; a man's due
Nomos	a law, convention or moral norm
Nous	for Plato, the highest form of the soul; more generally, mind
Oikonomia	household management
Orthodox	right way
Pagan	peasant (Latin pagus = country)
Pantheism	god everywhere
Pantheon	all gods
Paradosis	tradition
Physis:	instincts, appetites, impulses
Pistis	trust, pledge
Pleroma	the Gnostic fullness of the Godhead
Pneuma	spirit, breath (English = pneumatic)
Presbyters	elders
Pseudepigraphia	false or non-accepted writings
Psyche	soul
Rhema	one word
Scripture	writings
Synoptic	taken together
Sophia	wisdom
Sophosyne	moderation, discretion, temperance
Synagogue	gathering (see ecclesia)
Techne	art, craft
Telos	end, purpose (teleology = study of design in nature)

REFERENCES

Abelard, P. 1972. *The Story of My Misfortunes*. New York: Macmillan.

Ackroyd, P. 1999. *The Life of Thomas More*. London: Vintage.

Adkins, L. and R. Adkins. 1991. *Introduction to the Romans*. Secaucus, NJ: Chartwell Books.

Adler, M. 1986. *Drawing Down the Moon, Witches, Druids, Goddess-Worshippers, and Other Pagans in America Today*. New York: Penguin/Arkana.

Aeschylus. 1833. *The Tragedies*, translated by R. Potter. London: A. J. Valpy.

Aeschylus. 1965. *Aeschylus*, edited by R. W. Corrigan. New York: Dell.

Afnan, R. M. 1965. *Zoroaster's Influence on Greek Thought*. New York: Philosophical Library.

Ajami, F. 1998. *The Dream Palace of the Arabs, a Generation's Odyssey*. New York: Vintage Books.

Akenson, D. H. 1998. *Surpassing Wonder, The Invention of the Bible and the Talmuds*. New York: Harcourt Brace.

Aldred, C. 1998. *The Egyptians*. 3rd ed. London: Thames and Hudson.

———. 1988. *Akhenaten, King of Egypt*. London: Thames & Hudson.

Ali, A. H. 2006. *The Caged Virgin, An Emancipation Proclamation for Women and Islam*. New York: Free Press.

Allegro, J. 1956. *The Dead Sea Scrolls, A Reappraisal*. Baltimore: Penguin Books.

Allix, P. and S. R. Maitland. 1832. *Facts and Documents Illustrative of the History, Doctrine and Rites of the Ancient Aligenes and Waldenses*. London: Rivington, 344–50.

Aquinas, T. 1920. *The Summa Theologica*. Part 1, London: Burns Oates & Washbourne.

———. 1924. *The Summa Contra Gentiles*. Vol. 1. London: Burns, Oates & Washbourne.

Arendt, H. 1978. *The Life of the Mind*. New York: Harcourt.

Aries, P. and G. Duby. 1987. *A History of Private Life, from Pagan Rome to Byzantium*. Cambridge, MA: Harvard University Press.

Aristophanes. 1955. *Five Comedies of Aristophanes*, translated by B. B. Rogers. Garden City, NY: Doubleday Anchor Books.

———. 1968. *Clouds*, edited by K. J. Dover. Oxford: Clarendon Press.

———. 1979. *Clouds, Women in Power, Knights*, translated by K. Macleish. Cambridge: Cambridge University Press.

Aristotle. 1975. *The Nicomochean Ethics*, translated by D. Ross. London: Oxford University Press.

———. 1984. *The Complete Works of Aristotle, The Revised Oxford Translation*. Princeton, N.J.: Princeton University Press.

Armstrong, K. 2001. *The Battle for God*. New York: Ballantine Books.

———. 2000. *Islam, A Short History*. New York: Modern Library.

———. 1993. *A History of God, The 4,000-Year Quest of Judaism, Christianity and Islam*. New York: Ballantine Books.

Arndt, W. F., and F. W. Gingrich. 1979. *A Greek-English Lexicon of the New Testament and Other Early Christian Literature*. Chicago: University of Chicago Press.

Ashe, G. 1968. *Gandhi*. New York: Stein & Day.

Attridge, H. W., and R. A. Oden. 1981. *Philo of Byblos, The Phoenician History*. Washington, DC: Catholic Biblical Association of America.

Auden, W. H. 1948. *The Portable Greek Reader*. New York: Viking Press.

Auge, C., and J.-M. Dentzer. 2000. *Petra, the Rose-Red City*. London: Thames & Hudson.

Augustine, 1960. *The Confessions*. Garden City, NJ: Doubleday.

———. 1998. *The Confessions*, translated by H. Chadwick. Oxford: Oxford University Press.

———. 1950. *The City of God*. New York: Modern Library.

Aurelius, M. 1952. "Meditations." In *Great Books of the Western world*, edited by R. M. Hutchins. Chicago: Encyclopaedia Britannica.

Aveni, A. 2002. *Conversing with the Planets, How Science and Myth Invented the Cosmos*. Boulder: University Press of Colorado.

Avesta, Gathas. 1963. *The Hymns of Zarathustra*, translated by J. Duchesne Guillemin. Boston: Beacon Press.

Ayer, A. J. 1988. *Thomas Paine*. New York: Atheneum.

Backhouse, J. 1981. *The Lindisfarne Gospels*. Oxford: Phaidon.

Bacon, R. 1683. *Speculum Alchymiae, The True Glass of Alchemy*. London: William Cooper.

———. 1928. *Opus Majus*, translated by B. Burke. Philadelphia: University of Pennsylvania Press.

Bahn, P. G. 1997. *Lost Cities*. New York: Barnes & Noble.

Bailey, C. 1935, reprint 1969. *Religion in Virgil*. New York: Barnes & Noble.

Baker, K. M. 1976. *Condorcet Selected Writings*. Indianapolis: Bobbs-Merrill.

Balter, M. 2005. "The Seeds of Civilization." *Smithsonian* 36 (2): 68–74.

Bar, C. July 2003. "The Christianization of Rural Palestine During Late Antiquity." *Journal of Ecclesiastical History* 54 (3) 401–21.

Barber, M. 2003. *The Trial of the Templars*. London: Folio Society.

———. 2000. *The Cathars, Dualist Heretics in Languedoc in the High Middle Ages*. Harlow, Essex, England: Longman.

Bar-Efrat, S. 1989. *Narrative Art in the Bible*. Sheffield, UK: Almond Press.

Barnard, L. W. 1967. *Justin Martyr, His Life and Thought*. Cambridge, UK: Cambridge University Press.

Barnes, J. 1995. *The Cambridge Companion to Aristotle*. Cambridge: Cambridge University Press.

Barnes, T. D. 1998. *Ammianus Marcellinus and the Representation of Historical Reality*. Ithaca, NY: Cornell University Press.

——— 1993. *Athanasius and Constantius, Theology and Politics in the Constantinian Empire*. Cambridge, MA: Harvard University Press.

———. 1994. *From Eusebius to Augustine, Selected Papers 1982–1993*. Brookfield, VT: Variorum.

———. 1971. *Tertullian, A Historical and Literary Study*. Oxford: Clarendon Press.

Bartlett, J. R. 1982. *Jericho*. Guildford, Surrey: Lutterworth Press.

Bartlett, J. R., ed. 1997. *Archaeology and Biblical Interpretation*. London: Routledge.

Barzun, J. 2000. *From Dawn to Decadence, 1500 to the Present*. New York: Perennial.

———. 1989. *The Culture We Deserve*. Middletown, CT: Wesleyan University Press.

Bayral, M. 1985. *Secret Ephesus*. Izmir, Turkey: Ticaret Matbaacilik.

Bell, R., translated, with a critical re-arrangements of the Surahs. *The Qur'an*. Edinburgh: T & T Clark, 1937, 1960.

Benario, H. W. 1991. *Tacitus' Agricola, Germany, and Dialogue on Orators*. Norman: University of Oklahoma Press.

Bergman, C. 1996. *Orion's Legacy, A Cultural History of Man as Hunter*. New York: Dutton.

Bion of Smyrna. 1997. *Bion of Smyrna, The Fragments and the Adonis*, edited by J. D. Reed. Cambridge: Cambridge University Press.

Birley, A. 1993. *Marcus Aurelius, A Biography*. London: Batsford.

Blackman, E. C. 1948. *Marcion and His Influence*. London: SPCK.

Bleeker, C. J. 1973. *Hathor and Thoth, Two Key Figures of The Ancient Egyptian Religion.* Leiden: E. J. Brill.

Bloom, A. 1987. *The Closing of the American Mind.* New York: Simon & Schuster.

Bloom, H. 1990. *The Book of J.* New York: Vintage Books, Random House.

Bloom, P. 2005. "Is God an Accident?" *Atlantic Monthly* 296 (5): 105–12.

Boardman, J.,J. Griffin, and O. Murray 1991. *The Oxford History of the Roman World.* Oxford: Oxford: Oxford University Press.

Bock, K. 1994. *Human Nature Mythology.* Urbana: University of Illinois Press.

Bodanis, D. 2006. *Passionate Minds.* New York: Crown Publishers.

Boethius. 2001. *Consolation of Philosophy,* translated by J. C. Relihan. Indianapolis: Hackett Publishing.

Boisselier, J. 1993. *The Wisdom of the Buddha.* London: Thames & Hudson.

Bonaventure. 1993. *The Journey of the Mind to God.* Indianapolis: Hackett Publishing.

Borgal, C. 1972. *Beaumarchais.* Paris: Editiones Universitaires.

Bourbon, F. 1999. *Petra, Jordan's Extraordinary City.* New York: Barnes & Noble.

Bourke, V. J. 1993. *Augustine's Quest for Wisdom.* Albany, NY: Magi Books.

——. 1960. *The Pocket Aquinas.* New York: Washington Square Press.

Boutcher, W. October 2003. "The Analysis of Culture Revisited: Pure Texts, Applied Texts, Literary Historicisms, Cultural Histories." *Journal of the History of Ideas* 64 (3): 489–510.

Bovon, F. Summer 2003. "Canonical and Apocryphal Acts of Apostles." *Journal of the History of Ideas* 11 (2): 165–94.

——. 2000. "Fragment of Oxyrhynchus 840, Fragment of a Lost Gospel, Witness of an Early Christian Controversy Over Purity." *Journal of Biblical Literature* 119 (4): 705–28.

Bowen, J. 1972. *A History of Western Education, Vol. 1, The Ancient World.* London: Metheun & Co.

Bowler, P. J. 1992. *The Eclipse of Darwinsim.* Baltimore: Johns Hopkins University Press.

Boyer, B., and R. McKeon. 1976. *Peter Abelard, Sic et Non, A Critical Edition.* Vols. 1–6. Chicago: University of Chicago Press.

Boyer, P., and S. Nissenbaum. 1974. *Salem Possessed, The Social Origins of Witchcraft.* Cambridge, MA: Harvard University Press.

Brandscheid, F. ed. 1901. *Novum Testamentum Graece.* Friborg: Sumptibus Herder.

Brettler, M. Z. 1995. *The Creation of History in Ancient Israel.* London: Routledge.

Brewer, J. S. 1859. *Fr. Rogeri Bacon, Opera Quaedam Hactenus Inedita.* London: Longman, Green, Longman, & Roberts.

Bridges, J. H. 1914. *The Life and Work of Roger Bacon.* London: Williams & Norgate.

Bright, J. 2000, 1946. *A History of Israel.* 4th ed. Louisville: Westminster John Knox Press.

Brinton, E. S. 2003. *My American Eden, Mary Dyer, Martyr for Freedom.* Shippensburg, PA: Burd Street Press.

Brisson, L. 1998. *Plato the Myth Maker.* Chicago: University of Chicago Press.

Broder, J. M. March 11, 2006. "Muslim's Blunt Criticism of Islam Draws Threats and Some Hope." *New York Times,* A1.

Bronowski, J., and B. Mazlish. 1960. *The Western Intellectual Tradition.* New York: Harper & Brothers.

Bronowski, J. 1973. *The Ascent of Man.* Boston: Little Brown.

Broshi, M. 2003. "What Jesus Learned from the Essenes, the Blessing of Poverty, the Bane of Divorce." *Biblical Archaeology Review* 30 (1): 32ff.

Brown, M. P. 1998. *The British Library Guide to Writing and Scripts, History and Techniques.* London: British Library.

Brown, R. 1995. *Managing the Learning of History.* London: David Fulton Publishers.

Browne, J. 1995. *Charles Darwin.* London: Jonathan Cape.

Browne, L. 1946. *The World's Great Scriptures.* New York: Macmillan.

Browning, E. B. 1896. *Prometheus Bound and Other Poems.* London: Ward, Lock & Bowden.

Bruno, G. 1564; reprint, 1964. *The Expulsion of the Triumphant Beast,* translated by A. D. Imerti. New Brunswick, NJ: Rutgers University Press.

———. 1585; reprint, 2002. *The Cabala of Pegasus.* translated and annotated by Sidney L. Sondergard and Madison U. Sowell. New Haven, CT: Yale University Press.

———. 1583; reprint, 1998. *Cause, Principle and Unity, Essays on Magic.* translated and edited by Robert de Lucca and Richard J. Blackwell Cambridge UK: Cambridge University Press.

Brunschwig, J., and G. E. R. Lloyd, eds. 2003. *The Greek Pursuit of Knowledge.* Cambridge, MA: Belknap Press of Harvard University Press.

Brunwasser, M. January/February 2005. "The Gods Return to Olympus." *Archaeology* 58 (1): 63–70.

Buber, M. 1965. *Between Man and Man.* New York: Collier Macmillan.

Budge, E. A. W. 1983; reprint, 1910. *Egyptian language, Easy Lessons in Egyptian Hieroglyphics.* New York: Dover Publications.

———. 1911; reprint, 1973. *Osiris and the Egyptian Resurrection.* Vol. 1. New York: Dover Publications.

———. 1899; reprinted, 1980. *Egyptian Religion, Egyptian Ideas of the Future Life.* London: Routledge & Kegan Paul.

———. 1895, reprinted, 1967. *The Egyptian Book of the Dead, The Papyrus of Ani.* New York: Dover Publications.

Buell, D. K. 1999. *Making Christians, Clement of Alexandria and the Rhetoric of Legitimacy.* Princeton, NJ: Princeton University Press.

Bulfinch, T. 1855; reprinted, 1962. *The Age of Fable.* New York: New American Library.

Bullock, A. 1985. *The Humanist Tradition in the West.* New York: W. W. Norton.

Bulyer, E. 1872. *The Odes and Epodes of Horace.* London: George Routledge & Sons.

Burckhardt, J. 1979. *Reflections on History.* Indianapolis, IN: Liberty Fund.

———. 1880; reprinted, 1949. *The Age of Constantine the Great.* Berkeley: University of California Press.

Burke, P. 1997. *Varieties of Cultural History.* Ithaca, NY: Cornell University Press.

Burkert, W. 2004. *Babylon, Memphis, Persepolis. Eastern Contexts of Greek Culture.* Cambridge, MA: Harvard University Press.

Burkitt, F. C. 1925. *The Religion of the Manichees.* New York: AMS Press.

Burn, L. 1990. *Greek Myths.* London: British Museum.

Buruma, I. 2006. *Murder in Amsterdam, The Death of Theo Van Gogh and the Limits of Tolerance.* New York: Penguin Press.

Bury, J. B., S. A. Cook, and F. E. Peacock. 1925. *The Cambridge Ancient History.* Vol. 3. New York: Macmillan.

Cahill, T. 2003. *Sailing the Wine-Dark Sea, Why the Greeks Matter.* New York: Nan A. Talese/Doubleday.

Caldwell, C. April 3, 2005. "Daughter of the Enlightenment." *New York Times Magazine,* 26–31.

Callimachus. 1960. *Callimachus, Hymns and Epigrams,* translated by G. R. Mair. Cambridge, MA: Harvard University Press.

———. 1988. *Callimachus, Hymns, Epigrams, Select Fragments.* Baltimore: Johns Hopkins University Press.

Campbell, J., ed. 1955. *The Mysteries, Papers from the Eranos Yearbooks.* Bollingen Series. Vol. 2. Princeton, NJ: Princeton University Press,

————. 1987. *The Masks of God: Primitive Mythology.* New York: Penguin.

————. 1990 *The Hero's Journey, Joseph Campbell on his Life and Work.* San Francisco: Harper San Francisco.

————. 1988. *Joseph Campbell, the Power of Myth.* With Bill Moyers. New York: Doubleday.

Cann, R., and A. Wilson. 1987. "Mitochondrial DNA and Human Evolution." *Nature* 325: 31–36.

Cantor, N. 2004. *The Last Knight, The Twilight of the Middle Ages and the Birth of the Modern Era.* New York: Free Press.

————. 2003. *Antiquity, The Civilization of the Ancient World.* New York: HarperCollins.

————. 2001. *In the Wake of the Plague, The Black Death and the World It Made.* New York: Perennial.

————. 1993. *The Civilization of the Middle Ages.* New York: Harper Perennial.

————. 2001. *In the Wake of the Plague, The Black Death and the World It Made.* New York: Harper Perennial.

Carey, B. February 8, 2005. "For the Worst of Us, the Diagnosis May Be 'Evil.'" *New York Times*, D1–4.

Carmichael, C. M. 1996. *The Story of Creation, Its Origin and its Interpretation in Philo and the Fourth Gospel.* Ithaca, NY: Cornell University Press.

Carmichael, J. 1989. *The Birth of Christianity, Reality and Myth.* New York: Dorset Press.

Carson, C., and K. Shepard. 2001. *A Call to Conscience, The Landmark Speeches of Dr. Martin Luther King, Jr.* New York: Warner Books.

Carter, J. 1986. *The Blood of Abraham.* Boston: Houghton Mifflin.

Carter, J. B. 1906. *The Religion of Numa.* London: Macmillan & Co.

Casson, L. 1962. *Selected Satires of Lucian.* Chicago: Aldine Publishing.

Catullus, G. V. 1966. *The Poems of Catullus*, translated by P. Whigham. London: Penguin.

Celsus. 1987. *On the True Doctrine, A Discourse Against the Christians*, translated by R. J. Hoffmann. New York: Oxford University Press.

Chait, R. P. 2002. *The Questions of Tenure.* Cambridge, MA: Harvard University Press.

Chesterton, G. K. 1933. *St. Thomas Aquinas.* London: Hodder & Stoughton.

Choufrine, A. 2002. *Gnosis, Theophany, Theosis, Studies in Clement of Alexandria's Appropriation of His Background.* New York: Peter Lang.

Church, G. M. 2006. "Genomes for all." *Scientific American* 294 (1): 2006:46–55.

Churchill, W. 1956. *A History of the English-Speaking Peoples.* Vol. 2. London: Cassell & Co.

Churton, T. 1987. *The Gnostics.* New York: Barnes & Noble.

Cicero. 1950. *Brutus. On the Nature of the Gods. On Divination. On Duties*, translated by H. M. Poteat. Chicago: University of Chicago Press.

————. 1951. *The Basic Works of Cicero*, edited by M. Hadas. New York: Modern Library.

————. 1892. *Life and Letters.* Edinburgh: W. P. Nimmo, Hay, & Mitchell.

Clark, K. 1969. *Civilisation.* London: Penguin Books.

Clifton, C. S. 1992. *Encyclopedia of Heresies and Heretics.* New York: Barnes & Noble.

Clegg, B. 2003. *The First Scientist, A Life of Roger Bacon.* London: Constable.

Clement of Alexandria. 1715. *Opera Quae Extant.* Oxford: Georgii Mortlock.

————. 1953, 1972. *Clement of Alexandria*, translated by G. W. Butterworth. Cambridge, MA: Harvard University Press.

326   *References*

————. *Clement of Alexandria, Stromateis*, translated by J. Ferguson. Washington, DC: Catholic University of America Press.

Cobban, A. 1957. *A History of Modern France, Vol. 1: 1715–1799*. London: Penguin.

Cochrane, C. N. 1940; reprinted, 2003. *Christianity and Classical Culture, A Study of Thought and Action from Augustus to Augustine*. Indianapolis, IN: Liberty Fund.

Condorcet, A-N. de 1955. *Sketch for a Historical Picture of the Progress of the Human Mind*, translated b y J. Barraclough. London: Weidenfeld & Nicolson.

Conner, J. A. 2004. *Kepler's Witch*. San Francisco: Harper San Francisco.

Coope, J. A. 1995. *The Martyrs of Cordoba, Community and Family Conflict in an Age of Mass Conversion*. Lincoln: University of Nebraska Press.

Copeston, F. 1959. *A History of Philosophy*. Westminster, MD: Newman Press.

Covington, R. 2003. "Mesopotamian Masterpieces." *Smithsonian* 14 (5): 68–71.

Cremin, L. 1977. *Traditions of American Education*. New York: Basic Books.

Cresson, A. 1962. *The Essence of Ancient Philosophy*. New York: Walker & Co.

Crick, F. 1994. *The Astonishing Hypothesis: The Scientific Search for Soul*. New York: Charles Scribner.

Cross, F. M. 2005. "The History of Israelite Religion." *Biblical Archaeology Review* 31 (3): 42–45.

Crossan, J. D., and J. L. Reed. 2004. *In Search of Paul, How Jesus's Apostle Opposed Rome's Empire with God's Kingdom*. San Francisco: Harper San Francisco.

Cumont, F. 1956. *The Mysteries of Mithra*. New York: Dover Publications.

Cunningham, Scott. 1996. *Wicca, A Guide for the Solitary Practitioner*. St. Paul, MN: Llewellyn Publications.

Cupit, D. 1984. *The Sea of Faith, Christianity in Change*. London: British Broadcasting Corp.

Danielou, J. 1955. *Origen*. New York: Sheed & Ward.

Dante. 1966. *The Divine Comedy*, translated by L. Biancolli. New York: Washington Square Press.

Daraul, A. 1989. *Secret Societies*. New York: MJF Books.

Darwin, C. 1979. *The Illustrated Origin of the Species*. New York: Hill & Wang.

————. 1888. *The Descent of Man and Selection in Relation to Sex*. 2nd ed. London: John Murray.

————. 1958. *The Autobiography of Charles Darwin and Selected Letters*, edited by F. Darwin. New York: Dover Publications.

————. n.d., ca. 1890. *On the Structure and Distribution of Coral Reefs*, edited by J. W. Williams. London: Walter Scott Publishing Co.

————. 1998. *The Expression of the Emotions in Man and Animals*. London: HarperCollins.

Dawkins, R. 2004. *The Ancestor's Tale, A Pilgrimage to the Dawn of Life*. London: Phoenix Books.

Dawson, C. 1958. *Religion and the Rise of Western Culture*. New York: Image Books.

Dean, C. September 20, 2005. "Challenged by Creationists, Museums Answer Back."*New York Times*, D1.

Deane, H. A. 1963. *The Political and Social Ideas of St. Augustine*. New York: Columbia University Press.

Demurger, A. 2005. *The Last Templar, The Tragedy of Jacques de Molay Last Grand Master of the Temple*. London: Profile Books.

Dennis, C. August 31, 2005. "Chimp Genome: Branching Out." *Nature* 437, 7055, 17ff.

De Sandoli, S. 1984. *Calvary and the Holy Sepulcher*. Jerusalem: Franciscan Printing Press.

Descartes, R. 1941. *A Discourse on Method*. London: J. M. Dent.

De Selincourt, A. 1962. *The World of Herodotus*. London: Phoenix Press.

References 327

DeWitt, N. W. 1954. *St. Paul and Epicurus.* Minneapolis: University of Minnesota Press.

Diderot, D. 1986. *Jacques the Fatalist and His Master.* New York: Penguin Books.

———. 1979. *Les Pages Immortelles de Diderot.* Choisies et expliquees par E. Herriot. Paris: Editions Correa.

———. 1927; reprint, 1971. *Dialogues,* translated by F. Birrell. Port Washington, NY: Kennikat Press.

———. 1961. *La Religieuse.* Paris: Librarie Armand Colin.

Digeser, E. D. 2004. "An Oracle of Apollo at Daphne and the Great Persecution." *Classical Philology* 99 (1): 57–77.

Diodorus. 1985. *Diodorus on Egypt,* translated by E. Murphy. Jefferson, NC: McFarland & Co.

Diogenes Laertius. 1959. *Lives of Eminent Philosophers.* Vols. 1–2, translated by R. D. Hicks. Cambridge, MA: Harvard University Press.

Donovan, A. 1993. *Antoine Lavoisier, Science, Administration, and Revolution.* Oxford: Blackwell.

Donovan, M. S., and J. D. Bransford, ed. *How Students Learn: Science in the Classroom.* Washington, D.C.: National Research Council.

Drummond, J. 1888. *Philo Judaeus, or the Jewish-Alexandrian Philosophy in its Development and Completion.* Edinburgh: Williams & Norgate.

Duffield, G. E. 1965. *The Work of William Tyndale.* Philadelphia: Fortress Press.

Duncan, R. 1951. *Selected Writings of Mahatma Gandhi.* Boston: Beacon Press.

Dundes, A. 1984. *Sacred Narrative, Readings in the Theory of Myth.* Berkeley: University of California Press.

Durando, F. 1997. *Ancient Greece, The Dawn of the Western World.* New York: Barnes & Noble.

Durant, W., and A Durant. 1975. *The Age of Napoleon.* New York: MJF Books.

———. 1967. *Rousseau and Revolution.* New York: MJF Books.

———. 1926; reprinted, 1961. *The Story of Philosophy.* Garden City, NJ: Garden City Publishing Co.

———. 1935; reprinted, 1963. *Our Oriental Heritage.* New York: Simon & Schuster.

———. 1966. *The Life of Greece.* New York: Simon & Schuster.

———. 1944. *Caesar and Christ.* New York: Simon & Schuster.

———. 1950. *The Age of Faith.* New York: Simon & Schuster.

———. 1957. *The Reformation, A History of European Civilization from Wyclif to Calvin 1300–1564.* New York: Simon & Schuster.

———. 1961. *The Age of Reason Begins.* New York: Simon & Schuster.

———. 1953. *The Renaissance.* New York: Simon & Schuster.

Dyson, R. W. 1998. *Augustine, The City of God Against the Pagans.* Cambridge: Cambridge University Press.

Edman, I. 1956. *The Works of Plato.* New York: Modern Library.

Edwards, I. E. S. 1971. *The Cambridge Ancient History.* 3rd ed. Vols. 1–2. Part 2. Cambridge: Cambridge University Press.

Ehrman, B. D. 2003a. *Lost Christianities, The Battle for Scripture and the Faiths We Never Knew.* New York: Oxford University Press.

———. 2003b. *Lost Scriptures, Books that did not Make it into the New Testament.* New York: Oxford University Press.

Eisenman, R., and M. Wise. 1994. *The Dead Sea Scrolls Uncovered.* New York: Barnes & Noble.

Eliade, M. 1978. *A History of Religious Ideas, from the Stone Age to the Eleusinian Mysteries.* Vol. 1, translated by W. R. Trask. Chicago: University of Chicago Press.

Elitzur, Y., and D. Nir-Zevi. May/June 2004. "Four-Horned Altar Discovered In Judean Hills." *Biblical Archaeology* 30 (3): 35–39.

328   *References*

Elliott, D. February 2002. "Seeing Double: John Gerson, The Discernment of Spirits and Joan of Arc." *American Historical Review* 107 (1).

Ellis, J. J. July 31, 2005. "Founding Father of the American Left." *New York Times Book Review*, 15.

Elsner, J. 2003. "Archaeologies and Agendas: Reflections on Late AncientJewish and Early Christian Art." *Journal of Roman Studies* 83: 114–28.

Epictetus. 1942. *Moral Discourses*. New York: E. P. Dutton & Co.

———. 1952. *The Discourses of Epictetus*. In*Great Books of the Western World*, edited by R. M. Hutchins. Chicago: Encyclopedia Britannica.

Epicurus. 1995. *A Guide to Happiness*. London: Phoenix.

Easterling, P. E., and B. M. W. Knox. 1985. *The Cambridge History of Classical Literature*. Vol. 1. Cambridge: Cambridge University Press.

Euripides. 1996. *Heracles*, edited by S. A. Barlow. Warminster, UK: Aris & Phillips.

———. 1832. *Euripides*. Vols. 1–3, translated by R. Potter. London: A. J. Valpy.

———. 1832. *The Bacchae*. Vol. 1, Translated by R. Potter. London: A. J. Valpy. 1–50.

———. 1955. *The Complete Greek Tragedies*, translated byR. Lattimore. Chicago: University of Chicago Press.

Eusebius. 1965. *The History of the Church from Christ to Constantine*, translated by G. A. Williamson. New York: Dorset Press.

Evans, J. A. S. 1982. *Herodotus*. Boston: Twayne Publishers.

Fakhry, M. 2001. *Averroes (Ibn Rushd), His Life, Works and Influence*. Oxford: Oneworld.

Fellows, O. 1989. *Diderot, Updated Edition*. Boston: Twayne Publishers.

Ferguson, J. 1980. *Callimachus*. Boston: Twayne Publishers.

———. 1956. *Pelagius, A Historical and Theological Study*. Cambridge: W. Heffer & Sons.

Fernandez-Armesto, F. 2000. *Civilizations*. London: Macmillan.

Feuerbach, L. 1989. *The Essence of Christianity*, translated by G. Eliot. Amherst, NY: Prometheus Books.

Filoramo, G. 1990. *A History of Gnosticism*, translated by A. Alcock. Cambridge, MA: Basil Blackwell.

Fisher, I., and E. Povoledo. 2006. "Italy Grants Asylum to Afghan Christian Convert." *New York Times*, March 30, A12.

Flussas, F. 1574. *Mercurij Trismegisti Pimandras Utraque Lingua Restitutus Burdigale*: Apud Simonem Millangium Burdigallensium Typrograhum via Jacobea.

Foner, E. 1976. *Tom Paine and Revolutionary America*. New York: Oxford University Press.

Forde, N. W. 1975. *Cato the Censor*. Boston: Twayne Publishers.

Fowler, S. September 15, 2006. "Turkey, a Touchy Critic, Plans to Put a Novel on Trial." *New York Times*, A4.

France, P. 1983. *Diderot*. Oxford: Oxford University Press.

———. 1993. *Greek as a Treat, An Introduction to the Classics*. London: BBC Books.

Frankfurter, D. 1998. *Religion in Roman Egypt*. Princeton: Princeton University Press.

Franklin, B. B., and F. Rosenthal. 1976. *Shahrastani on the Indian Religions*. The Hague: Mouton.

Fraser, A. 1969. *Mary Queen of Scots*. New York: Random House/Delta.

Frayling, C. 1995. *Strange Landscape, A Journey Through the Middle Ages*. London: BCA.

Frazer, J. G. 1923. *Fork-Lore in the Old Testament*. New York: Tudor Publishing Co.

Freedman, D. N. 1998. *The Leningrad Codex*. Grand Rapids, MI: William B. Eerdmans.

Freeman, C. 2003. *The Closing of the Western Mind, the Rise of Faith and the Fall of Reason*. New York: Knopf.

Freeman, K. 1952. *God, Man and State, Greek Concepts*. Boston: Beacon Press.

Frenkel, K. 2007. "Why Aren't More Women Physicists?" *Scientific American* 296 (2): 90–92.

Friedly, M., and D. Gallen. 1993. *Martin Luther King, Jr., The FBI File*. New York: Carroll & Graf Publishers.

Friossart, J. 1901. *The Chronicle of Froissart*, translated by J. Bourcher in 1523. London: David Nutt.

Gainsford, P. 2003. "Formal Analysis of Recognition Scenes in the Odyssey." *Journal of Hellenic Studies* 123: 41–59.

Gaskill, M. 2005. *Witchfinders, A Seventeenth-Century English Tragedy*. Cambridge, MA: Harvard University Press.

Gaukroger, S. 1995. *Descartes, An Intellectual Biography*. Oxford: Clarendon Press.

Gaur, A. 1984. *A History of Writing*. New York: Charles Scribner's Sons.

Gaustad, E. S. 2005. *Roger Williams*. New York: Oxford University Press.

Gazda, E. K., ed. 2000. *The Villa of the Mysteries in Pompei, Ancient Ritual, Modern Muse*. Ann Arbor: University of Michigan Museum of Art.

Geertz, C. March 23, 2006. "Among the Infidels." *New York Review of Books*, 23–24.

Gernet, J. 2002. *A History of Chinese Civilisation*. Vol. 1. London: Folio Society.

Geronimo. 1970. *Geronimo, His Own Story*, edited byS. M. Barrett. New York: Ballantine Books.

Gerwirth, A., trans. and ed. 1967. *Marsilius of Padua, The Defender of Peace, The Defensor Pacis*. New York: Harper Torchbooks.

Gianakaris, C. J. 1970. *Plutarch*. New York: Twayne Publishers.

Gibbon, E. 1952. *The Decline and Fall of the Roman Empire*. New York: Penguin.

Gibson, M. 1981. *Boethius, His Life, Thought and Influence*. London: Basil Blackwell.

Gilgamesh. 1960. *The Epic of Gilgamesh*, translated by N. K. Sandars. Hammondsworth, England: Penguin Books.

Glover, T. R. 1920. *The Conflict of Religions in the Early Roman Empire*. 9th ed. London: Metheun & Co.

Goldman, M. December 2004. "The God Gene: How Faith is Hardwired into Our Genes." *Nature Genetics* 36, 1241.

Goldscheider, E. May 28, 2005. "Witches, Druids and Other Pagans Make Merry Again in the Magical Month of May." *New York Times*, A11.

Gollnick, J. 1999. *The Religious Dreamworld of Apuleius' Metamorphoses: Recovering a Forgotten Hermeneutic*. Waterloo, Ontario: Wilfrid Laurier University Press.

Goodenough, E. R. 1940. *An Introduction to Philo*. New York: Barnes & Noble.

Goodman, M. 1997. *The Roman World, 44 BC–AD 180*. New York: Routledge.

Goranson, S. 1994. "Qumran, A Hub of Scribal Activity?" *Biblical Archaeology Review* 20 (5), 37–39.

Gordon, C. H. 1962. *Before the Bible, The Common Background of Greek and Hebrew Civilization*. New York: Harper & Row.

———. 1968; reprinted, 1987. *Forgotten Scripts*. New York: Dorset Press.

Gordon, C. H., and G. A. Rendsburg. 1997. *The Bible and the Ancient Near East*. 4th ed. New York: W. W. Norton.

Gotoff, H. G. 1993. *Cicero's Caesarian Speeches*. Chapel Hill: University of North Carolina Press.

Gould, S. J. 1989. *Wonderful Life, The Burgess Shale and the Nature of History*. New York: W. W. Norton.

———. 1999. *Rocks of Ages: Science and Religion in the Fullness of Life*. New York: Ballantine Books.

———. 2002. *The Structure of Evolutionary Theory*. Cambridge, MA: Belnap Press.

Grant, F. C. 1957. *Ancient Roman Religion*. New York: Liberal Arts Press.

330 *References*

Grant, M. 1975. *The Twelve Caesars*. New York: Barnes & Noble.

———. 1977. *Jesus, An Historian's Review of the Gospels*. New York: Charles Scribner's Sons.

———. 1992. *Readings in the Classical Historians*. New York: Scribner's.

Grant, R. M. 1961. *Gnosticism, A Source Book of Heretical Writings From the Early Christian Period*. New York: Harper & Bros.

Graves, R. 1955; reprinted, 1992. *The Greek Myths*. London: Penguin Books.

——— 1951. *The Transformations of Lucius Otherwise Known as the Golden Ass*. New York: Farrar, Straus & Young.

Gray, J. 1969; reprinted, 1985. *Near Eastern Mythology*. New York: Peter Bedrick Books.

Green, J. 2005. "Roy and His Rock." *Atlantic Monthly* 296 (3), 77–82.

Greenslade, S. K. 1938. *The Work of William Tindale*. London: Blackie & Son.

Gregory, J. R. November 1, 2006. "P. W. Botha, Hard-Line Defender of Apartheid in 1980s, Is Dead at 90." *New York Times*, C20.

Grendel, F. 1977. *Beaumarchais, The Man Who Was Figaro*. New York: Thomas Y. Crowell.

Grube, G. M. A. 1974. *Plato's Republic*. Indianapolis, IN: Hacket Publishing.

Gruen, E. 1998. *Heritage and Hellenism, The Reinvention of Jewish Tradition*. Berkeley: University of California Press.

Guerlac, H. 1975. *Antoine-Laurent Lavoisier, Chemist and Revolutionary*. New York: Charles Scribner's Sons.

Guhl, E., and W. Koner. 1994. *The Greeks, Their life and Customs*. London: Senate.

Guthrie, W. K. C. 1950; reprinted, 1975. *The Greek Philosophers, From Thales to Aristotle*. New York: Harper Torchbooks.

Guzzo, P. G., and A. d'Ambrosio. 1998. *Pompeii*. Napoli: L'erma d' Bretschneider.

Hadas, M. 1951. *The Basic Works of Cicero*. New York: Modern Library.

———. 1962. *Greek Drama*. Toronto: Bantam Books.

Hadas-Lebel, M. 1993. *Flavius Josephus, Eyewitness to Rome's First Century Conquest of Judea*. New York: Macmillan.

Hamel, D. 2003. *Trying Neiaria, The True Story of a Courtesan's Scandalous Life in Ancient Greece*. New Haven, CT: Yale University.

———. 2004. *The God Gene, How Faith is Hardwired into Our Genes*. New York: Anchor Books.

Hamilton, E. 1930; reprinted, 1993. *The Greek Way*. New York: W. W. Norton.

———. 1932; reprinted, 1964. *The Roman Way*. New York: W. W. Norton.

———. 1948. *Witness to the Truth, Christ and His Interpreters*. New York: W. W. Norton.

Hargis, J. W. 1999. *Against the Christians, The Rise of Early Anti-Christian Polemic*. New York: Peter Lang.

Harmon, A. 2006. "Couples Cull Embryos to Halt Heritage of Cancer." *New York Times*, September 3, A1.

Harris, W. V. 2003. "Roman Opinions About the Truthfulness of Dreams." *Journal of Roman Studies* 83: 18–34.

Hart, A. January 14, 2005. "Judge in Georgia Orders Anti-Evolution Stickers Removed from Textbooks." *New York Times*, A12.

Hart, G. 1990. *Egyptian Myths*. Austin: University of Texas Press.

Hartog, F. 2001. *Memories of Odysseus, Frontier Tales from Ancient Greece*. Chicago: University of Chicago Press.

Hawkes, J. 1968. *Dawn of the Gods*. New York: Random House.

Head, P. M. 2000. "Some Recently Published NT Papyri from Oxyrhynchus: An Overview and Preliminary Assessment." *Tyndale Bulletin* 51, 1–16.

Hegel, G. W. F. 1888. *Lectures on the Philosophy of History.* London: George Bell.

Heibert, T. 1996. *The Yahwist's Landscape, Nature and Religion in Early Israel.* New York: Oxford University Press.

Herbstrith, W. 1985. *Edith Stein.* New York: Harper & Row.

Herenschmidt, C. 2003. "Zarathustra's Ritual: Conserving a Charismatic Domination." *History of Religions* 43 (1): 1–17.

Herodotus. 1830. *The Histories,* translated by William Beloe. London: Henry Colburn & Richard Bentley.

Heschel, A. 1962. *The Prophets.* New York: Harper Torchbooks.

Hesiod. *Theogony.* http://sunsite.berkeley.edu/OMACL/Hesiod/theogony.html

Hinchliff, P. 1974. *Cyprian of Carthage and the Unity of the Christian Church.* London: Geoffrey Chapman.

Hobbins, D., trans. 2005. *The Trial of Joan of Arc.* Cambridge, MA: Harvard University Press.

Hodder, I. 1986. *Reading the Past, Current Approaches to Interpretation in Archaeology.* Cambridge: Cambridge University Press.

Hogart, R. C. 1993. *The Hymns of Orpehus.* Grand Rapids, MI: Phanes Press.

Holland, R. 2004. *Augustus, Godfather of Europe.* Gloucestershire, UK: Sutton Publishing.

Holt, J. February 20, 2005. "Unintelligent Design." *New York Times Magazine,* 15–16.

Homer. 1966. *The Iliad,* translated by E. V. Rieu. Baltimore: Penguin Books.

———. 1963. *The Odyssey,* translated by R. Fitzgerald. New York: Anchor Books.

Horace. 1961. *The Odes of Horace,* translated by H. R. Henze. Norman: University of Oklahoma Press.

Horowitz, I. L. 1952. *The Renaissance Philosophy of Giordano Bruno.* New York: Coleman-Ross Co.

Howells, W. W. 1989."Skull Shapes and the Map: Craniometric Analyses in the Dispersion of Modern Homo." *Peabody Museum Papers* 79:1–189.

Hume, D. 1799; reprinted, 1990. *Dialogues Concerning Natural Religion.* New York: Penguin.

———. 1739; reprinted, 1967. *A Treatise of Human Nature,* edited by L. A. Selby Bigge. Oxford: Clarendon Press.

Hus, J. 1956. *Tractatus de Ecclesia,* edited by S. H. Thomson. Cambridge: W. Hefer & Sons, Ltd.

Hutchins, R. M. 1952. *Great Books of the Western World.* Vol . 45. Chicago: Encyclopedia Britannica.

Ibsen, H. 1910. *An Enemy of the People.* In *The Collected Works of Henrik Ibsen,* Vol. 3. New York: Charles Scribner's Sons.

Irenaeus, 1952. *Proof of the Apostolic Teaching.* Tranlsated by J. P. Smith. New York: Newman Press.

Irvin, T. 1989. *A History of Western Philosophy 1, Classical Thought.* New York: Oxford University Press.

Isaacs, H. 1972. *Idols of the Tribe, Group Identity and Political Change.* Cambridge, MA: Harvard University Press.

Iyer, R. 1983. *The Gospel According to Thomas.* New York: Concord Grove Press.

James, W. 1997. *The Varieties of Religious Experience.* New York: Simon & Schuster.

Johanson, D., and M. Edey. 1981. *Lucy, The Beginnings of Humankind.* New York: Simon & Schuster.

Johnson, G. September 27, 2005. "Agreeing Only to Disagree on God's Place in Science." *New York Times,* D2.

Johnson, P. 2000. *The Renaissance.* London: Phoenix Press.

———. 1976. *A History of Christianity.* New York: Atheneum.

Jones, B. W. 2000. *Suetonius Vespasian*. London: Bristol Classical Press.

Jones, J. 1979. *Thomas More*. Boston: Twayne Publishers.

Jones, S. 1993. *The Language of the Genes, Solving the Mysteries of Our Genetic Past, Present and Future*. New York: Anchor Books.

Josephus. F. 1960. *Jerusalem and Rome*. Selected by N. N. Glatzer. New York: Meridian Books.

Julian. 1913. *The Works of Emperor Julian*. Vol. 1, translated by W. C. Wright. London: William Heinemann.

Justinian. 1979. *The Digest of Roman Law*, translated by C. R. Kolbert. London: Penguin Books.

Juvenal. 1887. *Thirteen Satires of Juvenal*, translated by A. Leeper. London: Macmillan.

———. 1991. *The Satires*, translated by N. Rudd. Oxford: Clarendon Press.

Kemper, S. 2005. "Evolution on Trial." *Smithsonian* 36 (1): 52–61.

Kerenyi, C. 1992. *The Gods of the Greeks*. London: Thames & Hudson.

Kermode, F. June 15, 2003. "Another Gospel Truth." *New York Times Book Review*, 10.

Keys, D. 2003. "Pre-Christian Rituals at Nazareth." *Archaeology* 56 (6): 10.

Khaldun, I. 1967. *The Muqaddimah, An Introduction to History*. Princeton, NJ: Princeton University Press.

King, C. W. 1889. *Plutarch's Morals*. London: George Bell & Sons.

King, K. L. 2003. *What is Gnosticism?* Cambridge: Belknap Press.

King, M. L. 1988. *The Measure of Man*. Philadelphia: Fortress Press.

Kingsley, P. 1995. *Ancient Philosophy, Mystery and Magic, Empedocles and the Pythagorean Tradition*. Oxford: Clarendon Press.

Kinney, D. ed. 1986. *The Complete Works of St. Thomas More*. Vol. 15. New Haven: Yale University Press.

Kirk, G. S. 1965. *Homer and the Epic*. Cambridge: Cambridge University Press.

Kirk, G. S. J. E. Raven, M. Schofield. 1957; reprinted, 1983. *The Presocratic Philosophers*. 2nd ed. Cambridge: Cambridge University Press.

Kirsch, J. 1998. *Moses, a life*. New York: Ballantine Books.

Kitto, H. D. F. 1951. *The Greeks*. Baltimore, MD: Penguin Books.

Klosko, G. 1986. *The Development of Plato's Political Theory*. London: Metheun.

Koestler, A. 1959. *The Sleepwalkers, A History of Man's Changing Vision of the Universe*. London: Arkana.

Kraemer, R. S. 2004. *Women's Religions in the Graeco-Roman World, A Sourcebook*. New York: Oxford University Press.

Krahmalkov, C. R. 1994. "Exodus Itinerary Confirmed by Egyptian Evidence." *Biblical Archaeology Review* 20 (5): 55–62.

Kriwaczek, P. 2003. *In Search of Zarathustra, The First Prophet and the Ideas that Changed the World*. New York: Knopf.

Kugel, J. March 27, 2005. "God Speaks; Man Translates." *New York Times*, 20.

Kuhn, T. S. 1957; reprinted, 1985. *The Copernican Revolution, Planetary Astronomy in the Development of Western Thought*. Cambridge, MA: Harvard University Press.

Kung, H. 1976. *On Being a Christian*. Garden City, NY: Doubleday & Co.

———. 1980. "Why I Remain a Catholic." *Journal of Ecumenical Studies* 17 (1), 141–47.

Kurth, D. 2004. *The Temple of Edfu, A Guide by an Ancient Egyptian Priest*. Cairo: The American University in Cairo Press.

Landis, P. 1929. *Four Famous Greek Plays*. New York: Modern Library.

Lane Fox, R. 1992. *The Unauthorized Version, Truth and Fiction in the Bible*. New York: Alfred A. Knopf.

———. 1986. *Pagans and Christians*. New York: Viking.

Lange, K. 2005. "Unearthing Syria's Cult of the Dead." *National Geographic* 207 (2): 108–23.

Lanson, G. 1960. *Voltaire*. New York: John Wiley & Sons.

Lao-Tzu. 1994. *Tao Te Ching*. New York: Alfred A. Knopf.

Lasky, K. n.d.. *A Journey to the New World, The Diary of Remember Patience Whipple*. New York: Scholastic.

Lauring, P. 2004. *A History of Denmark*. Copenhagen: Host & Son.

Lavoisier, A. 1829. *Traite de Chimie Elementaire, Theorique et Pratique*. Brussels: Canongette et Compannie.

———. 1970. *Essays Physical and Chemical*, translated by T. Henry. London: Frank Cass & Co.

Lawler, T. M. C., G. Marc'Hadour, and R. C. Marius. 1981. *The Complete Works of St. Thomas More*. Vol. 6, Parts 1–2. New Haven, CT: Yale University Press.

Lawrence, T. E. 1926, 1935. *Seven Pillars of Wisdom*. London: Jonathan Cape.

Lazier, B. October 2003. "Overcoming Gnosticism." *Journal of the History of Ideas* 64 (4): 619–37.

Leeming, D. 2004. *Jealous Gods and Chosen People*. New York: Oxford University Press.

Lemaitre, G. 1949. *Beaumarchais*. New York: Alfred A. Knopf.

Levene, D. S. 1993. *Religion in Livy*. Leiden: E. J. Brill.

Lewy, H. 1946. *Selections from Philo*. Oxford: East and West Library.

Lilla, M. May 15, 2005. "Church Meets State." *New York Times Book Review* 39.

Linforth, I. M. 1919. *Solon the Athenian*. University of California Publications in Classical Philology. Vol. 6. Berkeley: University of California Press.

Little, A. G. 1914. *Roger Bacon, Essays on the Seventh Centenary of his Birth*. Oxford: Clarendon Press.

Loffreda, S. 1985. *Capharnaum, The Town of Jesus*. Jerusalem: Franciscan Printing Press.

Logan, A. H. B. 1996. *Gnostic Truth and Christian Heresy, A Study in the History of Gnosticism*. Edinburgh: T & T Clark.

Loisy, A. F. 1962. *The Birth of the Christian Religion*. Hyde Park, NY: University Books.

Lomperis, T. J. 1984. *Hindulinfluence on Greek Philosophy, The Odyssey of theSsoul from the Upanishads to Plato*. Calcutta: Minerva Publications.

London, G., and D. R. Clark. 1997. *Ancient Ammonites & Modern Arabs*. Amman, Jordan: American Center of Oriental Research.

London, G. A. June 1987. "Homage to the Elders." *Biblical Archaeologist* 70–74.

Long, A. A. 2002. *Epictetus, A Stoic and Socratic Guide to Life*. Oxford: Clarendon Press.

Loyn, H. R. 1989. *The Middle Ages, A Concise Encyclopaedia*. London: Thames & Hudson.

Lucretius. 1946. *On the Nature of Things*, translated by C. E. Bennett. Roslyn, NY: Walter J. Black.

Luhrmann, T. M. 1991. *Persuasions of the Witch's Craft*. Cambridge, MA: Harvard University Press.

Luibheid, C. 1987. *Pseudo-Dionysius, the Complete Works*. New York: Paulist Press.

Lutzow, Count. 1909. *The Life and Times of Master John Hus*. London: J. M. Dent.

Lyman, R. Summer 2003. 2002. "NAPS Presidential Address: Hellenism and Heresy." *Journal of Early Christian Studies* 11 (2): 209–22.

Maccoby, H. 1986. *The Myth-Maker, Paul and the Invention of Christianity*. New York: Harper & Row.

MacDonald, D. R. 2000. *The Homeric Epics and the Gospel of Mark*. New Haven, CT: Yale University Press.

———. 2003. *Does the New Testament Imitate Homer?* New Haven, CT: Yale University Press.

MacIntyre, A. 2006. *Edith Stein, A Philosophical Prologue, 1913–1922*. New York: Rowman & Littlefield.

Mack, B. L. 1995. *Who Wrote the New Testament? The Making of the Christian Myth*. San Francisco: Harper San Francisco.

Maclean, J. K. B., and E. B. Aitken. *Flavius Philostratus: Heroikus*. Atlanta: Society of Biblical Literature.

MacLeod, M. D. 1991. *Lucian, A Selection*. Warminster, UK: Aris & Phillips.

MacMullen, R. 1984. *Christianizing the Roman Empire*. New Haven, CT: Yale University Press.

MacMullen, R., and E. N. Lane. 1992. *Paganism and Christianity 100–425 CE*. Minneapolis: Fortress Press.

Magill, F. N. 1990. *Masterpieces of World Philosophy*. New York: HarperCollins.

Malandra, W. W. 1983. *An Introduction to Ancient Iranian Religion*. Minneapolis: University of Minnesota Press.

Malikow, M. 2006. "Engaging Students in Controversial Issues." *Kappa Delta Pi Record* 42 (3): 106–8.

Mann, V. B. 1992. *Convivencia, Jews, Muslims, and Christians in Medieval Spain*. New York: George Braziller.

Mansel, H. L. 1875. *The Gnostic Heresies of theFfirst and Second Centuries*. London: John Murray.

Marcellinus, Ammianus. 1986. *The Later Roman Empire (A.D. 354–378)*. New York: Penguin Books.

Marcilius. 1967. *Marsilius of Padua, The Defender of Peace, The Defensor Pacis*, translated and edited by A. Gerwirth. New York: Harper Torchbooks.

Marcus, J., and K. V. Flannery. December 15, 2004. The Coevolution of Ritual and Society: Ne14C Dates from Ancient Mexico. http://PNAS, 10.1073/pnas.0408551102

Maringer, J. 1960. *Gods of Prehistoric Man*. New York: Alfred A. Knopf.

Marsiglio of Padua. 1993. *Writings on the Empire, Defensor Minor and De Translatione Imperii*, edited by C. J. Nederman. Cambridge: Cambridge University Press.

Martial. 1963. *Selected Epigrams*, translated by R. Humphries. Bloomington: Indiana University Press.

Martines, L. 2006. *Fire in the City, Savonarola and the Struggle for Renaissance Florence*. Oxford: Oxford University Press.

Mascaro, J. 1962. *The Bhagavad Gita*. New York: Penguin Books.

———. 1965. *The Upanishads*. New York: Penguin Books.

Masson, G. 1968. *Queen Christina*. New York: Farrar, Straus, & Giroux.

Maurois, A. 1932. *Voltaire*. London: Thomas Nelson & Sons.

Mayr, E. 2001. *What Evolution Is*. New York: Basic Books.

Maziarz, E. A., and T. Greenwood. 1968. *Greek Mathematical Philosophy*. New York: Barnes & Noble.

McConnell, F. 1986. *The Bible and the Narrative Tradition*. New York: Oxford University Press.

McDowell, A. 1996. "Daily Life in Ancient Egypt." *Scientific American* 275 (6): 100–105.

McKechnie, P. 2001. *The First Christian Centuries*. Downers Grove, IL: InterVarsity Press.

McKeon, R. 1947. *Introduction to Aristotle*. New York: Modern Library.

Mead, G. R. S. 1960. *Fragments of a Faith Forgotten, The Gnostics, a Contribution to the Study of the Origins of Christianity*. New Hyde Park, NY: University Books.

———. 1966. *Apollonius of Tyana, The Philosopher-Reformer of the First Century A.D.* New Hyde Park, NY: University Books.

Meeks, W. A. 1983. *The First Urban Christians, The Social World of the Apostle Paul*. New Haven, CT: Yale University Press.

Meinardus, O. F. A. 1973. *St. Paul in Greece*. Athens: Lycabettus Press.

Mellor, R. 1993. *Tacitus*. New York: Routledge.

Mercatante, A. S. 1995. *Who's Who in Egyptian Mythology*. 2nd ed, edited by R. S. Bianchi. New York: Barnes & Noble.

Merenlahti, P. 2002. *Poetics for the Gospels? Rethinking Narrative Criticism*. New York: T&T Clark.

Merton, T. 1948. *The Seven Story Mountain*. New York: Harcourt Brace.

Miller, J. 1996. *God Has Ninety-Nine Names*. New York: Touchstone.

Moore, R. July 2002. "The Sad Status of Evolution Education in American Schools." *Linnean* 18 (3): 26–34.

Moorhead, J. 1999. *Ambrose, Church and Society in the Late Roman World*. London: Longman.

Morley, J. 1901. *The Works of Voltaire*. Limited edition of 190 copies in 42 volumes, Edition 39. Paris & London: E. R. Dumont.

Moynahan, B. 2002. *William Tyndale: If God Spare My Life*. London: Abacus.

Murray, C. 2003. *Human Accomplishment, The Pursuit of Excellence in the Arts and Sciences, 800 B.C. to 1950*. New York: Perennial.

Murray, G. 1946. *Greek Studies*. Oxford: Clarendon Press.

———. 1907; reprinted, 1934. *The Rise of the Greek Epic*. Oxford: Oxford University Press.

———. 1913, reprinted, 1947. *Euripides and His Age*. Oxford: Oxford University Press.

———. 1933. *Aristophanes, A Study*. Oxford: Clarendon Press.

Mururillo, H. A. 1954. *The Acts of the Pagan Martyrs*. Oxford: Clarendon Press.

Myers, C. 1998. "Kinship and Kingship, The Early Monarchy." Pp. 165ff in *The Oxford History of the Biblical World*, edited by M. Coogan. New York: Oxford University Press.

Nasr, S. H. 1968. *Science and Civilization in Islam*. New York: Barnes & Noble.

Negri, S. 1998. *Kartchner Caverns State Park*. Phoenix: Arizona Department of Transportation.

Nestorius. 1925. *The Bazaar of Heracleides*, translated by G. R. Driver and L. Hodgson. Oxford: Clarendon Press.

Newman, J. H. 1890. *The Arians of the Fourth Century*. 6th ed. London: Longmans, Green & Co.

Newport, F. 2004. "Third of Americans Say Evidence Has Supported Darwin's Evolution Theory." Gallop Poll, November 19.

Nietzsche, F. 1990. *Twilight of the Idols and the Anti-Christ*. New York: Penguin Books.

Nock, A. D. 1945 *Corpus Hermeticum*. Tome 1, Traites I–XII. Paris: Societe d'edition, Les Belles Lettres.

Norwich, J. J. 2003. *Byzantium, The Decline and Fall*. London: Folio Society.

———. 1988. *A Short History of Byzantium*. London: Penguin Books.

Noss, J. B. 1956. *Man's Religions*. New York: Macmillan.

Numenius. 1973. *Numenius Fragments*, translated by E. des Places. Paris: Societe D'Edition Les Belles Lettres.

Nye, A. 1999. *The Princess and the Philosopher, Letters of Elisabeth of the Palatine to Rene Descartes*. Lanham, MD: Rowman & Littlefield.

Oates, J. 1986. *Babylon*. London: Thames & Hudson.

336 *References*

Oates, W. J. 1948. *Basic Writings of Saint Augustine*. Vols. 1–2. New York: Random House.

O'Daly, G. O. 1991. *The Poetry of Boethius*. Chapel Hill: University of North Carolina Press.

Ogg, O. 1983. *The 26 Letters*. New York: Van Nostrand.

O'Grady, J. 1985. *Early Christian Heresies*. New York: Barnes & Noble.

Olson, R. G. 2004. *Science and Religion, 1450–1900, From Copernicus to Darwin*. Baltimore: Johns Hopkins University Press.

Origen. 1965. *Contra Celsum*, translated by H. Chadwick. New York: Cambridge University Press.

Orr, H. A. 2003. "What's Not in Your Genes." *New York Review of Books* 50 (13): 38–40.

Oulton, J. E. L., and H. Chadwick. 1954. *Alexandrian Christianity*. Philadelphia: Westminster Press.

Pagels, E. 1979. *The Gnostic Gospels*. New York: Vintage Books.

———. 1988. *Adam, Eve, and the Serpent*. New York: Random House.

———. 2003. *Beyond Belief, The Secret Gospel of Thomas*. New York: Random House.

Paine, S. W. 1961. *Beginning Greek*. New York: Oxford University Press.

Paine, T. 1993. *The Age of Reason, Being an Investigation of True and Fabulous Theology*. New York: Gramercy Books.

———. 1995. *Collected Writings*, edited by E. Foner. New York: Library of America.

Pamuk, O. May 25, 2006. "Freedom to Write." *New York Review of Books*: 53 (9).

Paris, M. 1853. *Matthew Paris's English History from the Year 1235 to 1273*. Vol. 2. London: Henry G. Bohn.

Parpola, S. 1997. *State Archives of Assyria*. Helsinki: Helsinki University Press.

Patti, T. S. 1995. *Manuscripts of the Bible*. London: British Library.

Pease, A. S. 1958. *M. Tullis Ciceronis De Natura Deorum*. Cambridge, MA: Harvard University Press.

Pelikan, J. 1971. *The Christian Tradition, A History of the Development of Doctrine. Vol. I. The Emergence of the Catholic Tradition (100–600)*. Chicago: University of Chicago Press.

Penella, R. J. 1979. *The Letters of Apollonius of Tyana*. Lugduni Batavorum: E. J. Brill.

Pernoud, R., and M-V. Clin. 1999. *Joan of Arc, Her Story*. New York: St. Martin's Griffin.

Perry, L. 1984. *Intellectual Life in America, A History*. Chicago: University of Chicago Press.

Perry, P. 2003. *Jesus in Egypt, Discovering the Secrets of Christ's Childhood Years*. New York: Ballantine Books.

Peters, E., ed. 1980. *Heresy and Authority in Medieval Europe, Documents in Translation*. Philadelphia: University of Pennsylvania Press.

———. 1988. *Inquisition*. New York: Free Press.

Peterssen, L. *Deserters*. 2005. Copenhagen: Danish Resistance Museum Publishing.

Petit, L. 1969. *Descartes et la Princesse Elisabeth, Roman D'amour Vecu*. Paris: Editions A. G. Nizer.

Petrarch. 1966. *The Sonnets of Petrarch*, edited by T. G. Bergin. New York: Heritage Press.

Philo of Alexandria. 1929. *Philo*, with an English translation by F. H. Colson and G. H. Whitaker. Cambridge, MA: Harvard University Press.

Philostratus, F. 1967. *Life and Times of Apollonius of Tyana*. New York: AMS Press.

Plato. 1956. *The Works of Plato,*. edited by I. Edman. New York: Modern Library.

———. 1956. *Protagoras*, edited by I. Edman. New York: Modern Library.

———. 1956. *Theaetetus*, edited by I. Edman. New York: Modern Library.

————. 1944. *The Republic*, translated by B. Jowett. New York: Heritage Press.

————. 1961. *The Collected Dialogues*. Princeton, NJ: Princeton University Press.

————. 1994. *Symposium*, translated by R. Waterfield. Oxford: Oxford University Press.

Plimpton, R. 1994. *Mary Dyer, Biography of a Rebel Quaker*. Boston: Branden Publishing.

Plotinus. 1962. *The Enneads*, ttranslated by S. MacKenna. London: Faber & Faber.

Plutarch. 1932. *The Lives of the Noble Grecians and Romans*, translated by J. Dryden. New York: Modern Library.

————. 1889. *Plutarch's Moralia*, translated by C. W. King. London: George Bell & Sons.

————. 1967. *Moralia*, translated by B. Einarson and P. H. Delacy. Vol. 14. Cambridge, MA: Harvard University Press.

————. 1969. *Moralia*, translated by F. H. Sandbach. Vpl. 15. Cambridge, MA: Harvard University Press.

————. 1888. *Plutarch's Miscellanies and Essays*, translated and revised by W. W. Goodwin. Vol. 4. Boston: Little Brown & Co.

Poirier, J. C. 2003. "General Reckoning in Hesiod and in the Pentateuch." *Journal of Near Eastern Studies* 62 (3): 193–99.

Polybius. 1960. *Polybius, The Histories*. Vol. 1. Cambridge, MA: Harvard University Press.

Porter, R. 2004. *Flesh in the Age of Reason, The Modern Foundations of Body and Soul*. New York: W. W. Norton.

Powell, B. 1989. "Why Was the Greek Alphabet Invented? The Epigraphical Evidence." *Classical Antiquity* 8 (2): 321–50.

Prabhavananda, S. and F. Manchester. 1975. *The Upanishads*. Hollywood, CA: Vedanta Press.

Pritchard, J. B. 1955; reprinted, 1969. *Ancient Near Eastern Texts Relating to the Old Testament*. 2nd ed. Princeton, NJ: Princeton University Press.

Radice, B. 1977. *Abelard and Heloise, The Story of his Misfortune and the Personal Letters*. London: Folio Society.

Randall, L. September 18, 2005. "Dangling Particles." *The New York Times*.

Reade, J. 1991. *Mesopotamia*. London: British Museum Press.

Redford, D. B. 1993. *Egypt, Canaan and Israel in Ancient Times*. Cairo: American University in Cairo Press.

Reiner, E. 1991. "First-Millennium Babylonian Literature." In *The Cambridge Ancient History*. Vol. 3, Part 2, edited by I. E. S. Edwards. Cambridge: Cambridge University Press.

Riley-Smith, J. 1997. *The Oxford Illustrated History of the Crusades*. Oxford: Oxford University Press.

Rives, J. B. 1995. *Religion and Authority in Roman Carthage from Augustus to Constantine*. Oxford: Clarendon Press.

Roach, M. K. 2002. *The Salem Witch Trials, A Day-by-Day Chronicle of a Community Under Siege*. Lanham, MD: Taylor Trade Publishing.

Roberts, A. 1995. *Hathor Rising, The Serpent Power of Ancient Egypt*. Totnes, UK: Northgate Publishers.

Robinson, J. M. 1986. "The Gospels as Narrative." Pp. 97–112 in *The Bible and the Narrative Tradition*, edited by F. McConnell. New York: Oxford University Press.

Robinson, J. M., P. Hoffman, and J. S. Kloppenborg. 2001. *The Q Gospel Sayings in Greek and English, with Parallels from the Gospels of Mark and Thomas*. Leuven: Peeters.

Rodis-Lewis, G. 1998, *Descartes, His Life and Thought*, translated by J. M. Todd. Ithaca, NY: Cornell University Press,

338 *References*

Rohde, D. March 13, 2005. "A World of Ways to Say 'Islamic Law.'" *The New York Times.*

Roquebert, M. 1988. *Cathar Religion.* Garonne, France: Editions Loubatieres.

Rosenberg, D., and H. Bloom. 1990. *The Book of J.* New York: Vintage Books.

Rosenblatt, J. P., and J. C. Sitterson. 1991. *Not in Heaven: Coherence and Complexity in Biblical Narrative.* Bloomington: Indiana University Press.

Rosin, H. 2005. "Beyond Belief." *Atlantic Monthly* 295 (1): 117–20.

Ross, J. 1994. *The Tudors.* London: Artus.

Ross, N. W. 1966. *Three Ways of Asian Wisdom.* New York: Simon &Schuster.

Rossetti, D. G. 1981. *The Early Italian Poets*, edited by S. Purcell. Berkeley: University of California Press.

Rossini, S. 1989. *Egyptian Hieroglyphics, How to Read and Write Them.* New York: Dover Publications.

Rothstein, R. September 8, 2005. "Seeking Justice, of Gods or the Politicians." *New York Times*, B1.

Rouse, W. H. D. 1956. *Great Dialogues of Plato.* New York: Mentor Books.

Rudolph, K. 1978. *Manaceeism.* Leiden: E. J. Brill.

Runciman, S. 1947. *The Medieval Manichee, A Study of the Christian Dualist Heresy.* Cambridge: Cambridge University Press.

Runia, D. T. 1990. *Exegesis and Philosophy: Studies on Philo of Alexandria.* Aldershot, Hampshire, UK: Variorum, 1–18.

Ruse, M. 2003. *Darwin and Design, Does Evolution Have a Purpose?* Cambridge, MA: Harvard University Press.

Ruskin, A. 1965. *Spy for Liberty.* New York: Pantheon Books.

Russell, B. 1935; reprinted, 1997. *Religion and Science.* New York: Oxford University Press.

———. 1955. *A History of Western Philosophy.* London: George Allen & Unwin.

———. 1932; reprinted, 1967. *Education and the Social Order.* London: Unwin.

Russell, J. B. 1971. *Religious Dissent in the Middle Ages.* New York: John Wiley.

———. 1992. *Dissent and Order in the Middle Ages, The Search for Legitimate Authority.* New York: Twayne Publishers.

Russell, L. 2004. "Drinking from the Penholder: Intentionality and Archaeological Theory." *Cambridge Archaeological Journal* 14 (1): 64–67.

Safire, W. 1992. *The First Dissident, The Book of Job in Today's Politics.* New York: Random House.

Saggs, H. W. G. 1989. *Civilization Before Greece and Rome.* New Haven, CT: Yale University Press.

Salmon, E. T. 1968. *A History of the Roman World, 30 BC to AD138.* London: Metheun & Co.

Sallust. 1992. *The Histories*, translated by P. McGushin. Vol. 1. Oxford: Clarendon Press.

Sandars, N. K. 1972. *The Epic of Gilgamesh.* New York: Penguin Books.

———. 1971. *Poems of Heaven and Hell from Ancient Mesopotamia.* London: Penguin Books.

Sanders, E. P. 2003. "Who Was Jesus?" *New York Review of Books* 50 (6): 49–51.

———. 2001. "In Quest of the Historical Jesus." *New York Review of Books* 48 (18): 33–36.

Sandmel, S. 1979. *Philo of Alexandria, An Introduction.* New York: Oxford University Press.

Saumagne, C. 1975. *Saint Cyprien Eveque de Carthage "Pape" d'Afrique.* Paris: Editions du Centre National de la Recherche Scientifique.

Schapiro, J. S. 1963. *Condorcet and the Rise of Liberalism.* New York: Octagon Press.

Schmidt, K. L. 2002. *The Place of the Gospels in the General History of Literature.* Columbia: University of South Carolina Press.

Schmidt, P. 1955. "The Ancient Mysteries in the Society of Their Time, Their Transformation and Most Recent Echoes." Pp. 93–118 in *The Mysteries, Papers from the Eranos Yearbooks.* Vol. 2. Bollingen Series, edited by J. Campbell. Princeton, NJ: Princeton University Press.

Schopenhauer, A. 1998. *The World as Will and Idea.* London: J. M. Dent.

Schowalter, D. N. 1998. "Churches in Context, The Jesus Movement in the Roman World." In, *The Oxford History of the Biblical World,,* edited by M. Coogan. New York: Oxford University Press.

Schuster, L. A., R. C. Marius, J. P. Lusardi, and R. J. Schoeck. 1973. *The Complete Works of St. Thomas More.* Vol. 8, Parts 1–2. New Haven, CT: Yale University Press.

Scott, C. 2005. "Stand by Science." *Edutopia* 1 (4): 52–54.

Segal, R. A. 1986. *The Poimandres as Myth, Scholarly Theory and Gnostic Meaning.* Berlin: Mouton de Gruyter.

Seneca. 1969. *Letters from a Stoic.* London: Penguin Books.

———. 1997. *Dialogues and Letters.* London: Penguin Books.

Serre, D., et al. 2004. "No Evidence of Neanderthal DNA Contribution to Early Modern Humans." *PLoS Biology* 2 (3) (March).

Settle, M. L. 2001. *I, Roger Williams, A Fragment of Autobiography.* New York: W. W. Norton.

Seymour-Smith, M. 1996. *Gnosticism, The Path of Inner Knowledge.* San Francisco: Harper San Francisco.

Shahrastani. 1976. *Shahrastani on the Indian Religions,* translated by B. B. Lawrence. The Hague: Mouton.

Sharpes, D. 1990. "Mandela One More Politician Caught in Country's Struggles." *Standard-Examiner,* July 15, D3.

Sharpes, D. K. 1987. "An Inquiry into Values of Islamic Fundamentalism." *Journal of Value Inquiry* 21: 309–15.

Sharpes, D. K., and M. M. Peramas. 2006. "Accepting Evolution or Discarding Science." *Kappa Delta Pi Record* (Summer): 156–60.

Sheed, F. J. 1957. *Theology for Beginners.* New York: Sheed & Ward.

Sherk, R. K. 1988. *The Roman Empire: Augustus to Hadrian.* Cambridge: Cambridge University Press, 1988.

Shermer, M. 2001. *The Borderlands of Science, Where Sense Meets Nonsense.* Oxford: Oxford University Press.

Shorter, A. W. 1939; reprinted, 1979. *The Egyptian Gods.* London: Routledge & Kegan Paul.

Sidelko, P. L. 1996. "The Condemnation of Roger Bacon." *Journal of Medieval History* 22 (1): 60–81.

Sider, D. 1981. *The Fragments of Anaxagoras.* Meisenheim: Verlag.

Simons, M. May 16, 2006. "A Critic of Muslim Intolerance Faces Loss of Dutch Citizenship." *New York Times,* A8.

Singer, D. W. 1950. *Giordano Bruno, His Life and Thought.* New York: Henry Schuman.

Sloan, C. November 2006. "The Origin of Childhood." *National Geographic* 210 (5): 148–59.

Smith, A. 1974. *Porphyry's Place in the Neoplatonic Tradition: A Study in Post-Plotinian Neoplatonism.* The Hague: Martinus Nijhoff.

Smith, D. B. March 25, 2007. "Can You Live with the Voices in Your Head." *New York Times Magazine,* 49–53.

Smith, M. S. 2002. *The Early History of God, Yahweh and the Other Deities in Ancient Israel.* 2nd ed. Grand Rapids, MI: William B. Eerdmans.

Sollberger, E. 1971. *The Babylonian Legend of the Flood.* London: British Museum Publications.

Solmsen, F. 1949; reprinted, 1995. *Hesiod and Aeschylus.* Ithaca, NY: Cornell University Press.

Solomon, R. C., and K. M. Higgins. 1996. *A Short History of Philosophy.* New York: Oxford University Press.

Solon. http://theosophy.org/tlodocs/teachers/Solon.htm

Speidel, M. P. 1980. *Mithras-Orion, Greek Hero and Roman Army God.* Leiden: E. J. Brill.

Spence, L. 1916. *Myths and Legends of Babylonia and Assyria.* London: George G. Harrap & Co.

Spinoza, B. 1894. *Ethic,* translated by W. H. White. London: T. Fisher Unwin.

———. *The Correspondence of Spinoza,* translated and edited by A. Wolf. New York: Russell & Russell.

———. 1862. *Tractatus Theologico-Politicus.* London: Trubner & Co.

Stacey, J. 1964. *John Wyclif and Reform.* Philadelphia: Westminster Press.

Stead, C. 1994. *Philosophy in Christian Antiquity.* Cambridge: Cambridge University Press.

Stendahl, K. 1984. *Meanings, The Bible as Document and Guide.* Philadelphia: Fortress Press.

Sternberg, M. 1998. *Hebrews Between Cultures, Group Portraits and National Literature.* Bloomington: Indiana University Press.

Stetkevych, J. 1996. *Muhammad and the Golden Bough, Reconstructing Arabian Myth.* Bloomington: Indiana University Press.

Stewart, M. 2005. *The Courtier and the Heretic, Leibnitz, Spinoza, and the Fate of God in the Modern World.* New York: W. W. Norton.

Steyn, M. 2005. "The Marrying Kind." *Atlantic Monthly* 295 (4): 142–43.

Stolpe, S. 1966. *Christina of Sweden.* New York: Macmillan.

Strauss, D. F. 1840; reprinted, 1972. *The Life of Jesus Critically Examined.* 4th ed., edited by P. Hodgson, translated by George Eliot. Mifflintown, PA: Sigler Press.

Suetonius. 1993. *Lives of Galba, Otho & Vitellius,* edited by D. Shotter. Warminster, UK: Aris & Philipps.

Sullivan, J. 2002. *Edith Stein, Essential Writings.* Maryknoll, NY: Orbis Books.

Sulloway, F. J. 1996. *Born to Rebel, Birth Order, Family Dynamics and Creative Lives.* New York: Pantheon Books.

Sungolowsky, J. 1974. *Beaumarchais.* New York: Twayne Publishers.

Sunstein, C. 2003. *Why Societies Need Dissent.* Cambridge, MA: Harvard University Press.

Sweeney, E. R. 1991. *Cochise, Chiricahua Apache Chief.* Norman: University of Oklahoma Press.

Tactitus. 1995. *The Histories,* translated by K. Wellesley. London: Penguin Books.

Tagore, R. 1931; reprinted, 1988. *The Religion of Man.* London: Unwin Paperbacks.

Tarnas, R. 1991. *The Passion of the Western Mind, Understanding the Ideas That Have Shaped Our World View.* New York: Ballantine.

Tattersall, I. 1998. *Becoming Human, Evolution and Human Uniqueness.* New York: Harcourt Brace.

Tertullian. 1790. *Q. Septimii Florentis Tertulliani Opera Omnia.* Wirceburgi: In Officina Libraria Staheliana.

———. *Tertullian's Prescription against hereticks; and the apologeticks of St. Theophilus Bishop of Antioch to Autolycus, against the malicious calumniators of the Christian religion, translated from their respective originals, with notes and preliminary dissertations.* By Joseph Betty, Oxford, 1722. 18th Century Collections Online. Gale Group. http://0-galenet.galegroup.com.library.lib.asu.edu:80/servlet/ECCO

———. 1956.*The Treatise Against Hermogenes*, translated by J. H. Waszink. Westminster, MD: Newman Press.

Thiede, C. P. 1992. *The Earliest Gospel Manuscript? The Qumran Papyrus 7Q5 and Its Significance for New Testament Studies.* Carlisle, UK: Paternoster Press.

Thomas, H. 2006. *Beaumarchais in Seville.* New Haven, CT: Yale University Press.

A Thousand Years of the Bible. 1991. Malibu, CA: J. Paul Getty Museum.

Thucydides. 1880. *A History of the Peloponnesian War.* New York: Harper & Brothers.

———. *Thucydides*, translated by W. Smith. Vol. 1. London: A. J. Valpy.

Tillich, P. 1955. *Biblical Religion and the Search for Ultimate Reality.* Chicago: University of Chicago Press.

Tishkoff, S. A., F. A Reed, A. Ranciaro, B. F Voight, C. C. Babbitt, J. S. Silverman, K. Powell, H. M. Mortensen, J. B. Hirbo, M. Osman, M. Ibrahim, S. A. Omar, G. Lema, T. B. Nyambo, J. Ghori, S. Bumpstead, J. K. Pritchard, G. A. Wray, and P. Deloukas. "Convergent Adaptation of Human Lactase Persistence in Africa and Europe." *Nature Genetics*, December 10, 2006.

Todd, M. 1957. "Sidelights on Greek Philosophers." *Journal of Hellenic Studies* 77: 137.

Townsend, J. W. 2003. "Reproductive Behavior in the Context of Global Population." *American Psychologist* 58 (3): 197–204.

Trevelyan, G. M. 1912. *England in the Age of Wycliffe.* London: Longmans, Green.

Trypanis, C. A. 1981. *Greek Poetry from Homer to Seferis.* London: Faber & Faber, 209–23.

Tsagarakis, O. 1977. *Nature and Background of Major Concepts of Divine Power in Homer.* Amsterdam: B. R. Grunder Publishing Co.

Tubb, J. N., and R. L. Chapman. 1990. *Archaeology and the Bible.* London: British Museum Publications.

Turcan, R. 1996. *The Cults of the Roman Empire.* Oxford: Blackwell.

———. 1975. *Mithras Platonicus, Recherches sur Hellenisation Philosophique de Mithra.* Leiden: E. J. Brill.

Turnbull, C. 1913. *Life and Teachings of Giordano Bruno, Philosopher, Martyr, Mystic, 1548–1600.* Philadelphia: David McKay.

Tyndale, W. 1848. *Doctrinal Treatises and Introductions to Different Portions of the Holy Scriptures.* Cambridge: University Press.

Ulansey, D. 1994. "Solving the Mithraic Mysteries." *Biblical Archaeology Review* 20 (5): 40–53.

———. 1989. *The Origins of the Mithraic Mysteries, Cosmology and Salvation in the Ancient World.* New York: Oxford University Press.

The Urantia Book,. 1955. No author. Chicago: Urantia Foundation.

Vail, T. 2003. *Grand Canyon: A Different View.* Green Forest, AR: Master Books.

Van Buskirk, W. R. 1929. *The Saviors of Mankind.* New York: Macmillan.

Van Doren, C. 1991. *A History of Knowledge: The Pivotal Events, People, and Achievements of World History.* New York: Ballantine.

Van Seters, J. 1983. *In Search of History, Historiography in the Ancient World and the Origins of Biblical History.* New Haven, CT: Yale University Press.

Vermaseren, M. J. 1963. *Mithras, the Secret God.* New York: Barnes &Noble.

Vermes, G. 1975. *The Dead Sea Scrolls in English.* New York: Penguin Books.

———. 1983. *Jesus and the World of Judaism.* London: SCM Press.

———. 2003. *Jesus in His Jewish Context.* Minneapolis: Fortress Press.

Vernant, J-P. 1982. *The Origins of Greek Thought.* Ithaca, NY: Cornell University Press.

342   *References*

Veyne, P. 1988. *Did the Greeks Believe in Their Own Myths?*, translated by P. Wissing. Chicago: University of Chicago Press.

Vine, A. R. 1937. *The Nestorian Churches.* London: Independent Press.

Virgil. 1983. *The Aeneid.* New York: Random House.

Viorst, M. 1994. *The Great Documents of Western Civilization.* New York: Barnes & Noble.

Voltaire. 1972. *Philosophical Dictionary.* New York: Viking Penguin.

———. 1956. *Candide and Other Writings.* New York: Modern Library.

———. 1940. *The Best Known Works of Voltaire.* New York: Greystone Press.

Von Balthasar, H. U. 1984. *Origin, Spirit and Fire, A Thematic Anthology of His Writings.* Washington, DC: Catholic University Press.

Wade, N. September 9, 2005. "Brain May Still Be Evolving, Studies Hint." *New York Times*, A14.

———. December 21, 2004. "7,000 Years of Religious Ritual is Traced to Mexico." *New York Times*, D4.

Wafa, A. W. 2006. "Kabul Judge Rejects Calls to End Trial of Christian Convert." *New York Times*, March 24, A3.

Waley, A. 1971. *The Analects of Confucius.* 6th ed. London: George Allen & Unwin.

Walker, A. T. 1907. *Caesar's Gallic Wars.* Chicago: Scott, Foresman.

Walters, V. J. 1974. *The Cult of Mithras in the Roman Provinces of Gaul.* Leiden: E. J. Brill.

Washington, J. M. *A Testament of Hope: The Essential Writings of Martin Luther King.* New York: Harper & Row, 1986.

Watson, B. 1996. *Hsun Tzu, Basic Writings.* New York: Columbia University Press.

Weatherford, J. 2004. *Genghis Khan and the Making of the Modern World.* New York: Three Rivers Press.

Weber, M. 1952. *Ancient Judaism.* Glencoe: IL: Free Press.

Weeden, T. J. 1971. *Mark, Traditions in Conflict.* Philadelphia: Fortress Press.

Wellesley, K. 1995. *Tacitus, the Histories.* London: Penguin Books.

Westerink, L. G. 1986. *Damascius, Traite Des Premiers Principes.* Vol. 1. Paris: Societe D'Edition Les Belles Lettres

Westfall, R. 1993. *The Life of Isaac Newton.* Cambridge: Cambridge University Press.

White, J. E. M. 1970. *Ancient Egypt, Its Culture and History.* New York: Dover Publications.

White, L. M. 2004. *From Jesus to Christianity, How Four Generations of Visionaries and Storytellers Created the New Testament and Christian Faith.* San Francisco: Harper San Francisco.

White, M. 2002. *The Pope and the Heretic, A True Story of Courage and Murder at the Hands of the Inquisition.* London: Little, Brown & Co.

White, N. 1983. *Handbook of Epictetus.* Indianapolis, IN: Hackett Publishing.

Whitfield, P. 2001. *Astrology, A History.* New York: Harry N. Abrams.

Wiles, M. 1996. *Archetypal Heresy, Arianism Through the Centuries.* Oxford: Clarendon Press.

Wilford, J. N. January 12, 2007. "Skull Supports Human-Migration Theory." *New York Times*, A10.

Wilgoren, J. Octobr 6, 2005. "Finding Creation and Evolution in Grand Canyon." *New York Times*, A1.

Williams, D. H. 1995. *Ambrose of Milan and the End of the Nicene-Arian Conflicts.* Oxford: Clarendon Press.

Williams, N. 1995. *The Life and Times of Elizabeth I.* New York: Shooting Star Press.

Williams, R. 1987; reprinted, 2001. *Arius, Heresy & Tradition.* Grand Rapids, MI: William B. Eerdmans Publishing Co.

Williams, S., and G. Friell. 1994. *Theodosius, The Empire at Bay*. New Haven, CT: Yale University Press.

Wills, G. 2003. *Saint Augustine's Sin*. New York: Viking.

Wilson, D. S. 2002. *Darwin's Cathedral, Evolution, Religion and the Nature of Society*. Chicago: University of Chicago Press.

Wilson, E. O. 1978. *On Human Nature*. Cambridge, MA: Harvard University Press.

———. 1998. *Consilience, The Unity of Knowledge*. New York: Knopf.

Wilson, I. 1984. *Jesus, The Evidence*. London: Pan Books.

Wilson, R. M. 1958. *The Gnostic Problem, A Study of Relations Between Hellenistic Judaism and the Gnostic Heresy*. London: A. R. Mowbray.

———. 1968. *Gnosis and the New Testament*. Philadelphia: Fortress.

Wilson, R. S. 1933. *Marcion, A Study of a Second-Century Heretic*. London: James Clarke & Co.

Winsten, J. 1999. *Moses Meets Israel, The Origins of One God*. Boston: Rumford Press.

Wolf, K. B. 1988. *Christian Martyrs in Muslim Spain*. Cambridge: Cambridge University Press.

Wolfson, H. A. 1947; reprinted, 1982. *Philo, Foundations of Religious Philosophy in Judaism, Christianity and Islam*. Vols. 1–2. Cambridge, MA: Harvard University Press.

Wong, K. February 2005a. "The Littlest Human." *Scientific American* 292 (2): 56–65.

———. 2005. "The Morning of the Modern Mind." *Scientific American* 292 (6), 86–95.

Woods, D. 1978. *Biko*. New York: Paddington Books.

Woolley, C. L. 1965. *The Sumerians*. New York: W. W. Norton.

Wunn, I. 2000. "Beginning of Religion." *Numen* 47 (4) (November): 417–52.

Wyclif, J. 1889. *Tractatus de Apostasia*, edited by M. H. Dziewicki. London: Trubner & Co.

———. 1929. *Select English Writings*, editd by H. E. Winn. London: Humphrey Milford for Oxford University Press.

———. 1992. *On Simony*, translated by T. A. McVeigh. New York: Fordham University Press.

Xenophon, n.d. *The Education of Cyrus*, translated by H. G. Dakyns. London: J. M. Dent.

Yadin, Y. 1957. *The Message of the Scrolls*. New York: Touchstone.

Yartz, F. J. 2004. "Myth, Knowledge and Homer." *Ancient World* 34 (1): 83–89.

Zaehner, R. C. 1956. *The Teachings of the Magi, A Compendium of Zoroastrian Beliefs*. New York: Oxford University Press.

———. 1962. *Hinduism*. New York: Oxford University Press.

Zernicke, K. August 23, 2002. "Georgia School Board Requires Balance of Evolution and Bible." *New York Times*, A8.

Zielinski, T. 1926; reprinted, 1975. *The Religion of Ancient Greece*, translated from Polish by George R Noyes. Chicago: Ares Publishers.

Zimmer, C. November 2006. "A Fin is a Limb is a Wing, How Evolution Fashioned its Masterworks." *National Geographic* 210 (5): 111–35.

———. 2006. *Evolution, The Triumph of an Idea*. New York: Harper Perennial.

Zimmermann, F. 1979. *The Aramaic Origin of the Four Gospels*. New York: KTAV Publishing House.

Zoroaster. 1963. *The Hymns of Zarathustra*, translated by J. Duchesne-Guillemin. Boston: Beacon Press.

Websites

http://nobelprize.org/peace/laureates/1991/kyi-bio.html

http://www.commondreams.org/views03/1211-03.htm

http://nobelprize.org/peace/laureates/2003/ebadi-bio.html
http://www.memritv.org/Transcript.asp?P1=1050
http://galenet.galegroup.com.ezproxy1.lib.asu.edu/servlet/ECCO
http://www.bigisland.com/~stony/redcloud.html
http://www.nationalacademies.org
http://www.thelatinlibrary.com/arnobius.html
http://www.geocities.com/Heartland/Valley/8920/churchcouncils/Ecum14.htm
http://ccat.sas.upenn.edu/~jmcgill/association.html
http://www.macalester.edu/~adupay/ElizabethViews.htm

INDEX